WITH EYES OF FLESH

The Bible in the Modern World, 10

Series Editors
J. Cheryl Exum, Jorunn Økland, Stephen D. Moore

Amsterdam Studies in the Bible and Religion, 2

Series Editor
Athalya Brenner

WITH EYES OF FLESH

The Bible, Gender and Human Rights

Carole R. Fontaine

SHEFFIELD PHOENIX PRESS

2008

Copyright © 2008 Sheffield Phoenix Press

Published by Sheffield Phoenix Press
Department of Biblical Studies, University of Sheffield
Sheffield S10 2TN

www.sheffieldphoenix.com

All rights reserved.
No part of this publication may be reproduced or transmitted in any form or by any means, electronic or mechanical, including photocopying, recording or any information storage or retrieval system, without the publishers' permission in writing.

A CIP catalogue record for this book
is available from the British Library

Typeset by CA Typesetting Ltd
Printed on acid-free paper by Lightning Source UK Ltd, Milton Keynes

ISBN 978-1-905048-54-0 (hbk)
ISBN 978-1-905048-55-7 (pbk)

*To Peace and Equality:
those who yearn for it;
those who work for it;
those who will achieve it.*

Contents

List of Figures	ix
Preface	xi
Acknowledgements	xxv
Abbreviations	xxxi

Chapter 1
'WITH EYES OF FLESH' (JOB 10.4): TOWARD A CONCEPT OF
HUMAN RIGHTS IN THE BIBLE AND THE ANCIENT NEAR EAST — 1
1. Baghdad Bound: On the Road between Wars — 1
2. The Problem with Terminology and Sources of Human Rights — 6
3. Back to the Religious Sources: The Shaping of Victim Consciousness and Ideology — 15
4. Conclusions: What Can We Take on the Journey toward Human Rights? — 26

Chapter 2
GENDERING THE CAPTIVE: REPRESENTATIONS OF THE ABUSE OF HUMAN DIGNITY — 31
1. Representation Studies — 32
2. Representation, Gender and Early Scenes of War — 39
3. C.S.I.: The Fertile Crescent — 54
4. The View from the Hebrew Bible — 66

Chapter 3
THE BODY BREACHED: INTIMATIONS OF HUMAN DIGNITY — 78
1. In their Own Words: Knowledge of the Impact of Torture and Mutilation in Ancient Empires — 78
2. Literary Evidence of Human Dignity — 93
3. The Book of Job: A 'Humanitarian Narrative'? — 104
4. 'I died there': Hearing the Silenced — 116

Chapter 4
READING FOR THE BEST: TOWARD DIVERSITY IN INTERPRETATION — 118
1. Standard Feminist Statement of Disclosure — 118
2. Toward a Multidimensional Aesthetic Theology — 122
3. Reading in Place: Reflections on Reading the Bible after September 11, 2001 — 126

    4. Aryan Christ or Matriarchal Jesus: On the Theology
       of 'Same-Old, Same-Old'   141
    5. What Is to Be Done?   147

Chapter 5
THE ABUSIVE BIBLE: ON THE USE OF FEMINIST METHOD IN PASTORAL CONTEXTS   150
    1. The Nature of the Bible   157
    2. The Content of the Bible   167
    3. We the Readers: The Function of the Bible, Revisited   173
    4. The Plain Sense of Abuse   175
    5. Accounting for Hope: The Four 'R's   176
    6. Afterword: The Bible Abused in the Wake of
       September 11, 2001   178

Chapter 6
'MANY DEVICES' (QOHELETH 7.23–8.1): QOHELETH, MISOGYNY, AND THE *MALLEUS MALEFICARUM*   181
    1. Foreword   181
    2. When Readers Respond…   181
    3. Establishing the 'Plain Sense' in Qoheleth 7.25–8.1a   186
    4. Qoheleth among the Commentators: A Selective Sampling   194
    5. Qoheleth among the Christians: Literary Proverb
       Performance in the *Malleus maleficarum*   198
    6. Many Devices of the Modern Commentators   205

Chapter 7
'COME, LIE WITH ME!': THE MYTHOLOGY OF HONOR KILLINGS AND FEMALE DESIRE IN BIBLICAL ISRAEL AND THE ANCIENT NEAR EAST   215
    1. What's All the Fuss About?   215
    2. The Wages of Sin: Women's Desire in the Ancient World   218
    3. Female Desire in the Bible and among the Neighbors   221
    4. The Primary Texts   222
    5. Concluding Remarks on the Mythology of Female Desire   237
    6. Watching Out for Watchmen in the Song of Songs   246
    7. Listening through the Textual Veils   250
    8. Epilogue   258

Chapter 8
YOU SHALL NOT STAND IDLY BY   262
    1. Prologue: Jesus in the Human Rights Community   262
    2. A Final Word on the Bible and Human Rights Abuses
       in its World and Ours   266

Epilogue   280
Bibliography   281
Indexes   302

LIST OF FIGURES

All drawings are by the author unless otherwise noted.

Fig. 1.	Cemetery, Mound A, Kish: 'Candy Dish'	36
Fig. 2.	Naqada III Era Knife	45
Fig. 3.	Oxford Palette: Human shaman (?) dressed as jackal	47
Fig. 4.	The Hunter's Palette	48
Fig. 5.	Narmer Palette, Reverse, Middle Register	49
Fig. 6.	Narmer Palette, Reverse, Bottom Register	51
Fig. 7.	Narmer Palette, Obverse, Bottom Register	52
Fig. 8.	Bull Palette, Top Register	53
Fig. 9.	Battlefield Palette	54
Fig. 10.	The Siege of Lachish	55
Fig. 11.	Assyrians flaying two men from Lachish	55
Fig. 12.	Terracotta Execration Figures	57
Fig. 13.	Syrian Dea Nutrix	58
Fig. 14.	Bas-relief from Nimrud	59
Fig. 15.	*Coitus a tergo* Tavern Drinking Scene	60
Fig. 16.	Assyrian Bas-relief: Assyrians attack city walls	61
Fig. 17.	Impaled prisoners at Lachish	71
Fig. 18.	Lachish prisoner	72
Fig. 19.	Egyptian cartouche for the name glyph of a conquered enemy	86
Fig. 20.	Egypt: Beheaded Prisoners	86
Fig. 21.	Assyrian scribes	97
Fig. 22.	Egyptian scribes	101
Fig. 23.	Chart of K2111 Variants	224-226
Fig. 24.	Motif Index of K2111 Variants in the Ancient Near East	240-245

Preface

1. *How This Book Came to Be*

Gentle Reader, I thank you for approaching this book with its scary, ambivalent title: is it another entry in the 'biblical apologies' genre? you might wonder. Is it some new attempt at 'values' talk by a member of one of *those* groups (feminists, religious and otherwise) that most offend the political, corporate, and moral guardians of fundamentalist America?

In short, is it *safe* or *useful* to read this book?

I hope that you answer in the affirmative after reading, but I would like to speak to you simply, straightforwardly, about the grief and outrage that has prompted me to write, collect, and rework these particular essays at this particular time in history. The work presented here uses gender and a focus on universal Human Rights, especially the rights of women and girls, to explore the roles that biblical religion interpreted in the present may play in both empowering and obstructing such concepts.

Quite frankly, this was not a book I wanted to write. I was happily engaged in other research when the photographs of prisoner abuse at Abu Ghraib appeared in 2004. Like many persons of all nationalities, I was sickened by what I saw.[1] As biblically inspired rhetoric was enlisted by military officials to teach US citizens that *anything* was permissible in the protection of our world from 'smoking guns', 'mushroom clouds', and (a personal favorite) militant 'Islamo-fascism', I began to question aloud the content of the beliefs displayed by my countryfolk.

But I had other questions as well. Where in all the photographs were the women captives of Abu Ghraib? As a Human Rights activist with ties to the Middle East, I knew perfectly well from personal reports that women were indeed held, tortured, and sexually abused in Abu Ghraib, but it was not *those* pictures that the world saw at first. Why the silence? Granted that the use of 'Saddam's Rape Rooms' for that very same purpose by the liberators from the US Military is a *bit* embarrassing, but

---

1. I am quite sure that if photos were allowed out of Guantanamo Bay, they would be sickening, too.

no more so than the missing weapons of mass destruction, the theft of millions of dollars meant for Iraqi reconstruction, or the shocking treatment of wounded returning soldiers.

What *was* the point, then, of the forms of torture and humiliation practiced at Abu Ghraib? Hapless cab-drivers and street vendors from Baghdad had no particular valuable, time-sensitive information about al-Qaeda in Iraq at that time. Conservative pundits tried to claim it was no more than the 'venting' of tension by guards, a sort of hi-jinks, college frat party approach to decoding the events, or that it was only a 'few rotten apples' spoiling the barrel of American goodness, even in the prosecution of illegal wars of pre-emption. So, what was to be gained by the actions brought to Abu Ghraib by the torturers of Guantanamo? Since the perpetrators seldom discuss what they really thought or hoped, we can only draw conclusions based on what we see in the pictures. As America's truth-telling comedic talent Jon Stewart asked on his *Daily Show*, why do all the pictures from Abu Ghraib look like bad gay porn?

Indeed. What had struck me about the photos was precisely the emphasis on homoerotic activity to foster shame in the captive, and give the captors a future power to control and exploit through threats of exposure of such shameful activity. Clearly, the young prison guards from the American South, given no explicit training as a policing force in prisons or anywhere else, were not astute enough to know that such photographs would bear a particular meaning in Islamic cultures. Yet, latent homophobia and misogyny were clearly a code shared by both captives and captors, making the feminizing of the captives a perfect way to shame them by casting doubts on their manhood, understood sexually. The practices at Abu Ghraib and Guantanamo also served to render a success of sorts to the US, still smarting from the attacks in 2001 which had *no* origin or connection with Iraq. The taking of manhood in one case restored the taken manhood of the outraged victim, and so it goes on (and on).

In the midst of contrasting accounts coming out of the US and Islamic countries, I was interested to see who might have picked up on the deliberate use of gender codes to manipulate ideologies of war and torture. Some of the Abu Ghraib materials looked quite similar to depictions of enemies during the rise of historic Empires in the ancient Near East. The more I studied scenes of war, the more I saw gender everywhere, constantly inscribed on real bodies in the worst of ways. I was much inspired by the scholarship of a particular author. Following the model of the scholar Joshua Trachtenberg, who wrote *The Devil and the Jews: The Medieval Conception of the Jew and its Relation to Modern Antisemitism* in 1943, I thought perhaps I could contribute a small piece toward the redemption of my people through a scholarly study of the history of war in our religious traditions, its ideologies and its images. Trachtenberg had wondered, as he wrote, whether his study was really a suitable response to the massive atrocities taking place against the Jews as part of World War II. But a scholar must do what a scholar does, and a resisting one all the more so.

As I rewrite this Preface in August, 2007, I am happy to relate that the story begun in this volume has had a least a partial end in real life. The government architects of the Iraq War, torture at Guantanamo Bay military facility in Cuba, and widespread curtailment of domestic civil liberties in the name of protection from a 'new' enemy of Evil-Doers have finally fallen, due less to moral outrage than outright incompetence. As the United States seems set to reclaim its Constitutional protections, neoconservatives openly yearn for another September 11-type attack to cover their own ineptitude, sex scandals, and other high crimes and misdemeanors.

As I sit safely — well, more or less — in a 'Blue State' in the Northeast of the USA, I freely admit that I am modestly heartened by the display of sanity in the American Congressional elections of 2006, and subsequent developments in the US body politick. Perhaps deliverance and redemption of the United States are at hand; perhaps not. If we have learned one thing over the years since the terrorist attacks of September 11, 2001, it is that if one wants justice, the price is eternal vigilance.

Triggered by the war crimes, I still wonder at how easily and effectively the Bible that I love was turned into a justification for war. How did we come to read the Bible as we do? I wonder how religious ethics came to be so narrowly focused on the areas between the waist and the knees, while actual, living children go hungry at an alarming rate.[2] I wonder how 'values' became so 'value-less' in a country that proudly declares itself to be overwhelmingly Christian and run by 'Compassionate Conservatives': as recently as 2006, the president-elect of our so-called 'Christian Coalition' was asked to step down for daring to suggest that the agenda of these good Christian people should include eliminating poverty and addressing global warming. Above all, I wonder what the Bible has to say about the part it plays in the one-sided values debate where patriarchal sexuality is All and the 'Word' of God is merely a mocking cover for political and moral corruption.

Scholars of the modern era are of several minds, of course: the Bible might be the innocent victim of deliberate misinterpretation — but then, there's the Book of Joshua, whose story and interpretation seems fairly plain. Or, perhaps the Bible is itself *part* of the problem, and the

---

2. We learned from the US government in the Fall of 2006 that there is no 'hunger' in the United States, only persons experiencing 'low food security'.

readers of it simply inscribe the same old desiccated principles of a self-identified 'Chosen' on each new generation of innocents as they are indoctrinated into the 'faith of the fathers'. Or, it may be that we, experts and ordinary readers alike, have a paucity of imagination in our approaches to the Bible, restrictive expectations that insure certain readings and not others, with certain conventions of reading and departures approved and others forbidden.

The essays presented here take the form of controlled probes into different layers of some of the big issues of reading, interpretation, and intention, all of which come together whenever any text is read by a community. You are not wrong if you perceive an archaeological metaphor here: I really *am* digging small, defined trenches into a much bigger mound of compositional complexities when I choose gender as a tool to focus my gaze and subsequent critique. Though I do not pretend to excavate a whole biblical book, text, or motif, I believe that the results of the studies done here give shape to the bigger sets of issues. My goal is to provide the critical factual details that make wholesome, integrative interpretations more likely than restrictive, literal, world-killing ones. The results offered here suggest outcomes and approaches that will give insight into the much bigger compendium of texts that is the Bible, even if you have no particular interest in the use of gender analysis as a methodology.

These days, reading the Bible (or the Qur'an for that matter) is a life-and-death proposition for some of us. The world of biblical criticism has recently made much of 'autobiographical criticism' in its methodology. While it is not my primary method, since this topic became so personal to me, I have adopted a way of interjecting the voice of the Human Rights Activist to stand before, after, or to the side of the Scholar's voice. They are indeed the same person, but the Activist voice is rendered in *italics* in Prologues, Epilogues, and occasionally footnotes. This is because the Activist is speaking out of experiences which do not derive from a text-based model, but rather from the real experiences of the people working in the area of religion and Human Rights. Since those experiences now inform my scholarship, it seemed only fair that I let them be voiced on their own terms—partisan, weeping, hoping, gasping. Since this book began with Abu Ghraib placed alongside other atrocities of empires of the past, the present had to find a way to represent itself in the interplay of epochs, concerns, and methodologies. I chose a change of fonts as the simplest way to let you know.

Since we do speak here of ultimate matters, I shall treat them as such, and adopt language which eschews the finest minutiae of the expert's methodological tool-kit. I shall not always feel obliged to pelt you with pages of footnotes or extensive reviews of the background issues, whether in Human Rights discourse, *or* in feminist biblical hermeneutics.

I am assuming that you, Gentle Reader, will take up *your* solemn role as Reader and pursue such questions as seem good in your eyes if you find that you need more than I have given.

2. *Shocked and Awed on the Road to Abu Ghraib*

Scholars of gender and religion are in a strange position, whether male or female or some combination of the two. When we simply *describe* religious practices concerning sex and gender, to the best of our limited abilities and with our various biases, we may have done our jobs as researchers into the past or present—but have we really done our *duty* if that is as far as we dare go? Formerly our commitments, political or religious, have seldom been considered appropriate subject matter for exploration as part of our topic by the mainstream academic academy. That, however, was the position *before* women and 'underrepresented minorities' entered as experts into those very disciplines. Often, it may seem to the newcomer that biblical studies possesses a *raison d'etre* of providing the intellectual and historical foundations of their exclusion from the hallowed halls of knowledge. Experts were trained to become 'disembodied', forgetful of their sex, working class background, or history as a people, so that 'knowledge' was able to masquerade as whole, positive, and objective. So were we all trained: give nothing personal away, as the personal had been effectively exiled as a grounding source of knowledge by any who were *not* white, male, European, usually Protestant, heterosexual elites. The very fact that some of us, by nature of race, class, sexual orientation and gender identity, nationality and so on, are having drastically different experiences is *itself* a critical spanner thrown into the machine of the academic pursuits. To acknowledge such socially conditioned differences in experience is to question the very claims upon which the Western establishment is founded: that experience and truth are unitary, indivisible, and invariable.

The scholarly situation has now changed; at least on the fringes where women and other excluded Others tend to work. We can speak of such things as 'autobiographical criticism' and 'post-Modern discourse', not to mention feminist readings, politics of identity, queer theory, representation of the gendered body, and classical deconstruction. We can blog, post, or set up websites; we can stream our videos and lectures (if we have the equipment); we can write letters to the Editor, or aspire to Greater Chomsky-hood, with a fair degree of impunity—at least here in True Blue America...so far.[3] Yet, even the Blues in the Free States feel

---

3. The news of January 15, 2006 brought word, for example, that not only has the National Security Agency been 'data-mining' and spying on US citizens without

a chill in the air as civil liberties disappear: our Muslim colleagues are targeted by right-wing supporters in the West and in their own countries of origin. American Muslim clerics returning from peace and interreligious dialogue conferences are removed from US airplanes when they pray; right-wing students are exhorted to turn in professors who teach any sort of view of peacemaking which departs from the agenda of the New American Century. Nice, white liberation theologians wonder if they will be able to board airplanes; former government workers swear that their email and phones are being monitored. This was our condition in the world of the 'Unitary Executive' (*L'état c'est moi?*) whose Christianity went right out the window whenever it was judged time to 'protect America' and stay the course of imperial conquest for control of disappearing resources.

Have we the strength to realize the depth of our losses and the tasks before us? Most of America, polls tell us, is singularly distanced from our war of conquest and occupation in terms of personal effect on their lives. Closer to home, the loss of civil liberties and the decimation of the Constitution at the hands of incompetents and hucksters have led to a rejection of the principles of the Unitary Executive and his permanent majority. The war in Iraq drags on, and the US public rejects both the causes for it and its continuing debacle.

So, although those formerly excluded from the creation of knowledge have experienced a modicum of theoretical openness, an ability to experiment with finding a voice for dangerous thoughts, how long will that last if we consent to an era of post-Constitutional totalitarian corporate rule in the United States? Those who cannot permit the TV-viewing public to watch Spielberg's *Saving Private Ryan* due to its pungent language and realistic portrayal of the violence of war (you mean it's *not* just a video game?) will scarcely permit *real* inquiries into the way certain kinds of biblical interpretation support corrupt political institutions. Old timers tell us to 'pick our battles', but sometimes that can easily turn into a decision to remain behind the desk. What sane person would willingly choose the option to 'come out' and join the popular discussion over faith-based government policies that just somehow *always* work out to support multinational corporate interests against the well being of the body politick? Scholars may not be up for 're-election'

benefit of warrant or any judicial oversight, but it seems the Internal Revenue Service is also taking more than a peek at political affiliations, class membership, etc. The loss of habeas corpus as part of the Military Commissions Act, passed by the Republican held Congress on its way out of office, means that no citizen who criticizes the government is really safe from Homeland Security and may expect no fair trial, hearing of evidence, or deliverance from long-term internment without charges ever being brought.

once they receive tenure in that time-honored system of maintaining seniority and exacting the most work out of the least secure, but they *can* lose their health insurance, their students, their job, their travel money, their promotions, and so on.⁴

Even in the faith-based communities that view themselves as liberal and activist, the old phantom of 'congregational divisiveness' is still a boogeyman with which one must reckon. Many Liberal churches, even in the Free States, had a difficult time raising the moral question of pre-emptive wars during the recent past. The specter of Vietnam and the havoc it wrought on congregations was still fresh in the minds of many a Vestry Committee. The prophet Micah would have been right at home in the Pastor's Study these last several years ('Do not preach' — thus they preach — 'one should not preach of such things; disgrace will not overtake us!', 2.6), as decent church leaders tried to raise questions of morality with a people fully bent on believing the best of their government, now endowed with god-like prescience and a parent's all-powerful ability to keep the children safe from harm. And the government *is* watching. It is now the case that pastors in this country who choose to preach sermons questioning the war in Iraq (and the upcoming one in Iran) run the risk of their church losing its tax-exempt status. Right-wing churches who pray death-wishes onto Supreme Court Justices in their biblically inspired 'Justice Sundays', however, are 'home free': no one questions *their* right to agitate for political appointees who will enforce patriarchal morality on a somnolent population.

For the present scholar, the deadening silence by church and society imposed on the experiences of the Iraqi women victims of abuse at Abu Ghraib constituted one more straw than this camel's back could hold. Blessed with employment, a generous, long-suffering editor, and a degenerative disease, I am uniquely situated as a biblical scholar with a list of feminist publications. My form of religious observance has made me a 'grunt' in Human Rights work — an 'HR defender', as we call ourselves.⁵ I am free to speak as others are not. This has also turned out to mean that I am 'free' to be harassed, accused of treason, heresy, non-heterosexuality, personal bias, and many other things besides. However, no amount of denunciation erases either my freedom or my responsibility. I simply find it impossible to write

---

4. Indeed, the Right prides itself on keeping track of and 'exposing' 'activist' or radical professors. For one chilling example currently at UCLA, see the site <http://www.uclaprofs.com>, accessed June, 2006, a nasty little project by the Bruins Alumni Association.

5. No one can afford to be called 'activist' anymore, thanks to the Right Wing 'sound machine'. Like the term 'liberal', activist now means 'traitor'.

about abuses in the past—standard feminist fare—and then 'pass by on the other side' when they occur right in front of my face—whether in the blog *Baghdad Burning*, in a swing state, in tribunal testimonies, or on Al-Jazeera.

3. A Word About the Illustrations

You will notice as you read many illustrations, executed in a variety of ways. The drawings were made by me with assistance from my photographer mate, Dr Craig Fontaine, spiffed with a whiz-bang 'Natural Media emulation' program for Windows, and then refined for whatever use I intend them. Drawings are made from reference shots taken from several angles, if possible. My husband's great height has given me the gift of 'aerial views' of the *inside* or tops of many artifacts viewed through glass cases, which have yielded their own surprises. While it is always best to examine the artifact itself before drawing it, not many museums permit an artist to set up shop before a major display, or come equipped for art when allowed into a back room for personal study of objects (don't forget to bring your transparent acetate and marking pen.). In only three cases (the Naqada period knife from Gebel el-Arak in the Louvre, the Oxford Palette in the Ashmolean Museum, and the wall painting in a Fifth Dynasty Egyptian tomb at Saqqarah) was I forced to resort to a selection of art books showing the same image. Travel to museums and other academic expenses were covered by a generous Lilly Foundation grant for Theological Research from the Association of Theological Schools in 2002–2003 to study visual theology in ancient Israel. This volume appears in fulfillment of that grant.

The drawings vary greatly, from simple schematics that attempt to keep scale for illustrative purpose, to artistic responses to some of the images. You will note that Sennacherib's reliefs of the siege of Lachish (modern Tell ed-Duweir), Judah in c. 710 BCE, as well as other Assyrian bas-reliefs in the British Museum, take a particular pride of place in cataloguing the abuse of bodily integrity in war. Studies on another topic took me to Lachish in the Late Bronze Age in a study of iconography in the southern Levant, but the solemn and horrific discovery in Tomb 120 claimed my attention,[6] and made me return to Lachish in its iconographic form on Assyrian palace walls. I watched as my own style progressed from the far distant past of Narmer's braggadocio claims

---

6. Fifteen hundred skeletons, a meter deep, all with skulls disarticulated. Skulls had fallen down the sides of the skeletal mound and not one had its lower jaw still in place where it should be. Early excavators of the site broke down the remains into approximately 750 males, 500 females, and all the rest too young to be sexed.

on an impractical palette to the stark woodcut or etching style of later drawings. Once I had real visual and tactile experience of Narmer's foes, usually deprived of genitals and expression by most schematics, they seemed to require of me a certain dimensionality and depth: these became more than simple outlines as I shifted away from the smiters to the smitten. While drawing the abuses at Lachish I found myself unable to do more than indicate the children, though with depth and nuance: like Hagar, I could not bear to look upon their faces. Where earlier drawings had been crisp, now the eighth century of Assyrian aggression took firm hold of the artist. Light, shadow and texture now dominate. The final drawing in this series is one of the impaled elders of Lachish in Chapter 3. It seems to this artist upon examination of close up photographs that the second captive is most certainly dead; the other two have postures which suggest their continuing pain and horror.

Chapter 1, ' "With Eyes of Flesh" (Job 10.4): Toward a Concept of Human Rights in the Bible and the Ancient Near East', has been substantially revised and reprinted with permission from its original appearance as 'Strange Bed Fellows: Scriptures, Human Rights and the UU Seven Principles' in the *Journal of Liberal Religion* 4 (Winter, 2003); <http://www.meadville.edu/journal/2003_fontaine_4_1.pdf>, given as an address at the General Assembly of the Unitarian Universalist Association in 2002. Here, I raise the question of 'rights' talk. Taking up the issue of Human Rights Foundationalism, we will explore where and how precisely our claims of universal human dignity (even for women and enemies) may be grounded. Are such claims essentially religious in nature? If so, what might that mean for the way we read the Bible? Selected texts from all three Peoples of the Book will be explored: Leviticus 19, the Sermon on the Mount, and Qur'anic passages on freedom of religion and conscience. I will attempt to answer the enduring questions that come up when trying to teach the Bible and Human Rights: do Human Rights *need* God? Does God *need* Human Rights?

Chapter 2, 'Gendering the Captive: Representations of the Abuse of Human Dignity', argues for a contextualized (that is, a view situated in the world of the ancient Near East) study of neighboring traditions on war and abuse. The role of gender in defining the 'Other' as a resource for exploitation will be explored in the medium of the artistic representation of combat art. Visiting the early dynastic periods of Sumer and Egypt, we find many of the humiliating practices now so familiar to us from the photos of Abu Ghraib. Even more chilling than the debased and enduring history of humans tormenting other living creatures, we will discover the relationship between the hunt and the war. What begins in the prehistoric representations of people with animals becomes the hunt; the hunt is then transmuted into the 'heroic' deeds of the Empire: smiting the Other. The Empire needs its prey, and it is easier all around if the prey is also female. We will find here that the Hebrew Bible speaks of women in war in ways seldom found in surrounding cultures.

Turning to the ancient texts again in Chapter 3, 'The Body Breached: Intimations of Human Dignity', we will explore attitudes toward bodily harm in ancient law codes and practice. Along with the historical notices of kings bragging of their brutality, we will explore scribal responses to war and abuse. Taking up the genre of the 'Humanitarian Narrative', I discuss the uses to which the Book of Job's 'Oath of Innocence' in chapter 31 is put, along with its Egyptian forerunner in the *Book of the Dead*. Both texts—and in the case of Egypt, the iconography—allow us to propose a biblically, cross-culturally grounded notion of both the 'good life' of any body and a concept of its fundamental violations. From these varied materials, I hope to propose a basic understanding of a nascent 'universal human rights' concept and the dignity which is its epistemological underpinning.

From matters theoretical and visual in the first three chapters, we turn our attention to the biblical text, set in ancient Near Eastern context in Chapters 4 through 8. Since we have no visual corpus of combat art to examine from ancient Israel and Judah—or rather, no *native* representations—textual abuse of captives, slaves, women and Others is explored. Combat art concerning our targeted biblical societies *does* exist, but only in the records of the conquerors, who have their own agendas in portrayal of wars. It is only fair to let the biblical texts speak back to the conquerors, even though both might share the same codes of gender, power, and difference. While we might properly say that in the text we are dealing with *'verbal abuse'* of the type-figures of prisoner, enemy, woman, slave, I would also argue that behind the law codes, the prophetic diatribes, and the narrative stories, *real* practices of abuse are present, ones which affect lives, then and now. Certainly, the biblical texts are no more representations of reality than are the iconographic schemes of the Empires, but neither are they divorced from the social, psychological and political realities of the communities for which they were written. By exploring the nature of text and interpretation, textual turns and twists, and discordant voices within those very texts or in neighboring people's versions, I hope to model responsible interpretation that is fair to the past and relevant to the present and future.

Chapter 4, 'Reading for the Best: Toward Diversity in Interpretation', began as part of 'Watching out for the Watchmen (Song of Songs 5:7): How I Hold Myself Accountable' and has been reprinted with additions from Charles Cosgrove (ed.), *The Meanings We Choose: Hermeneutical Ethics, Indeterminacy and the Conflict of Interpretations* (The Bible in the

21st Century; London: T&T Clark International, 2004). Here, I present an 'aesthetic hermeneutic', essential to my idea of a biblical 'Partnership Theology' — a theology that brings ancient text and modern society into their very best mutually informative affiliation. A new addendum explores the Christian practice of anti-Judaism in our theological readings, and wonders what impact those practices will have on the new tendency to demonize Islam and its texts.

Chapter 5, 'The Abusive Bible: On the Use of Feminist Method in Pastoral Contexts', appeared earlier in *A Feminist Companion to Reading the Bible: Approaches, Methods and Strategies* (ed. Athalya Brenner and Carole Fontaine; Sheffield: Sheffield Academic Press, 1997), reprinted here with permission. This work deals with the 'plain meaning' of biblical texts on purity, sexual infractions, and gender, and grew out of my pastoral work with survivors of rape, incest, and abuse.

Chapter 6, ' "Many Devices" (Qoh 7.23–8.1): Qoheleth, Misogyny and the *Malleus maleficarum*' is reprinted with permission from *A Feminist Companion to Wisdom and Psalms (Second Series)* (ed. Athalya Brenner and Carole R. Fontaine; Feminist Companion to the Bible, 2; Sheffield: Sheffield Academic Press, 1998). This essay looks at text reception: what happens when a fairly standard piece of misogyny from the biblical text falls into the hands of torturers? This piece uses folklore analysis and close literary readings to search out the method of proof-texting found in Kramer and Spengler's great early modern witch-hunting manual, a 'religious book' responsible for the outright torture of so many women in Europe. On the basis of statistical analysis of raw data, it turns out that the classical philosophers are more to blame than the Bible for the misogyny of this book, but the Bible plays its part — and only too well. A new section in this essay compares the state and religion-inspired torture of women as a class during Europe's witch craze with the actions and pronouncements of the Mullahs of Iran's fundamentalist Islamic state, where women serve as a projection screen from which all Western traces must be expunged — for the health of society and the women's own good, of course. Again, the use of proverbs by women or about women will become a lens that helps us view the intersection of gender, power, and politics.

Chapter 7, ' "Come, Lie with Me!" The Mythology of Honor Killing and Female Desire in Biblical Israel and the Ancient Near East', investigates the motif of the seductress who entices the young, virile male and, by doing so, suborns the authority of the older patriarchal husband. Texts from Mesopotamia, Egypt, Anatolia and the Hebrew Bible will explore the different appearances of this motif. The ritual of the 'Sotah' in Numbers 5, the case of Mrs Potiphar, and the Beloved in the Song of Songs all show a significant wrinkle in how biblical Israel viewed such situations and resolved them into honor killings which never take place. The final section on the Song is reprinted from Charles Cosgrove (ed.), *The Meanings We Choose: Hermeneutical Ethics, Indeterminacy and the Conflict of Interpretations* (The Bible in the 21st Century; London: T&T Clark International, 2004), with permission. The questions raised by these texts about sexual crimes under patriarchy, capital punishment (extra-judicial or not) for them, and the role of religion in shaping traditional cultural practices are powerful ones with ongoing effects in our own world: a recent Christian honor killing in Iraq shows this only too well.

Chapter 8, 'You Shall Not Stand Idly By', takes a fresh look at the 'historical Jesus' as a Human Rights Hero who can serve as a fitting and inspiring model of a witness for human dignity and worth. The findings of previous chapters are summarized, and interpretive strategies are explored. Partnership Theology is developed as a viable, principled option for interpretation among all three Peoples of the Book.

Those who wish to understand Human Rights discourse with respect to the Hebrew Bible are invited to pursue their studies further, or lead them for others, by using a self-paced study guide which was designed for the Non-Governmental Organization, the Women's United Nations Report Network (WUNRN), as part of a workshop given in Boston in October, 2005. WUNRN is the only body of its kind, based on a United Nations Report on women and religion, and has as its mandate the study of the rights of women and girls from the perspective of freedom of religion, which is guaranteed by numerous international instruments. This web-based course can be viewed on the WUNRN website (<http://www.wunrn.com/reference/pdf/ants.pdf>), where it provides many interactive links for leading discussions of Bible and Women's Rights, and introduces some basic features of Human Rights international conventions. You are quite welcome, Gentle Reader, to make use of this material in any way you may wish: as a leader's guide, as a tool for self-study, as an example for what needs to be done also for Islam, Judaism, and other world religions.

Finally, there is an Epilogue in poetry form. 'Only When Women Sing' was submitted as testimony in a Women's War Crime Tribunal in Mumbai in 2004, headed by Former Attorney General Ramsey Clark, concerning the legality of the US invasion and occupation of Iraq. From there, it made its way all around the globe on the WUNRN daily list-serve. It was subsequently reprinted in *Disciplesworld*, the pastoral magazine of the Disciples of Christ denomination.[7] The Human Rights institutions of the University of Minnesota discovered it from that source, and

---

7. *Disciplesworld* 3 (2004), p. 53.

requested permission to include it as a conclusion to a women's cantata consisting of speeches by Shirin Ebadi, the first Iranian woman to win a Nobel Peace Prize for her work on women's rights. Sung by hundreds of women's voices in a special event to honor Ebadi, the content of the poem engendered its own real-world manifestation. That words about women's rights and war could turn into songs of hope and courage instead of lament was a signal moment for this author.

Can such endings—poems and on-line educational activities—really be legitimate for a biblical scholar?, we must all wonder. Yet, when I used to complain that there is so little that speaks to a woman's experience in the Psalms, a highly esteemed European scholar of that book said, 'Then you must write them. Do you think inspiration ended with the canon? Do you think God approves of a book that has nothing in it for women? You must write'.

So, I do.

Naturally, Dear Reader, I long to transmute my own shock and awe at the collapse of moral and religious discourse in the United States. By writing, I hope to breed in myself some species of the endurance and rebirth that I have witnessed in the real lives of bodies which have been tortured, raped, humiliated, and imprisoned. By suggesting other ways to read the Bible, human eyes wide open for gender and dignity, I hope to make some small repair to the world that weeps on my neck, and clutches at my hand. I offer this book, in hopes that none of us can any longer bear to stand idly by in the presence of our neighbors' blood (Leviticus 19), whether those neighbors be close or far, blood kin, co-religionist, or personally known to us. Those among the People of the Book must educate themselves about their own traditions and those of their neighbors. Everyone needs to become familiar with basic concepts of Human Rights as a form of global repentance and dedication to the survival of *homo sapiens* and other land mammals on Planet Earth. Human Rights talk and faith talk must be viewed as two sides of a single coin. Like Peace and Righteousness in the Bible (Ps. 85.10-11), they must embrace, for neither makes much sense without the other.

It will be up to *you* to partner *this* book into its best, most useful reading.

And therein squats the toad: we are none of us innocent or uninvolved. As feminist Algerian poet Zineb Laoudj said of the repression of women in her own closed country at a Human Rights conference in 2005, 'What began in words ended in crimes...' This is a chilling observation for those raised on concepts of the Word, and that old saw that 'Sticks and stones can break my bones, but words will never hurt me'. I have seen, in my refusal to turn away, that words do indeed kill, make war, and destroy lives.

It is time for other kinds of words now.

Peace.
Shalom.
Salaam.
Salom.

We will give the Living Torah, writ large, the last word from a prophetic text on women, war, captivity and justice:

> Thus says the Lord: Do not let the wise boast in their wisdom, do not let the mighty boast in their might, do not let the wealthy boast in their wealth; but let those who boast boast in this:
> that they understand and know me,
> that I am the Lord;
> I act with steadfast love,
> justice, and righteousness in the earth,
> for in these things I delight,
> says the Lord (Jer. 9.23-24 NRSV).

Acknowledgements

No one writes a book filled with traumatic content spanning epochs without all kinds of assistance—moral, intellectual, spiritual and technical. The people in my life have put up with me and this awful topic during the completion of this book, and they deserve more than thanks. My husband, Professor Craig W. Fontaine, serves as the abiding backdrop for my pursuit of adequate notions of male honor; his assistance to me and my Human Rights friends at all levels of this enterprise has been quiet, powerful, and beneficent. Some global friends have called him my true 'secret weapon' in confronting male violence against women and children. I believe them.

My biblical colleagues and editors have been exemplary, continuing to encourage me when this project dragged on and seemed to have no end in real life: Athalya Brenner and David Clines have been more than patient, and bracing, too, when I could not see an end to the abuse that I was documenting. The humanist readings of Professor Hector Avalos have kept me company on this journey; the biblical insights of Professor Norman Habel, the famous ecologist and Joban scholar, have served as a place in my own discipline where I could turn for brief respite and refreshment. Charlie Cosgrove is to be credited with making me finally write up my own personal hermeneutical statement in his book, *The Meanings We Choose*; the reworked version of that progressive manifesto appears in this volume in sections of Chapters 4 and 7. Colleagues Mark Burrows and Elizabeth Nordbeck from the Worship, Theology and the Arts program at Andover Newton Theological School have provided encouragement to meld an art project with biblical studies. William Childs Robinson, III, has also had his hand in it: the cynical voice echoing pious sentiments sometimes heard in my writing must be attributed to his careful nurture of the will to resist saccharine theological assertions.

Beloved mentors have passed on to their reward since this book was undertaken. Claus Westermann, dying before the terrorist attacks of Sept. 11, 2001, nevertheless was constantly in my thoughts as I wrote. His experiences as a prisoner of war in World War II, which he shared with me as a companion piece to my personal Tales of the Ghetto reminiscences, reminded me that one can write, even if only a scrap of torn paper picked up in the barren exercise yard of the compound—his seminal book *Praise and Lament in the Psalms* began in just such a way. His is the voice that says 'Write, write!' when faced with the terrible lacunae around women's lives in the biblical text. Fr. Roland E. Murphy died after the September 11, 2001 attacks, but reflected with me before his death on the 'uphill battle' of trying to speak to American citizens of violence against Muslim women and in defense of a balanced reading of the Qur'an. He blessed me on my journeys of conscience, but persisted in hoping I would keep up with my Egyptian language study. I hope he would be pleased with this volume, because I took his advice seriously. Edward Platzer, my Jewish papa-of-choice, also died early in the new century; I know he would approve my mixture of art and living Torah! His was the very first printer's studio I ever visited, and clearly it left its mark. 'You won't despise me, will you, if I cannot believe in anything?' he once asked me; 'A Jew cannot believe, not after What Happened'. I reminded him that as his own, personally raised theologian, I had plenty of left-over belief for us both, and more. Without his love and interest in me as a child, I would never have known I was 'sharp as a matzo ball', and I would not be here writing. Little did he know what he was willing to the world when his family bought me my first library card!

This work has also brought me very close to my days at Duke University and the teachers who encouraged me there. Professor Harry Partin taught me methodology like no other, and directed my studies in Islam on women in the Qur'an, offering me my first glimpse of feminist criticism. Orval Wintermute, a student of Albright's, was my Comparative Semitics and Egyptian professor, and I have recalled fondly reading the Tale of Two Brothers and the Westcar Papyrus under his able guidance. Eric and Carol Meyers, the archaeologists, provided my first introduction to field work and they are the ones who assigned me to Small Artifact Registry when they discovered my drawing abilities. The Scholar Who Draws is partly of their making, and hot afternoons in Meiron, Israel excavating in 1977 frequently came to mind.

My thoughtful and rigorous drawing masters have impacted the work done here in a major way. Irish painter Tim Hawkesworth of the School of the Museum of Fine Arts in Boston is the relentless critic who weaned me away from the view that photo-realism was somehow more true than expressionist art. He told me I should daily thank my shaking hands (so troublesome if one is trying to be Norman Rockwell) for delivering me from a life of Hallmark Cards of 'Great Moments from the Bible'. 'Your greatest pitfall', he told me, 'is that you will someday bow to mere illustration. Don't!!' White South African artist Paul Stopforth honed my understanding of political art when he shared his etchings of the corpse of Human Rights hero Stephen Biko, which he made at the Biko family's request. Using only regular floor wax and the charcoal-like leavings of a Xerox machine, he preserved what oppressive governments tried so hard to hide from view. That brave body battered and scarred has not left my visual memory, even though the event was long ago. The dignity, power and witness of artistic attention to the 'voice' of the corpse—the body itself—formed a key impulse behind my own drawings of captives, prisoners, and scribes at war.

The staff at Andover Newton Theological School has been exceptionally supportive and helpful in my meanders through ancient and modern history. Cynthia Bolshaw and Diana Yount are enduring reminders that libraries do not contain only books! Their assistance has been timely, careful and cheerful. Jennifer Shaw, Faculty Assistant, has assisted me in the technical details, research, and served as careful reader looking over my shoulder as I wrote. This book would not be here without her careful, gracious attention to details and love of the Hebrew Bible. Student research assistants have had their part to play, too, and I name them here: Richard Hanks, Christina Sillari, Deborah Vickers, and Dawn Sorenson provided much assistance for which I remain very grateful indeed. YoungJoon Kim of Boston University School of Theology also provided me with much needed support in technical and research matters, and I am deeply grateful.

My friends and companions in the work of Human Rights deserve some special attention in my list of personal heroes. Lois A. Herman, the facilitator of WUNRN, and Elizabeth Sydney, O.B.E., head of the International Federation of Women United against Fundamentalism and For Equality (www.wafe-women.org) both serve as examples I can only hope to emulate. Women of power and purpose, they extend their energies across the globe, and they are a sight to behold in their indefatigable good works on behalf of women and girls. Angela Harris, Baroness of Richmond, is the fabulous sponsor of the work of WAFE in British governmental circles, and is another example of what a woman with power can do. Islamic scholar Riffat Hassan gave me my first introduction to the modern phenomenon of honor killings in Muslim societies. Her jurist brother, Farooq Hassan, Senior Advocate of Pakistan's (former) Supreme Court and visiting professor at Harvard, is my faithful Shari'a expert and conversation partner on the theological currents that sweep through the modern world. Jila Kazerounian, women's rights activist, has been a companion, partner, and friend of open generosity and support. Likewise, her husband Kazem has repeatedly shown his merit as a Human Rights mate: no delayed flight nor ice storm deters him from fetching the weary traveler home at last. Sarvi Chitsaz of the National Council of Resistance-Iran has also been a key person in understanding that theologians must be brought on board to confront matters theological, and her hard work and dedication to her people are inspirational to us all. Mrs Maryam Rajavi, President-Elect of a 'new' democratic Iranian resistance, has likewise served as a stirring example of global women who do not shirk from taking up the hardest of tasks. She has been the kindest of hostesses and a tireless worker for democracy and a moderate Islam free of gender bias. Her use of proverbs, and personal leadership style characterized by womanly warmth and wisdom empower all who know her. It is little wonder that she is loved by many and feared by some.

Part of the research for this book was undertaken during a sabbatical semester in 2004, graciously granted by Andover Newton. The drawings appearing in the book were made possible by a study grant from the Association of Theological Schools for Theological Research in 2002–2003, and this work appears in fulfillment of that grant. I was ably assisted by the staff of many fine libraries and museums. I would particularly like to thank Jonathan Tubb, of the Ancient Near Eastern Collection at the British Museum, and Drs Nigel Strudwick and Neal Spencer of the Department of Ancient Egypt and Sudan, also at the British Museum. I also wish to thank Ian Carroll, Collections Manager at the Institute of Archaeology at the University College of London. In Amsterdam, connections were made for me by Professor Athalya Brenner, and the curators of the Allard Pierson Museum at the University of Amsterdam were particularly gracious: Geralda Jurriaans-Helle, Drs Rene van Beek and Willem van Haarlem literally opened the glass cases for me and allowed me to rummage about in their non-provenanced 'trash'.

I would also like to thank Continuum Press, Sheffield Academic Press, and the *Journal of Liberal Religion* for their permission to reprint earlier versions of some of the material found in Chapters 1, 4, and 7. The material on anti-Judaism in Chapter 4 was prepared for a conference on Jewish-Christian dialogue, 'No Cause to Boast: The Teaching of Contempt', sponsored by the US Holocaust Museum, and held jointly by Andover Newton Theological School and Hebrew College in 1997.

During the writing of this book, many women made captive by misogynist traditions attributed to religion have been tortured and were murdered in so-called 'Honor' Killings. While it was not possible to collect all their names, the following list acknowledges the death by torture that took place while I was safe, researching and writing. Each star represents five women whose deaths were reported but not their names.

Thank you for remembering them.

Newton Centre, Massachusetts
2007

Acknowledgements xxix

The Remembered

United Nations statistics estimate that approximately 5,000 women worldwide are victims of so-called 'honor killings', and many more incidences go unreported. Each star below represents 5 women. The names listed here represent only a small handful of the women whose lives have been taken during the writing of this book.

```
* * * * * * * * * * * * * * * * * * * * * * * * * * * * * * * * * * * * * * * * * * * * * * * * *
* * * * * * * * * * * * * * * * * * * * * * * * * * * * * * * * * * * * * * * * * * * * * * * * *
* * * * * * * * * * * * * * * * * * * * * * * * * * * * * * * * * * * * * * * * * * * * * * * * *
* * * * * * * * * * * * * * * * * * * * * * * * * * * * * * * * * * * * * * * * * * * * * * * * *
* * * * * * * * * * * * * * * * * * * * * * * * * * * * * * * * * * * * * * * * * * * * * * * * *
* * * * * * * * * * * * * * * * * * * * * * * * * * * * * * * * * * * * * * * * * * * * * * * * *
* * * * * * * * * * * * * * * * * * * * * * * * * * * * * * * * * * * * * * * * * * * * * * * * *
* * * * * * * * * * * * * * * * * * * * * * * * * * * * * * * * * * * * * * * * * * * * * * * * *
* * * * * * * * * * * * * * * * * * * * * * * * * * * * * * * * * * * * * * * * * * * * * * * * *
* * * * * * * * * * * * * * * * * * * * * * * * * * * * * * * * * * * * * * * * * * * * * * * * *
* * * * * * * * * * * * * * * * * * * * * * * * * * * * * * * * * * * * * * * * * * * * * * * * *
* * * * * * * * * * * * * * * * * * * * * * * * * * * * * * * * * * * * * * * * * * * * * * * * *
* * * * * * * * * * * * * * * * * * * * * * * * * * * * * * * * * * * * * * * * * * * * * * * * *
* * * * * * * * * * * * * * * * * * * * * * * * * * * * * * * * * * * * * * * * * * * * * * * * *
* * * * * * * * * * * * * * * * * * * * * * * * * * * * * * * * * * * * * * * * * * * * * * * * *
* * * * * * * * * * * * * * * * * * * * * * * * * * * * * * * * * * * * * * * * * * * * * * * * *
* * * * * * * * * * * * * * * * * * * * * * * * * * * * * * * * * * * * * * * * * * * * * * * * *
* * * * * * * * * * * * * * * * * * * * * * * * * * * * * * * * * * * * * * * * * * * * * * * * *
* * * * * * * * * * * * * * * * * * * * * * * * * * * * * * * * * * * * * * * * * * * * * * * * *
* * * * * * * * * * * * * * * * * * * * * * * * * * * * * * * * * * * * * * * * * * * * * * * * *
* * * * * * * * * * * * * * * * * * * * * * * * * * * * * * * * * * * * * * * * * * * * * * * * *
* * * * * * * * * * * * * * * * * * * * * * * * * * * * * * * * * * * * * * * * * * * * * * * * *
```

Banaz Agha
Chnar Akram
Shwbo Rauf Ali
Rabiakhatun Ansari
Du'a Khalil Aswad
Janna Bibi
Shakeela Bibi
En'am Deifallah
Ileshvah Eyvazimooshabad
Zahra Ezzo
Reem Abu Ghanem
Sabrin Abu Ghanem
Shirihan Abu Ghanem

Hamda Abu Ghanem
Faten Habash
Samar Hasson
Nahed Hija
Suha Hija
Lina Hija
Kifaya Husayn
Karolin Kooshabeh
Samina Korkani
Karmin Koshabeh
Banaz Mahmod
Samaira Nazin
Nejat (no last name)
Hina Saleem
Amani Shakirat
Rudaina Shakirat
Shahzadi Shar
Rafayda Qaoud
Heshu Yones

ABBREVIATIONS

AAR	American Academy of Religion
AB	Anchor Bible
AEL	Miriam Lichtheim, *Ancient Egyptian Literature: A Book of Readings* (3 vols.; Berkeley: University of California, 1975).
ANE	Ancient Near East
ANEP	James B. Pritchard (ed.), *The Ancient Near East in Pictures Relating to the Old Testament* (Princeton, NJ: Princeton University Press, 2nd edn, 1974).
ANET	James B. Pritchard (ed.), *Ancient Near Eastern Texts Relating to the Old Testament* (Princeton, NJ: Princeton University Press, 3rd edn, 1969).
BA	*Biblical Archaeologist*
BARev	*Biblical Archaeology Review*
BASOR	*Bulletin of the American Schools of Oriental Research*
BIS	Biblical Interpretation Series (Leiden)
BJS	Brown Judaic Studies
BL	Bible and Literature (Sheffield)
BM	British Museum
BT	Babylonian Talmud, Isidore Epstein (ed.), *The Soncino Hebrew-English Talmud* (London: Soncino Press, 1935-48).
BTB	*Biblical Theology Bulletin*
CANE	Jack M. Sasson (ed.), *Civilizations of the Ancient Near East* (4 vols.; New York: Scribner, 1995).
CBQ	*Catholic Biblical Quarterly*
CBQMS	*Catholic Biblical Quarterly*, Monograph Series
CIS	Culture and Ideology Series, Sheffield Academic Press
CTH	*Catalogue des Textes Hittites*
EA	*El Amarna* (refers to the numbering of the letters in VAB 2/1 and Rainey, AOAT 8^2)
EAS	Elkunirsa, Asherah, and the Storm-God
FCB	Athalya Brenner (ed.), *The Feminist Companion to the Bible* (1st series; Sheffield: Sheffield Academic Press, 1993).
GE	Gilgamesh Epic
Gos. Thom.	*Gospel of Thomas*
HB	Hebrew Bible
HR	*History of Religions*
HSM	Harvard Semitic Monographs
HTR	*Harvard Theological Review*
JANES	*Journal of the Ancient Near Eastern Society*
JARCE	*Journal of the American Research Center in Egypt*

JBL	*Journal of Biblical Literature*
JCS	*Journal of Cuneiform Studies*
JELS	*Journal of Egyptian Language Studies*
JES	*Journal of Ecumenical Studies*
JFS	*Journal of Feminist Studies in Religion*
JNES	*Journal of Near Eastern Studies*
JSOT	*Journal for the Study of the Old Testament*
JSOTSup	*Journal for the Study of the Old Testament Supplement Series*
JPF	Judean Pillar Figurines
KMT	*Kemet*
KUB	*Keilschrifturkunden aus Boghazköi* (34 vols.; Staatliche Museen zu Berlin [Germany]. Berlin: Akademie-Verlag, 1921–1944).
LAE	W.K. Simpson (ed.), *The Literature of Ancient Egypt: An Anthology of Stories, Instructions, Stelae, Autobiographies, and Poetry* (New Haven: Yale University Press, 3rd edn, 2003).
LBA	Late Bronze Age
LXX	The Septuagint
MAL	Middle Assyrian Laws
MI	Myth of Illuyanka
MIO	*Mitteilungen des Institut für Orientforschung*
NK	New Kingdom
NT	New Testament
NTS	*New Testament Studies*
OBT	Overtures to Biblical Theology
OMCT	*Organisation Mondiale Contra la Torture* (World Organization Against Torture)
OTL	Old Testament Library
RA	*Revue d'assyriologie et d'archéologie orientale*
RB	*Revue biblique*
RHA	*Revue Hittite et asianique*
SBL	Society of Biblical Literature
SBLDS	Society of Biblical Literature Dissertation Series
SBLMS	Society of Biblical Literature Monograph Series
THeth	*Texte der Hethiter* (Heidelberg)
TDNT	*Theological Dictionary of the NT*
TTB	Tale of Two Brothers
TToday	*Theology Today*
UN	United Nations
UNHCHR	United Nations High Commission on Human Rights
VAB	*Vorderasiatische Bibliotek*, vol. II (J.A. Knudtzon, *Die El-Amarna-Tafeln: mit Einleitung und Erläuterungen / hrsg.*, Anmerkungen und Register bearbeitet von Otto Weber und Erich Ebeling, 1-2 [Neudruck der Ausg., 1915; repr., Aalen: O. Zeller, 1964]).
VTSup	*Vetus Testamentum*, Supplements
WAW	Writings from the Ancient World Series (SBL; Atlanta: Scholars Press)
WBC	Word Bible Commentary
WUNRN	Womens United Nations Report Network
ZAW	*Zeitschrift für die alttestamentliche Wissenschaft*

Chapter 1

'WITH EYES OF FLESH' (JOB 10.4):
TOWARD A CONCEPT OF HUMAN RIGHTS IN THE BIBLE AND THE ANCIENT NEAR EAST

1. *Baghdad Bound: On the Road between Wars*

I often tell my students, when sharing my personal strategy for stress management, 'When the going gets tough, the tough go to the Bronze Age...' I am fortunate that electronic resources allow me to visit far away museums, access long ago texts, and perform my research without ever leaving my desk, should I so choose. My biblical interests are broad, but include a strong commitment to contextualization—setting the Bible in its aesthetic, cultural, and historical milieu—as a key hermeneutic for my interpretations and their modern applications. The focus on the ancient Near Eastern setting of our biblical texts also operates as a 'diffusing activity' that trauma specialists are so enthusiastic in recommending for mending survivors of conflict.[1] Since no one in my work world particularly cares about Assyrian law codes, for example, absolutely no theological stigma of radicalism is attached to their study. The same is true of the iconographic traditions that are so often transmuted into text by the biblical authors, so this is one place where I have safely pitched my tent out of the line of fire. I freely admit it: sometimes expediency is the mother of scholarship, too.

Working on a much longer project that tries to take the Song of Songs seriously in all sorts of theological ways, I received a grant that allowed me to do a significant amount of work in museums cataloging my motifs of choice: gazelles and trees in ancient Israel, Judah, and the surrounding regions. Visiting Oxford, London, Paris, Amsterdam,

---

1. I work at a free-standing Protestant seminary (not attached to a university). Denominational approval is the life blood of survival and taken very seriously indeed. I do not belong to the institution's traditional constituent denominations, and hence, have diplomatic immunity on most struggles. However, I have been working in the area of religion and Human Rights as an independent content expert since 1999.

New York City, and Boston museums, sketch book and camera in hand, I was also intrigued by other research options beyond my gazelles. In particular, I realized there was both incredible variation *and* standardization of scenes featuring couples—all kinds of couples: paired warrior buddies, romantic partners, mother-and-child, father-and-son, deity and worshipper...king and captive. I did some documentation as I found couples, and put that work aside for a later time.

As is often the case, my *Big, BIG Book of Gazelles and Trees* has begun in piecemeal fashion, as I publish various studies drawn from the project while preparing for more research trips and studies to round off my corpus of evidence. Working on relating the image of the 'woman well', female-gendered artifacts holding liquid, to the teachings of the Book of Proverbs on promiscuity, I began with a mother-goddess handled jug found at Kish, in ancient Mesopotamia, now in the Ashmolean Museum in Oxford.[2] My artifact came from Cemetery A, carved into the palace complex of Mound A at the end of the Early Dynastic Period. While the Iraq war and the US military's push to 'clean out' insurgents in their 'death throes'[3] swirled through the news of the modern world, I quietly sorted the evidence from the first Sumerian city to go from local to regional leadership, thereby becoming a symbol of imperial power and conquest for later wannabe-kings. I thought I would be safe in the past, quiet in the grave. It was not to be.

Since excavations of Kish had begun in the 1920s, the site had the misfortune to see both its excavations and the recovered items split up between several excavators and museums in different parts of the world. The lack of continuity in recording of the excavations necessitated a lot of geographical and ancillary study just to gain a cognitive map of the region and the city's commanding position at the spot where the Tigris and the Euphrates lay closest together. Oddly, it seemed all the works on Kish of the early twentieth century were eager to give geographic orientation based on locally known coordinates. Quite literally, I found myself, day after day, being pointed between 'Ghraib' and 'Faloojeh', according to the British team of excavators. It was inevitable, I suppose, that one such search should take me to the bend in the river where the Girl Blogger of Baghdad, 'Riverbend', writes her diary entitled *Baghdad*

---

2. Carole R. Fontaine, 'Visual Metaphors and Proverbs 5:15-20: Some Archaeological Reflections on Gendered Iconography', in Ronald L. Troxel, Kelvin G. Friebel and Dennis R. Margary (eds.), *Seeking out the Wisdom of the Ancients: Essays Offered to Honor Michael V. Fox, on the Occasion of his Sixty-Fifth Birthday* (Winona Lake, IN: Eisenbrauns, 2005), pp. 185-202.

3. These days, the Summer of 2007, we are now told those rending struggles are not civil war, but the 'birth pangs of democracy'.

Burning.[4] It was Riverbend, through the eyes of her family and neighbors, who showed the world the horrors of the US attack on civilians in Fallujah with outlawed weaponry like white phosphorus (napalm), long before military whistle-blowers and the mainstream media said a word.

My scholarly searches of internet databases, then, looking for materials from older journals of archaeology with full-text articles routinely also turned up sites on Abu Ghraib, Fallujah, and Baghdad. As I contemplated the beginnings of empire in an oil-rich region of the world, ancient and modern melded in image and impact. The photos of abuse of Iraqi prisoners at the hands of their American *liberators* at Abu Ghraib were latter-day reinventions of the mother-of-pearl inlays displaying prisoners of war in the banqueting hall of Palace A at Kish. The outrages taking place at Fallujah where the United States was illegally using weapons of mass destruction outlawed by international treaty had blended into the imperial ruler's ideological, gendered delight in the destruction of his male captives.

There was no peace to be found in the past, only the beginnings of the kinds of atrocities in which modern people also indulge. 'No human dignity there', I thought, as I pondered the vicissitudes of empire and expansion. I was put in mind of the biblical Psalms' attention to the prisoner and the captive, and began to wonder whether the Hebrew Bible might not have made a significant break with the tradition of display and open torment of captives. Male captives were replaced, of course, with the figure of Israel and Judah as the battered whoring wife on public, pubic display in the prophetic writings, everywhere justified as a well-deserved punishment from God. Was this an improvement?, I wondered. Clearly, the topic deserved more attention, and since there was no escape, and finally, no desire for one, I set out to

---

4. <http://riverbendblog.blogspot.com>, cited August 3, 2007; Riverbend's blogs have now been collected and published as *Baghdad Burning: Girl Blog from Iraq* (New York: Feminist Press at CUNY, 2005). Go, read it. David Clines called my attention to Fallujah's earlier life as *Pumbeditha*, a home of the Babylonian Talmud, so it is no surprise that the destruction of this famous center of learning was mourned by the founder of the peace organization, The Shalom Center. Rabbi Arthur Waskow writes of the US military action there, ' "Love your neighbor as yourself." For your neighbor IS yourself. If we forget thee, Pumbeditha, the right arms of our young men will wither into shreds and stumps of flesh. God help us, God help us, God help us' ('Falluja is the Birthplace of the Talmud', December 1, 2004), cited February 8, 2008 <http://www.shalomctr.org/node/729>. For videos and first hand survivor accounts, see <http://www.rememberfallujah.org/index.html>, which shows some significant signs that religious groups in Britain condemn the action of the military coalition in Iraq.

study the depiction of captives and women in the art of the ancient Near East. What follows is the result of that study, and its relationship to our modern thinking about gender, rights, abuse, and morality, religious or otherwise.

Why even ask?
One of the frequent experiences that a person in Human Rights work often encounters is marked hostilities between religious groups and the 'Human Rights Agenda'.[5] Whether standing on the religion side of 'ministry' (however that may be construed) or the Human Rights side of international law aimed at mitigating abuses, we find rather similar views: the Other Side is part of the problem, *not* part of the solution. Human Rights workers are viewed with suspicion by indigenous religions that chafe at the idea of any international consensus interfering with their right to practice religion as they choose (*also* a right guaranteed by the *United Nations Declaration of Universal Human Rights [UNDUHR]*). Secular Human Rights defenders, for their part, find religious leaders and traditions to be obstructive, narrowly-focused, and certainly no defenders of universal rights. Even when a common goal is clearly identified—like mounting international criminal tribunals to bring justice to victims of genocide,[6] there is likely to be a clash. As one doctor from Physicians for Human Rights told an interfaith group with whom I work, 'We really *need* you, your knowledge and your expertise!' She related a story where religious authorities, based on *their* views of human dignity residing in the corpse or bones of a victim, attempted to thwart exhumations by international commissions trying to establish identities and causes of death, much needed documentation for war crimes proceedings. 'Can't you find some way from *within* to help us do our work?' Here at last was someone asking for a theological entry point to rectifying real abuses. *Could* we help?

Yes, as a matter of fact, there *is* much to be said to the physician and her commission. From the Bible's point of view, the 'bloods' of Abel (Gen. 4.10-11) cry out from the ground for justice in Genesis, constituting the first human prayer. If we were like God and could see into the inner heart of things, we would not need to exhume bodies for the testimonies they have to give. In recognition of our humility as created beings, we also recognize our duty to render justice in ways that are appropriate to the kind of creatures we are. Exhumation and autopsy,

---

5. For some persons, this agenda is every bit as godless and threatening as the 'Homosexual Agenda' we hear so much about in Right Wing America.

6. Such activities are also keys in providing resolution for families, allowing grief and survivor guilt to be processed and eventually integrated into the psyche.

then, should be understood as fulfillments of the imperative that one should not 'stand idly by in the presence of your companion's blood' (Lev. 21.20). Return of the body to relatives (or appropriate group, if no relatives exist) and/or reburial of the body responds to the belief that human dignity that still resides in the corpse or its remains. Thus the twin concerns of justice and respect for the dead are met.

Maybe contextualized theology *can* help.

Theological Abuse

In an age of growing, worldwide religious fundamentalism that is most often known through its attempts to abridge the rights of others in order to build a better theocracy, it is important to recognize the religious shaping of many of the abuses of the body that we will be discussing. Ideologies may appeal to religious texts or national law, but they always need to appeal to *something* to mask their genuine motives of domination (for our own good, of course). These issues are particularly worthy of study when they concern women and girls, a group that the New Testament might very well have referred to as 'the least of them' (Mt. 25.40). Yakin Ertürk, Special Rapporteur on Violence against Women reporting to the UN High Commission on Human Rights, calls upon community leaders, academicians, including religious scholars and leaders, media, government entities, national and international NGOs to engage in 'cultural negotiation' of group interests versus the rights of women.[7] Her analysis shows that when states or groups seek to repress women it is often in the service of group interests: they routinely sacrifice the women to bolster group identity—only witness the problem women's rights caused in the attempt to draft an Iraqi constitution, making Iran the *real* winner of the war in Iraq. As one Muslim scholar has remarked, nowhere does the standard of 'cultural relativism' hold more sway than in the treatment of women and girls.[8] When international law seeks to respond to charges of cultural imperialism, they allow states to 'balance' the rights of women against the needs of group survival—but the balance is routinely tilted away from those needing the most protection. Sunder notes that the law's view of religion and its practice is the same as that of the fundamentalists: by assuming that

---

7. UN doc E/CN.4/2004/66; para. 55(b) (2003), 'Integration of the Human Rights of Women and the Gender Perspective: Violence against Women', cited September 26, 2007 <http://www.unhchr.ch/Huridocda/Huridoca.nsf/TestFrame/b0ec728d91b871d8c1256e610040591e>.

8. Madhavi Sunder, 'A Culture of One's Own: Learning from Women Living under Muslim Laws', in Betsey Reed (ed.), *Nothing Sacred: Women Respond to Religious Fundamentalism and Terror* (New York: Thunder's Mouth Press, 2002), pp. 149-63.

religion is 'homogeneous, static, discrete, God-given, and imposed on individuals from the top down', Human Rights becomes complicit in stifling the very dissent from within that it claims to champion.[9] Yet, the States of the world need to understand that the practice of religion can be subjected to moral scrutiny and debate, and that they are accountable to women and other Others for the guarantee of their rights, full access to legal protections, and bodily integrity.

For scholars of the Bible and the religious authorities in charge of passing on the tradition, 'rights talk', whether of universals or particulars, is seldom part of our discourse. The patriarchal formulation of the scriptural religions of Judaism, Christianity, and Islam does not easily permit the claim that intrinsically *all* human beings are of equal worth or destiny, since some are owners and others are owned. Indeed, the profound impact of the concept of the 'election' of a particular group for divine favor makes it unlikely that rights talk will ever 'catch on' in religious circles if it requires the Elect to hold themselves equal to the Others who are not so fortunate as to be them.

Of course, one need not explain this lacuna in scriptural anthropologies solely by reference to theological origins. Survey of Human Rights instruments show that traditions of the West around limitation of state power over the individual or groups have shaped this current dialogue. Certainly, it would be impossible to claim that universal rights in the way we think of them today—everyone everywhere, regardless of circumstances, having the same standing from the global point of view— were ever a salient feature of antiquity's thinking about the nature and destiny of *man*. These are modern concepts that owe much to the Protestant Reformation, the Enlightenment, and seven hundred years of Anglo-Saxon jurisprudence. While many of the Human Rights treatises gesture toward a supposed underpinning in religion, the more common bond in these documents is not religion's theoretical profound respect for all life, but rather the international conventions of law which developed during modernity.

2. *The Problem with Terminology and Sources of Human Rights*

Feminist critical analysis of religion and ethics often differs substantially from that of the traditional male experts who tended to dominate this field of discourse,[10] and so feminist theory ought always to be a part of the discussion—but all too often it is not. There are considerable challenges and difficulties in any attempt to anchor basic notions

---

9. Sunder, 'A Culture', pp. 149-63 (150).
10. Thank Go(o)d/dess!

of Human Rights in the traditional patriarchal forms of the Scripture-based religions of the world. Since the ambiguities which I present here are especially observable with reference to establishing rights for women and girls, I will be using that group as a lens for focusing my topic. I will speak primarily of the Peoples of the 'Book' and what is in their Book—the Bible, not just because this is what I know best, but also because it is to *this* Book as read by Jews, Muslims, and Christians that one may trace many of the founding ideas that influenced philosophers of Human Rights. However, according to some experts on the status of women, the questions raised here about the content and effects of Scriptures[11] on Human Rights apply equally to other classical religions like Hinduism and Buddhism,[12] but as those religions are outside my area of expertise, I will concentrate on the Bible, especially the First Testament, as it is held in common by all three groups.

The dramatic political changes of the last century form a backdrop to epistemological dialogue about Human Rights which began as long ago as the Reformation and Enlightenment in particular, and in British jurisprudence before that. What exactly *are* Human Rights and from where do they come? *Is* it true, as Natural Law philosopher John Locke said, that certain rights are inalienable? Are rights really present if one cannot enjoy them, or if there is no way to enforce them? How do we establish universal rights in a plural world,[13] still dogged by the racist legacies of imperialism? Indeed, does not all this focus on the worth of a single individual suggest that the whole concept is beholden to a

---

11. A word on our choice of terminology: with capitalization, I use 'Scripture' to refer to the biblical text as it is held to be of special authority and origin as believed by communities of faith. The term 'Hebrew Bible' or 'New Testament' will be used where I refer to the text as an object of study, not laden with the theological understandings of postbiblical faith communities. 'Scriptures' here refers to the Torah, New Testament, and Qur'an which are held in common by believers in the Abrahamic religions.

12. M.T. Whyte, *The Status of Women in Preindustrial Societies* (Princeton, NJ: Princeton University Press, 1978). Although women have lower status in the cultures which follow the religions of the Book, the researcher feels this is not *necessarily* to be related to the teachings and practice of those religions, but may in fact reflect that those societies tend to be more formally organized, hierarchical, and stratified, situations in which women and children fare less well.

13. 'Biocentric Pluralism' refers to the ethical position that just like individual living entities, ecosystems and species can be benefited or harmed, and therefore have an ideal 'good' which inheres for them. Hence, they are moral subjects, capable of having interests and rights (James P. Sterba, *Three Challenges to Ethics: Environmentalism, Feminism, and Multiculturalism* [New York and Oxford: Oxford University Press, 2001], pp. 29-31). From the point of view of this ethical framework, the claim of the human species to be superior to other species becomes unsupportable.

Eurocentric individualism, and so cannot be considered especially normative? Does the recognition that someone does in fact have a right (such that they are considered a *right-bearer*) always imply a *duty-bearer* who must respect or, at least, not hinder the enjoyment of the right-bearer's right? And is the right itself the real matter at stake or is it the object of the right which the right-bearer is seeking to enjoy?[14] Do rights emerge as a function of hypothetical contracts, or are contracts only possible in the context of rights? Are we obliged to be able to show rational grounds for positing Human Rights before we can enforce them? Are Human Rights *absolute* — that is, should they be considered a normative requirement regardless of culture, tradition, national laws, race, gender and so on?[15]

These are only some of the questions of juridical and moral philosophy that beset those of us who would like to establish universal Human Rights, and space precludes discussion of all of them here. I will just say that for those of us in a pragmatic, advocacy position (religiously inspired or otherwise)[16] with respect to understandings of entitlement to rights, we do *not* cede that a right does *not* exist simply because a group is not allowed to enjoy it (or its object), no one is willing to enforce it, or because the religious teachings of the community in question do not choose to recognize that right. Wherever we choose to lodge the source of universal human rights, be it God, Natural Law, or feminist anthropology, we *do* believe them to exist, even in the absence of their enjoyment, enforcement, or cogent philosophical foundation. This point will become especially important later as religious reformers attempt to argue that Human Rights are ceded in their Scriptures and only require recognition or enforcement to correct their denial to certain groups, such as women, outsiders, and dissenters — the three great groups who are largely marginalized in most religions' thinking about rights.

Simply put, Human Rights are rights which belong to every human, simply by virtue of being born human. The extended effect of these

---

14. Jack Donnelly, *The Concept of Human Rights* (New York: St. Martin's Press, 1985), pp. 11-44. Donnelly concludes that Human Rights are rights every human has just by being born human; Martin E. Marty, 'Religious Dimensions of Human Rights', in John Witte, Jr and Johan D. van der Vyver (eds.), *Religious Human Rights in Global Perspective: Religious Perspectives* (The Hague: Martinus Nijhoff Publishers, 1996), pp. 1-16; Michael J. Perry, *The Idea of Human Rights: Four Inquiries* (Oxford: Oxford University Press, 1998), pp. 16-20.

15. Sterba, *Challenges*, pp. 27-49, 77-103; Donnelly, *Concept*, pp. 80-88; Perry, *Idea*, pp. 87-106.

16. When operating in a religious sphere, such work is considered a 'ministry', even though it may operate outside the borders of one's own group of believers.

intrinsic rights is that there are some things which should *never* be done to *any* human, just as there are some things which *ought* to be done for *every* human. Simple enough, or so you would think until you wade into the discourse on how to ground those rights. (This quest for lucidity has been dubbed Human Rights Foundationalism, and is sometimes felt to be a theoretical barrier to the activity of securing and enforcing Human Rights.)

In the last two or three centuries there has been a radical shift in thinking about the role of religion in the obtaining and enforcing universal Human Rights. Philosophers of the Enlightenment noted, not without reason given Europe's bleak religious history, that historically religious groups had largely neglected the rights of many: slaves, women, children, homosexuals, and most especially, those who dissented from the doctrinal statements of the given religion. Human Rights, almost always conceived as the 'rights of Man', were anchored in both historical moments when rights were secured by secular groups—the signing of the Magna Carta, for example—and in the philosophies of Natural Law, most especially in John Locke, the hypothetical social contracts of Kantian ethics, or the Utilitarianism of John Stuart Mill. From the point of view of the Enlightenment, the 'supernaturalism' permeating most of the religions then known rendered them both irrational (in a very narrow sense of rationality) and outdated as a source for universal ethical norms.

We should not dismiss, however, the historical evidence of successful inculturation of Christianity as a source for universal rights within the framework of Anglo-Saxon jurisprudence.[17] If the Reformation freed the Old World from a clerically mediated Scripture and encouraged individuals and groups to read Scripture for themselves and decide, we must not overlook the way culture shaped those readings. If we look at one of the most successful 'Historic Peace Churches', the Religious Society of Friends (Quakers), we note that its founding ideas come from a deep engagement with British common law as well as Scripture, meditated upon in community.[18]

The following features constitute identifying markers of this British legal tradition:

---

17. Actually, in the realm of women's rights, Christians owe much to the traditions of Nordic tribes who simply would not convert without some safeguards to women's rights (see the present writer's *Smooth Words: Women, Proverbs and Performance in Biblical Wisdom* [JSOTSup, 356; Sheffield: Sheffield Academic Press, 2002], pp. 65-71).

18. Ann K. Riggs, 'Inculturation: Building on the Cultures of our Past', in Fernando Enns, Scott Holland and Ann K. Riggs (eds.), *Seeking Cultures of Peace: A Peace Church Conversation* (Telford, PA: Cascadia Publishing House, 2004), pp. 97-108.

- a body of general rules prescribing social conduct,
- enforced by ordinary royal courts,
- and characterized by the development of its own principles in actual legal controversies,
- by the procedure of trial by jury, and
- by a doctrine of the supremacy of law.[19]

These elements will look quite familiar to those who proceed in Human Rights work from the perspective of international law—all, except that modern states have no particular passion for the enforcement of rights. The theology of the Quakers, especially in key thinkers like George Fox of the seventeenth century and John Woolman of the eighteenth century, is deeply *biblical* theology that sees the role of individual conscience attuning itself to God's true wisdom, but does not see this in opposition to legal traditions. Rather, the legal traditions are initially informed by this inner knowledge available to all. Terms like 'reason', 'rationality', 'good sense', and 'conscience' are used to link human sentiment and perception to a grounding in God, and law serves as a useful tool in the implementation of what is 'morally' right (and not simply 'not illegal').[20]

Woolman's comments on the impact of slavery on the American psyche show these complex interactions among law, society, social ills, and biblical concepts ('covetousness', etc.), though the latter are never made explicit since all knew his scriptural reference points:

> A covetous mind which seeks opportunity to exalt itself is a great enemy to true harmony in a country. Envy and grudging usually accompany this disposition, and it tends to stir up its likeness in others. And where this disposition ariseth so high to embolden us to look upon honest, industrious men as our own property during life, and to keep them to hard labor to support us in those customs which have not their foundation in right reason, or to use any means of oppression, a haughty spirit is cherished on the one side and the desire of revenge frequently on the other, till the inhabitants of the land are ripe for great commotion and trouble; and thus luxury and oppression have the seeds of war and desolation in them.[21]

---

19. Arthur R. Hogue, *Origins of the Common Law* (Indianapolis, IN: Liberty Press, 1985), p. 190.

20. Riggs, 'Inculturation', pp. 97-108 (98-103). Interestingly, as the Archdiocese of Boston has dealt with pedophilia scandals within the Catholic Church, activists suing for victim's rights and restitution were wont to say of child rape by priests, 'It's not just a sin; it's a *crime!*'.

21. John Woolman, *Considerations on Keeping Negroes (Part 2), 1762* (New York: Grossman Publishers, 1976), quoted in Riggs, 'Inculturation', pp. 97-108 (97).

1. 'With Eyes of Flesh' (Job 10.4)

Although traditionally praised for their 'quiet' spiritual practices, the writings of Quaker theologians and activists are redolent with phrases from the Ten Commandments and the biblical wisdom tradition. In Quakerism, law, reason, and faith sit comfortably in the same prayerful space, and make common cause for just action and lived hope.

However, those living in the United States find themselves in a new post-Constitutional world in response to the terrorist attacks of September 11, 2001, and the grab for power by the 'Unitary Executive' in the wake of the events (i.e., by the executive branch as dictator with no oversight by judicial or legislative branch). The rationality and orderliness of checks and balances provided by the United States Constitution seem like golden treasures to us now, but it should be recalled that rationality is not all it has been claimed to be, and that it has not successfully shaped humanity's quest for meaning in the modern period. The Enlightenment's high hopes for rationality or new, better systems capable of replacing religion seem unfounded. Nazi extermination of the Jews was profoundly rational, 'legal' on its own national terms, and guided by a freedom of inquiry (just how long will it take a Jew to die under certain circumstances?) and a profound belief in scientific method. Fed by the streams of literalistic and exclusive interpretations of faith and belief, any notion of rationality, law, and good sense in popular American Christianity are hard to find at present writing. At the same time, the notion of universal Human Rights gets harder and harder to anchor in a pluralistic world, where even a 'super power' would rather be 'secure' than 'moral'. It has been shown cogently that our philosophies of rights are largely Eurocentric—a sort of 'acquired taste' (like philosophical escargot) of Western communities.[22]

Further, rights philosophies are indeed guilty of a kind of moral relativism that has allowed philosophers and politicians to pursue their self-interested or national goals as though they were universally normative. Contradictory views abound: while nationalist Muslims angrily dismiss some Human Rights documents as reeking of Western taint and Judeo-Christian bias, it is just as typical to hear Westerners talk as though all these concepts can be lifted directly from Holy Scriptures (and not from property laws forbidding seizure of property by the king). So, we are left with competing theories of the philosophical and legal grounding for Human Rights in an arena where three separate areas of jurisdiction intersect: religious law, national laws, and international law.

How *do* we adjudicate when the traditions of a religion about ethics cause a person or group to violate either national or international law? As Westerners, are we supposed to condemn Muslim 'honor killings'

---

22. And a Good Thing, too!

as murder, extra-judicial summary executions, or absolve them under the banner of group rights to live out their religious traditions without interference?[23] The laws that come from religions are usually held by their adherents as having some sort of divine authorization, and hence, they outrank all civil and international considerations for the believer. For some interpreters of the tradition, it is legal to prosecute a *jihad* that makes no distinction between the innocent and the guilty, although international and most national laws forbid that. Fundamentalist Christians, who 'hate the sin but love the sinner', raise no particular outcry when homosexuals are murdered or women's health professionals are subjected to violence for their willingness to abide by constitutional rulings of law in providing women with reproductive choices. When charged with promulgation of hate speech or commitment of crimes, believers simply quote the Bible (*selectively!*). Of course, Christian countries are not the sole offenders. When religion shapes policy in a vacuum where all competing claims and sources of authority are scorned, no one is safe. The government of the modern state of Israel feels perfectly free and justified in violating UN Security Council rulings on the state of affairs in the Occupied Palestinian Territories, based on grounds of national interest and right to self-defense. This political position tacitly includes some quasi-religious arguments of religious extremists as a given in understanding national right and destiny. We could say the same of notorious Human Rights violations taking place in Iran, where they are packaged as the harbinger of a 'true' Islam that will straddle East and West under control of the Mullahs. The Egyptian government's

---

23. Compare, for example, the different approaches on this topic exemplified by John Pilch and the present writer in Chapter 7 below ('Family Violence in Cross-Cultural Perspective: An Approach for Feminist Interpreters of the Bible', pp. 306-23 in Athalya Brenner and Carole R. Fontaine [eds.], *A Feminist Companion to Reading the Bible: Approaches, Methods, Strategies* [Sheffield: Sheffield Academic Press, 1997]), with Women's United Nations Report Networks' (WUNRN) resources on Honor Killings and Human Rights <http://www.soas.ac.uk/honourcrimes/Directory_Contents.htm>; Special Rapporteur Asma Jahangir's report 'Civil and Political Rights, Including the Question of Disappearances and Summary Executions' to the UNHCHR, cited September 26, 2007, <http://www.wunrn.com/research/factual_aspects/stories/04-20-04ReportUNHRCommis04full.htm>, para. 66-71. Jahangir concludes in para. 96, §8: 'The main reason for the perpetuation of the practice of "honour" killings is the lack of political will by Governments to bring the perpetrators of these crimes to justice. Governments are urged to make legislative changes to ensure that such killings receive no discriminatory treatment under the law and to sensitize their judiciary to gender issues. Those threatening the life of a female victim should be brought to justice. Correctional and custody homes run by Governments should not be permitted to detain forcibly women whose lives are at risk. Prisons should never be used to detain potential victims of honour killings…'

1990 charter on Human Rights simply eschews all international legal or philosophical resources in favor of resolving every issue through *Shari'a* (even when *Shari'a* can be shown to have compromised Qur'anic values).[24] Certainly, the situation for Human Rights fares no better under authoritarian communist rule, transitions between types of governments and economies, or during intensely nationalistic struggles.

In this climate, some ethicists and philosophers are again making the case that Human Rights talk makes sense *only* in the context of religious talk and assumptions.[25] Cogent analysis shows that without privileging humankind as a divine creation with special rights (usually based on 'divine image'), no genuine explanation can be given for why humans have more rights than elephants or ecosystems. What a reversal. But what *are* those religious ideas, principles or sources that ought to ground our notion of universal Human Rights, and will they indeed save us? For Judaism, Christianity and Islam, all possessing interrelated Scriptures claiming some sort of normative values, we must begin with an understanding of the those Scriptures. I think it is fair to say that a key principle of Human Rights,[26] the 'inherent worth and dignity of every person', while perhaps implicit in each Scripture, has been honored more in its breach than its practice. However, if it *is* true that all 'rights talk' is inherently 'religious talk', then we must attend closely to the themes of human dignity in our Scriptural data-base, because it is clear that a literalistic and exclusivist patriarchal interpretation of texts promotes no such thing. It takes the eye of the beholder to find the tiny tendrils of universal worth and dignity of all life in our favorite Holy Books.

'Does the truth really matter?'
One learns to expect a range of questions in trying to relate Human Rights to religious traditions;[27] a wise woman replies guardedly until

---

24. 'Cairo Declaration on Human Rights in Islam' (August 5, 1990), UN GAOR, World Conference on Human Rights, 4th Session, Agenda Item 5, UN Doc. A/CONF.157/PC/62/Add.18 (1993); for original see <http://www1.umn.edu/humanrts/instree/cairodeclaration.html>, cited September 26, 2007.

25. Perry, *Idea*, pp. 11-42, among others.

26. Ian Brownlie (ed.), *Basic Documents on Human Rights* (Oxford: Clarendon Press, 1971), p. 106. For a discussion of Christian influence on the formulation of the UN Declaration, see Robert Traer, *Faith in Human Rights: Support in Religious Traditions for a Global Struggle* (Washington, DC: Georgetown University Press, 1991), pp. 173-87. It also happens to be the First of the 'Seven Principles' of Unitarian Universalism.

27. Favorites so far include 'Do you believe in armed resistance?'; 'Are you going to go all Western if we need to pay a bribe?'; 'How does it feel to be living in the most powerful, wealthy empire the world has ever known?'; and 'Do you *really* want the United States to turn into Belgium?' (Answers: Sometimes. No. Terrible. Yes, please.)

she understands the *real* question implied by the one she was actually asked. After a presentation in the House of Lords on religious resources for confronting extremism by breaking up the hegemony of interpretation by the powerful,[28] a wealthy donor and global businessman asked me at lunch if the truth really mattered any more—if in fact the truth even existed. In such circumstances, I try to answer from the plainest, most easily verifiable grounds for my position. Well, I replied, certain things are absolutely true: a body is alive or dead; it has been raped and tortured or it has not; it has had access to fresh water and food or it has not. 'Oh, well, *material* truth!', he replied; 'naturally on a practical level, truth exists'. His point was that given that the claims of religion are not subject to proof, and their Scriptural basis is interpreted through the lens of the ideology of the moment, did it actually matter that the Qur'an stands against slavery? No one cares about what it actually says, he opined, because they will interpret how they will, no matter what a scholar says about the text.

It was a nicely post-modern observation, but a chilling one, nevertheless. Certainly, the disconnect this Lord of the Manor had identified was not unfamiliar to me: as a young student, I never thought philosophy particularly valid for it failed to address any of the material issues I had known from an upbringing in poverty in the racist American South of childhood. If any ancient or modern philosopher had been capable of making it from my house to the bus stop in one piece, while holding the positions that they did, I would have been thoroughly amazed. It takes a different set of ethics to negotiate unremitting violence and squalor in a differently colored, female body, and of *these* realities, the great men had little to say. If material truth has no relation to historical or philosophical truth, perhaps the problem is that truth has been separated into many competing compartments, so that all is eternally relative and no defense against any abuse can be sustained. If all those little, local truths do not have some connection at a deeper level to material truths, then as a biblical scholar, I might as well stop writing and simply declare my own interpretation as eternal, infallible, and universal. As heir to many centuries of biblical scholarship and many archaeological finds which refine our understanding of Bible and history, I have as much claim as anyone that my interpretations are the best informed and most useful to date.

Of course, a historian and literary critic of feminist bent living in the world of post-modern discourse can do no such thing. Meanings must be adjudicated with one's biases held firmly in the forefront so they may be nullified when they interfere with liberative meanings. If a Scripture

---

28. Available in PowerPoint format on <http://www.wafe-women.org>.

scholar would have some voice in the world of those who still honor her source material, then the text and its study must continue to play a foundational role in our discourse. True, this approach is old-fashioned, and may only represent one small candle flame in the dark night of relativity, but this is the path I must choose if my passions for justice are to be heard, much less understood.

3. Back to the Religious Sources: The Shaping of Victim Consciousness and Ideology

Perhaps some history with respect to the biblical witness might be in order.

It is the hope here that a re-examination of particular themes and motifs in the biblical text and its ancient Near Eastern cousins can help us clarify what the Bible actually *does* say on the general topic, what it does *not* say, and the usefulness of either of those things to current global debate on balancing competing rights and claims. This is, of course, a very abstract way of putting something that has actually assumed the role of a deeply personal quest. As I have explained, I did not gain my curiosity in an objective or abstract way. I was, rather, caught between a rock and a hard place; as usual, I reached for a Hebrew Bible.

The Formation of Classical Religions of 'the Book'
The trio of religions which call the Torah sacred all began in the Fertile Crescent of the ancient Near East: those regions we speak of today as the 'Middle East', 'Near East', 'Levant' or other such term. Each of the three religions emerged from within sociopolitical contexts in which the new faith was forced to struggle for acceptance and its very survival. Each, to a different degree, spoke a message of increasingly radical monotheism or its reinterpretation with the inclusion of a divine messiah, a message which was at odds with the dominant forms of faith in its culture.[29] This legacy of persecution and difference in message or practice accounts for much of the three Scriptures' xenophobic attitudes towards the Other, understood as anyone outside the community of the new 'true' faith. Yet Human Rights philosophies make clear that the human being who is to be accorded the rights that must be carefully guarded and enforced

---

29. For a more extensive introduction to the Religions of the Book, see Karen Armstrong, *A History of God: The 4000-Year Quest of Judaism, Christianity, and Islam* (New York: Ballantine, 1993). Armstrong argues that some of the problems around violence and the Other can be understood as a function of the religions' origin in the Axial Age (800–200 BCE), a time of formative new ideologies in response to changing economic arrangements (p. 27).

is that very Other we have been taught to suspect. (No group, religious or otherwise, ever seems to question its *own* intrinsic qualifications for having 'rights'.) How, then, do the religions of the Book find a way to overcome the rooted suspicion and devaluation of the Other?

In Judaism, Christianity, and Islam, all value, including morality, derives from God, *not* humanity. Humans are deserving of salvation not because of anything to do with *their nature or rights*, but because God has created them and would redeem them. It is safe to say that the Human Rights concepts of the Peoples of the Book are rooted in what Christian theologian David Tracy calls the 'analogical imagination'[30]: all humans are understood as children of One Fathering Parent, a loving God, who binds us all into One Family, will we or nil we.[31] Given each religion's fundamental affirmation of this paternal Creator God, almost always imaged as male and referred to as male,[32] we find that the enactment of the goals of religious Human Rights often falters at the point where generalizations are to be applied to the female half of humanity. We may all be children of God the Father, but some have always been the 'favorites' while others are the step-children. Contrary to some theorists who emphasize the inherently religious nature of Human Rights discourse,[33] feminists often find it difficult to unearth a great deal within the Scripture of each group which supports the notion of *intrinsic* human value and dignity for women and girls (it should be noted that the religions differ from each other in the nuances of how they regard the concept of universality). In secular Human Rights debates, it is much easier to find straightforward support of Human Rights for *all* humanity, even though the classic documents of Western philosophy which serve as source material for these rights usually are narrowly framed in ways that exclude women, children, slaves and those who do not hold property. (The 'threshold' for having rights is almost always one's maleness, inscribed via rationality, property, superiority). If we find that religion has betrayed the rights of some of the human family, it should at least be remembered that secular society had done no better, at least so far.

Judaism. Scholars debate with considerable vigor the possibility of fixing a time of origin for the emergence of the earliest of these Scripture-based thought systems. Here we look not simply for texts, but the people and groups who created them. By the Iron Age (approx. 1000–587 BCE

---

30. David Tracy, *The Analogical Imagination: Christian Theology and the Culture of Pluralism* (New York: Crossroad, 1981).

31. M. Perry, *Idea*, pp. 16-20.

32. For many feminists, this male-exclusive way of imaging the Creator presents serious problems, both in theory and practice.

33. See M. Perry, *Idea*, pp. 11-42, 57-86.

in the Levant), we are able to point to numerous archaeological finds and literary texts that witness to the emergence of a nation of 'mixed' tribes who identified themselves as 'Israel' and 'Judah'. Some experts would argue that the foundational group whose progeny later emerged as Israel were in fact already in the area by the time of the Bronze Age (3200–1000 BCE, divided into Early, Middle, and Late archaeological periods), existing as a social class of outcasts, runaway slaves, mercenaries, and those displaced for whatever reason (the so-called 'apiru' of Late Bronze Age texts). Newer scholarly theories argue forcefully that the bulk of those who made up the 'tribal' proto-Israelites of the Iron I age (1200–1000 BCE) are in fact *not* outsiders but indigenous Canaanites fleeing the collapsing cities of the valleys to clear new territory in the isolated Central Hill Country.[34]

However we choose to understand the origins of the groups who created the Hebrew Bible, the 'in-house story' of their theology is proclaimed by the Hebrew Bible: this people who worshiped a deity known as 'the God of the Fathers' found themselves enslaved, and were delivered from that slavery by the direct intervention of their god. In grateful response to this social and material 'redemption', the people agreed to follow the laws of that God and forgo the worship of any other entity. Respect for slaves, foreigners, the widow and orphan were made part of the law code the people were to follow; foreigners, homosexuals, and others were not so fortunate. This early codification of 'rights', if one wants to call it that, is based on the theoretical idea that the people, marginal groups or freed slaves themselves, knew the bitterness of oppression and so should seek to ameliorate it for others.[35] In fact, the ancient Near East routinely expected its kings and gods to protect the rights of a few particular groups: widows and orphans disadvantaged by having no patriarchal male to care for their economic provision; the 'stranger' within the gates was also protected, at least in part because the law codes presume such a sojourner to be a merchant or diplomat from another country with whom one has trade or treaty agreements. Ancient Israel added two new groups to the social concerns protected by its god. The first of these groups is slaves, especially slaves of one's own ethnic group held in slavery by someone of another nationality; the second was the 'citizen army', an all-volunteer force dedicated to

---

34. William Dever, *Who Were the Israelites and Where Did They Come from?* (Grand Rapids, MI: Eerdmans, 2003). For a splendid critique of both the logic and outcome of Dever's historical reconstructions, see Hector Avalos, *The End of Biblical Studies* (Amherst, NY: Prometheus Books, 2007), pp. 109-84.

35. In the Decalogue, see Deut. 5.15; on slaves, see Deut. 15.12-18; 21.10-14; 23.15-17; on the poor, see Deut. 15.7-11.

protecting the newly settled and amalgamated group from the surrounding city states, nations and empires. Together, these five groups: widows, orphans, sojourners, slaves, and military volunteers make up what one scholar has called 'Yahweh's special interest groups'.[36] Note please that they are 'groups' who are thought to have right of special appeal to the Hebrew God for protection—in other words, we have a 'class' of right-bearers identified and the hearers of these laws are constituted as 'duty-bearers' who empower the enjoyment of those rights. By extension, an individual in that protected class has rights as an individual to claim the redress promised to the whole protected group. So, while it is quite true that individual fulfillment[37] must be viewed as a modern concept that does not find much support in antiquity in general, rights of a certain sort do exist. This also leads us to wonder if even more individual and group rights might exist, were we to search for them properly.

While scholars debate whether this Exodus (from slavery in Egypt) is historical or an imaginative liturgical narrative, whether it is early Iron Age or Saiidic in time, its impact on the theology and thought world of the people who made this story 'Scripture' is indisputable.[38] Eventually, Judaism is the name given to the system of religious beliefs and laws belonging to the descendants of the people of Israel and Judah. Long after their states had been conquered and annexed by various imperial kingdoms—the Assyrians, the Babylonians, the Persians, the Greeks and the Romans—the teachings of lived Torah continued to be a vital force for survival and group identity. Because of these vicissitudes in its national fortunes, the Jews had to find a way to remain a people after they were no longer a nation. This was done through zealous guardianship of standards of endogamous marriage[39] and focus on religion as a distinctive feature of that people. At the same time the people were struggling for their survival in all their 'uniqueness', they found themselves scattered throughout the Roman Empire in the West and the former provinces of the Persian Empire in the East. Hence, *all* their laws had to be continuously reinterpreted to fit new cultural and geographical conditions. Torah could not change and did not need to change—indeed, it was held to contain all one ever needed

---

36. Norman Gottwald, *The Hebrew Bible: A Socio-literary Introduction* (Philadelphia: Fortress, 1985).

37. Understood here as the ability to fully enjoy one's rights as a human living in a group.

38. Niels Peter Lemche, *The Israelites in History and Tradition* (Louisville, KY: Westminster/John Knox Press, 1998).

39. Claudia Camp, *Wise, Strange and Holy: The Foreign Woman and the Making of the Bible* (JSOTSup, 320; Sheffield: Sheffield Academic Press, 2000).

to know — but *interpretation* of the Torah was ongoing, diverse, and was held to be as binding and normative as the original written laws. This is Good News for interpreters.

Christianity. The later development of Christianity in the first and second centuries CE was originally viewed by its first adherents as a liberation and reform movement within Judaism. At its inception, the Jesus-movement proclaimed the real arrival and presence of the 'Kingdom of God', a golden era marked by peace and justice in every aspect. The vision of such a kingdom was the people's response to the ongoing political and economic oppression by Imperial Rome and the Jewish community's struggle against Greek cultural domination. When Roman officials overseeing the province of Judea executed the Jew, Jesus of Nazareth, as a political criminal, his life and death served as the central rallying point for his followers. When a large portion of the Jewish population failed to accept the claims of the early 'Jesus movement', the message was then taken to Gentile (non-Jewish) populations. A new religion was born, but one that was aware of its earlier origins in Judaism, although much of that uneasy legacy had to be translated for its non-Jewish audience into the very Hellenistic idioms of pagan mystery cults it had originally opposed.[40] For the next 300 years, this religion spread throughout the Roman Empire, making ample use of the Roman road system to reach the urban centers where its message seemed to take hold with the most fervor. Finally, Christianity became the official religion of the Roman Empire under Constantine in 325 CE at the Council of Nicea. For some, it remains a question as to *whose* triumph this actually represents: did Christianity win out over the Roman Empire, or did the Roman Empire successfully assimilate Christianity to its hierarchical, imperial worldview? Answers to this question are varied.

Membership in the household of Christ was not predicated upon one's birth or nationality. This innovation was required of the nascent movement, since eventually Gentiles had become the dominant group, replacing Christian Jews as the proponents of this faith. Slaves and masters, men and women, Gentiles and Jews were all to find a place at this new table of salvation which God had set, but the price of a seat was a firm and universally required profession: 'Jesus is Lord'. In the early centuries, this came to mean a rejection of the dominion of the Roman Emperor, *and* an exodus from the heritage of Judaism or one's previous belief system.

---

40. See John Dominic Crossan, *The Birth of Christianity: Discovering What Happened in the Years Immediately after the Execution of Jesus* (San Francisco: HarperCollins, 1998). See also James Carroll, *Constantine's Sword: The Church and the Jews: A History* (Boston: Houghton Mifflin, 2001).

Christian Empire. With its adoption as the imperial religion by Constantine, the faith of the Galileans became a state religion whose heavenly goals just happened to mirror the imperial aspirations of the empire, the internal struggles of the Roman Empire. At the same time, Rome's external rivalry with the Sassanian Empire, the inheritors of the Persian Empire, set much of the agenda of the Church's struggles against 'wrong' belief and 'wrong' action. These conflicts eventually ended in a schism which split the Western Empire and its church from the Eastern Empire, each with its version of the one, true Faith.

Islam. During these centuries of squabbles, the populace of the Near East remained largely under the rule of the Christian Roman Empire, much to the detriment of the quality of life of Jewish communities, whose religious and political rights were steadily abridged. The rise of Islam in seventh century Arabia was itself a response to the political, theological, and moral disarray in its own world and the local impact of the rivalries of the two great imperial powers of Byzantium and Persia. A reaction to the materialism and ethical bankruptcy of the wealthy merchant class of Mecca, Muhammad's message was heard as a threat to that reality.[41] Born in the crucible of political as well as theological opposition, Islam was spread by faith and sword in contexts determined to suppress it, and like Christianity before it, achieved much in its centuries of expansion, until it ranged from the Indian continent to the Atlantic Ocean.

Like Christianity before it, the nation of Islam, the *'Umma*, had different rules for membership from Judaism. While it is true that most Muslims in the early period of establishment of the religion came primarily from Semitic groups, Islam was much like Christianity in allowing for true and authentic membership by converts who professed the one-ness of Allah (*Shahada*) and the exalted status of Muhammad as Allah's messenger.[42] The Qur'an was viewed then as the unmediated word of Allah, delivered to Muhammad verbatim and without error by the angel Gabriel. Thus, the Qur'an and its profession of Allah became the ultimate rule of faith and source of all authority. In the seventh century, the Qur'an was quite 'forward-looking' for its time in its view of right relations between humanity and Allah.

Those who know the history of the Prophet, and the profound support, respect, and dignity accorded him by the women in his life cringe at what we now see in so-called 'Islamic Fundamentalism'.[43] Among the

---

41. W. Montgomery Watt, *Muhammad: Prophet and Statesman* (Oxford: Oxford University Press, 1961).

42. In theory; many non-Arab Muslims question whether the *'Umma* is all *that* welcoming to other ethnicities.

43. I believe we must question the appropriateness of naming a movement in

three 'Book' Scriptures—the Hebrew Bible or Torah, the Christian New Testament, and the Qur'an—it is the Qur'an which insists on the dignity of slaves and the necessity of setting them free. It is the Qur'an which forbids female infanticide. It is the Qur'an which provides that women must be consulted for their agreement on any marriage arranged by their families (that is, they cannot be 'inherited' against their will, and this is amplified through *Ahadith*). It is the Qur'an which provides women with some guarantee of inheritance rights, and the right to freedom of religion, and so on. The Qur'an's teachings on social justice, and especially women and slaves, were revolutionary for their time, and could be revolutionary even now.[44]

Interpretation, however, eventually became necessary as cultural conditions shifted. This was accomplished by the collection of *Ahadith*: a *Hadith* (sg.) is an originally 'oral' tradition about the life of Muhammad and his practices (*Sunnah*). These were later collected, and committed to writing. Once all the *Ahadith* had been found, written, and collated, it was still necessary to assess and clarify how they were to be applied to daily life. Traditions of interpretation of this originally oral body of teachings arose: some *Hadith* were considered 'strong'—coming from multiple sources and standing in clear continuation of Qur'anic teachings. Others are considered *Hasan*, less reliable, because of the quality of the narrators of the account. Other *Hadith* were considered 'weak': these had only a single source and/or questionable authenticity of content when compared to the Qur'an or strong *Ahadith*. In this way, cultural opinion and context could make its weight felt in the interpretation of a Qur'an that never changed.[45]

The Rights of Woman?: *Patriarchal Interpretation of the Religions of the Book*
Violence against women has a long and substantial history. It did not begin with the Hebrew Bible (the Torah) and its dogged determination to submerge all female aspects of the Hebrew God.[46] It did not come

---

Islam after a faction of Christianity descended from the warped religion of the slave-owning South in the United States.

44. Jamal A. Badawi, 'Gender Equity in Islam' (2002), cited September 27, 2007 <http://www.islamicity.com/articles/articles.asp?ref=IC0210-1757&p=1>.

45. An excellent discussion of Qur'anic exegesis and the role of *Ahadith* may be found in Asma Barlas, *'Believing Women' in Islam: Unreading Patriarchal Interpretations of the Qur'an* (Austin: University of Texas Press, 2002), pp. 42-50.

46. In fact, it would be wrong to assume that the presence of the Female Divine automatically creates improved status or worth of living women (see Susan Pollock and Reinhard Bernbeck, 'And They Said, Let Us Make Gods in our Image: Gendered Ideologies in Ancient Mesopotamia', in Alison E. Rautman, *Reading the Body: Representations and Remains in the Archaeological Record* [Philadelphia: University of Pennsylvania Press, 2000], pp. 150-64).

into being when the Christian Messiah was born male. Islam did not make it up; it did not arrive with the Prophet Mohammed. Patriarchy is the economic ideology in which the father owns all other members of his family, and has absolute rights of disposition of them (we will find no texts that challenge a man for murdering a wife, daughter, or female relative). This is the source of much violence in Scripture, though it is not often identified as such by mainstream scholars. My own work has suggested to me that to write the history of patriarchy in the ancient world is also to write the history of the rise of cities and states. If that is true, then it follows that we always need to 'follow the money' and ask material, economic questions of our textual and theological sources.

From its earliest times, patriarchy operated as a strategy for state formation and male dominance. In order to acquire land and hold it, a man must be able to trust and count on support from those men to whom the land is given. If a man can control marriages and give his womenfolk to the right men, he will suddenly have brothers he can trust. So women's bodies must be controlled, in order for this strategy to function properly. Little girls were 'trafficked' to other countries to seal political bargains and treaties; slave women were kept for personal exploitation or freely passed around as rewards to the men who did their masters' bidding. Violence was used to punish and enforce this economic reality, and so securing women's chastity should be understood as an attempt to protect an economic resource, and not a matter of morality. Myth, text, and law code all attempt to establish this male ownership over everyone else as natural, normal, desirable, and divinely authorized.

Hence, the three religions of the Book came into being in patriarchal cultures whose male-biased organization and thought-world was well established long before their arrival. This simple fact has left a profound mark on the interpretation of the potentially liberating content of the different faiths, and dismissive Neo-Pagans and others would do well to note that their traditions *also* bear the same stamp of patriarchal origin. Whether tribe or state, cultures throughout the ancient Near East and classical world agreed in their estimation that women were somehow more fallible, more 'sinful', more imperfect than their male counterparts, and used those biased beliefs to limit the rights of women as persons and as a group.[47] Though *many* women are present in the stories of the foundation and spread of each of the religions of the Book, clearly exercising power and serving their god with their whole selves, their accomplishments and commitments were trivialized, ignored,

---

47. Carole R. Fontaine, '"A Heifer from thy Stable": On Goddesses and the Status of Women in the Ancient Near East', in Alice Bach (ed.), *Women in the Hebrew Bible: A Reader* (New York: Routledge, 1999), pp. 159-78.

hidden, or distorted by the androcentric bias of their societies. Ironically and tragically, as godly accomplishments of women in their religions were slowly obscured by male authorities and popular interpretation, that same trend in interpretation simultaneously made Woman solely responsible for the entrance of evil into the world, thus justifying for many the curtailment of her rights as a moral necessity approved—nay, required—by God of all true believers.

Hence, the 'Scripture' of all three religions has been the victim of biased interpretation, almost from its inception. However the group may think of its Book as 'inspired' by a deity in whatever way, the *texts themselves* were largely edited, copied, transmitted and interpreted *by* males for the benefit *of* males.[48] At the materialist level, the exclusion of women from the public, male world of power was justified by their status as mothers and potential mothers who would be the primary care-givers to children. This made it unnecessary to educate them as one would a man who was expected to deal with the world outside the home. Denied education and the advancement made possible by the acquisition of professional skills, women were seldom able to become qualified 'experts' as interpreters of their faith traditions, and so could mount no authoritative, theological opposition to the curtailment of their personhood. Women who 'succeeded' as saints usually did so at the expense of renunciation of female sexuality, and so the exemplar of their holy lives could be deemed irrelevant to the existence or abilities of 'regular' women who had embraced their lives as wives and mothers.

Depending on the religion's view of 'spirit', 'body', 'flesh' and 'sex', women might fare better or worse. Jewish women were valued as mothers of an embattled minority, so were less likely to be despised for their reproductive roles or told to forgo them. Under later persecution in European Christian nations, Jewish women became the public negotiators for their families in the marketplace and village. The preferred high-status roles of Torah-scholar and student went to the males of the community, who were less at risk from Christian violence when they remained sequestered in study.

Christian women were burdened with the gynophobia of Hellenistic philosophy which feared and debased women as inferior 'matter'

---

48. Extensive research has been done on this topic, and cannot be detailed here. I refer readers to the following 'classics': Carol Newsom and Sharon Ringe (eds.), *The Women's Bible Commentary* (Louisville, KY: Westminster/John Knox Press, 1992); Elisabeth Schüssler Fiorenza (ed.), *Searching the Scriptures* (2 vols.; New York: Crossroad, 1993–1994); and the many volumes of *A Feminist Companion to the Bible*, Athalya Brenner (ed.), (1st Series; Sheffield: Sheffield Academic Press, 1993), especially Athalya Brenner and Carole R. Fontaine (eds.), *A Feminist Companion to Reading the Bible: Approaches, Methods, Strategies* (Sheffield: Sheffield Academic Press, 1997).

in contrast to male 'spirit', bearers of 'emotion' instead of 'rationality'. For Christian theologians, motherhood itself still partook of the material, fallen part of the world, so some women found other options more appealing in the quest to secure their authenticity before their god. These variations took several forms. The appeal of the monastic celibate life might well have been a refuge both from male authority and early death in childbed, and must have been an especially welcome option for lesbians of the time. Further, with some wonderful maneuvering, experienced women seized upon the New Testament's and Greek world's hatred of female sexuality to affirm a widow's right *not* to remarry, thus retaining control over her own economic resources. Unmarried women were celebrated when they became virgin martyrs of the early Church. Those who had no taste for chastity or death as a means of securing their salvation looked to the heretical practices of so-called 'witchcraft', better understood as wise women's healing traditions from non-Christian groups. All of these options must be understood as women's *resistance* to the religious classification of the female body as morally defective and in need of constant control by male relatives or authorities. Since the Christian community is 'born by faith' (a work of the 'spirit'), rather than 'by flesh' as the Jewish community is reproduced, mothers and sex partners are less necessary to the group's ultimate viability, even though the New Testament proclaims that it is through childbirth that women shall be 'saved' from their guilt of bringing sin into the world. One new Gnostic gospel found in Egypt in the twentieth century takes the point further, going so far as to state that for women Jesus Christ exercises his ultimate, redemptive power by making them into men: 'Jesus said, "I myself shall lead her in order to make her male, so that she too may becomes a living spirit resembling you males. For every woman who will make herself male will enter the Kingdom of Heaven"' (*Gos. Thom.* 114.20).[49] Such formulations, whether enforcing compulsory motherhood or spiritual sex-change, do not represent good news for the women of these faiths from a Human Rights perspective, which argues that no matter what sex one is, one has equal value and dignity.

In the world of Islam, we see perhaps the most glaring disparity between the teachings of its Holy Book and their popular interpretation in patriarchal societies.[50] The Qur'an speaks more of the rights and duties to obtain

---

49. Helmut Koester and Thomas O. Lambdin, 'The Gospel of Thomas (II, 2)', in James M. Robinson (ed.), *The Nag Hammadi Library in English* (San Francisco: Harper & Row, 1977), pp. 124-38 (130). This is also how it works with the 'academic salvation' of tenure, too.

50. Here I follow the work of Muslim feminist theologian Riffat Hassan (*Women's Rights and Islam: From the I.C.P.D. to Beijing* [Louisville, KY: NISA Publications, 1995];

between family members than any other topic in the realm of 'Human Rights'. The Qur'an provides explicit protections for women within and without marriage, based on the *recognition* of their disadvantaged status under patriarchy. (This is *not* the same as *prescribing* that patriarchal devaluation as normative.) Along with its position on the evils caused by the existence of slavery, a topic neither Judaism nor Christianity attacks so directly in *their* source Scriptures, the Qur'an's view that each person, male and female, owes primary allegiance to God without bowing to any intermediary has indeed allowed some Muslim scholars to refer to their book as the 'Magna Carta of Human Rights'. However, these principles were consistently eroded by the traditional, androcentric bias of its interpreters and the inculturation of the religion in tribal societies. The role of motherhood continued to be a sanctified, approved one, but the 'materiality' of human women who sneeze, menstruate, and give birth was negatively contrasted with the fantastical Houris, the highest expression of femaleness. These exotic, sexual servo-mechanisms meted out to heroes of the faith in Paradise had renewable hymens, and never, ever required a handkerchief or a midwife. If such beings constitute the heavenly *reward* for men, then real Muslim women could be understood as an earthly antithesis, a punishment or burden of sorts compared to the virgins of paradise. In the realm of official theology, the on-going lack of expert female participation in interpretation has left us with an Islamic world in which many, if not most, average Muslims firmly believe that woman's inferiority is a major tenet of their faith, and that any 'Westernized' appropriation of concepts of Human Rights for women must *necessarily* entail a betrayal of their most fundamental religious commitments.[51] At least some of the hostilities between Sunni and Shi'a groups stem from their differing practices concerning marriage and female inheritance (Shi'a permit *sigheh*, temporary marriage, but have more female-friendly inheritance practices).

Parenthetical, but not unrelated, are the problems raised for the natural world, slaves, and children by each Book's externalized, sky-god

---

'Religious Human Rights and the Qur'an', in *Religious Human Rights in the World Today* [Emory International Law Review, 10 (1996)], pp. 85-96; plus a chapter in Arvind Sharma and Katherine K. Young [eds.], *Through her Eyes: Women's Perspectives on World Religions* [Boulder, CO: Westview Press, 1999]).

51. In part, this has occurred because of the introduction of misogynist 'less reliable' or 'weak' *Ahadith* into normative collections during the eleventh century long after the canon of reliable *Ahadith* had been closed (Barlas, *Women*, p. 45 *et passim*). For a statement differentiating Islamic views from 'fundamentalist' ones, see Farooq Hassan, Special UN Ambassador for the Family, 'Women in Islam: Distinction between Religious and Fundamentalist Approaches?' (2005), cited August 6, 2007 <http://www.greaterdemocracy.org/archives/000408.html>.

theologies. Both slaves and children were clearly regarded as property of the patriarchal household, and though the Hebrew Bible and the New Testament attempt to ameliorate the conditions of these biologically functional 'objects', they do not really address anything like a concept of intrinsic worth, which *is* a concern in the Qur'an. But in all three religions, the Earth and all its creatures—Gaia, the biosphere, the interdependent web—however we might name it—are simply matter created by God with no inherent value or rights, except those assigned by the Creator, and placed at the disposal of in-group males. Modern feminist readers, along with traditional groups practicing Earth-based spiritualities from around the world, find this ontological situation with respect to the interdependent web of being totally unacceptable. In ecofeminist interpretive projects, we find the Bible turned on its head with respect to planet Earth.[52] Using the format of a prophetic covenant lawsuit, the God of the Book has been put on trial for murdering trees in Ezekiel, for flooding all the earth in Genesis, and consigning all life on this Water Planet to the fires in Revelation. Outcome? Guilty as charged. Some of us conclude that classical Scripture traditionally interpreted cannot save polar icecaps or the ozone layer if read within its dominant patriarchal framework.

4. *Conclusions: What Can We Take on the Journey toward Human Rights?*

Human Dignity and the Imago Dei

The scriptural record on Human Rights for women and girls associated with the classical religions of the Book is, frankly, abysmal in application, because each faith was traditionally interpreted in a gender-biased or culturally parochial fashion. Nevertheless, each of the three religions contains significant insights and theological warrants for the establishment of universal Human Rights, even though those insights derive from theological ideas about divine authorization which are anathema to secularists. For all three religions of the Book, the concept of 'human dignity' is the key. It is usually understood to be derived from the view that all humans are created in God's image (*imago dei*). In the Hebrew Bible, it is made explicit that 'male and female' are both part of the image of God which was stamped on humanity, or expressed through humanity, at its creation (Gen. 1.27). Both sexes are pronounced 'good', along with the rest of the created earth (v. 31).

---

52. See the multivolume set, *The Earth Bible,* Norman C. Habel and Shirley Wurst (eds.) (New York: Pilgrim Press with Sheffield Academic Press, 2001-2004). For a Jewish exposition of the same principles, see Ellen Bernstein, *The Splendor of Creation: A Biblical Ecology* (Cleveland: Pilgrim Press, 2005).

Judaism fully endorses the dignity of humans bestowed by the Image of God.[53] Judaism's most fundamental ethical concept for humans emerges out of the book of Leviticus, a work not largely hailed for its liberating impulses: in a verse which has been given a variety of translations, Lev. 19.16, we read: 'You shall not go around spreading scandal among your people; you shall not stand idly by in the presence of your neighbor's blood; I am the Lord'. The ethical principle of all the Law and Prophets is seen here: because God's nature is just and holy, believers must behave in harmony with those principles, and this cannot be limited to relations only in one's own family or among one's own sex. It is easy enough to give the whole essence of the Torah as the rabbis did, 'standing on one foot',[54] or as Jesus repeatedly taught: 'You shall love the Lord your God with all your heart, and with all your soul, and with all your strength, and with all your mind; and your neighbor as yourself' (Lk. 10.27). Though early apocalyptically minded Christianity opted for an 'other-worldly' solution[55] to this world's problems, the execution of its innocent leader on trumped-up political charges creates a natural affinity for a religious openness toward a pursuit of 'Human Rights'.

The Qur'an, too, weighs in on the subject of Human Rights: part of the 'sacred duty' Allah has commanded is 'that ye slay not life which Allah hath made sacred, save in the course of justice' (Sura 6.151), and that all persons, male or female, who believe in God and do 'justice' will be rewarded by Allah (Sura 2.62; 4.124; 9.97).[56] Likewise, the Qur'an affirms the right to freedom of religion, freedom of movement, and the importance of individual ethical choice, and reserves dire punishments for those who choose to disregard these God-given rights:

> Who is more wicked than the one who fashions lies about God?
> Such men shall be arraigned before their Lord,
> And the Witnesses will testify:
> 'These are those who imputed lies to God'.
> Beware! The scourge of God will fall on the unjust (Sura Hud [11], Ayat 18).

Following the logic of all three Scriptures, I make the claim here that 'All embodied life is sacred', which then leads to the claim that the rights of the living entity, in our case Human Rights, must also be held

---

53. Shlomo Fischer, '*Kevod Ha'adam, Tzelem Elohim* and *Kevod Habriot* (The Dignity of Man, the Image of God, and the Honor of the Fellow-Creature)', in Adam B. Seligman (ed.), *Religion and Human Rights: Conflict or Convergence* (Interreligious Center on Public Life; Hollis, NH: Hollis Publishing Company, 2004), pp. 15-26.

54. That is, in concise form.

55. Through right belief, one is 'saved' for eternal life in the afterlife, making this world's problems of less critical importance to the committed believer.

56. Abdullah Yusuf Ali, *The Holy Qur'an* (Brentwood, MD: Amana Corporation, 1989).

sacred as part of the whole. This empirical *and* revelatory insight is the prime foundation of the origin and source of all rights, whether those currently ascribed to humans, or to other species or ecosystems in the future. Such 'Entity Rights' are sacred by both function and origin.

Human Rights are sacred by *function* because they operate as the *point non plus*, the 'bottom line' by which all (human) atrocity and injustice may be known and judged, just as Entity Rights will become the measure for abuses to a living, complex environment. The term in International Law for this is *jus cogens* (Latin: 'compelling law', developed from case laws, etc.): peremptory norms to which all agree (or ought to agree). While such norms are not listed anywhere by any authoritative body, they tend to include 'prohibitions on waging aggressive war, crimes against humanity, war crimes, piracy, genocide, slavery, racial discrimination, and torture'.[57] Such norms cannot be violated by any state, and according to the Vienna Convention on the Law of Treaties, any treaty which violates a peremptory norm is automatically null and void. Peremptory norms form the basis of the international laws used to construct and prosecute the World War II Nuremburg Tribunals, as set down in the London Charter of the International Military Tribunal.[58]

In origin, Human Rights are made sacred by their objective universality. By the very fact of existence, all (created) life-forms have the inherent worth of simply *being embodied here*.[59] Some may claim that 'what exists' is here because God created it so, and blessed the creation. Others may reject that account, choosing instead the complexities of evolution and science as explanation, but that does not obviate the ethical implications of the existence of being. From either perspective, religious or secular, the evidentiary function of simply being, as a part of known creation, conveys a dignity proper to whatever form of existence we may be speaking of, and creates a duty in the one who perceives it. The Other does not need to disappear, be done away with, or contained; the Other needs only to be acknowledged, truly and properly *seen*, through

---

57. Wikipedia contributors, 'Peremptory Norm', Wikipedia, The Free Encyclopedia, <http://en.wikipedia.org/w/index.php?title=Peremptory_norm&oldid=35680056>, cited August 6, 2007. Note also that 'domestic abuse' is now classed as a form of torture by the OMCT (*World Organization against Torture*; <http://www.omct.org>), headquartered in Geneva, and human trafficking is covered by all laws against slavery.

58. Wikipedia contributors, 'Crime against Humanity', Wikipedia, The Free Encyclopedia, <http://en.wikipedia.org/w/index.php?title=Crime_against_humanity&oldid=36696265>, cited August 6, 2007.

59. Some may argue that my definition of life does not include spiritual entities or energy fields, but since I view all rights as based in embodiment and the experience of an embodied entity who hopes to experience them, I can only address the realities I know (at the present time).

the fleshy eyes of another embodied entity. It is no mistake that one of the most important legal principles of Human Rights is named in Latin *habeas corpus*,[60] 'you produce the body'. It is through the impact on the body, especially the female one, that we will trace Scripture's contribution to normative rights.

The Bible's quintessential sufferer — an Other, no less — Job, the Edomite sage, asks God poignantly in Chapter 10:

> Do you have eyes of flesh? Do you see as humans see?
> Are your days like the days of mortals, or your years like human years?
> (vv. 4-5)

Job is suggesting that God remember that, to Job, things appear very differently, precisely because he is embodied and experiencing life from a particular angle of vision. He is wracked by pain and disgrace, all undeserved, and God appears to him like the Divine Warrior, a combatant against whom none can stand. Job suggests that *his* embodied perceptions of the situation have something to say to the construction of his theological problem. God needs to recall how little, how fragile, how brief human life actually is, and judge by that benchmark of vision — who on earth could ever live up to God's divine standards? A bit further on, Job makes clear on what philosophical grounds he pelts God with these existential questions:

> Your hands fashioned and made me;
>   and now you turn and destroy me.
> Remember that you fashioned me like clay;
>   and will you turn me to dust again?
> Did you not pour me out like milk
>   and curdle me like cheese?
> You clothed me with skin and flesh,
>   and knit me together with bones and sinews.
> You have granted me life and steadfast love,
>   and your care has preserved my spirit.
> Yet these things you hid in your heart;
>   I know that this was your purpose (10.9-13).

Job's wisdom is to appeal to the evidence of his existence: he is here. He is made by God just like everything else, and God has some relationship

---

60. This legal concept gives the right to know the reasons for which one has been incarcerated, the right to judicial hearing and appeal, rather than indefinite detainment for unspecified reasons. It should be noted that it is in the form of a subjective command: '(We command) that you have the body'. More specifically, the writ of *habeas corpus ad subjiciendum* requires that a state custodian produce a prisoner in court to determine if the state has the actual right to detain such prisoner (Wikipedia contributors, 'Habeas Corpus', Wikipedia, The Free Encyclopedia, <http://en.wikipedia.org/wiki/Habeas_corpus>, cited January 14, 2008).

to both his foibles and his future destiny. Even though a human is malleable like clay or cheese, there is a dignity and an inherent right to fair treatment hidden in being that demands an acknowledgement from God or, at the very least, an explanation for divine violence. In other words, the living body has an 'honor' appropriate to it, and a 'way' that ought to be observed. Seeing with 'eyes of flesh' means a multifaceted, embodied vision in the midst of context and complexity, while simultaneously recognizing the limitations to full knowledge such embedded seeing implies. Potters, after all, have *some* responsibility to and for the clay beneath their hands.

In the present context of argument, I would also claim that this kind of perception—embedded, fleshy, frail, angled, and human—is perhaps especially to be found in those who take up the cause of Human Rights. It takes considerable effort to hold oneself to the discipline of being informed about the world, and its travails. It is hard to hear the stories of prisoners, survivors of natural disasters, war, and famine. It is heartbreaking to take those stories into an uncaring, narcissistic religious setting and watch the believers turn away from seeing and acting. Seeing as a human sees implies a willingness to know of a full range of vulnerabilities that most of us would just as soon keep hidden. To allow this kind of perceiving-in-solidarity to take place, we must finally and thoroughly acknowledge our own susceptibility to the same circumstances, along with our involvement in both the problems and the solutions.

Only humans can declare where Human Rights come from and if they are universal.

Sometimes what we see with eyes of flesh will shock and assail us—like the recognition that captives in ancient imperial 'smiting' scenes are implicitly and routinely gendered as *female* (see below, Chapter 2). Such iconography morphs into standard images of the Redemptive God in the Hebrew Bible, who delivers with 'a mighty and outstretched hand'. It has been all too easy to forget that those delivering limbs were in the act of smiting the Other, thus inspiring the sentiment, 'better him than us.' Elsewhere what we see in Scriptures will transform us: it is hard to buy into the New Testament's view of the 'Law' after sitting with a page of Talmud; even harder to sit still while Islam is debased and slandered by its heretical, self-professed protectors. We need not always claim that to dishonor the human is to dishonor the Creator God (though we could.); looking with eyes of flesh, we need only understand and see that in dishonoring any human[61] we dishonor ourselves, because we are all connected.

That might be lesson enough.

---

61. Or dishonoring any other part of creation, but that, Reader, is beyond the scope of this particular book.

Chapter 2

GENDERING THE CAPTIVE:
REPRESENTATIONS OF THE ABUSE OF HUMAN DIGNITY

We have seen in our short historical survey that various socio-cultural configurations of oppression were the crucible in which the Bible and Qur'an were formed. This is reflected in both the interest of those texts in the topic of judgment, and in the social need to continually reinforce the survival of a people whose text presented a significant challenge to their worlds. Were we to evaluate the 'Book(s)' for their conformity to the norms of international law, especially those which explicate 'crimes against humanity', we would find, sadly, that our three Scriptures have plenty to offer by way of negative examples.[1] For every wonderful passage like Matthew 25, a cosmic judgment scene which privileges 'right action' over right piety, group membership, or worship, we have another where the dissenting enemy is gleefully consigned to eternal damnation.[2] Some legal scholars have suggested that the ancient world was not nearly so violent as the modern one (when calculated in terms of persons per million to die in wars), but the data do not look at everyday abuses like spousal or child abuse, nor do they include situations of structural violence short of death, such as chattel slavery.[3]

Our task here is to understand the depiction of the abuses of human dignity, using the archaeological record and ancient texts to set the Bible in context. Since human dignity was an important concept in all three Scriptures, albeit one which places human value as derived from divine origins, the treatment of the divinely created body should leave a trace, positive or negative, in our source materials.

---

1. Hector Avalos, *Fighting Words: The Origins of Religious Violence* (Amherst, NY: Prometheus Books, 2005); Charles Kimball, *When Religion Becomes Evil* (San Francisco: HarperCollins, 2002). Kimball advises us to look for the following signs that a religion has gone wrong: absolute truth claims, blind obedience, establishing the 'ideal' time, ends justify any means, and declarations of 'holy war'.
2. Mt. 23.29-33, for example.
3. Calum Carmichael, 'Women's Offences and Biblical Law', *forum historiae iuris* (February 14, 1998), p. 9; cited September 27, 2007 <http://www.rewi.hu-berlin.de/online/fhi/articles/9802carmi.htm>.

To write the history of the treatment of the body in antiquity is also to write the history of its ideological manipulation in representations and the violation of its margins — precisely the arena where the act of 'gendering' occurs. No form of 'political correctness' obtained in the ancient world: it was not against the rules to treat one's captives (or one's women or slaves, by extension) however one wished.[4] Not only did abuse routinely take place, but there was no stigma attached to it for the perpetrator — only shame for the victim — and it is proudly portrayed in the public art of the great empires. As a final note, we should not forget that 'battle' and war-making were positive and important aspects of the divine (for their worshippers, at least).[5] Fiercesome and violent actions were freely attributed to the gods, male and female, and celebrated in myth, cult, and the arts. When the Hebrew Bible proclaims, 'Yahweh is a man of war!' (Exod. 15.3), it is only echoing the common world view of its time. A deity with no 'warrior portfolio' simply wasn't of much use in a dangerous world of competing powers. The value of war-making, with all it entails, became 'canonical' in both art and text, and despite the presence of warrior goddesses like Inanna/Ishtar; Hathor/Sekmet, and the Maiden Anat, all 'positive' aspects of war are gendered as male behaviors and character traits.

1. *Representation Studies*

It is probably no accident that representation studies are flourishing methodologically at the same time the role of gender as a social construction has been problematized by researchers. Neither art history nor psychology, representation studies partake of both of those bodies of knowledge and more to study their target subject: how and why is the human body represented materially, and what meanings should be attached to those representations? Are the rules for representing male and female humans the same when applied to the gods and goddesses? Are there ideal body types, and when a portrayal deviates from the

---

4. Damages caused to the property of another male, of course, required legal restitution, but the captive, woman, or slave was not viewed as a legal entity themselves deserving of compensation. The Hebrew Bible deviates here in its treatment of slaves who have been permanently injured: the slave shall go free (Exod. 21.26-27).

5. See the present writer's ' "A Heifer from thy Stable": On Goddesses and the Status of Women in the Ancient Near East' in Alice Bach (ed.), *Women in the Hebrew Bible: A Reader* (New York: Routledge, 1999), pp.159-78, and 'The Deceptive Goddess in Ancient Near Eastern Myth: Inanna and Inaras', in J. Cheryl Exum and Johanna W.H. Bos (eds.), *Reasoning among the Foxes: Female Wit in a World of Male Power* (Semeia, 42; Atlanta: Scholars Press, 1988), pp. 84-102, for the trope of the militant goddess.

ideal—one thinks here of Akhenaton, the heretic Pharaoh of the New Kingdom and patron of a radically redeveloped artistic style—what should we make of those deviations?[6] While modern persons might tend to see the category of 'the nude' as operating somewhere between 'art' and 'the erotic', should we so easily project our own understandings back onto prehistory and antiquity? Are only female subjects represented as erotic in the ancient world of the Bible, or are males and ambiguously gendered bodies also capable of yielding erotic potency?[7] Can we, using ancient sources, distinguish between the representation of acceptable erotic activity and depiction of sexual abuse, or is the meaning of such depictions in the eye of the beholder, ancient or modern? To answer many of these questions we must ask about the *edges*, surfaces, or boundaries of the body, and the way transgressive acts against them or at their margins are portrayed in context.

There are, of course, some things that we *can* say definitely about representation of the body, even though the study is in its infancy and growing all the time.[8] Archaeology has shown that representations, human and otherwise, appear with the arrival of modern humans (*homo sapiens*) in the evolutionary record. About 50,000 years ago during the Late Pleistocene, an explosion of representation occurred as modern humans successfully competed with and eventually replaced

---

6. Egyptian specialists are still arguing over whether portrayals of Akhenaton are ironic parodies or genuine attempts at a more *realistic* representation of someone with physical disabilities. Close examination of the designs, stylistic treatment, and overall composition of bas-reliefs of Akhenaton in the Metropolitan Museum of Art (New York) suggest a fine sensitivity and affinity for the subject portrayed, to this artist-historian's eye.

7. What, for instance, should we make of Naram-Sin's extremely bodacious, almost demonic, buttocks? (Irene J. Winter, 'Sex, Rhetoric, and the Public Monument: The Alluring Body of Naram-Sin of Agade', in Natalie Boymel Kampen [ed.], *Sexuality in Ancient Art: Near East, Egypt, Greece, and Italy* [Cambridge: Cambridge University Press, 1996], pp. 11-36). Is his depiction as ultra-male, semi-human more related to his textual afterlife as a city god, or to his disastrous act of ignoring divine oracles about war-making, and looting the Enlil temple at Nippur, thereby leading to the destruction of his city Akkad? (Sabina Franke, 'Kings of Akkad: Sargon and Naram-Sin', in Jack M. Sasson (ed.), *CANE*, II [New York: Scribner, 1995], pp. 838-39).

8. Elizabeth Grosz, *Volatile Bodies: Toward a Corporeal Feminism* (Bloomington: Indiana University Press, 1994); Janet Price and Margrit Shildrick (eds.), *Feminist Theory and the Body: A Reader* (New York: Routledge, 1999); Alison E. Rautman (ed.), *Reading the Body: Representations and Remains in the Archaeological Record* (Philadelphia: University of Pennsylvania Press, 2000); Judith Butler, *Gender Trouble: Feminism and the Subversion of Identity* (New York: Routledge, 1990); Kampen (ed.), *Sexuality in Ancient Art*.

Neanderthal humans.[9] During the incubation of modern humans in the previous ten millennia in Africa, little symbolic representation had been created, although brain capacity for it existed.

Specialists debate the origin of this ancient epiphany of the visual: it could represent a neurological mutation that gave rise to this new form of perceptual language; it may be linked to the rise of language itself, or it may be seen as the result of a long development from Middle Paleolithic markings (probably animal tracks). Its sudden arrival in the archaeological record may exist as an illusion in the record simply because earlier examples have not been preserved as well. Most probably this tradition of visual depictions ought to be understood as the product of cultural and social processes, rather than biological or neurological changes.[10] However one resolves those questions, there does seem to be clear consensus that the ability to make visual representation must have had dramatic *adaptive* value for the success of human cultures.

What kind of adaptive use might representation have served for those earliest bands of humans? One of the most interesting aspects of material representation is its profound, almost alchemical, ability to take a form out of context and place it into a new one: now bison stalk the walls of underground caves, and ivory is carved into the shape of shells. This is a major step on the way to forging metaphorical thinking: making (new) meaning by means of joining elements in a new configuration. Writes one historian of prehistoric art:

> The new ability to isolate attributes and forms, and transfer them to another context, had profound organizational and adaptive implications. Ornamenting the body was a way of constructing a set of social distinctions that do not otherwise exist. Socially defined categories of persons do not have obvious physical correlates. By abstracting certain formal properties of natural objects and bestowing them on certain classes of people, the earliest Cro-Magnon cultures were able to make manifest gradations of social status and identity.[11]

So, the representation is *not* the actual thing represented (*sic*), and in that very realization lay the seeds of symbolic thinking, where one thing can stand for another. However, this difference between subject and depiction also operates in the realm of technological challenges; representation is bound by certain constraints placed upon it by the

---

9. Neanderthals and *homo sapiens* in Africa around 200,000 BCE might, of course, have possessed all kinds of *non-material* representation (language, music, etc.) which are lost to modern researchers.

10. Randall White, *Prehistoric Art: The Symbolic Journey of Humankind* (New York: Harry Abrams, 2003), pp. 10-15.

11. White, *Art*, p. 16.

artistic process of representation and the medium chosen. Hands, for example, offer the sculptor a full range of problems—fingers are simply too fragile to execute realistically in certain kinds of media or sculpture.[12] Egypt solved this problem much as the sculptor of the Lincoln Memorial approached Abraham Lincoln's swollen and deformed arthritic hands: hands of important Egyptian figures are shown clasped around a small wooden (?) dowel whose use is unknown. Could it be a simple artistic strategy to make the hand and fingers more fully visible and easily rendered?[13]

Next, it should be pointed out that all representation is *purposive*: it is not an accident when the human body is sculpted, drawn, carved, painted, decorated, or indicated by iconic symbols (like stick figures or glyphs). When we work in the pre-historical time frame in cultures without texts but whose artistic representations still survive, we must face the fact that we will *never* know the entire ancient meaning of those representations, but we are secure in believing that they did *indeed* have meaning.

It is important as well to *unlearn* Western art historical conceptions about what 'art' is and how it works, since these presuppositions can confound our attempts at empathetic understanding of the ancient context. For example, thinking that the process of representing is a kind of cognate of the biological process of visual perception, one which aims at 'accurate' technical depiction, leaves no room for other modes of representing space or time. Photorealism is not the necessary goal of all authentic art, just as the linear time the West experiences is not necessarily relevant to the cyclical worlds of nature in which ancient art is embedded. Inuit carvings can convey *all* of the elements of a hunting scene in a single whole (dogs and sled approaching ice hole, human breaking through ice to hunt, seal approaching the opening from below, spear thrown at the seal through the opening). Such profound differences in representation teach us

> ...how environment, everyday life, and culturally specific ways of thinking, acting, and believing must be woven together to provide a contextualized understanding of the acts of constructing and interpreting representations; whether they be stories, sculptures, songs or engravings.[14]

---

12. Just try carving finely detailed fingers into a limestone rock with a stone chisel and wooden mallet! Painting around the hand outline with a pigment which contrasts with the rock surface is a *much* more forgiving technique!

13. Sometimes, as Freud commented, 'a cigar is just a cigar'. The out-turned base of the Judean Pillar Figurines (JPFs) of biblical times may *not* represent a tree trunk, but simply reflect the sculptor's desire to make the figure vertical and stable.

14. White, *Art*, p. 30.

We can find a very nice example of difference in understanding space in the ancient world, a difference which does not necessarily derive from the artist/artisan's inability to invent or master Western perspective. From the Sumerian cemetery in Mound A at ancient Kish, we find an ornamented 'candy dish' among grave goods (Fig. 1).[15]

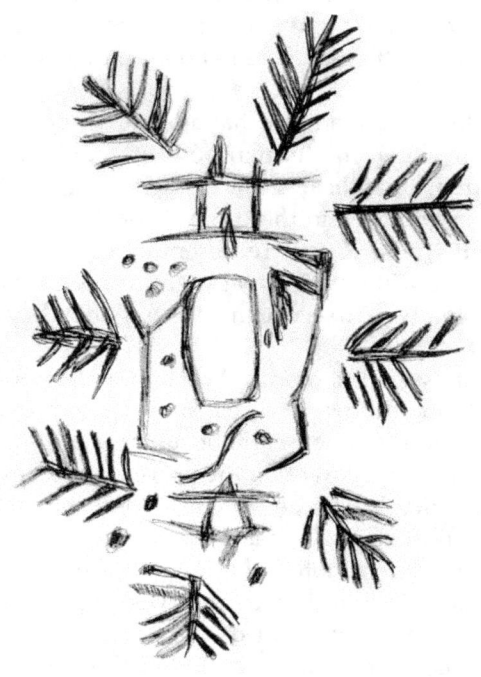

Fig. 1. *Cemetery, Mound A, Kish, Inside of 'Candy Dish' (Pottery Type 'A').*

Excavators of the early twentieth century frankly admitted that the illustration on the small dish stumped them. While the representation is clearly of *something*, and something important enough to include in a high-end burial, the subject was not at all clear to archaeologists of those early decades. However, the researcher following along in their

---

15. Ernest MacKay, *Report on the Excavation of the 'A' Cemetery at Kish, Mesopotamia* (Anthropology Memoirs; Chicago: Field Museum of Natural History, 1925), Plate L-7, #1860 (In other numbering systems, Pl. XLV, #3; on problems with the documentation of the Kish excavation, see Carole R. Fontaine, 'Visual Metaphors and Proverbs 5:15-20: Some Archaeological Reflections on Gendered Iconography', in Ronald L. Troxel, Kelvin G. Friebel and Dennis R. Margary [eds.], *Seeking out the Wisdom of the Ancients: Essays Offered to Honor Michael V. Fox, on the Occasion of his Sixty-Fifth Birthday* [Winona Lake, IN: Eisenbrauns, 2005], pp. 185-202.)

footsteps, guided by later aerial, geological, and topographical maps, and subsequent excavations,[16] could 'see' that what lay before her was a map of the two great temples at either end of the city square or market area. Forested areas—*wild nature*, from which the city and temples were carved out as an act of ordering the social world—are indicated by large symbolic sprouts that circle the city area. It may be that the linear strokes represent a schematic of the streets that verge on the open area guarded by the two temples. The 'dots' must indicate points of note (steles? statues? buildings of note?), but what they might be cannot be determined...yet.

Clearly, we have here a very sophisticated representation of important items: three dimensional objects and environmental features are both depicted visually in two dimensions; symbols are used metonymically to indicate whole forested regions, and both kinds of features, natural and human-made, are shown existing together in a single field of vision. Someone at Kish knew how to 'look down and out' on the general layout of the settlement and reproduce what they saw in another format. That it was found in a grave piques the imagination: what is a grave but a human 'cut' into the natural world, an imposition of one thing on top of or next to another at the site of boundaries? Just as the pious elite at Kish were often buried with 'mother goddess' images on the handle of ritual jugs,[17] here is another burial practice that speaks to the human condition: how better to go down into the underworld than with a memory of the two great temples that guard human society from the unknown wilds. The grave serves the same symbolic purpose as the temples that guard the human spaces: imposing human categories onto external world, with the hope that their order will hold chaos at bay. To remember the temples within the space of the grave is to invoke a known power in the face of the unknown.

The Body in Representation
Our task in examining the visual record of representations of the body encounters another methodological snag beyond the consideration of the meaning of the act of representation itself and its use or meaning in societies. The jury is in, and the body is out. There is no longer a non-problematic view of body nor any sense of self-hood which may attach to it. The body as a unified, discrete entity in space or over time has

---

16. McGuire Gibson, *The City and Area of Kish* (Coconut Grove, FL: Field Research Projects, 1972), and L. Ch. Watelin and Stephen Langdon, *Excavations at Kish* (Field Museum, Oxford University Joint Expedition to Mesopotamia; Paris: Librairie Orientaliste Paul Geuthner, 1930).

17. Carole R. Fontaine, 'Visual Metaphors', pp. 185-202 (189-90).

disintegrated under the same close scrutiny afforded to notion of 'fixed' immutable gender.

For most theorists in corporeal studies, there *is* no body as we have generally understood it, and indeed, it is this very difficulty which accounts for the cultural tasks of repeatedly inscribing meaning at the body's edges. This will be of particular concern when we turn to the Human Rights genre of 'Humanitarian Narrative', a legal and medical literary form that aims at describing very concretely the particular circumstances in which a discrete body met its demise: *how* is one to protect the boundaries of this fluid, semi-metaphorical, constantly morphing illusion of a vertical container which holds us 'in'?[18] Clearly, we have a tangle of impulses, illusions, and cultural meanings whose component parts must be carefully teased apart and differentiated. The sensation of being inside a vessel of skin, flesh, and bone is one of the hallmarks of bodily consciousness; the presumption of a real, physical body is foundational to all criminal, property, and inheritance law. How shall we speak, much less protect and defend, without a stable body at the center of our concerns?

Gender, because it is multiply constructed just like the concept of a stable, discrete body, offers us yet another tool for seeing through our collective fantasy of the fixed body. Peter Brooks fruitfully uses the concept of the eroticized body in narrative to explore the paradox between the body in theory and in individual consciousness:

> One tradition of contemporary thought would have it that the body is a social and linguistic construct, the creation of specific discursive practices, very much including those that construct the female body as distinct from the male. If the sociocultural body is clearly a construct, an ideological

---

18. George Lakoff and Mark Johnson argue in their experientialist approach to semantics and categories in metaphor that our most basic bodily metaphors are that of being 'contained' within our skin in upright orientation (George Lakoff, *Women, Fire and Dangerous Things: What Categories Reveal about the Mind* [Chicago: University of Chicago Press, 1987]), and make the case that even preconceptual experience/ cognition is *not independent* of the entity doing the experiencing: '...no metaphor can ever be comprehended or even adequately represented independently of its experiential basis' (George Lakoff and Mark Johnson, *Metaphors We Live By, with a new Afterword* [Chicago: University of Chicago Press, 2003], p. 19). By this view, woman is a leaky container whose human verticality is often compromised in sexual congress. We should imagine these categories as influencing the negative view of emissions of semen, 'spilling one's seed': the actor entirely misses the upended or sideways-lying container. This carries over to female post-coital emissions of semen, which render the woman cultically impure (Mayer Gruber, 'Purity and Impurity in Halakic Sources and Qumran Law', in Kristin De Troyer *et al.* (eds.), *Wholly Woman, Holy Blood: A Feminist Critique of Purity and Impurity* [Studies in Antiquity and Christianity; Harrisburg, PA: Trinity Press International, 2003], pp. 65-76).

> product, nonetheless we tend to think of the physical body as precultural and prelinguistic: sensations of pleasure and *especially pain* [present author's italics], for instance, are generally held to be experiences outside language; and the body's end, in death, is not simply a discursive concept. *Mortality may be that against which all discourse defines itself, as a protest or as attempted recovery and preservation of the human spirit, but it puts a stark biological limit to human constructions.*[19]

If the body causes a 'fall from language', as Brooks argues, it is at least encouraging to know that we have a net of iconography upon which to land.

It is in the face of pain and mortality that the work of representing the body falls into line with aims of abusers of bodies, those torturers, the victorious commanders, the priestly rituals that invade or curse, such as that in Numbers 5. The precise point of abuse of the body is to re-inscribe a different world-view in the person whose body is violated: new power relations that favor the physically dominant are introduced as the abuse, terror, and fear continually drive the victim into a pre-linguistic, almost inhuman collection of moans, shrieks and cries. Even where torture is concerned, the true purpose is *never* the need to obtain critical information (because the tortured are just as likely to lie to stop the pain as to tell the truth). Rather, it is to unmake the world of the victim in favor of a paradigm where the tortured finally accept and articulate the world-view and goals of the torturer, as Elaine Scarry's seminal work, *The Body in Pain: The Making and Unmaking of the World*, has shown.[20] Just as patriarchy would teach women to think of themselves and their power primarily in terms of their potential to shame and pollute their men, so the torturer and captor advance their own fictions of power. From Scarry's point of view, the ability to inflict pain becomes a structural sign of power.[21] The regime is strong *because* it is brutal, not in spite of it.

2. *Representation, Gender and Early Scenes of War*

Those in ancient Near Eastern studies find themselves in a far more enviable position with respect to understanding material representations than those who work in pre-history. We have texts, and traditions about interpreting them, and we work in one of the most excavated regions in the modern world. Often our public art comes complete with

---

19. Peter Brooks, *Body Work: Objects of Desire in Modern Narrative* (Cambridge, MA: Harvard University Press, 1993), p. 7.

20. Elaine Scarry, *The Body in Pain: The Making and Unmaking of the World* (New York and Oxford: Oxford University Press, 1985).

21. Scarry, *Body in Pain*, p. 56.

explanatory inscriptions. Further, although some die-hards might still pooh-pooh the notion of gender as an analytic category, it is hard to sustain that argument when dealing with our slice of antiquity: ancient Egyptian artists obligingly 'gendered' their human figures as male or female, whether divine or human.[22] Mesopotamian artists were happy to give us clear indices of gender and power: how many 'horns' are on the crown of that bearded figure? Differences in portrayal by different cultures may well be symbolic of a differing thought–world. Or not: we may never understand properly why nipples, male and female, are routinely represented in Egyptian art but not in Mesopotamian artifacts. Whether it is the glyph that stands for male or female (a 'determinative' used to mark gender in Egyptian hieroglyphs) or ideogram (the first 'symbol' for 'woman' in ancient Sumerian is a triangle marked with a line, indicating the pudenda), gender was incontrovertibly a category for ancient people. This is beyond dispute for anyone who has seriously considered the material record.

However, it is worth remembering that gender, as it is currently understood in feminist thought, is not an ontological given (like biological sex, although even that is in dispute), but a constructive process, repeated again and again, to form a normative social construct. Working on the lack of images of female agency in Mesopotamian art, Zainab Bahrani writes:

> When we speak of the 'construction of gender' in representation, it is not the real essence of man, woman, and so on, whether historically contingent or universal, that is being constructed within society and then passively reflected in the image; nor is it a false image divorced from reality, as in a coercive type of image or propaganda. Rather, the construction of gender is theorized as being intimately linked to the visual realm. Art must then be seen as the site of process, a site of the inscription of sexual difference, and not the place of its reflection. The order of gender is inserted into the social order through, among other areas, visual cultural representation. Such a representation configures and underscores, rather than reflects, the reality of gender categories.[23]

So, again, the image is not the reality, but neither is it divorced from it. We will not be surprised, then, to find that the human captive in war or slavery is ambiguously gendered, showing deliberate female markers

---

22. For more discussion of gendering in Egyptian art, see the present writer's '"Be Men, O Philistines!" (1 Sam. 4:9): Iconographic Representations and Reflections on Female Gender as Disability in the Ancient World', in Hector Avalos, Sarah J. Melcher, and Jeremy Schipper (eds.), *This Abled Body: Rethinking Disabilities in Biblical Studies* (Semeia Studies, 55; Atlanta: Society of Biblical Literature, 2007), pp. 61-72.

23. Zainab Bahrani, *Women of Babylon: Gender and Representation in Mesopotamia* (London and New York: Routledge, 2001), p. 32.

of gender, but this need not require us to assume the humans so represented were in fact male effetes, androgynes, Amazons, or persons crippled by having been born without a penis.

Paleolithic Representations of Living Beings
While prehistoric representations contained some human figures, the majority of representations are of animals and therianthropic humans (human–animal hybrids). Art historians speculate at length as to whether or not the art from prehistory is in fact magico-religious in nature (no 'art for art's sake' in the Neolithic, apparently, given the incredible inaccessibility of some of these images from the zones of ordinary, daily life). For many decades it was assumed that meaning and context of the animal parades in the cave art of Old Europe was 'the hunt', and that representations were designed to strengthen the success of that activity. Yet, in many contexts, the animals shown are *not* the animals which made up a major portion of the settlement's diet, which suggests they might have been either especially valued but rare objects of organized hunting activity, or that they bear some other meaning altogether for the communities creating these scenes.

The earliest Paleolithic hunting scenes, if they are indeed that, found deep in caves of Europe are nevertheless remarkable for one particular feature, especially compared to what will come later in the ancient Near East. The more ancient scenes seldom-to-never show the violence of the hunt in terms of dying or wounded animals, an actual death blow, or the butchering of animals prior to their transport back to a community. Likewise, the geometric objects often shown in context of human–animal encounters may *not* be weapons, traps, or wounds as theorized by previous generations of art historians. Instead, they may be linked to the entoptic images seen on the retina (caused by chemical processes in the brain without an external visual stimulus) by shamans in a trance. The representation of them in the caves may reflect the use of the environment for shamanic activity, with these symbols helping to induce the altered consciousness from which they originally sprang.[24] If this interpretation holds true, then the representations themselves are not simply representations, but a threshold or portal to the spirit world of altered consciousness, with all its denizens, difficulties, and opportunities for making meaning.

24. White, *Art*, pp. 119-22, 166. In this interpretation, the therianthropic figures are not to be understood as demonic, but as humans wearing animal masks. The understanding of some of these art traditions as linked with shamanism is bolstered by the mass of bone flutes recovered in such contexts, as the acoustic accompaniment to trance is a key instigator of the state.

As we move into the period of history in the ancient Near East, we see a different situation with respect to the representation of animals and humans. While the Levant may have been an important land bridge for movement of early human population types, by the Neolithic period it can no longer be linked to the art traditions of southern Africa or the cave paintings of Europe. Neanderthals and modern humans coexisted together in our region of interest for over 60,000 years. There is no explosion of representational objects to be found with the advent of early modern humans as in Europe, so assigning what objects we *do* have to modern humans is considerably more complicated than elsewhere. The Levant has a low percentage of representational objects compared to other regions until the beginnings of the Natufian period (c. 13,000 years ago). As agricultural pre-pottery Neolithic communities succeed the Natufians, the distinctive traditions of representation of the ancient Near East are set by the conditions of the agricultural, stratified societies that grew up in the region. In such a context, scenes of a hunt must be related to the complex interaction of new environmental configurations, rather than seen as a continuation of the much earlier traditions described above.[25]

Hunting scenes may reflect an economic reality for the communities who created these scenes in the Neolithic, early dynastic, and empire periods in the ancient Near East, but they also serve some more symbolic purpose. They present the notion of humans successfully manipulating an environment in which they are usually at a disadvantage, something like the triumph of the Gothic cathedral or modern sky-scraper in symbolizing the 'ascent of man'.

What we *can* say is that so-called 'hunting' scenes and animals are one of the earliest themes represented in Near Eastern artistic images, prioritizing this violent yet risky form of human activity within the category of that which was thought worthy or needful of representing. Like later war scenes, hunting scenes are gendered male, yet we know from both nature and culture that females *do* hunt (and not just for men.).[26] The erect penis of hunters as they hunt, found at Lascaux eons before, has been replaced by the 'mighty outstretched hand' ready to deliver the death blow. One might be tempted to draw a connection there between *that* triumph and the successful provision of economic resources to the group, but, given that we are now dealing with much later royal art of successful empires,[27] we may need to posit a more complex symbol-

---

25. White, *Art*, pp. 168-72.

26. A theriomorphic figure of a hybrid lioness/woman from mammoth ivory from the Aurignacian period in Hohlenstein-Stadel, Germany, makes this point very nicely in material form (White, *Art*, p. 72, Plate 32).

27. See White, *Art*, pp. 100-101, Plate 69, from the shaft at Lascaux, in France,

ism. The tropes of the hunting scene may include representations of weapons, use of weapons by hunters, animals penetrated by weapons, wounded hunters, animals dying, and hunters rejoicing. Members of a hunting party, or servants, beaters, and game handlers may also form part of the scene. When found in the later 'royal nexus' of artistic idioms, the king or pharaoh is shown as the key figure among the humans, or else takes on noble or impressive features of lordly animals associated with physical power and prowess.

Drawing on Palettes: Tales of the 'Raging Catfish'
With the coming of more highly organized communal structures in ancient Egypt during the early Pre-dynastic period (Naqada I or II), we can clearly see a transition in images to meet the needs of internal and external conquest ideologies. We turn now to a set of artifacts known as 'ritual palettes', one of the earliest places in the visual record to find the themes and figures which will become canonical in the art of ancient Egypt.[28] This is not tangential to our biblical interests, as archaeology has shown a considerable number of points of contact between pre-Dynastic Egypt and our target cultures in the Levant, even at such an early period.[29] Both the *serekh* sign, which references Narmer's palace façade, as well as this pharaoh's name sign ('the raging catfish'), have been found in Canaan (Nahal Tillah and elsewhere), indicating a trading network between Egypt and southern Canaan, if nothing else.

---

from the Magdalenian period. The figure is bird-headed, and may have a spear-thrower lying at his feet; however, the huge horned mammal definitely seems to be the winner in this encounter, as the figure is leaning/lying at a 45-degree angle. Anthropologist Felicitas Goodman associates this particular posture with shamanic trance states which can be induced in modern subjects lying in the same angled position (*Where Spirits Ride the Wind: Trance Journeys and Other Ecstatic Experiences* [Bloomington: Indiana University. Press, 1990], compare Pls. 3 and 5).

28. Whitney Davis, *The Canonical Tradition in Ancient Egyptian Art* (Cambridge: Cambridge University Press, 1989). See also Whitney Davis, *Masking the Blow: The Scene of Representation in Late Prehistoric Egyptian Art* (Berkeley: University of California Press, 1992).

29. Thomas E. Levy *et al.*, 'New Light on King Narmer and the Protodynastic Egyptian Presence in Canaan', *BA* 58 (1995), pp. 26-35; Thomas E. Levy and Edwin C.M. van den Brink, 'Interaction Models, Egypt and the Levantine Periphery', in Edwin C.M. van den Brink and Thomas E. Levy (eds.), *Egypt and the Levant: Interrelations from the 4th through the early 3rd Millennium BCE* (London: Leicester University Press, 2002), pp. 3-38; Pierre de Miroschedji, 'The Socio-Political Dynamics of Egyptian-Canaanite Interaction in the Early Bronze Age', in van den Brink and Levy (eds.), *Egypt and the Levant*, pp. 39-57; Jean-Daniel Stanley, 'Configuration of the Egypt-to-Canaan Coastal Margin and the North Sinai Byway in the Bronze Age', in van den Brink and Levy (eds.), *Egypt and the Levant*, pp. 98-117.

The heavily decorated ritual palettes in question (the Oxford Palette; the Hunter's Palette; the Battlefield Palette; Narmer Palette;[30] Bull Palette; etc.) have a counterpart in the plain stone palettes commonly used for the grinding, moistening and application of eye make-up, worn by both women and men. Almost all are made of the easily worked mudstone, greywacke or siltstone (not to be confused with the flaking sedimentary rocks of shist/slate). Rudimentary decoration in the forms of marks, usually representing animals, or carved double bird heads at the top are found on numerous common funeral palettes, many of which can be securely dated, starting with the Naqada I period. By the Naqada II period, these palettes may be decorated with a deity's symbol (the Min Palette in the British Museum) or fantastical animal figures of unknown purpose, but perhaps heraldic devices. The palettes continue the representational themes found in Nile valley rock art starting around the fifth millennium: humans and animals in association with one another, divisions of labor, and activity, themes also evident on carved knife handles from the same pre-Dynastic eras.

Also to be classed with this set of artifacts is an ivory knife handle, currently in the Louvre, from Gebel el-Arak (though that is disputed) from the Naqada III period. It shows hunt, battle, and processional themes on separate registers, perhaps with some 'proto-narrative' arrangement.[31] The warlike actions on this knife handle are of interest because they show a relatively 'equal' presentation of 'own' and 'enemy': the 'social perspective' which features the Big Man in larger size than his enemies or retainers is not present, nor are the special royal trappings of weapons, or military uniform (no one is wearing a bull's tail, for example). While some glyphs and medallions in the lowest register represent the group to which some of the combatants belonged, on the whole we have a balanced portrait of conflict (see Fig. 2).[32] Not only are opponents shown fighting back, they seem to carry the same simple weapon, a knife in its sheath. They are all roughly the same size, but it should be noted that the clearest sign of dominance falls to the character on the far left: he holds an upraised mace, and seems to have the fellow before him in a rudimentary form of the captive 'position' (arms pinned behind the

---

30. The Narmer Palette, our main focus here, may be viewed in full at <http://academics.stonehill.edu/Fine-Arts/page.asp>, cited August, 2007; see also James B. Pritchard (ed.), *ANEP* (Princeton, NJ: Princeton University Press, 2nd edn, 1974), Plates 296-97.

31. See Figure 6.6 in Davis, *Canonical Tradition*, p. 128.

32. Registration # E11517, the Louvre, Guillemettre Andreu, Marie-Hélène Rutschowscaya and Christiane Ziegler, *Ancient Egypt at the Louvre*, (trans. Lisa Davidson; London and New York: I.B. Tauris, 1999), pp. 14, 16-17, and *ANEP*, Plate 290.

back, usually above the elbow, in the Egyptian idiom). We will see this trope translated to the hero Pharaoh and gods in later art.

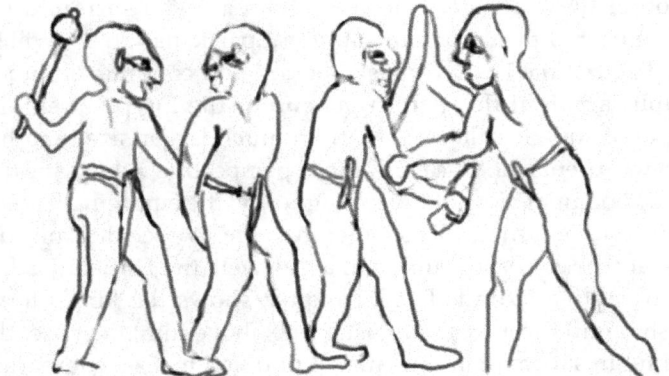

Fig. 2. *Detail, Top Register, Naqada III Era Knife of Hippopotamus Ivory from Gebel el-Arak.*

Artistically, the large ritual palettes show the same constraints often found on practical items with limited space: focus on line and outline, some differentiation of registers, 'bird's eye view', stylized themes and preference for frontal-profile depiction of humans.[33] Their existence and content testifies to the rise of luxury and ritual items in Upper Egypt at the beginning of the fourth millennium immediately prior to and just at the time of state formation.

Mostly from Hierakonpolis, the ritual palettes are much, much larger than the non-ritual ones, usually carved in relief on both sides, but they still bear the general shape of a rhomboid or tomahawk blade. Although their 'ritual' use has not been confirmed, the association of pharaonic glyphs, copious illustration, and oversize style has led historians and archaeologists to posit a ritual, commemorative, or royal use as the only possible explanations. In theory, the eyes of the deity's idol are outlined with eyeliner made on these palettes as a preparation for awakening the god and pressing him into leading (or at least approving) the upcoming battles and wars of the Pharaoh. At present, no more likely explanation for their use presents themselves (they are far too heavy to have been easily used as a personal toiletry item). Some have argued for signs of Sumerian or Elamite influence in some of the motifs used, such as serpent-necked feline predators (serpopards) or a man standing between and separating two rampant lions.[34]

33. Davis, *Canonical Tradition*, pp. 120-34.
34. Davis, p. 134.

What is of interest in the iconography of the change from local organization to state structure is the depictions of animals, enemies, and heroes recorded there. Many of the themes—the king as lion or bull, the depiction of the king as larger-in-life than all who surround him, the stock character of the barbarian entity in a particular pose—will become standardized in the Early Dynastic period and continue on in personal and public art right through to the end of the Egyptian empire. The technique of showing the 'Big Man' in much larger size than his companions represents the so-called 'social perspective' which speaks to the ideological point of view of the iconography: the emerging leadership is determined to present itself as larger than life. We see the same dynastic impulse at work in early Sumerian art as well: the Ur Standard, replete with war captives paraded at a banquet, shows the king's head literally pushing up through the register line above him; likewise, the Stele of Naram-Sin shows that king almost doubled in size, compared to his enemies who fall back or cower before him.[35]

The Oxford Palette challenges our artistic notions that all animal scenes from antiquity must, of necessity, represent the hunt, or at least have some relationship to material human needs (such as food). There, birds, dogs, serpopards, foxes, and all kinds of corvine creatures (ram, ibex, goat, gazelle) move together, licking and showing congenial relations in this earliest Peaceable Kingdom.[36] No humans appear at all on the obverse; there is one puzzling human figure on the reverse. There we find an upright jackal figure, playing on a pipe as he follows along after a giraffe (see Fig. 3). While he may be performing some sort of hunting magic, this is only conjecture, for no other signs of violence or human–animal competition appear anywhere on these reliefs. The human is entirely integrated into nature as one of the crowd, neither less nor more than the creatures that surround him in non-threatening stances.[37]

The Hunter's Palette (Naqada IIIa; see Fig. 4) which is dated after the Gebel el-Arak but before the Narmer Palette is of interest for its visions of the hunt, now standardized and shown with many organized males, sporting horned hats (either their tribal symbol or a ritualized fetish used to secure a successful hunt), bull-tails, and carrying ropes,

---

35. Dominique Collon, *Ancient Near Eastern Art* (Berkeley: University of California, 1995), pp. 67-75.

36. For a wonderful site bringing together the entire pre-Dynastic and Early Dynastic palette corpus, please visit online at <http://xoomer.alice.it/francescoraf/hesyra/palettes.htm>, created by Francesco Raffaele; cited July 2007.

37. Davis, *Canonical Tradition*, pp. 141-43. The giraffe looks as though she is not too sure about the jackal's performance.

Fig. 3. *Oxford Palette Detail: Human shaman (?) dressed as jackal pipes for/to a giraffe.*

throwing sticks, insignia or bows.[38] The figures of animals now share rather than dominate the stage and though they are shown in flight with hunters, we still have a sense that they and the hunters are fairly well matched.

In our detail we see not only a variety of types of animals — no scorning of small animals in favor of the more impressive — but even a hint that humans do not have it all their own way with animals on their own turf. The lion, already stylized with his interlocking scallops of mane, is down but not out: though wounded by arrows, he makes his best attempt at taking a bite or two out of the hunter with the bow. Further, the male lion defeating the hunter is protecting a lion cub which is shown just behind his tail. Nearby in the mélange of figures to the left, a gazelle is taken by a hunter with a rope, while a dog/fox and rabbit run past. Here, two forms of the hunt are placed in sharp juxtaposition: the hunt for grazing animals in which humans are at great advantage, and the chase of dangerous predators where the predator has an equal chance at victory. With the lines of uniformed hunters processing across the top register of the palette, we have a clear sense that Culture has met Nature, and humans stand out as 'overlords' of all they

---

38. *ANEP*, Plate 12.

Fig. 4. *The Hunter's Palette: Detail of Wounded Hunter and Captured Gazelle*

survey, even if they are still occasionally in jeopardy. At the other end of the palette from the fallen hunter, we see a male lion that has been wounded with six arrows (as opposed to the two arrows in the lion mauling the hunter). The lion's tail is held erect, and an arrow seems to have pierced his genitals between his legs, suggestive of symbolic rape by a hunter. The image of conquest of man over animal, even if perilous, is a natural inference in this new presentation.

As we move to the Bull, Battlefield and Narmer Palettes,[39] we find some significant changes as the culture of the state begins to advance. Now, it is neither *dangerous animals* nor peaceful grazers who are

---

39. Vivian Davies and Renee Friedman, 'The Narmer Palette: A Forgotten Member', *Nekhen* 10 (1998), p. 22; Davis, *Masking the Blow*; Orly Goldwasser, 'The Narmer Palette and the Triumph of Metaphor', *Lingua Aegyptia* (*JELS*, 2; 1992), pp. 67-85; Jacques Kinnaer, 'What is Really Known about the Narmer Palette?', *KMT* 15.1 (2004), pp. 48-54; E. Christiana Köhler, 'History or Ideology? New Reflections on the Narmer Palette and the Nature of Foreign Relations in Pre- and Early Dynastic Egypt', in van den Brink and Levy (eds.), *Egypt and the Levant*, pp. 499-514 (505-507); Levy *et al.*, 'New Light', pp. 26-35; van den Brink and Levy, 'Interaction Models', pp. 3-38; Nicholas B. Millet, 'The Narmer Macehead and Related Objects', *JARCE* 27 (1990), pp. 53-59; David O'Connor, 'Context, Function and Program: Understanding Ceremonial Slate Palettes', *JARCE* 39 (2004), pp. 5-25; David O'Connor, 'Narmer's Enigmatic Palette', *Archaeology Odyssey* (September–October, 2004), pp. 16-52.

hunted, but *people*—an Enemy has taken on shape and function for the first time. On the Narmer Palette, we finally have a name associated with the scene—Narmer, whose name appears clearly marked with the *serekh* (ritualized palace) containing the catfish and chisel glyph. Instead of the equal sized combatants of the Gebel el-Arak knife, now there is a world of difference between the pharaoh-hero and his prey (see Fig. 5). Narmer not only towers over his kneeling, fallen enemy on the reverse side; he is also shown far larger than any of his attendants or any other figure, with the exception of the bulls and serpopards.

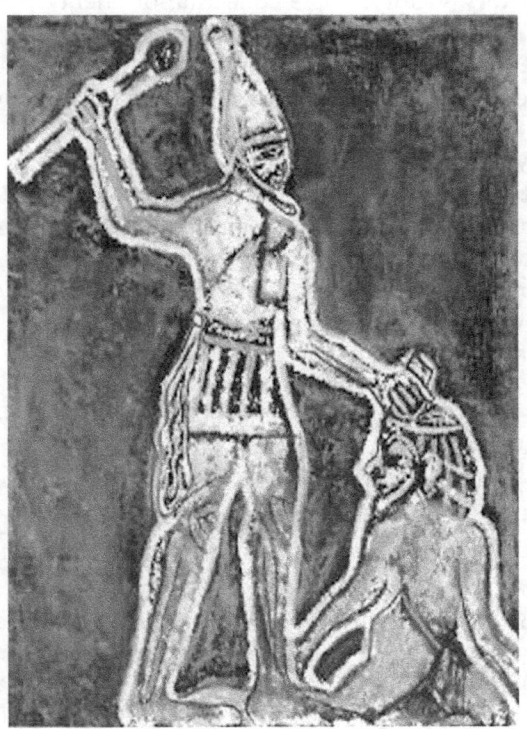

Fig. 5. *Narmer Palette, Reverse, Middle Register (not to scale): Narmer smites an enemy.*

Narmer grasps his enemy's hair or forelock in preparation for smiting with his mace, a scene which will be repeated many times in the art of the Egyptian empires right down into the Roman period. Above this unfortunate captive, a Horus-falcon uses a hook or rope to pull the nose of an enemy's head, nicely emerging from a glyph of reeds (perhaps indicating the geographical origin of the foe in the Delta) up and back for easier access for beheading. The message is clear: Narmer's actions are echoed by his god, giving the ultimate blessing thereby.

Beheadings and (perhaps) other mutilations are seen on the obverse of the palette (see Fig. 6): the mutilated corpses of ten captives in two rows have been lined up for counting, the head of each placed between their feet. Nine of the captives have been castrated, and these figures wear 'sausage-like' objects on the top of their severed heads. The tenth captive, who still has his member, wears no sausage upon his head, leading one archaeologist to suggest that we have here a deliberate image of the feminizing of the foe. It is not sufficient simply to cut off the head; the severing of the other 'head' serves to complete the Pharaoh's totally satisfactory victory.[40] The collection of enemy penises to serve for a body-count is attested in New Kingdom times, when 'civilized' enemies were counted by their severed hands,[41] but tribal enemies were counted by penises, especially if uncircumcised or showing the notched circumcision foreign to the Egyptian practice.[42] Since the Narmer Palette comes to us well before historical records of any such practice, no more can be said about whether or not this might be one of the origins of the New Kingdom custom. It is of note, perhaps, that the penis shown on the right in the detail of two kneeling enemies beneath Narmer's oversized image of smiting is notched, indicating 'Other'. The enemy on the left is shown without male genitalia.

Other elements complete the troubling feminization: captives are placed on the right or looking to the left, the 'female' position of the less important figure in Egyptian art. They are often shown with long, flowing tresses, and they kneel or vainly attempt flight. They are often shown naked, with flaccid penis, or in penis-sheaths or loin cloths, while the Pharaoh's genitals are always safely garbed. To highlight his hypermasculinity, the Pharaoh wears a large bull's tail, and is shown wearing

---

40. Davies and Friedman, 'A Forgotten Member', p. 22. Here the researcher with interests in gender encounters a major road-block in 'text-reception': early modern archaeologists and art historians often censored what was portrayed in ancient art when it transgressed existing boundaries of sexual modesty; later studies which followed their expurgated schematics make little or no mention of gendered representation because they did not examine the rather interesting and varied visual record of this iconic element on the original artifacts. The cast of the Narmer Palette in the British Museum which was examined by the author also showed a tendency to blur or erase genitalia clearly visible on clear, modern reference photographs.

41. *ANEP*, Plates 319, 348.

42. Egyptian circumcisions followed the Semitic practice of removal of the foreskin. The drive to parade prisoners naked, with particular form of circumcision clearly indicated, makes its way into Canaan by the time of the Late Bronze Age. Shasu prisoners are shown in headdress and 'own-style' circumcision in a procession before the king or ruler of Megiddo on an etched ivory in the Rockefeller Museum in Jerusalem (Sophie Laurant, 'Megiddo: Questions sur le Royaume de Salomon', *La Monde de la Bible* 180 (November-December, 2007), pp. 30-33 (30).

Fig. 6. *Narmer Palette, Reverse: Detail of Bottom Register*

the typical crowns of Egypt (the White Crown of Upper Egypt on the reverse, the Red Crown of Lower Egypt on the front). This Super-Male is followed by a much smaller functionary who carries his sandals, one of the highest status personal items in the iconographic lexicon, and not unknown in folklore for the shoe/sandal's relationship to the vagina. In the colored art of tomb paintings of later centuries, enemies will also be gendered by color, painted with the yellow ochre typically reserved for female representation.

Another feature of the desire to gender the enemy as the female complement to the king as Über-male is the use of animal imagery found on the Narmer, Bull, and Battlefield Palettes. All three of these palettes are usually associated with the early period of unification of local nomes into a national unit, but the historicity of the imagery or the identification of the various groups represented is not our focus here, since we are dealing with representation, which takes us into the realms of ideology and cultural idiosyncrasy. It is for Egyptologists and other specialists to puzzle out the exact relationship of the iconography to anything like historical truth, contested though such studies may be in a post-modern dialogue with the past.

The bull makes multiple appearances on the Narmer Palette: on both sides, the bull's head is doubled and depicted on the top register, flanking the *serekh* with Narmer's signifying glyphs. On the bottom register on the obverse, a bull, genitals prominently displayed, is seen battering down a town wall, as it tramples another naked, fleeing foe with long hair from the back (see Fig. 7). The foe is clearly an 'Other',

Fig. 7. *Narmer Palette, Obverse, Bottom Register*

as seen from his notched circumcision. Testicles may also be indicated: close examination of photographs suggests that the 'blur' so tastefully rendered on the plaster casts of the palette in the British Museum may in fact be a small echo of the bull's rampant display.

On the Bull Palette from the Louvre, bulls are used similarly to cow and trample the defeated enemies (see Fig. 8).[43] Again, the hapless enemy is shown beneath the bull, with trampling of his legs in progress, and the scene is repeated on each side in the top register. The hooves, head, face, and genitalia of the bull, though stylized, are given significant attention in their rendering. As the captive falls to the ground, the bull's head leans over his shoulders. The foe's entire body is shown between the bull's two front legs, and the enemy's penis sheath echoes the two-part generative member of the bull. Though the sheath is shown larger than the bull's genitals, there is no question about who is 'on top' in this vignette. Glyphs for towns and assorted groups are used as design features but, because of the fragmentary nature of the artifact, no more can be said of their use than that.

Completing the transition from Über-male human to fierce male animal of prodigious endowments is the Battlefield Palette. Now, the lion, formerly a worthy and dangerous foe on the Hunter's Palette,

---

43. *ANEP*, Plates 291-92.

2. *Gendering the Captive*

Fig. 8. *Bull Palette Detail, Top Register*

has morphed into a fitting symbol of the conquering king (see Fig. 9). With corpses all around, many of them being eaten by birds, the lion-king holds his naked prey in an almost lover-like embrace as he mauls his mid-section. The notched penis on the partial figure to the right of the unfortunate victim clearly marks the foe as foreign and deserving of such a deadly encounter. One hopes, on the basis of the small bird pecking at the foe's body, that the human is already dead before the lion has his way with him.

As we will see in the next section, one of the ways that war is prosecuted is through its sexual codings, which are then repeated in real actions. It is interesting that one of the most powerful ways of feminizing an enemy is to commit rape upon them, but this literal figuration is absent, not only from the pre-Dynastic art we have surveyed, but through all periods. For instance, in scribal texts, the present writer has found only one scant mention of homosexual activity between men: a variant line in the *Book of the Dead* can read either 'I have not copulated' or 'I have not copulated with a man-boy'.[44] We will also find images of

---

44. Translators suggest that this protestation of innocence relates to one's state of sexual purity before entering sacred precincts, and is not a condemnation of homo-erotic behavior as such (Robert K. Ritner, 'Book of the Dead 125: "The Negative Confession" ', in W.K. Simpson, *The Literature of Ancient Egypt: An Anthology of Stories, Instructions, Stelae, Autobiographies, and Poetry* [New Haven: Yale University Press, 3rd edn, 2003], pp. 267-77 [269-77]).

Fig. 9. *Battlefield Palette, with Highlighted Detail of Bottom Fragment*

homosexual or heterosexual rape missing from the Mesopotamian art corpus, as well as historical notices of campaigns (see below). Given the way the newly created kingship chooses to image its leader as a wild, male natural predator, and the compromising, pseudo-sexual positions in which the victim and the animal are presented, there is a strong possibility that scenes like those from the Bull Palette, the Battlefield Palette, and Narmer Palette may be symbolic, yet discrete,[45] suggestions of this act of violation.

3. C.S.I.: *The Fertile Crescent*[46]

Recently, much work has appeared on the gendering of the language of warfare, some of it even drawing implications for the visual assault of sado-homoerotic images from American torture of Iraqis at Abu Ghraib.[47] Certainly, the records of war from Assyria and Babylon show

---

45. It may be that even being the dominant player in same-sex rape attaches *some* shame to the rapist, given views of purity and natural orders of sexuality.

46. 'Crime Scene Investigation' is currently a very popular series on US television, taking place in various cities, and teaching the public how to use deductive reasoning.

47. Among the most notable entries are Bruce Lincoln, 'From Artaxerxes to Abu Ghraib: On Religion and the Pornography of Imperial Violence', *Religion and Culture Web Forum* (January 2007); Cynthia R. Chapman, *The Gendered Language of Warfare in*

many examples of abuses which make clear that while human dignity *may* have been attributed to the occasional elite, it had no place in the figuration or treatment of one's enemies (see Figs. 10-11), and this is a lesson even children must learn.

Fig. 10. *Detail of Top of Middle Register of the Siege of Lachish: Two women ride in a baggage cart; the second figure is comforting a child, while another holds on from behind; See Fig. 11 for vignette appearing directly beneath this cart. Palace of Sennacherib, Nineveh.*

Fig. 11. *Detail of Assyrians flaying two men from Lachish while children look on from behind and above (see Fig. 10). Palace of Sennacherib, Nineveh.*

the Israelite–Assyrian Encounter (HSM, 62; Winona Lake, IN: Eisenbrauns, 2004); T.M. Lemos, 'Shame and Mutilation of Enemies in the Hebrew Bible', *JBL* 125 (2006), pp. 225-41.

The Gendering of War

All researchers have recognized the habitual association of warfare with masculinity, particularly the way that feminizing the enemy serves to both shame the foe and hearten one's own troops. Worldwide, the gender coding of war requires the enemy, subordinates, and civilians to be gendered as female within the male warrior's psychology. This is achieved in ways both symbolic and tangible. In concrete terms, armies may choose one or all of the following: (1) gendered massacre (kill all the men, rape all the women and take them captive); (2) castration and sexual mutilation, and (3) homosexual rape.[48] The Hebrew Bible seems quite familiar with many of these practices; consider the war notice in Numbers 31 for its implications in terms of human suffering for non-combatants:

> Moses sent them to the war, a thousand from each tribe, along with Phinehas son of Eleazar the priest, with the vessels of the sanctuary and the trumpets for sounding the alarm in his hand. They did battle against Midian, as the LORD had commanded Moses, and *killed every male*. They killed the kings of Midian: Evi, Rekem, Zur, Hur, and Reba, the five kings of Midian, in addition to others who were slain by them; and they also killed Balaam son of Beor with the sword. The Israelites *took the women of Midian and their little ones captive*; and they took all their cattle, their flocks, and all their goods as booty. All their towns where they had settled, and all their encampments, they burned, but they took all the spoil and all the booty, both people and animals. Then they brought the captives and the booty and the spoil to Moses, to Eleazar the priest, and to the congregation of the Israelites, at the camp on the plains of Moab by the Jordan at Jericho. Moses, Eleazar the priest, and all the leaders of the congregation went to meet them outside the camp. Moses became angry with the officers of the army, the commanders of thousands and the commanders of hundreds, who had come from service in the war. Moses said to them, *'Have you allowed all the women to live? These women here, on Balaam's advice, made the Israelites act treacherously against the LORD in the affair of Peor*, so that the plague came among the congregation of the LORD. *Now therefore, kill every male among the little ones, and kill every woman who has known a man by sleeping with him. But all the young girls who have not known a man by sleeping with him, keep alive for yourselves* (Num. 31.6-18, NRSV).

Even the great Law-Giver Moses feels the necessity of adding a bit of justification to the slaughter of innocents: the women aren't really innocent, but deserve death as a sort of public health measure. Nevertheless, somehow the virgins have escaped the blight of their mothers, grandmothers, and older sisters and are 'easy pickings' for the victorious men.

48. Joshua S. Goldstein, *War and Gender: How Gender Shapes the War System and Vice Versa* (Cambridge: Cambridge University Press, 2001), pp. 332-80.

2. Gendering the Captive

How odd that our comparative documents and monuments are so willing to tell one part of that story, but seldom allude, except through symbolic means, to the rape incidents against either sex. The Incantation texts from the Levant are replete with the use of male and female physical imagery—weapons for men and spindle-whorls and mirrors for women—to express the orderly categories of gender and provide a magical method for subverting them (see Figs. 12 and 13): when males are made into females, they are much easier to control, thinks the magical work of execration. 'May your enemies be turned into women!'[49] is the consistent refrain in the Bible and its surrounding cultures, a hope that finds its echo in the Holy Grail of Pentagon. This is the much discussed, fondly wished-for armament known as the 'Gay Bomb': it infects enemy soldiers (only?) with sudden erotic desires which they turn on their comrades.

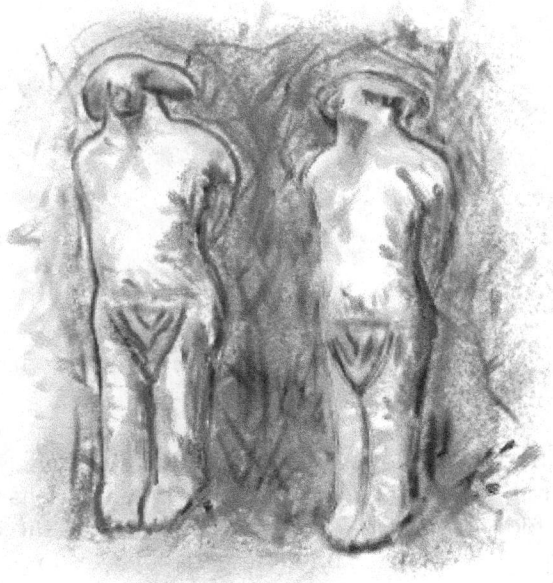

Fig. 12. *Terracotta Execration Figures: Bound Enemy Males Shown with Female Pubic Triangles. Thirteenth–Twelfth century, New Kingdom Egypt, the Louvre.*

Sexuality is a primary realm in which the honor and shame cultures of antiquity attempted to spell out roles appropriate to different groups, and the mutilation and mistreatment of enemies quite naturally makes

---

49. Isa. 19.16; Nah. 3.13; Jer. 50.37; 51.30.

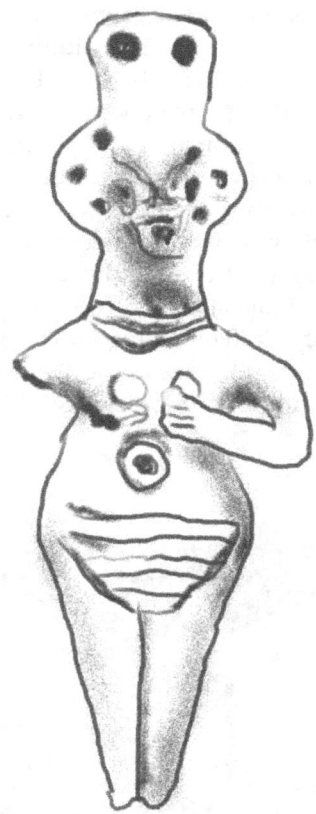

Fig. 13. *Bronze Age Syrian Dea Nutrix, with Exaggerated Pudenda. Allard Pearson Museum, University of Amsterdam.*

use of one of the key tools of ideology: gendering the male as female and substituting him for animal prey. While the hunt had as its purpose the provision of food—as well as honor and glory to the successful hunters—the purpose of the new hunt of imperial kings is to provide 'food' for the empire. When we think of the placement of such moments as Assyrian bas-reliefs in palaces, there is a clear message aimed at visiting dignitaries, war captives on display, and any locals who might feel that they could provide for themselves better than the conquering state: *this captive could be YOU! You are no more than meat set out for the banquet, or dogs beneath the overlord's table who must compete for scraps.*[50] The use of animal imagery and the trappings of female gender play a huge part in stifling malcontent among one's own, and breeding fear among fractious

50. Judg. 1.6.

Others (see Fig. 14; note the prostrate captive/enemy at the conqueror's 'feet', a typical metaphor for male genitalia).

Fig. 14. *Detail of Bas-relief from Nimrud: Assyrian elite humiliates a captive. Ninth century. British Museum.*

What remains a puzzle, given the Bible's record of viewing warfare as the rape and humiliation of the erring city or country, personified as the god's adulterous wife,[51] is the lack of direct sexual imagery used in

---

51. Copious amounts have been written on this metaphor; for articles, see Athalya Brenner and Carole R. Fontaine (eds.), *A Feminist Companion to the Latter Prophets* (FCB, 8; Sheffield: Sheffield Academic Press, 1995), and Renita Weems, *Battered Love: Marriage, Sex, and Violence in the Hebrew Prophets* (OBT; Minneapolis: Augsburg-Fortress Press, 1995). Pamela Gordon and Harold C. Washington explore the relationship between a 'rape culture' and military imagery in 'Rape as a Military Metaphor in the Hebrew Bible' (Brenner and Fontaine, *Latter Prophets*, pp. 308-35), while F. Rachel Magdalene calls our attention to treaty curses as a source for the prophetic use of rape and abuse as its 'marriage metaphor' ('Ancient Near Eastern Treaty-Curses and the Ultimate Texts of Terror: A Study of the Language of Divine Sexual Abuse in the Prophetic Corpus', *ibid*, pp. 326-53). See also Gerlinde Baumann, *Love and Violence: Marriage as Metaphor for the Relationship between YHWH and Israel in the Prophetic Books* (trans. Linda M. Maloney; Collegeville, MN: Liturgical Press, 2003). I must object at this point to the use of 'marriage metaphor' terminology to reference the prophetic propensity for showing Israel and Judah as Yahweh's errant adulterous wife who is publically humiliated by 'her' 'husband'. Domestic violence under patriarchy does not represent the whole extent of the domain of marital imagery, and ought not to be made the monolithic category by which we consider social relations between the sexes, especially in past societies where we lack full ability to document abuses. This is not to deny that abuses

battlefield or aftermath of warfare scenes. Mesopotamian reliefs show captive women being marched out of their cities and into slavery by the conquering troops; records show that rations were allotted to feed them. While this certainly shames enemy males who are shown up as incapable of performing one of the key roles of the masculine gender, protector of women-folk and other unfortunates, it could hardly do that as effectively as the open display of behaviors like wide-scale rape of enemy women or other sado-erotic uses of the captive body. Certainly, the erotic and magico-religious art of the great river valley empires shows no tendency to delicacy in the depiction of body parts in erotic scenes for purposes of magic (see Fig. 15).[52]

Fig. 15. Coitus a tergo *Tavern Drinking Scene; Bronze Age Terracotta Plaque, Mesopotamia. Allard Pearson Museum, University of Amsterdam.*

certainly did exist, nor that the Bible accepts them as reasonable and customary; rather, my view seeks to find a place for texts like Proverbs 31 and the Song of Songs in our analyses. The Song, while not referring explicitly to a married couple, certainly does make use of marriage imagery here and there.

52. Julia Assante, 'Sex, Magic and the Liminal Body in the Erotic Art and Texts of the Old Babylonian Period', in Simo Parpola and R.M. Whiting (eds.), *Sex and Gender in the Ancient Near East: proceedings of the XLVII Rencontre Assyriologique Internationale, Helsinki, July 2-6, 2001* (University of Helsinki: Neo-Assyrian Text Corpus Project), pp. 27-52.

2. *Gendering the Captive* 61

Cynthia Chapman has suggested[53] that the associations of architectural features like entry ways, doors, gates, and so on may yield the meaning of penetration in Assyrian war scenes, along with the tropes of piercing weapons and nakedness, a point also made by J. Assante (see n. 52, this chapter) in her evaluation of Old Babylonian erotic magical plaques (see Fig. 16). Nakedness as a category, however, goes through many different variations, and cannot be said either to be exclusively negative or female.[54] While naked enemies fall from the towers they could not defend (and were certainly not trying to defend while naked, given the entire scene), the Assyrian siege engine with battering ram is suggestively posed near the entrance of the city. As a nude foe falls from the walls, the battering ram cuts him in half, perhaps a trope for rape, given the angle of the battering ram.

Fig. 16. *Assyrians attack city walls with a siege machine and battering ram while corpses fall and litter the ground. Bas-relief, Nimrud, Central Palace of Tiglath-Pileser III.*

Another relief from Shalmaneser III's campaign against Dabigu in Syria (not shown here) depicts city leaders or fleeing captives impaled outside the city walls, with the wooden shafts piercing them through

---

53. *Gendered Language*, pp. 46-47, 159-63.
54. Julia M. Asher-Greve, 'The Essential Body: Mesopotamian Conceptions of the Gendered Body' in Maria Wyke (ed.), *Gender and the Body in the Ancient Mediterranean* (Oxford: Blackwell Publishers, 1998), pp. 8-37.

the genitals,[55] supporting Chapman's hypothesis. Of course, the most common scene of piercing to viewers of Western art is the copious illustrations of the New Testament scene where a Roman soldier pierces the side of Jesus with his spear to determine whether or not he is dead yet. The sexual overtones of this scene are not lost on women survivors of rape who are Christian: the piercing is a clear sign to them at least that Jesus shares their bodily vulnerability and humiliation. He too has been violated by penetration and so he becomes a feminized Redeemer, one who can share their pain and transmute it, as they share in his Resurrection, whether that is viewed bodily or in psychological terms as emergence from post-traumatic stress.[56]

Is it History?
'I hope you aren't taking all of this too seriously', said the Assistant Curator of the British Museum's Egyptian Reading Room when I arrived for my appointment to examine the Victorian casts made of the Narmer Palette, the original of which lives in Cairo. 'I beg your pardon?' I asked. 'Oh, well, people come here looking for "history", and whatever Narmer might be, it certainly isn't *that!*', he told me. I told him that my project was looking at development of a particular motif over time and relating it to sentiments expressed in texts, and he seemed a bit relieved. I nodded wisely, as I had once been led down the garden path by Ramses II on the walls of Karnak. A good scholar learns to tell the difference between propaganda, magical wish-fulfillment, and actual data.

Attacking this question full on, however, requires a bit more than an anecdote. Like the inflated genocidal wars related by the Deuteronomistic Historians of the Bible, the Narmer Palette (and other images surveyed here) may or may not have much relationship to actual fact. Just like narrative, it is *an interpretation*, not a one-for-one representation. Any interpretation requires a departure from objectivity, as a Narrator or Interpreter must be present in all their embodied particularity to draw the conclusions and craft meaning. Just because we are seeing an

---

55. This may be viewed online at <http://www.islamic-awareness.org/Quran/Contrad/External/crucify.html>, cited July 2007; for other images of battering rams and weapons used in sexual positions, see Chapman, *Gendered Language*, Plates 1-14.

56. This observation is based on work with many survivors of rape, domestic, and political torture. Christian women do seem to find an 'edge' that functions to enhance their recoveries: their humiliation and defilement, when shared by Jesus, provides them with the possibility of another outcome than suicide because of dishonor. Jesus is one who shares experience and thereby gives it new meaning not available to secularists in similar situations. This is the power of the theologically disturbing (to some) image of the *Christa*.

ideological interpretation of pre-Dynastic ideas and perhaps events does not rob the artifact of its interest or importance to us. As with the Deuteronomistic History's xenophobic zeal for genocide, we must take the ideology presented in text and artifact very seriously indeed for what it may tell us about values and world-views. Of course it is *not* history—but it wishes that it was, and for *that* the critic must account, especially in a world hell-bent on reading ancient texts for ideological justification for violence of any sort.[57]

The Female Question: Where Are They?
History or not, there are no rapes portrayed in all the scenes of brutalities on the battlefield and beyond. This seems a shock to moderns, that such an elementary scene of horror and humiliation has gone neglected in the iconographic arsenal of the great kings.[58] Are we wrong in thinking that rape is an inevitable accompaniment to organized human violence? Have the 'Rape' of Nanking,[59] Hitler's 'Rape of Poland', the fate of Korean 'comfort women', and the deliberate use of rape as a tool of war in Bosnia and Darfur rendered us hyper-sensitive?[60] Can the artist or historian look at the evidence of the past without the blur caused by the images of Abu Ghraib and Guantanamo obstructing our eyes?

The absence of women in the iconography of imperial war is not the only lacuna to be found, however, and perhaps other omissions give a hint of the agenda of the composers of the war art. No Egyptian or Assyrian soldier was shown as wounded, dead or mutilated; no Pharaoh or Great King ever lost a battle, fought to a draw, or had anything other than a

57. For similar thoughts on the relationship between facticity and narrative in the account of the destruction of Lachish, see Philip R. Davies, 'This is What Happens...', in Lester L. Grabbe, *'Like a Bird in a Cage': The Invasion of Sennacherib in 701 BCE* (JSOTSup, 363; European Seminar in Historical Methodology; Sheffield: Sheffield Academic Press, 2003), pp. 106-19; Christoph Uehlinger, 'Clio in a World of Pictures—Another Look at the Lachish Reliefs from Sennacherib's Southwest Palace at Nineveh', *idem*, pp. 221-307.

58. So, too, in classical art and texts on war, where the depiction of abduction of a specially chosen woman is preferred to rape (Ada Cohen, 'Portrayals of Abduction in Greek Art: Rape or Metaphor?', in Kampen [ed.], *Sexuality in Ancient Art*, pp. 117-36).

59. Susan Brooks Thistlethwaite, ' "You May Enjoy the Spoil of your Enemies": Rape as a Biblical Metaphor for War', in Claudia V. Camp and Carole R. Fontaine (eds.), *Women, War and Metaphor: Language and Society in the Study of the Hebrew Bible* (Semeia, 61; Atlanta: Scholars Press, 1993), pp. 59-78.

60. Let us hope so! Only in this century are we beginning to understand the special circumstances of women and girls during episodes of conflict (to view the United Nations initiatives around this special group, see <http://www.un.org/children/conflict/english/girlsinwar101.html>, cited August 1, 2007).

thoroughly satisfactory 'slam dunk' in their prosecution of the wars. Further, soldiers of the empire are never themselves shown as captives, though we know from the attention given in Babylonian and Assyrian law codes to the returning captive and his reclamation of his property after escape, that the war-makers did not have it all their own way.[61] War was intrinsically linked to a divine purpose of imposing imperial order, whether it was desired or not, but it did not mean that one had to show every little set-back that commonly occurs in any human enterprise. In other words, anything that might shame the aggressors goes unreported.

It is perhaps to *this* realm of ideological cover-up that we must add the lack of attention to the treatment of women, other than forced exile and enslavement. Horrifying as those fates are, they do evince a certain positive aspect: women were valued as slaves and mothers producing even more slaves for their captors. Further, women are more docile and easily intimidated, especially when their children are at risk, so this again makes them the superior choice in a captive.[62] Cross-culturally, wisdom literature and inscriptions tell us that *all* kings and pharaohs were, by nature, construed as the special guarantors of the well-being of widows, orphans, and foreigners: Ur-Namma (c. 2100 BCE) writes of his commitment to justice in Ur:

> I did not deliver the orphan to the rich. I did not deliver the widow to the mighty. I did not deliver the man with but one shekel to the man with one mina (c. 60 shekels); I did not deliver the man with but one sheep to the man with one ox […] I did not impose orders. I eliminated enmity, violence and cries for justice. I established justice in the land.[63]

Since the conquering king has just converted women and children into widows and orphans, he has, in effect, become their protector. Perhaps showing attacks on women might provoke some question as to just what kind of protector the king actually was, even if we were to

---

61. 'Laws of Eshnunna', para. 29, in Martha T. Roth, *Law Collections from Mesopotamia and Asia Minor* (WAW, 6; Atlanta: Scholars Press, 2nd edn, 1997), p. 63; 'Laws of Hammurabi', section 32 (column xi 13-38), p. 87; 'Middle Assyrian Laws', section A45, pp. 170-71.

62. The first recorded ideogram for any kind of slave is the Sumerian ideogram made of a pudenda flanked by three small mountains, or 'mountain (foreign) female', since mountainous regions were the territory of their enemies (especially so of the Guti: 'the snake of the mountain made his lair there' (Piotr Michalowski, *The Lamentation over the Destruction of Sumer and Ur* [Mesopotamian Civilizations, 1; Winona Lake, IN: Eisenbrauns, 1989], p. 45, line 145). The first slave in history, then, is a captive female, desirable for exploitation for both of those reasons. Sisera's mother makes a similar metonymic statement about the rape of captives in Judges 5.

63. 'Laws of Ur-Namma' (Roth, *Law Collections*, pp. 16-17).

overlook his role in creating the very conditions which require him to serve as guarantor of rights of the bereaved.

Even in modern times, this impulse to present oneself as the protector of the weak (= women and children) is still fully at work.[64] While we heard many stories and saw many pictures of the abuse of male detainees by American soldiers, intelligence operatives and contractors in Iraq, precious little information can be found about the rapes of women and girls at US facilities, although we know that such took place. Having used the 'rape rooms' of Iraq as one of the supposedly many compelling reasons to launch a war of choice—the damsel in distress *must* be protected by the caring, civilized West[65]—the display of women detainees' experience in Iraq would have been a brutal irony. US troops and others immediately began to use the same tactics and even buildings as their enemy to practice their very own version of the Geneva Conventions.[66] The shaming of male Iraqis in detention with homoerotic or sadistic sexual imagery had the purpose of feminizing these unfortunate souls, thereby conferring hyper-masculinity on the perpetrators, still smarting from a terrorist attack on their own soil. When real perpetrators or enemies are not captured and brought to justice, something must be done to redistribute honor and shame among the parties involved. Showing what has happened to women under American occupation would bring shame to the conquerors, given their previous rhetoric,[67]

---

64. John Kane, 'American Values or Human Rights? U.S. Foreign Policy and the Fractured Myth of Virtuous Power', *Presidential Studies Quarterly* 33 (2003), pp. 772-800.

65. I am indebted to my colleague Professor Valerie Elverton Dixon for calling my attention to this 'righteous defender'/knight in shining armor trope in our current wars.

66. How does one learn of things which are quite literally unspeakable and held close as a military/governmental secret? One often comes across those who can bear witness in the Human Rights community which deals with issues of torture as part of its daily bread. In this particular case, I cannot share names, but was privileged to offer comfort to a person who had taken the transcripts for testimony coming out of Abu Ghraib. The release of any of this available material would put lie to all the ideologies of humanitarian intervention currently trotted out by leaders in the United States. For a general discussion of the culpability of leadership at Abu Ghraib and names that *can* be shared, see eye-opening and on-going work by New Yorker writer, Seymour M. Hersh (*Chain of Command: The Road from 9/11 to Abu Ghraib* [New York: HarperCollins Publishers, 2004]). Talks with women NGO workers from Iraq continue to highlight the impossibility of addressing the experiences of these women prisoners, given the cultural context of female shame. The backlash against women in Iraq can be seen as way to 'let off steam' over the dishonor of occupation, as well as a slap in the face of secular factions.

67. One could also argue that this group has shown decisively that they *have no*

and expose them, not the women, to the eyes of the world. So, the voice of the tortured female is silenced in the present, just as it was in the earliest times of imperial aggression.

To be fair, we must add to this analysis in the present that the women so abused and later released have an incentive *not* to discuss their experiences. The honor and shame paradigm in which their culture is steeped would put them at risk from the males of their own family. Honor killings are seldom about female honor; it is rather a response to the supposed shame females bring upon their male relatives. The woman trapped by the enemy becomes an immediate 'orphan': no family member can protect her, and no power works in her favor. Usually, death is the outcome for a woman in a traditional society who manages to survive her 'fate worse than death'. If she did not have the decency to die of shame, her culture is all too willing to take care of that detail.

4. *The View from the Hebrew Bible*

War in the Hebrew Bible cannot be viewed as a unified concept, because the texts that speak of it and attempt to regulate it come from different times and circumstances. Further, final editors of the historical books, the Deuteronomistic Historians of the seventh century, imposed a decidedly lop-sided ideological reading onto the war narratives they collected, sorted, edited and appended: the tribal period was characterized by violence because 'there was no king in Israel and every man did what was right in his own eyes'. The monarchic period, though filled with civil wars, border wars, and imperial invasions, is nevertheless heralded as a better State to be in, because now, like the nations, the people have a divinely chosen leader to conduct their wars.[68] For these writers, the wars of the Lord are an example of divine justice, executed on Israel's behalf, and the violence visited upon the Other is a deserved punishment for various idolatries and differences. Of course, this view of 'holy war', where all living things are slain, was not Israel's sole invention or practice: the Moabite Inscription of King Mesha in the ninth century shows that the god Chemosh also ordered such practices, carried out with glee equal to the Deuteronomists' by the faithful king.[69] In these ideologies of war, the enemy

---

shame. People who reclassify the hungry among their own people as suffering from 'low food security' will do or say anything, without a backward glance.

68. See the excellent study by Susan Niditch, *War in the Hebrew Bible: A Study in the Ethics of Violence* (New York: Oxford University Press, 1993), pp. 56-77, 123-33.

69. *ANET*, pp. 320-21.

2. *Gendering the Captive* 67

is an evil-doer who opposes cosmic order (that is, the State's avatar), and as such, deserves no mercy. The life of such evil-doers has no human value, except for the occasional lovely virgin or two. The community is 'cleaner' when they are removed. If we consider the nature of the *ḥerem* or 'ban' as a conventional cultural practice, we need not consider it a theological directive which constitutes a unique biblical revelation and as such, always and everywhere worthy of emulation. Hence, we may dismiss the so-called 'Yahweh-alone' group's genocidal proclivities as a form of cultural captivity in a violent world. It forms no particular deterrent to a modern construction of a biblically based theological praxis of non-violence or peace.

Later, during and after the Babylonian Exile, Priestly writers were responsible for much of the legal material as well as the general editing of the entire Torah which was to become biblical Israel's legacy to a now-scattered people. The taking of life in war was now theorized by those for whom the letting of blood and exposure to dead flesh posed significant problems for ritual purity. They chose the model of the Temple sacrifice to understand a different meaning for such a liminal and irreparable act: the ban was authentic and good because it was dedicated as a sacrifice to God. In this paradigm, the human is offered as a sacrifice because their life has an intrinsic value. War is metaphorized as a ritual of surrendering life to its Creator, not a cleansing of the land of undesirables.[70]

Although there is an element of superiority in the Priestly writers' view—after all they are not the ones getting sacrificed, but rather legitimating it—at least the value of human life is upheld, and considered more worthy than an animal's.[71] It is with the view of the earlier historians of late Judah that we find the most similarity to the theories espoused by imperial states about underlying the meaning and necessity of war.

Is it accidental that the Hebrew Bible includes a whole area of war normally suppressed in image and word by their neighbors? Compared to the river valley empires, the Hebrew Bible tells us a very different story concerning the fate of women in wartime. Judges 5 presents a fabricated scene:[72] the queen mother of the Canaanite hero Sisera wonders why he has not yet returned from battle. Intelligent women know what is going on:

70. Niditch, *War*, pp. 28-55.
71. I must dispute this last priestly claim, but that is another book.
72. This is, of course, yet another way of showing one's enemy to be brutal: the rape of captives is the subject of approving conversation by the women of the enemy (Mieke Bal, *Murder and Difference: Gender, Genre and Scholarship on Sisera's Death* [trans. Matthew Gumpert; Bloomington: Indiana University Press, 1988]).

> Her wisest ladies make answer,
>> indeed, she answers the question herself:
> 'Are they not finding and dividing the spoil? —
>> A *womb* or two for every man;
> spoil of dyed stuffs for Sisera,
>> spoil of dyed stuffs embroidered,
>> two pieces of dyed work embroidered
>> for my neck as spoil?' (5.29-30).

In this brief interchange, the metonymy of a 'womb or two' to stand for the entire woman is telling—what else is a female captive, after all? Her worth is clearly inscribed by her sexual availability and fecundity.

Likewise, the resolution of the complex situation following the gang rape of the Levite's concubine (or better, patrilocal wife) by the Benjaminite men of Gibeah in Judges 19 shows again that in this rough and ready period of 'no king in Israel', women were at risk no matter their state of sexual experience. Virgin daughters and married women alike are offered to a crowd for sexual gratification, in order to spare males any such stain upon their honor. The women of the town in Gibeah are 'put to the sword' just like everyone else when Israel takes revenge on Benjamin, though they certainly had no say whatsoever about the fate meted out to their unfortunate sister from Bethlehem (Judg. 20.48). The outcome of this revenge *itself* puts even more women at risk: since Israel swore an oath that no one should give their daughters to Benjamin as brides, now a tribe of Israel will die out, and male seed cannot be permitted to go to waste in such a fashion. The town of Jabesh-Gilead, which failed to participate in the general call-up of troops to punish Benjamin, is put to the sword—except for 400 virgins with no sexual experience. These are 'spared' and forced into marriage with the rape-hungry men of Benjamin. Yet, there are not enough women for their purposes, so next they are counseled by elders to abduct wives from among the young women of Shiloh who come out to dance in worship at a festival. Now, all is well: the men of Shiloh (no doubt glad to be spared the fate of Jabesh-Gilead) are to be 'generous' to Benjamin: after all, it has been engineered that they have not dishonored their oath because their daughters were taken captive (Judg. 21.19-22). Male honor is satisfied all around, and the fate of the women, much less those in cities put to the sword for the purpose of capturing virgin brides, requires no comment.

Do biblical women fare any better when there *is* a king in Israel? The books of Samuel tell the same old story, but now in the register of royal shenanigans, shaped as much by political impulse as by lust. David's appropriation of Bath-sheba without a word on her part, the rape of Tamar, the transfer of Michal from one husband to another, and

2. Gendering the Captive

Absalom's public sex with his father David's concubines in order to dishonor his father and secure his own claim to the throne leave us to wonder if monarchy had any particular benefits for women. The writers of Deuteronomy in the seventh-sixth centuries at least decide it is time to promulgate a law to govern what must have been commonplace: the legal disposition of female captives who have been 'taken' sexually:

> When you go out to war against your enemies, and the LORD your God hands them over to you and you take them captive, suppose you see among the captives a beautiful woman whom you desire and want to marry, and so you bring her home to your house: she shall shave her head, pare her nails, discard her captive's garb, and shall remain in your house a full month, mourning for her father and mother; after that you may go in to her and be her husband, and she shall be your wife. But if you are not satisfied with her, you shall let her go free and not sell her for money. You must not treat her as a slave, since you have dishonored her (Deut. 21.10-14).

Here at last we see a taste of the much-vaunted justice of the laws of the Covenant Community. Yes, of course, you may capture the woman, you may enslave her, you may desire the slave, you may have the slave, but let the decencies of normal practice all be honored. Pretend she has *not* been made into an orphan, but is simply a guest in your house observing the period of mourning. Force her into marriage if you will, but should it not turn out as desired, leave her some small honor—let her go free to beg on the streets, or hire herself out for more exploitation, or become a prostitute. After all, niceties must be observed if the conscience of the victor is to be at rest.

As we come to later notices of the monarchy's failures to protect their populace, we see the fate of women in war used as the penultimate example of the whole people's humiliation. Mothers eat their young (Lam. 2.20; 4.10); mothers are like widows (Lam. 5.3); young women are killed (rather than taken as slaves for sex and labor, Lam. 2.21), all as result of the Lord's jealous anger against Daughter/Mother Zion, the adulteress who preferred her 'lovers' (i.e., made treaties with foreigners) to her covenant master. Lamentations, so similar yet so different from Mesopotamian city-laments (see Chapter 3 below), finally says straight out what art and inscription have so politely hidden:

> Women are raped in Zion, young maidens in the towns of Judah (Lam. 5.11)

We must consider ourselves grateful for the Bible's remarkable candor on the subject all others omit. Of course, that very statement of fact is itself ideological, as it supports the notion of God-the-enraged-husband, who hands over his wife for public abuse by others. The implication throughout Lamentations is that Daughter Zion deserved everything that happened to her; there is no touch of injustice attributed to God. To further the motif of the abject realizations of sin on the part of the survivors, the final humiliation is added: the men of Judah are helpless to protect their females, and hence, have been thoroughly shamed in one of the most potent arenas pertaining to masculinity, the power to preserve.

Returning to our earlier iconographic sources, what shall we say, then, concerning the strange absence of enemy women in text and imagery from the ancient, imperial past? What makes 'woman' such a fine metaphor for male abjection, such that aspects of her are transferred onto the male, while she herself is erased?

Our ancient sources had plenty of opportunity to tell us of the numbers of women who were raped and mutilated, more details of the fate of the female captives who march so docilely before their truncheon-wielding military handlers. What creates that orderly line of women and children going into slavery? The reliefs of the capture of Lachish around 710 BCE, found in Sennacherib's palace in Nineveh, are worth a thousand words: as the line of captives march out of the city gate, they are flanked on the right by three nude men impaled upon stakes by the Assyrians.[73] Further along in the panel section to the right of this, they are treated to scenes of beheadings and flaying (see Figs. 17 and 18; cf. also Figs. 10 and 11 above).

On the whole, we must consider the artistic and monumental silence on the fate of women in wartime and their standing among captives with respect to gender to be a either a deliberate attempt to hide the customary truth *or* testimony to a truth so commonplace that no one bothers to document it. The silence is a covert tribute to the fact that sexual exploitation of captives was *so* routine, just like one's own soldiers

---

73. These events may have some bearing on the actions related in Num. 25, where God orders the harlotrous elders executed and displayed in the sun by Moses, in order to avert even greater punishments to the people. Later suggestive sexual terminology is employed to describe the slaying of Cozbi and Zimri in vv. 26-28, 14, pierced together through Cozbi's body in the 'inner room' by Phin'ehas, the grandson of Aaron. God's order (never carried out by Moses) seems to refer to impalement and display. Phin'ehas' action spared the elders, 'got' the deadly 'foreign woman', and is rewarded by God with a 'covenant of peace' and perpetual priesthood. For the dire implications for those in mixed marriages, see the White Supremacist reading of this text, which proposes a revival of a Phin'ehas priesthood to enforce racial purity (for the AntiDefamation League's review of such a priesthood, see <http://www.adl.org/Learn/ext_us/Hoskins.asp?LEARN_Cat=Extremism&LEARN_SubCat=Extremism_in_America&xpicked=2&item=Hoskins>. I am indebted to my students Brian Jenkins, Rasheed Townes, and Jeremiah Rood for bringing this movement to my attention.)

2. *Gendering the Captive* 71

Fig. 17. *Impaled prisoners at Lachish city gate, while women captives (not shown) walk past. Sennacherib's Palace, Nineveh.*

being wounded or killed, that it did not merit discussion or had to be deliberately covered up for the sake of honor. Just as all female slaves are at the sexual disposal of their owners,[74] perhaps we should presuppose that captive females taken into slavery receive that treatment from the outset of their captivity.[75] Rather than assuming that the Hebrew Bible chose to manufacture a gendered meaning for war—that of rape and public humiliation of the 'erring wife'—that no other people found necessary or apparent in *their* ideology of war,[76] we must now consider

---

74. Exod. 21.7-8.
75. The sheer amount of space in ancient Near Eastern law codes devoted to the legal status and potential inheritance of children born to slave women of the household provides evidence of the sexual exploitation of women slaves.
76. We will see in Chapter 3 that this image is derived from the Weeping Goddess of Mesopotamian city-laments, but in those texts the city goddesses are never raped, only dispossessed of temple, glory, town, people, and possessions. While it takes some 'cheek' to take a profoundly comforting metaphor like the protective goddess

Fig. 18. *Lachish prisoner beheaded as line of captives (not shown) passes by. Sennacherib's Palace, Nineveh.*

the subject position of those who do the writing. Given the absence of women from the iconographic world of war and captivity, the Hebrew Bible's focus on gender in war and war crimes is a testament to a reality others ignore, for whatever reason. Consider Amos's general curse upon a non-covenantal people of Ammon:

> Thus says the LORD:
> For three transgressions of the Ammonites,
>   and for four, I will not revoke the punishment;
> because they have ripped open pregnant women in Gilead
>   in order to enlarge their territory (Amos 1.13).

Amos refers here to wars of expansion and wars that create captive populations (e.g. vv. 3, 6, 9 concerning Damascus, Gaza and Tyre), and those crimes against innocent(?) populations of Others rate a call for

in solidarity and intercession for her people into the image of a raped and naked adulteress crying on a heap of rubble (Zion, see the Book of Lamentations), we nevertheless must consider the biblical version of the fate of women in war to bear a kernel of historical truth missing from the earlier version.

2. Gendering the Captive

divine punishment just as strong as the prophet's condemnation of the 'Own' community's disregard of Yahweh's covenantal duties and laws. The Hebrew Bible is astonishing in that it takes up issues bearing on a sense of universal human dignity and bodily integrity, apparently ethical values that should even be known to and observed by foreign makers of war. In such openings to the perception of diverse sufferings, we have an expression of a nascent universal ethic that is not far from the modern world's concept of 'crimes against humanity'. By the time of the great empires, the Hebrew Bible has come a long way in its thinking from the accounts of Moses on the fields of Moab.

It is time to account for the striking metaphorical distance between the reports of the Hebrew Bible, and the witness of the military empires at whose hands the writers of the Bible suffered. Can it be that the testimony of the *losers*—the defeated and exiled—records the events from a different subject position, ultimately a *female captive's* position, that causes such a sharply divergent point of view? Do we have access to the voice of the survivor, so routinely silenced by the winner, the torturer, the conqueror, the historian, in the Hebrew Bible's description of the experience of losing, again and again, to powers more well supplied and perhaps more brutal then their own...? If so, the Bible has given us a 'confession' the torturer never could: a living testimony[77] of the tortured, viewed with eyes of flesh that do not seek to look away from the captive or survivor in the particularity of their suffering, even when they do not belong to the preferred group.

When we look at the witness of Scripture we find not just the wishes and fond prayers of a people long past, but a view of history, which, whether accurate or not, has been a significant template for Western thinking about war and whatever human dignity may be found therein, or even nearby, dying beneath the wheels of the siege machine. Much has been made of the 'historical consciousness' of the writers of the Bible, their 'long view' of history unfolding according to promise or hope, and the distinctiveness of that world view within a setting of cyclical subsistence agriculture and mighty empires who make the rules. Whether we endorse that reading of Hebrew historical narrative and poetic theology, we do have remnants of an unusual shift in vision in the Hebrew Bible: the perspective of those who went through the flame and lived to write and speculate about that experience.

So what was it about the female experience, the metaphor of the violated female body, that so caught the imagination of the prophets, the

---

77. By 'living', I mean that it lives in our culture as part of a foundational text, and not simply as a long-forgotten inscription of empires only a few specialists remember.

legalists, the storytellers who gave us the Bible? We need only turn to the word for female, *neqevah*, to seek our explanation. Athalya Brenner has pointed out long ago that the asymmetry between the sexes is prosecuted even at the level of language or semantics. While the male is *zakar*, remembrance, that which endures to be reenacted and reinscribed again and again, *neqevah*, female, is simply a gap, an empty space to be filled, a hole.[78] In our understanding of the body represented, then, the defining mark of the female experience, according to the orders of biblical patriarchy, is that 'female' is a boundary which exists to be crossed, penetrated, violated, or annexed as an extra-corporeal boundary of a more powerful creature. In other words, the identity of the female is shaped semantically by her ability to be violated and made a vessel in service of the one who has successfully transgressed her edges to make them an extension of his own.

Horror of female biology as almost counter to normal life (contained, upright) can be viewed in the most female-gendered arenas. Woman is the upended, leaking pot which is only capable of containing something if she is horizontal. This image is invoked in incantation rituals to begin a childbirth or aid in a difficult birth in pre-Sargonic Mesopotamian texts. When the woman's water has not broken, the analogy of the woman-pot spilling downward is invoked:

> ...after you over the vagina of the troubled woman
> From which a cord hangs
> Have cast the incantation from Eridu,
> May it be released like rain from heaven,
> May it run away like drain-pipe water from a high roof,
> May it [x-x] like a river pouring into a lagoon,
> May it be smashed like a smashed pot.
> If it is male may it a weapon (and) an axe, its strength of heroism,
> Seize in the hand;
> If it is female, may spindle and hair clasp be in its hand...[79]

Since the creature walking upright and copulating with fertile outcome is 'up' and alive, if death is associated with being 'down' and horizontal, then female biology combines some very frightening positions indeed. Life and Death meet in her very flesh. She challenges the male to be always able to measure up to her, her capacity to retain his seed reflects on *his* honor and masculinity, and when she belongs to

---

78. Athalya Brenner, *The Intercourse of Knowledge: On Gendering Desire and 'Sexuality' in the Hebrew Bible* (BIS, 26; Leiden: E.J. Brill, 1997).

79. Graham Cunningham, *'Deliver Me from Evil': Mesopotamian Incantations 2500–1500 BC* (Studia Pohl, Series Maior, 17; Rome: Pontificio Istituto Biblico, 1997), p. 72; cf. p. 85.

him, there is always a possibility that someone else may fill the man's pot,[80] causing shame.

For *this* reason, not some lack of physical strength, failure of intellect, defect of moral capacity, the female has been gendered as a receptacle for all masculinity's fears—she is everything that male heterosexism simultaneously desires and then denigrates as it seeks to define itself. It is not nakedness itself which is shameful or symbolic of conquest—the many exposed males of art and literature show us that; rather, it is permeable edges of the female body which form the basis of the male nightmare of powerlessness. Here is the ultimate homophobic figuration: what is desirable with a female can have no place in a male's conception of his own sexuality. Males penetrate; they are not to be penetrated without a signal loss of honor and a double dose of shame. No wonder a conquered people calls up this metaphor, and the most violent (yet bearable) use of it in their symbolic repertoire.

In a world of honor and shame, honor inheres in acting in accordance with the *hoq*, or 'way', allotted to each form of created being. The wind has its own way, so too the snake and the ship on the water.[81] The 'way' of the male is to penetrate, engender, father, project, extend; the *hoq* of the female is to endure and sometimes even welcome, that intensely personal boundary breach. In the best of contexts, she transmutes it into new life, via the connectedness of kinship, which is the social 'glue' that holds a traditional society together. The violent transgression of that living boundary is a perfect metaphor for war and its 'way', and the expression of this in the Bible offers a poignant critique of the violence of the (male) state and tribe.

The choice of a female metaphor to express the emotions and experience of shamed and humiliated men, men deprived of what they felt was their natural right to some self-determination and honor, is deeply telling. On the one hand, we might simply take it as a sign that all things female, even when positive in nature (like intercourse which produces children and pleasure), become negative and dishonorable when applied to men. We could see the military curses which ask the gods to feminize the enemy as a statement of women's relative low value to the society during stressful times or in militaristic societies, their physical weakness, tendency to nest, or dither in an emergency.

---

80. We will not recount the many texts about the love and war goddess Inanna's lusty, hairy 'mouth' which is filled with wondrous beer in her tavern...but we could.

81. Norman C. Habel, 'The Implications of God Discovering Wisdom in Earth' in Ellen van Wolde (ed.), *Job 28: Cognition in Context* (BIS, 64; Leiden: E.J. Brill, 2003), pp. 281-97.

We could even learn to hate the female body which places half of humanity at physical risk from the other.

Or, we could deliberately opt for a more nuanced, broader interpretation, one which makes no excuses for the negative aspects of the metaphor, but finds positive ones as well, thus destabilizing the meaning of both. That men can speak of their own personal horror as in some sense *female* betrays the very consciousness that believes women exist to be penetrated by males. There is a more than a hint of bad conscience here, surely; the shaming of one's own group by a particular image shows the power and horror that image evokes. From a Human Rights' analysis, the display of brutality against the adulterous wife, the Bible's trope for the conquered city, shames not just the wife who is publically humiliated and whose dignity is a thing written on the wind; it also shames every watcher of this calamity. When acts of torture are public—beatings, rape, exposure—they create a right-bearer, the woman who deserved whatever due process[82] existed and consideration of her dignity as a human person. But the events also create duty-bearers in the bystanders who were and are obliged to object and offer aid and support. We must not underestimate the ethical responsibilities that bind the bystander to the traumatic event; failure to act or protest, however muted or ineffectual, carries severe psychological burdens for survivors and bystanders as well, as modern trauma studies show.[83]

The Bible's use of the violated boundary, the female body, offers us a view into the staggering reversals that war and the treatment of captives creates, more evidence that such activities are as much about un-making a world view as they are about any necessities of war. The writers of the Bible most certainly 'got the message' of their own vulnerability, even though they chose to understand it as a matter of human sin, and a gendered one at that,[84] instead of divine forsakenness or the simple fact of being in the way of more ruthless, acquisitive powers. We have a modern parallel here from trauma studies. Most abused children would prefer to think of themselves as guilty and deserving of punishment or abuse than deal with the horrifying reality that the adults and abusers in their world are simply brutal, crazy, powerless, or untrustworthy. It is better to have *some* sort of order, however skewed,

---

82. It must be noted that even due process under patriarchy leaves women at risk when sexual actions are categorized as capital crimes. The guilty daughter stoned at her father's doorstep in Deut. 22.13-21 got all the due process she could handle and then some. Law is no guarantee of justice.

83. Judith L. Herman, *Trauma and Recovery: The Aftermath of Violence from Domestic Abuse to Political Terror* (New York: Basic Books, 1992).

84. For example, the people's behavior *made* God hit them; 'he' hits Israel because 'he' loves them.

than none at all, by which to chart a path to safety among the chaos.[85] The very 'victim subjectivity' that we have noted as a natural result of the historical processes at work in the formation of the Bible and the Qur'an operates to shepherd the community toward believing in its own guilt, rather than coping with the notion that their god is impotent to save, or worse, entirely non-existent. A violent god is preferable to an impotent or non-existent one.

Yet, the guilty community simultaneously proclaims itself also a *chosen* one, and in fact, that chosen status becomes the mechanism that creates the theological guilt. Adultery was the common political metaphor in the ancient Near East for the parties who broke their covenant with another, usually superior partner. The gendered nature of the metaphor carried a powerful impact; no patriarch could stomach a topsy-turvy world in which his possessions violate his wishes. It would be equivalent to having one's big toe walk away from its body and start a career of its own. Patriarchal fears shaped the vision of the ideal family and home; it also shaped the political vision between aggressors and victims.

Extending this metaphor, the 'adultery' against one's god (whether conceived of as personal or political) is even worse when that god is portrayed as beneficent creator and redeemer: the sense of personal and community failing is all the more shameful because it was committed against such a very good and responsible heroic male. Who are we humans to have standards, to complain, to ask for recognition of a basic dignity that honors our bodily integrity, even during moments of profound alienation? As the created, the handmade pot, we are supposed to accept any treatment from the potter who holds himself entirely above our fate and takes no personal responsibility at all for any part of our destiny.[86] All Job's friends tell him so, as he continues to lament and challenge God concerning his disproportionate suffering.

Has *knowledge* of torture and brutality, up close and personal, its own part to play in the ideologies of war and sexuality which we have been discussing? Or, has the modern consciousness in the midst of struggle caused us to overestimate the impact of brutality on a society at large? How do we tell? What did *they* think, and when did they think it? We need texts.

---

85. Herman, *Trauma*, pp. 96-110.
86. But whose thumb-print is that on the inside of the pot? The potter's! So, too, with Eve (Gen. 4.1).

Chapter 3

THE BODY BREACHED: INTIMATIONS OF HUMAN DIGNITY

1. *In their Own Words:*
Knowledge of the Impact of Torture and Mutilation in Ancient Empires

What kind of world does the practice of torture and physical abuse create? The United Nations' 'Convention against Torture and Other Cruel, Inhuman, or Degrading Treatment or Punishment' defines torture in its first article as '...any act by which severe pain or suffering, whether physical or mental, is intentionally inflicted on a person for such purposes as obtaining from him or a third person information or a confession, punishing him for an act he or a third person has committed or is suspected of having committed, or intimidating or coercing him or a third person, or for any reason based on discrimination of any kind, when such pain or suffering is inflicted by or at the instigation of or with the consent or acquiescence of a public official or other person acting in an official capacity. It does not include pain or suffering arising only from, inherent in or incidental to lawful sanctions'.[1] In other words, the pain and fear of execution inflicted on someone who has been convicted of a capital crime with due process of law would not be considered torture by modern standards; savaging the convict before execution would. Thinking in terms of our earlier discussions of representation and gender, torture is the transgression of the body's boundaries in such a way as to create intolerable pain,[2] for some official,

---

1. <http://www2.ohchr.org/english/law/cat.htm>, cited February, 2008. Torture is also forbidden in Article 5 of the *United Nations Declaration of Universal Human Rights (UNDUHR)*. One needs to ask here precisely who legislates 'legal sanctions' and vouches for their fair and impartial implementation. Nazis made laws which they followed religiously; that they were totally evil laws would not seem to enter into the standard definitions in international law.

2. Does 'intolerable pain' also cover the psychological and social pain of treating the male torture subject as a female, or catamite? Since US torture methods at Abu Ghraib and Guantanamo are predicated on inflicting precisely this kind of pain and shame on subjects, perhaps the discussion of what constitutes torture needs to become far more nuanced in its treatment of misogyny, homophobia and

tolerated purpose. While we certainly don't expect to see in the ancient Near East any statements *per se* forbidding torture along the order of those we see in modern international law, we *can* trace practice, knowledge and strategy of ancient torture and its converse, respect of bodily integrity, by paying attention to the contours of the body and their violation. From this definition, too, we see the inherent problem with attempting to gender torture: the female is already predisposed by her biology to having her bodily integrity breached. How exactly will we know if that breaching is torture or just a more extreme example of her daily lot?

Modern discussions of torture, as may be seen in the United Nations' statement, draw distinctions between the goals of torture, with much focus (especially since September 11, 2001 and its accompanying fears of the 'ticking bomb' that must be discovered at all costs) on the obtaining of information (where it might actually happen that the tortured did indeed *know* something the state claims it needs to know for its own protection), and the use of torture as a form of social control, where no amount of confession, repentance, or information sharing will stop the torture for knowledge was not its goal. We will find both sorts of torture in our ancient texts. Some in conflict resolution even suggest that if we study torture as a 'game' of strategy where concealing and revealing, assessments of one's type of torturer ('professional', 'zealot', or 'sadist') and type of victim (strong, weak, innocent, guilty) are the salient variables, we can better discriminate between the goals of torture, and hence, 'solve' the game.[3] Whether there is *any* outcome to this embodied power game which would be acceptable to the tortured and the activist is another question entirely.

'Legal' Punishments in Mesopotamian Law Codes

Torture and humiliation of one's enemies seems to have been a commonplace of war in the ancient Fertile Crescent, but we must be clear: in the law codes of the ancient Near East, we find many forms of punishment provided by due process which moderns would reject out of hand or find very close to 'torture'.[4] Further, we should not assume that law

---

Orientalism (Jashir K. Puar, 'Abu Ghraib: Arguing against Exceptionalism', *Feminist Studies* 30.2 [Summer 2004], pp. 522-34; Barbara Ehrenreich, 'Prison Abuse: Feminism's Assumptions Upended', *Los Angeles Times* [May 16, 2004], cited May, 2004; no longer available <www.latimes.com/news/opinion/commentary/la-op-ehrenreich16may16,1,190206>).

3. Leonard Wantchekon and Andrew Healy, 'The "Game" of Torture', *Journal of Conflict Resolution* 43 (1999), pp. 596-609.

4. Law codes surveyed include Sumerian (Ur-Namma, Lipit-Ishtar), Babylonian (Eshnunna, Hammurabi, Neo-Babylonian), Assyrian (Middle Assyrian Laws = MAL),

codes give a one-on-one correspondence of real legal practice, nor that jurisprudence remains unchanged over centuries. Attempts at reform (fines rather than death penalties; freeing of slaves; removal of debt; movement away from vicarious liability) appear in the law codes of the ancient Near East, so we may certainly say that legal practice changed over time, even if we cannot fully document those different phases.[5]

Penalties for serious offenses (treason, adultery, theft of temple or state property, and sorcery) usually required the death penalty. In other less serious circumstances (slander, false witness, fraud, theft, injury, etc.), persons would be forced to take a magically active oath as to their innocence, often coupled with the River Ordeal in Mesopotamia. In the River Ordeal, the accused were forced to jump into the river; if innocent, they did not drown; if guilty, 'the river god overwhelmed' them.[6] Such practices clearly favor the strong and healthy, if not the innocent.[7]

The cost of bringing a false accusation against someone was severe: death or mutilation was a common punishment for the one who lost such a case in Code of Hammurabi or Assyrian laws. Other law codes like the Sumerian Laws of Ur-Namma and the Babylonian Laws of Eshnunna provided for the payment of a fine instead of commensurate retaliation.[8] Similarly, the legal price for compassion was death: harboring a runaway slave, or a woman innkeeper's failure to report on criminal activity in her tavern all carried a death sentence.[9] Otherwise, various forms of mutilation, physical punishment and fines were meted out, based on the seriousness of the offense and the social class to which the offender and victim belonged. Runaway slaves could be shaved, branded, mutilated, beaten or have their mouths scoured with lye for back talk or cursing; prostitutes could be stripped, beaten and have hot pitch poured on their heads for the crime of not wearing a veil.[10] Wives could be treated in any way the husband liked: public disrespect of a

---

and Hittite law codes (Martha T. Roth, *Law Collections from Mesopotamia and Asia Minor* (WAW, 6; Atlanta: Scholars Press, 2nd edn, 1997).

5. Samuel Greengus, 'Some Issues Relating to the Comparability of Laws and the Coherence of Legal Tradition', in Bernard M. Levinson (ed.), *Theory and Method in Biblical and Cuneiform Law: Revision, Interpolation and Development* (JSOTSup, 181; Sheffield: Sheffield Academic Press, 1994), pp. 60-90.

6. Some scholars of folk traditions like sorcery believe that the Mesopotamian River Ordeal is the origin of the practice of 'swimming witches', especially in Russia.

7. Samuel Greengus, 'Legal and Social Institutions of Ancient Mesopotamia', in Jack M. Sasson (ed.), *Civilizations of the Ancient Near East*, I (New York: Scribner, 1995), pp. 469-84 (474).

8. Roth, *Law Collections*, pp. 17-21; 59-68.

9. 'Laws of Hammurabi', para. 15-19, *idem*, pp. 71-142 (84-85).

10. MAL para. 40, in Roth, *Law Collections*, pp. 167-69.

husband and even failure to be thrifty with household accounts condemned a wife to the River Ordeal, as did any unproved suspicions brought against her chastity.[11] As long as he did not transgress property law concerning bride price and dowry, inheritance, or make accusations which could not be proved, the husband's power over the women of his household was nearly complete, as the reference in MAL §A 59 makes clear:

> In addition to the punishments for [a man's wife] that are [written] on the tablet, a man may [whip] his wife, pluck out her hair, mutilate her ears, or strike her, with impunity.[12]

For slaves, especially slave women who had borne children to the household that owned her, the legal situation was often complex, since laws concerning them partook of both property *and* inheritance laws. No doubt ethnicity and ideology played a part in the valuing of slaves: most slaves appear to have been foreign captives of war, but some were members of the community who had been enslaved due to debt. The latter were more likely to be redeemed by families than the former, who had been bereaved and displaced by war. It should also be noted that slaves 'donated' to temples at the death of their owners served in perpetuity, with no hope of manumission. For women, this could include duties as a secular prostitute, whose fees were paid into temple treasuries.

Yet, the law codes also show a sense of the value of life and bodily integrity. Clearly, the permanent wounding of a citizen or even a slave was considered a sufficient violation to warrant wounding in kind or a fine. The sense of property value vested in the owned persons at the disposal of the father's patriarchal authority attests the value of life, at least as an economic resource if nothing else. Causing a woman to lose her fetus was punished by fines or corresponding 'eye for an eye' retribution. Of course, the fetus of a free woman (member of the *awīlu* class) was due more compensation for the father's property loss than the fetus of a slave woman. Naturally, under patriarchy, a female fetus was worth only half the compensation of that of a male, but even a prostitute's lost fetus required compensation.[13] A woman who aborted her fetus on purpose was impaled and her body was left unburied (MAL §A 53).

Given our brief description here, we must posit a general background of public tolerance and approval of physical punishments meted out by the state to offending citizens. Since enemies in war are considered

---

11. 'Hammurabi', paras. 132, 141-43, in Roth, *Law Collections*, pp. 106-108.
12. Roth, *Law Collections*, pp. 175-76.
13. MAL paras. A 21, A50-52, in Roth, *Law Collections*, pp. 160, 173-74.

by the state to be the greatest of offenders in their failure to bow to the conqueror's authority or surrender quickly to any demands, it is perhaps natural that we should see the most extreme forms of the power to punish enacted upon the Other at war.[14]

'Legal' Punishments in Ancient Egypt
Our understanding of legal process in Egypt is hampered by the fact that no law codes have been discovered there. Legal procedures must be established through other kinds of archival records, court proceedings, narrative texts, inscriptions, and the *gestalt* of ethical behavior presented in the *Book of the Dead* (see below). Such materials tell us that families could produce documents concerning land transfers, official appointments and gifts of land and usufruct covering up to three hundred years of a family's legal history.[15] At the local level, both criminal and civil crime was handled by the community in tribunals that met as needed. Village tribunals would render a decision and involved parties would take an oath to abide by the decision, but tribunals had little or no enforcement mechanisms. Hence, community values and shaming for dishonorable conduct were the ultimate guarantors of compliance with verdicts. Cases concerning temple or state properties, or intractable serious situations which could not be resolved by tribunals were referred up the chain of the social ladder to visiting royal functionaries. Elites constituted about five percent of the population, and functioned as ad-hoc judges in cases referred to them from the local level. Should this intermediate stage fail to provide relief, the case would then be referred to the Vizier for that region, a 'federal' position, if you will. Finally, viziers could refer the most serious, state or temple-oriented cases, like grave-robbing or treason to the Pharaoh for final deliberations. At any level, it was possible to ask for a divine oracle, officiated by tribunal members. Corrupt officials were removed from office, but might also be sentenced to death if their malfeasance rose to the level of treason. Death sentences were rare, and usually referred to the state, or Pharaoh himself for sentencing and execution.[16]

14. Sadly, this same attitude could be seen in conservative supporters of the Iraq war in their response to the abuses at Abu Ghraib: 'Not so fast!', they opined. 'We treat our *own* prisoners this way, and besides, this is war! Why, this was no more than a version of fraternity high-jinks commonly performed on pledges to the fraternity' (*The Bill O'Reilly Show*, Fox 'News' (*sic*!) Network, occasions too numerous to list!).

15. David Lorton, 'Legal and Social Institutions of Pharaonic Egypt', in Sasson (ed.), *CANE*, I, pp. 345-62 (346).

16. Lorton, 'Pharaonic Egypt', pp. 345-62. The 'middle class' community of artisans and state employees of the Ramesside period at Dayr al-Madina (Deir el-Medina) provides us with the bulk of this information about community legal processes.

3. The Body Breached

As seen in Mesopotamian law codes, the penalties for false accusations could be quite severe: beatings,[17] open wounds (usually five), fines, and restitution of lost work-days (where appropriate) were typically levied all together on the one who lost the criminal case. Civil infractions usually called for restitution with interest, and occasionally forced labor (for assault and levied by the state). Both slavery and punishment by mutilations are extremely rare in the Old and Middle Kingdoms, but in the time of New Kingdom imperialism, large numbers of foreign captives were imported as slaves, and mutilation becomes a more common punishment as noted in legal proceedings. Activities common in war or derived from its aftermath start to influence life in Egypt toward more brutal standards.[18]

Yet, Egypt shows some particular variations that are of interest in our search for a sense of how ancients viewed bodies and their violations. Women were 'legal entities' in ancient Egypt, able to buy and sell property, bequeath it to whomever they pleased, own and free slaves, and sue in court. Adultery was considered a personal matter, rather than a crime against the state, and often did not even seem to qualify as grounds for divorce. Revenge and honor killings of women, though found in narrative texts, are not borne out by the practices in Dayr al-Madina: while there are records of proceedings concerning adultery, there are no records of any revenge-based homicides. Slaves, too, might own property and even other slaves. They could marry free persons, and be manumitted or adopted by free people.[19]

Unlike the Mesopotamian empires, which used torture of war captives and civilians to enforce social domination and create a victim subjectivity in their unfortunate targets, the Egyptians practiced torture to gain information. This is particularly noticeable from Ramesside texts concerning questioning of tomb robbers who had already confessed. The state authorities continued to torture the criminal (using 'the stick, the birch, and the screw') to make sure that he had indeed entered only one pyramid. Once satisfied that he had confessed everything, they stopped torturing him. Objects of disclosure would be names of accomplices, methods used to circumvent security and perform the crime, and the whereabouts of stolen items. Prevention of future break-ins was

---

17. One or two hundred blows were the typical punishment, compared to 20 blows in Mesopotamia. For anyone wishing to see the results of a flogging of 50 blows, simply use the internet and type in the key words, 'woman' and 'Iran'.

18. Lorton, 'Pharaonic Egypt', pp. 345-62 (355-59).

19. One woman of the thirteenth Dynasty even sued her father over possessions which he took from her and gave to his second wife! (Lorton, 'Pharaonic Egypt', pp. 345-62 [349, 352]).

considered a priority so information obtained from those apprehended was crucial.[20]

On the whole, what we know of Egyptian legal proceedings from documentary texts must be sifted carefully and, ultimately, given more weight than myth or popular narratives in establishing a sense of real, common practice: deeds and legal decisions tell us more than folklore. In turn, the words of those imposing and carrying out secular sentences at the local level, or cosmic, ideologically conditioned brutalities against enemies at the state level of war may tell us more than any amount of monumental art celebrating victorious battles. When we add all these kinds of evidence together with evidence of material culture (like the cult of the dead in Egypt or the reliefs of Sennacherib in Nineveh, coupled with excavation evidence from Lachish in Judah) we gain a far more balanced portrait—even if one supplemented by imagination and poetry of lament—than we would have by only viewing the evidence through one lens.

Somewhere in the Middle: Legal Punishments in the Hebrew Bible

The law codes and legal practices found in the Hebrew Bible comprise a specialization all on their own, and owe much to their ancient Near Eastern neighbors. Much of what we have seen elsewhere in Mesopotamia in law codes and *haven't* seen in Egypt in practical application of jurisprudence operates in biblical Israel: laws by the state vied with authority and overlapped with village systems of justice administered by local elders.[21] If the text is to be believed, death penalties were frequently levied, for rape, incest, male homosexuality, sorcery, bestiality, child sacrifice to an alien god, and cursing parents (Lev. 20). It is not clear how literally we are to take the frequent judgment that offenders are to be 'cut off' from the community.[22] Mutilation as a punishment may be found readily (Deut. 25.12; Exod. 21.24), but payment of fines or restoration of property were also provided as remedies. Punishment for adultery varied by classification of partners, ranging from death for both parties in consensual adultery with a betrothed or married woman (Deut. 22.22-24), to death for the man who rapes a virgin, but no punishment for the victim (Deut. 22.25). Women given in marriage and found *not* to be virgins were to be stoned to death at the door of their father's house, to provide greatest maximum shaming and horror for the girl's family

---

20. Lorton, 'Pharaonic Egypt', pp. 345-62 (356).

21. Hector Avalos, 'Legal and Social Institutions in Canaan and Ancient Israel', in Sasson (ed.), *CANE*, I, pp. 615-31 (622-23).

22. Would they really have killed a legal couple having consensual sex during the woman's menses? (Lev. 20.18).

(Deut. 22.13-21). If the accusations were found to be false, the accuser receives a beating, a stiff fine and forfeits his right to ever divorce the lucky woman he has accused so publically, if unsuccessfully. If fighting men caused a woman to lose her fetus, they paid a fine of compensation to the husband 'if no harm follows' (Exod. 21.22-23). In the event that more than a miscarriage occurs, then the *lex talionis* was invoked and injury of like body part was inflicted. Ezekiel's diatribe against the lecherous Oholibah, female personification of Judah, in 23.25-26 replicates the Assyrian provisions for punishing an erring wife: nose and ears will be cut off and the woman stripped and left naked.

Crimes committed against slaves were considered less serious than crimes against free people (sex with a slave woman is covered in Lev. 19.20-22, and requires only a sin-offering from the man, whereas in Mesopotamian codes, the owner of the virgin slave who has been defiled receives a payment). Damages were usually paid to the slave's owner, but permanent mutilation of the slave resulted in the slave going free (Exod. 21.26-27), and anyone who beat their slave to death, and death was instantaneous, was to be 'punished' but the text does not specify what that might be (Exod. 21.20-21). Further, legal distinction was made between foreign slaves (war captives?) and Hebrew slaves, usually in that state of servitude due to debt (Lev. 25.45-46). Contrary to Mesopotamian standards, an escaped slave was *not* to be returned to his master, but given good refuge (Deut. 23.15-16; this probably refers to a Hebrew slave who has escaped from a foreign master).

In Their Own Words: the State Speaks of the Other
We turn now to various sorts of epigraphic evidence about the knowledge and tolerance of brutality and any sense of human dignity and right to bodily integrity. How much did those outside of the armies committing such acts know, care or understand its meaning, symbolic or otherwise? In Ancient Egypt, the 'smite makes right' scenes attributed to Pharaoh throughout all periods become 'canon', so much so that even queens must be shown that way.[23] Where table legs in the pre-dynastic period used to be made as elegant depictions of bull legs, under the state the bound foreign captive now takes over the position of holding up the powerful ruler's table or chair. The image of the kneeling, bound captive becomes the glyph which is used to encompass the names of foreign countries and scenes of dismemberment are proudly displayed on sarcophagi, monuments, and inscriptions (see Figs. 19-20).

---

23. Nefertiti is shown in full smiting position over a long-haired, male captive (Gay Robins, *Women in Ancient Egypt* [Cambridge, MA: Harvard University Press, 1993], p. 54).

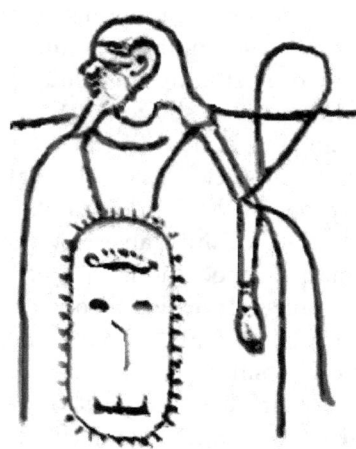

Fig. 19. *Bound Captive Focalized as the Cartouche for the Name Glyph of a Conquered Enemy. Sarcophagus of Rameses III, the Louvre.*

Fig. 20. *Beheaded Prisoners; Sarcophagus of Rameses III, Louvre.*

Beheadings, exhibitions of decapitated heads, impalements, and piles of body parts are routinely displayed in the art of the river valley Empires.[24] In myth, Osiris is the husband of the magical mother goddess Isis and post-mortem father of Horus, the Falcon god patron of Pharaohs. His brother Seth dismembers him and flings his body parts over the wide earth, but especially in the Egyptian delta. Grieving Isis undertakes a quest to re-unite the body parts of her dead husband. She does so successfully, and Horus is born. While Osiris rules the land of the dead as king,

---

24. James B. Pritchard, *The Ancient Near East in Pictures Relating to the Old Testament* (Princeton, NJ: Princeton University Press, 2nd edn, 1974), Plates 319, 348, etc.

Horus becomes lord of the great skies. In the Levant, the (battle) Maiden Anat loves her bloody trophies so much that she fashions jewelry out of them, anticipating by centuries the iconography of Kali-Ma, the Indian goddess of assassination and revenge. If the gods can be dismembered or take trophies, then the human community can in some sense rationalize those behaviors as part of the cosmic scheme of things. Of course, the likelihood that humanity projected those delightful traits upon their gods for precisely that ideological reason never occurs to those promoting the 'as above, so below' relationship between sacred and profane realms.

The horror of the disarticulated body and its ability to strike dismay into most humans[25] seems an ongoing icon for the decisive disruptions of war, a symbol which somehow seems to touch humans across geographic region and historical epoch. How much of the horror of the extremist websites of Islamic terrorists and internet videos is directly related to this ancient form of execution being displayed to the fastidious West? Riverbend, the Girl Blogger of Baghdad, commenting after seeing local pictures of Iraqis with their skin on fire from the use of internationally banned white phosphorus in the Battle of Fallujah[26] wonders why only Muslims making use of beheading traditions are branded as brutal. Beheadings occur in the Bible and they are not condemned as such, as long as it is 'our side' which is performing them. Clearly, only bias labels one form of execution better than another, and one could argue that beheading is swift and painless, whereas death-by-napalm is agonizingly painful and protracted.

Texts from Egypt and Mesopotamia, along with their accompanying iconography, not only make clear that the war-makers knew what they were doing, they find it worthy of celebration as the state (theirs) must

---

25. Note that Hollywood has a new genre for its storytelling, named in the press as 'torture porn': movies which depart from the typical 'slice-and-dice' horror film to include sexual acts and brutalization as components of the torture (*The Hostel, II*, etc.). Like Fox Network's brutal series, *24*, where US counter-terrorist 'good guys' routinely torture to find the ticking bomb, torture porn has the effect of normalizing the practices and making the audience into bystanders. Seldom do those who oppose torture on principle as duty-bearers who must speak for the victims gain any limelight in these productions, where they are used as illustrations for the trope of weakness and inadequate patriotism.

26. White phosphorus has a better known name, napalm, but was only used for 'lighting the battlefield'—needed in the daytime?!—according to the Coalition of the Killing in Iraq. Use of it with significant civilian casualties is considered a war crime in legitimate international circles. For more information, see internet sites like Truthout.org, Information Clearing House, and the many blogs and sites put up by veterans of Operation Iraqi Freedom. Riverbend's blog is called *Baghdad Burning*, and represents a major voice of a woman testifying to the real situation for women and others on the modern battlefield of insurgency.

drive back chaos by whatever means. In most cases, the river valley empires employed torture and mutilations of the enemy living and dead as a form of social control to create a docile conquered populace. Accordingly, there was little the victims could do (other than surrendering immediately and suing for mercy, which they often did) to stop the violence. Mutilations, flaying, and display of bodily trophies are the stuff of which the memoirs of great kings are made; one can only imagine what international war crimes tribunals could do with so much testimony. Consider Ashurnasiripal II's incriminating statements, so boldly made:

> I felled 50 of their fighting men with the sword, burnt 200 captives from them [and] defeated in a battle on the plain 332 troops... With their blood I dyed the mount red like red wool, [and] the rest of them the ravines [and] torrents of the mountain swallowed. I carried off captives [and] possessions from them. I cut off heads of their fighters [and] built [therewith] a tower before their city. I burnt their adolescent boys [and] girls'.[27]

Special, brutal attention is given to those who have revolted against this great king: those who had attempted to put up a boundary between their territory and Assyrian plunder found themselves subjected to the removal of their personal boundary while still alive:

> I flayed as many nobles as had rebelled against me [and] I draped their skins over the pile [of corpses]; some I spread out within the pile, some I erected on stakes upon the pile... I flayed many right through my land [and] draped their skins over the walls.[28]

According to modern definitions, flaying constitutes a form of death by torture, and so has everything to do with power and very little to do with obtaining information. Ashurnasiripal may have started out with rebellious vassal lords on his borders, but he soon learns that applying the same techniques within his own land serves as an excellent object lesson to the people. At other times, the display of *more* of the defeated body provides a little variation in the king's educational efforts:

---

27. Quoted in Erika Bleibtreu, 'Grisly Assyrian Record of Torture and Death', *BARev* (January–February, 1991), pp. 52-61 (57). For other discussions of torture episodes and war crimes, see T.M. Lemos, 'Shame and Mutilation of Enemies in the Hebrew Bible', *JBL* 125 (2006), pp. 225-41; Bruce Lincoln, 'From Artaxerxes to Abu Ghraib: On Religion and the Pornography of Imperial Violence', *Religion and Culture Web Forum*, January 2007; Pauline Albenda, 'An Assyrian Relief Depicting a Nude Captive in Wellesley College', *JNES* 29 (1970), pp. 145-50; Jean Kellaway, *The History of Torture and Execution: From Early Civilization through Medieval Times to the Present* (Guildford, CT: Lyons Press, 2003).

28. Quoted in Bleibtreu, 'Grisly Assyrian', pp. 52-61 (57).

3. *The Body Breached* 89

> In strife and conflict I besieged [and] conquered the city. I felled 3,000 of their fighting men with the sword... I captured many troops alive: I cut off of some their arms [and] hands; I cut off of others their noses, ears, [and] extremities. I gouged out the eyes of many troops. I made one pile of the living [and] one of heads. I hung their heads on trees around the city.[29]

The taking of trophies is naturally very gratifying to the victor, and their display can add the perfect touch to a lovely day by giving proof positive of the enemy's death: from Ashurbanipal's north palace in Nineveh we have just such a scene. The royal couple recline and enjoy a drink while attendants fan them and harpers strum for their entertainment in the garden. Adjacent, a rebel's head (one Teumann of Elam, by name) hangs, pierced with a ring, from a shade tree. Previously the head had been rushed by chariot to the Assyrian king, so that he could hang it around the neck of another traitor during a torture session (also recorded visually).[30] Suitable for public torture or private entertainment, the versatility of body parts in Assyrian ideologies of power and purpose would be the envy of any Hollywood special effects factory.

Beheading, Trophy Taking, and Mutilation in the Bible
The 'shock' value of the disarticulated head is double: it symbolizes both broken leadership (in Hebrew, the same word for head, *rō'š*, also means 'chief' or leader) and the disappearance of the body of the traitor, whose grisly fate and the manner of it is both known and unknown. Because the head is a metonym for the entire body (and its death) and for leadership, it is an excellent tool for building a particular view of the world: strike the head of the snake and the body will writhe helplessly.

The Bible knows this very well and makes much of the wordplay between head and leader. When the trophy head is displayed, it usually symbolizes the collapse of a threat, or challenge, and even symbolic beheadings serve their narrative purposes of delicious horror. 2 Samuel 4 gives us the defeat of the last of Saul's family who might have challenged David. In 2 Samuel 20, the wise woman of Abel prevents a potential siege of her city by throwing the head of Sheba the rebel over the city wall to Joab and his men. In Genesis, Pharaoh's unfortunate baker features mainly as an amusing pun—Pharaoh lifts up his head, but from off his body—because he is actually hanged for his poor service. Structurally, we must consider this a symbolic beheading, the flip side of the cupbearer's positive dream, in a plot whose main purpose is to show off the theological acumen of the foreign prisoner/slave, Joseph the Dream

---

29. Bleibtreu, 'Grisly Assyrian', pp. 52-61 (57-58).
30. Dominique Collon, *Ancient Near Eastern Art* (Berkeley: University of California, 1995), pp. 146-51, Fig. 120.

Interpreter.[31] In 2 Sam. 18, a rebellion is crushed when Prince Absalom comes to a 'heady' end. His long, flowing tresses catch in a tree branch, leaving him helpless to defend himself from his father's general.

In Judith 12-13, this redoubtable Jewish heroine defends her people by cutting off the head of General Holofernes, the 'Assyrian' besieging her town, in another 'reclining' banqueting setting similar to Ashurbanipal's garden party. Some of Judith's rhetoric again makes plain the plight of all women in conflict situations, whether domestic, local, or international:

> O Lord God of my father Simeon, to whom thou gavest a sword to take revenge on the strangers who had loosed the girdle of a virgin to defile her, and uncovered her thigh to put her to shame, and polluted her womb to disgrace her; for thou hast said, 'It shall not be done'—yet they did it. So thou gave up their rulers to be slain, and their bed, which was ashamed of the deceit they had practiced, to be stained with blood, and thou didst strike down slaves along with princes, and princes on their thrones; and thou gave their wives for a prey and their daughters to captivity, and all their booty to be divided among thy beloved sons, who were zealous for thee, and abhorred the pollution of their blood, and called on thee for help—O God, my God, hear me also, a widow (9.2-4).

The blood of rape so defiles the beds of the perpetrators that only repayment in kind, the rape and enslavement of their own womenfolk, can restore the situation to its former stasis. Further, all of these crimes which Judith's prayer submits for God's consideration become a motivation for action which she clearly expects to be efficacious in her petition for help. Together with her membership in a preferred class under God's protection—widows—and we have a splendid example of the bloodthirsty wisdom of a woman tired of war. Display of Holofernes' head has all the potency this wise woman expected: not only is the enemy shamed and dismayed by the death of their leader at the hands of a woman, but also 'fear and trembling' falls upon them (15.2). Judith has saved the day, and kept her chastity to boot. Add Salome's dance to acquire the head of John the Baptist on a platter (Mark 6; Mt. 14), thereby removing a threat to Herod's domestic arrangements, for a negative example of a woman and a head, and we have a smattering of scriptural accounts to go with our symbolic beheadings and trophy display.[32]

Of course, heads are not the only item worthy of capture and display. Saul sets the brideprice David must pay for his daughter Michal at one

---

31. Gen. 40.
32. Other beheadings occur in 1 Sam. 17.51 (post-mortem), 1 Sam. 5.4 (along with hands of Dagon's statue), 1 Sam. 21.9 (post-mortem, body displayed as trophy), 2 Sam. 4.12 (killers of Ishbaal, plus hands and feet cut off), and in the martyrdom stories of Maccabees (1 Macc. 7.47; 11.17; 2 Macc. 1.16; 7.4 [only scalped, not beheaded]; 15.30), and Rev. 20.4 (beheaded martyrs honored).

hundred Philistine foreskins—what new bride wouldn't be delighted with such a show of affection. Still, given the New Kingdom Egyptian practice of castrating the uncircumcised or differently circumcised enemy instead of taking hands for the body count, Saul's price, though hefty, is not without some historical precedent. Of course, Saul is hopeful that he has just put an end to David's insidious alienation of his family's and followers' affections by setting him a fairy-tale type task designed to get him killed, using Michal's love as the fulcrum of his cunning plan. Since the Lord is with David, naturally the Philistine's contribution to the wedding festivities comes off without a hitch.

Mutilation, whether of citizens for legal reasons, or of captives for political reasons carries a special impact in honor-and-shame cultures, signaling 'a newly established power dynamic between the victim and the aggressor', bringing 'shame upon the victim and their community by associating the victim with a lower-status group and/or by effecting an actual status change in the victim'.[33] Not only is the marking of certain body parts clearly symbolic of sexual imagery (hands, feet, thumbs, big toes), but it is an enduring, public disgrace. Shaved hair may grow back, nakedness may be covered, but a brand on the face or the loss of nose or ears is permanent. Further, the ancient fetish with bodily purity meant that the mutilated person might well be excluded from ritual activities of worship or other community events.

The permanence of the shame implied by the mutilation is the goal here, not so much the terror or shame of the actual experience of being mutilated. The torture of the act is incidental to its power to coerce 'right' behavior. It is the public, indelible mark of shame and its social impact upon the offender which is desired: the story of Nahash the Ammonite's mutilation (eyes gouged out as a symbolic marking of covenant relations) and shaming of males of the tribes of Gad and Reuben in 1 Sam. 10.27–11.11 makes this explicit. The gouging of eyes in the inferior covenant partner is devised, says Nahash the Snake, 'so that I may put shame upon all Israel' (11.2). Whether it is the disfigured wife who shows her husband's opinion of her to everyone she meets or the humbled captive, citizen, or slave, the practice continually re-inscribes the political male elite or the socially privileged husband as the ranking arbiter of justice, honor and shame.

The Egyptian Evidence: The 'Good God' at War
In Egypt, the more grisly details of the battlefield and its aftermath are found represented visually, while historical texts of campaigns generalize the mayhem and tend to highlight lists of booty and plunder derived

---

33. Lemos, 'Shame and Mutilation', pp. 225-41 (225-26).

from the always 'wretched enemy'. Still, the stock phrases of praise for Pharaoh's prowess, when read alongside the iconographical record, leave no doubt that general havoc was considered both appropriate in war-making and a sign of the god's favor. A flowery summation of Seti I's attitudes toward his Asian campaigns highlights the ideology that the enemy is always wrong in his earthly assault on Egypt's cosmic position of Guarantor of Right Order, whom Pharaoh delights in suppressing for the best of reasons. It reads:

> ...Then one came to say to His Majesty: 'The foe belonging to the Shasu are plotting rebellion. Their tribal chiefs are gathered in one place...They have taken to clamoring and quarreling, one of them killing his fellow. They have no regard for the laws of the palace.' The heart of his majesty (l.p.h.) was glad of it.
>
> Now as for the good god [Seti I], he exults at undertaking combat; he delights at an attack on him; his heart is satisfied at the sight of blood. He cuts off the heads of the perverse of heart. He loves an instant of trampling more than a day of jubilation. His majesty kills them all at one time, and leaves no heirs among them. He who is spared by his hand is a living prisoner, carried off to Egypt.[34]

Notice that the crime of disloyalty to Egypt, the *real* reason for the campaign, is bolstered by a subtle 'humanitarian' justification for invasion (quite common for aggressors of the twentieth and twenty-first centuries, especially where the land in disarray has oil): the Shasu are killing each other and have no respect for law or palace. Pharaoh is delighted by this, as it presents him with another opportunity for his favorite divinely ordained sport, which he prefers even to the solemn and festive assemblies of worship. The reference to 'living prisoners', quite familiar from the lists of plunder, clearly implies dead prisoners, as shown by piles of hands, other body parts, and the battlefield dead on monuments. Further, the occasional references to the premature glee of despoiling the enemy before the battle is fully completed suggest the possibilities of further war crimes, rape included. Still, the extensive lists of living prisoners of various types, carted off to Egypt as workers and elite hostages, may tilt the balance of crime enacted toward the living, rather than the full decimations of population found in Assyrian records.

---

34. John A. Wilson (trans.), 'Campaign of Seti I in Asia', in James B. Pritchard, *Ancient Near Eastern Texts Relating to the Old Testament* (Princeton, NJ: Princeton University Press, 3rd edn, 1969), pp. 254-55 (254). Tuthmoses III's taking of Megiddo was delayed by the acquisitive behavior of his troops in looting too soon (pp. 234-41 [236]); so, too, the Hittite army at the Battle of Qadesh, where premature booty-stashing caused them to lose their significant advantage over Ramses II's troops, causing the battle to be fought to a 'draw'.

The kings, commanders, and foot-soldiers know the reality of their actions, and find them reasonable, necessary, moral and even pleasurable, if we are to credit the self-serving historical notices and texts. Ideology triumphs over the universal human experience of revulsion and dismay at the sight of the violated body, alive or dead, male or female. Things have changed very little, at least among those who articulate that ideology. Whether triumphantly bringing democracy to benighted parts of the world, the claims of just protection of one's own ethnic enclave (such a useful strategy for Hitler's wars of aggression), or the Pharaoh's goal of pacifying the Shasu, the story on the lips of the war-maker and torturer is always the same. The awful increase in suicides among the US military, along with the soaring incidence of Traumatic Stress Disorder in returning combatants (not to mention the population of Iraq) suggests that there is a silenced voice of pain in response to all this violent brutality.[35] Historical notices of war written by the conquerors and occupiers alone cannot be trusted; the potential for self-deception and outright political gutting of the truth is simply too overwhelming. As the saying goes, 'The first casualty of war is Truth'.

If the ancient makers of war are aware of its brutality, what might the elite or average citizen of the Empire make of it all? Is there a simple acceptance of the national mythology of their divine mandate to impose order, or do other, less positive, more morally uncertain responses lurk beneath the official stories? We *do* have some access to the thought-world of non-royal elites — scribes and authors — that suggest they understand the brutality around them, and how they respond to it.

2. *Literary Evidence of Human Dignity*

Texts from the Elite of Sumer and Akkad: Lamentations for the Destruction of Cities

Lamentations over the destruction of cities became a common form in the warlike context of Mesopotamia, and they undergird the sentiments and form found in the biblical book of Lamentations, as well as other biblical texts that reference the destruction of Jerusalem and the Exile (cf. Ps. 137, etc.), which have been studied extensively for their connections to this ancient genre.[36] While we seldom hear *human* persons other than

---

35. Dreadful details and statistics may be found at www.truthout.org: The Associated Press. 'Army Suicide Highest in 26 Years', cited September 27, 2007 <http://www.truthout.org/docs_2006/081607J.shtml>.

36. Margaret W. Green, 'The Eridu Lament', *JCS* 30 (1978), pp. 127-67; Jerrold S. Cooper, 'Genre, Gender, and the Sumerian Lamentation', *JCS* 58 (2006), pp. 39-47;

the poet (probably a temple scribe, given his interests and knowledge) speak in the classic 'Lamentation over the Destruction of Sumer and Ur' (probably Ur III), we hear the laments of the gods Nanna-Sin and his wife Ningal for their broken city. The destruction was brought about by cruel decrees of the god Enlil through either supernatural disasters or the agency of enemies like the Guti and Elamites who are allowed to humble once proud Sumer and its cities. Like the Hebrew Bible, this cycle of lament texts imagines that the gods are angry with the city, and use foreign groups making war to punish the city. The main features of destruction and war are lamented: fire in the city, destruction of architectural features, fields, and temples, captivity of one's leaders, mass deaths of the populace and livestock at the hands of soldiers, desertion of the populace, drying up of canals (which had to be maintained regularly against salinization), destruction of trees and crops, famine and hunger, loss of divine protection, and forced captivity of the surviving citizens. While there is no specific mention of rape or mutilation during the devastation of the city, the emphasis on the destruction of gates, entries, doorposts and the god's bedroom accoutrements may be symbolic allusions to such events. As the poet goes city by city in Sumer, telling their fates, each section ends with the town's goddess's outcry: '"O my destroyed city, destroyed house!", bitterly she cried'.[37] The devastation has caused every city goddess to lament 'as if she were human' (l. 174), leaving her beautiful possessions behind, fleeing into enemy land 'like a slave' (ll. 272-78). Captivity is a plight that even the gods do not covet: a lament to lure Enki to return once more to his city of Eridu cries out to him, 'Living in an alien city is miserable! To your city (return) your attention! Living in an alien temple is miserable! To your temple (return) your attention!'[38] More than direct acts of war afflict the cities of Sumer in the onslaught of enemies from Guti and Elam:

> In Ur, no one went to fetch food, no one went to fetch drink,
> Its people rush around like water *churning* in a well,
> Their strength has ebbed away, they cannot (even) go on their way.
> Enlil afflicted the city with an inimical famine.
> He afflicted the city with something that destroys cities, that destroys temples,

---

S.N. Kramer (trans.), 'Lamentation over the Destruction of Sumer and Ur', in Pritchard (ed.), *ANET*, pp. 614-16; F.W. Dobbs-Allsopp, *Weep, O Daughter of Zion: A Study of the City-Lament Genre in the Hebrew Bible* (Biblica et orientalia, 44; Rome: Pontificio Istituto Biblico, 1993); George Savran, ' "How Can We Sing a Song of the Lord?": The Strategy of Lament in Psalm 137', *ZAW* 112 (2000), pp. 43-58.

37. Piotr Michalowski, *The Lamentation over the Destruction of Sumer and Ur* (Mesopotamian Civilizations, 1; Winona Lake: Eisenbrauns, 1989), pp. 37-69.

38. Green, 'The Eridu Lament', pp. 127-67 (141).

He afflicted the city with something that cannot be withstood with weapons,
He afflicted the city with dissatisfaction and treachery (ll. 293-99).[39]

In one brief stanza, we hear the people of the city speak as they suffer from famine. The temple poet turns from description of the ruination of all the things he knew best to outline the plight of the survivors:

Its people dropped (their) weapons; (their) weapons hit the ground,
They struck their necks with their hands and cried.
They sought counsel with each other, they searched for clarification,
'Alas, what can we say about it, what can we add to it?
How long until we are finished off by (this) catastrophe?
Ur—inside it there is death, outside it there is death,
Inside it we are being finished off by famine,
Outside it we are being finished off by Elamite weapons .
In Ur the enemy has oppressed us, oh, we are finished!'
They *take refuge* behind it (the city walls), they were united (in their fear)...
Elam, like a swelling flood wave, *left only the spirits of the dead*
In Ur (people) were smashed as if they were clay pots,
Its refugees were (unable) to flee, they were trapped inside the walls,
Like fish living in a pond, they seek shelter... (ll. 394-407a).[40]

In the 'Curse of Akkade/Agade', however, we find perhaps the first instance of the genre, if not its actual beginning: the same repertoire of images are used to narrate not a wondrous rise to power, but its inverse. The evil actions of King Naram-Sin led to a curse on the cities which was to become a cause of lament once the curse had been fulfilled.[41] Survivors of the Guti invasion live to perform a lamentation at the town of Nippur, in which all sectors of the populace seem to take place:

The old women who survived those days,
The old men who survived those days,
The chief gala who survived those years—
For seven days and seven nights
Put in place seven balag-drums, as if they stood at heaven's base, and
Made ub, mexe, and lilis-drums resonate for him (Enlil, the god) among them.
The old women did not restrain (the cry) 'Alas my city!',
The old men did not restrain (the cry) 'Alas its people!',
The gala did not restrain (the cry) 'Alas the Ekur! (the temple)'.
Its young women did not restrain from tearing their hair,
Its young men did not restrain from sharpening their knives.
Their laments were the laments for Enlil's ancestors...[42]

---

39. Michalowski, *Lamentation*, p. 55.
40. Michalowski, *Lamentation*, pp. 61-63.
41. Dobbs-Allsopp, *Weep, O Daughter*, p. 20; Cooper, 'Genre', pp. 39-47 (40).
42. Cooper, 'Genre', pp. 39-47 (41). The 'old women' here speak in the dialect *Emesal*, used by women, goddesses, and castrates for ritual lament. They are probably

In these lament texts, we find a recognition by the entire populace of the displacement and destruction of war, so much so that even the gods must join in the lament for their broken cities and temples. While the deities weep for the annihilation of their own temples and accoutrements as much as they do for the dead, we are allowed a glimpse of the grueling struggle to survive the aftermath of battle. The unburied corpses make impossible the ritual purity that accompanied most forms of intercessory worship, so the situation renders the survivors not just displaced and dispossessed, but unclean. Moderns may think primarily of public health issues raised by siege, war and the aftermath of battle, but there was considerable suffering in the 'spiritual' realm for ancient survivors, too. Unburied bodies also raise the threat of unsettled spirits of those denied burial, attracting both demons and carrion-eaters to the scene, and shame the survivors by their inability to provide proper burial and ritual duties for their dead.

Once we reflect upon the authorial class producing laments, inscriptions, poetry, and legal texts in Mesopotamia we have entered the world of the scribe, member of a class with a powerful *raison d'être*, the documentation of the state. Scribes are shown as part of military campaigns (see Fig. 21), accoutrements of court scenes, and were even critical in medical situations: if they could not get the prescribed tablets for a specific ritual ready and copied on time, the poor patient and his fish-garbed doctor must wait to begin their cure! Though they exist to do their master's bidding, the scribes are themselves equipped with eyes as well as the ideology of the aggressor.

Lions on a Leash: Human Dignity in an Old Kingdom Magic Tale
The knowledge of bodily integrity is found in the outraged cry of a wise man dragged into the Pharaoh's court to show his prowess in magic. This is found in the Fourth Wonder Tale of the Westcar Papyrus, a series of stories within a story of entertaining storytelling at the court of Khufu (Cheops). While set in the Old Kingdom under Khufu, this group of magic tales was probably composed in the Twelfth Dynasty.[43] Dedi,

---

to be understood as forerunners of the Hebrew Bible's 'wise/skilled' women who are trained in laments (Jer. 9.17; 2 Chron. 35.25; Ezek. 32.16) as we hear in Gudea's Statue B inscription of post-war disharmonies, '…The pickaxe was not wielded in the city's cemetery, corpses were not buried, the gala did not set up his balag-drum and bring forth laments from it, the woman lamenter did not utter laments' (quoted in Cooper, 'Genre', pp. 39-47 [42]). The young men with knives may be about to engage in ritual cutting.

43. W.K. Simpson, 'King Cheops and the Magicians', in W.K Simpson (ed.), *The Literature of Ancient Egypt: An Anthology of Stories, Instructions, Stelae, Autobiographies, and Poetry* (New Haven: Yale University Press, 3rd edn, 2003), pp. 13-24 (13-14).

Fig. 21. *Assyrian scribes take orders while captives are taken away on carts.*

the miraculous, has lived to a prodigious old age (110 years), every day eating 500 loaves and a shoulder of beef and drinking 100 jugs of beer. Whether this accounts for his abilities—he can reunite a detached head from its body and can make a lion follow him on a leash—is not clear, but it does describe the ideal lifespan to which Egyptians aspired. Escorted by the crown prince Hardjedef to the court of Pharaoh, the wise man insists on bringing his students and writings (papyrus rolls) along in support.[44] The scene with Khufu unfolds:

> His Majesty said: Is it true, the saying that you know how to reattach a head which has been cut off? Dedi said: Yes, I do know how, Sovereign (*lph*), my lord. His Majesty said: Let there be brought to me a prisoner who is in confinement, that his punishment may be inflicted. And Dedi said: But not indeed to a man, Sovereign, my lord! For the doing of the like is not commanded unto the august cattle.[45]

Pharaoh obviously does not agree that all humans, even condemned prisoners, are sacred as part of the cattle herd of the gods, but he does not try to convince the sage of that. Instead, a goose is brought for

---

44. This may be the first reference in history to the 'graduate assistant' accompanying the professor on a lecture tour.

45. Simpson, 'Cheops', pp. 13-24 (20). Literally, the last line reads 'not to the noble herd'; that is, people are the cattle of the gods.

demonstration, followed by an ox, both successfully brought back to life after decapitation. [46] We note with approval that the wise man has outdistanced his godlike ruler in understanding the value of human life, even in those destined for death. Even though Dedi shows by his subsequent actions that the condemned prisoner would have been in no real jeopardy from serving as magician's apprentice, such a thing ought not to be done: humans are not fit subjects for casual experimentation and entertainment for the court. Dedi has used his response to a particular stimulus to raise respect for human life to the level of a categorical imperative even a king must obey. Although Dedi derives human dignity and worth from an external source, the gods, rather than from some recognition of intrinsic human worth, he has found a point upon which he can turn as he attempts to steer the Pharaoh away from a signal abuse of bodily dignity and integrity.

Bad Faith in New Kingdom Thebes: The Book of the Dead
The *Book of the Dead* is a compendium of incantations, hymnic interludes, magic spells, and pictorial vignettes of mythic action needed for a mummy's successful reanimation in the afterlife. Originating as Old Kingdom pyramid texts, by the Middle Kingdom mortuary prayers were inscribed inside coffins, becoming known as the Coffin Texts to modern researchers. By the New Kingdom period, the spells and illustrations were made into a specially commissioned or ready-made scroll used in elite and upscale non-royal burials. The most lavish example is the 78 ft long Papyrus of Ani, now in the British Museum.[47] One hundred and eighty-nine chapters in total, not every *Book of the Dead* contains every spell, and they are not always in the same order.[48]

The Book outlines the various processes through which the body of the mummy must go in order to achieve bodily resurrection. In substance, it draws on the mythology of Heliopolis where the Sun God Amon-Re regenerated nightly. This imagery later merged with the cult of Osiris, God-King of the Dead, which was associated with the lucrative funerary industry at Abydos run by the Theban scribal bureaucracy. The *Book of the Dead* helped its patrons make the perilous journey after

---

46. Obviously, a third episode with a lion is expected but appears to have dropped out of the text.

47. Raymond Faulkner (trans.), *The Egyptian Book of the Dead: The Book of Going Forth by Day* (San Francisco: Chronicle Books, 2nd rev. edn, 1998); Erik Hornung and David Lorton (trans.), *The Ancient Egyptian Books of the Afterlife* (Ithaca, NY: Cornell University Press, 1998).

48. Only 18 chapters of the 189 seem to be 'must-haves' which are non-negotiable for a successful afterlife: 1, 6, 17-18, 22-23, 30A, 30B, 44, 50, 58-59, 74, 91-92, 110, 125, 148.

death to the Field of Offerings, providing special information, helpful pictures and incantations, and no doubt provided a nice little income on the side for entrepreneurial scribes and artists.

The high point of the underworld journey occurs in chapter 125, The Negative Oath of Innocence, where the deceased's heart, witness to all deeds performed in life, is weighed on a scale against the goddess Ma'at (represented by an ostrich feather). Like 'Lady Wisdom' of Proverbs 8, Ma'at stands for cosmic order and human justice, and undergirds all rulership and authority. 'She' symbolizes the very cosmic order that Pharaohs were called upon to defend, with conquest and war if necessary. During the heart's 'weigh-in' ceremony, mummies recited lengthy descriptions of all the sins they had *not* committed, and made a short profession of their good deeds. The scribal god Thoth ('Beaky', since he has the head of an ibis) recorded the verdict: the successful dead merged with Osiris, living again bodily and forever. The hearts of the wicked were eaten by the hybrid monster, Ammit (part hippopotamus, part lion, part crocodile), representing the final annihilation of the human person.

Most telling for our purposes are not the forensic reflections on Egyptian views of the multiply constituted personality which includes several hearts, souls, a spirit, a double, a shadow, a good name, and so on, but the descriptions of bodily fates to be avoided at all costs. The land of the Dead was clearly a place beset by multiple dangers, and the deceased needed not just a geographical chart, but effective magic spells to summon the items needed to combat the evil fortunes that lurked through every guarded doorway.

The general structure of the journey was to find the path to the Great Hall of Judgment, and from there, hopefully, to the Field of Reeds, a paradise of all good things where they would be reunited with loved ones already gone on before. Obstacles included menacing demonic gatekeepers who must be propitiated by recitation of their proper name, confusing waterways and caverns, pitch black darkness, the Lake of the Jackal, walls of flames, the 'slaughtering block of the god', not to mention enemies and common plagues of the desert: snakes, beetles, and scorpions. To combat all these, quite a bit of equipment was necessary, which could take a lifetime to assemble for burial with the corpse. Ladders, *ushabtis* (like 'doubles' of the deceased provided to do any assigned work in the afterlife), amulets, incense, storms, hail, sunlight, birds, beetles, locusts, incantations, information,[49] and of course, the help of

---

49. The sheer amount of information needed accounts for the need for this genre. One needed to know (by heart, but a scroll is always helpful for jogging the memory of the dead): all the geographical information about the Lake of Fire, the Walls of

the gods were all a prerequisite for warding off fates worse than death itself. Many bad things could happen while attempting to board the Solar Barque of the Sun God and share his victorious voyage of turning night to day: falling out of the boat; being present while the snake-god Apophis attacks the boat; losing one's way; running out of provisions; not finding a mooring; and getting on the wrong boat, or failing to successfully hail the ferryman.[50] The particular horror of 'missing the boat' is thought to underlie the practice of concerted attempts to recover the bodies of soldiers or the drowned, so they could make their journey successfully despite their fall. Chapter 93 in Ani's *Book of the Dead* even gives a spell for not getting onto the wrong ferry (cf. 98, 99) and for escaping the net and the Catcher of Fish (153A, 153B).[51]

The book contains, of course, many positive remedies for the body of the corpse: spells invoking amulets and gods' help, for turning into some other creature (lotus, benu-bird, good beetle, heron, etc.), for breathing pure air, for being able to go in and out with power in one's legs and so on. But the list of preventive spells reads as though it were cribbed from a list of tortures and mutilations drawn from the military monuments. The mouth of one's mummy must be 'opened' in a special ceremony right after burial, so that the deceased could give testimony at judgment; this is counter to the practice of pulling out tongues, or the silence of the mutilated corpse. The *Book of the Dead* gives spells for not having one's head severed from one's body (chapter 43); not having the heart give unhelpful testimony during questioning (chapter 30B); not being hung upside down and not eating one's own excrement or drinking one's own urine (chapters 53, 189); not being tormented by creepy crawlies and other pests who prey on exposed bodies on the battlefield and in the tomb (chapters 33, 34, 35, 36, 39, 163); not being burnt by fire (chapter 63A) or scalded by water (chapter 63B); not putrefying in the grave (chapter 45); and not dying a second death (chapters 44, 175, 176). We also find aid for not entering the Slaughterhouse of the God (chapters 50, 41, 42); not being forced to labor (chapters 5, 6);

Flint (knives), the God's Slaughtering Block, the River of Flame, on to the Field of Offerings, in which one finally arrived at the Field of Reeds. One also needed to know the names of every guardian being, every gatekeeper (numbering at least seven, depending on the period), and in one astonishing ritual, over hundreds of specialized parts of a boat (Leonard H. Lesko, 'Death and the Afterlife in Ancient Egyptian Thought', in Sasson (ed.), *CANE*, III [New York: Scribner, 1995], pp. 1763-74 [1767-71]).

50. Anyone familiar with urban challenges in New York City understands the inherent threats of not being able to hail a taxi.

51. All chapter numbers for the *Book of the Dead* here are taken from the Papyrus of Ani (Faulkner's translation).

passing over the Circle of Fire (chapter 136B); and of course, the ever-relevant spell for driving off Him Who Swallowed an Ass (chapter 40).

All the things done to enemies and captives in war are those which the mummy is particularly interested in avoiding—could it be that we have a bit of 'bad faith' here? Is there perhaps an element of the 'act–consequence' relationship at work, the folk idea of wisdom that one's own deeds breed an outcome, good for good deeds and evil for evil? The very elites making use of the *Book of the Dead* are also those who write for the state, keeping accounts of military campaigns as well as tallying the goods and resources of the temples and other state-run enterprises. One can only wonder if the realm of the Dead might not also have offered an opportunity for 'pay-back time'. The scribes are perfectly well acquainted with their roles in coercion (see Fig. 22). 'What is hateful to you, do not do to another', taught the rabbis who interpreted the Hebrew Bible, and the founder of Christianity. Perhaps this lesson was also known to those who were in charge of marketing and documenting the ways of the state in earlier times.

Fig. 22: *Egyptian scribes take testimony while debtors are hauled in for questioning. Tomb of Ti, Saqqarah, Dynasty 5 (After Richard H. Wilkinson,* Symbol and Magic in Egyptian Art,[52] *p. 208, Pl. 151).*

It is easy to deduce from this array of magical aids that the fate of the corpse is of intense interest to those hoping to be reanimated. There is a nascent sort of 'human dignity' here, even if it is applied to the bodily

---

52. (London: Thames & Hudson, 1999).

remains only of the elite. Every corpse wants the positive treatments during burial and beyond described in the *Book of the Dead*. Similarly, *no* corpse wants to be treated the way Egypt treated its enemies. There is knowledge of the extremes of suffering, humiliation, and the disintegration of the body, and a desire to avoid them at all costs. While what we have here is only a 'humanitarian narrative' of a dead body, with no focus whatsoever on the cause of death, there is nevertheless a betrayal of some sense of human dignity in our magical text.

The Negative Confession: Dignity and Bodily Integrity in Chapter 125 of the Book of the Dead

When we come to the high point of the ritual journey, the Hall of Double Ma'at, we are presented with a *précis* of daily elite ethics, as the successful mummy recites not a list of their good deeds, but a list of things they *haven't* done on earth. In form, structure and placement, this text resonates with the Oath of Innocence taken by Job in chapter 31 of that book. The oath holds a key place in the legal proceedings in Job just as it does in the Egyptian underworld: part magic, part testimony, it is notable that the Egyptians did not entirely count on their earthly deeds as being enough or of the proper sort. Magic spells of protection are just as important in getting through the Hall of Judgment as are one's own oaths.

Compared to Job's oath (chapter 31), the *Book of the Dead*'s negative confession has slightly more emphasis on ritual sins, but only 25% of the *Book of the Dead*'s confessions have to do with ritual matters (22 professions out of a total of 88). Modern persons are less likely to categorize the ritual failings as falling within the sphere of morality, but this was not the view from the past. If ritual sins, like presenting a poor sacrifice to the gods or failing to observe purity laws before entering the sanctuary, brought down as severe a punishment on the doer as a moral sin, then clearly they had to be dealt with in the magical economy of prevention of negative outcomes in the Hall of Double Truth. Still, it is interesting to note that the Bible believes this too (cf. 1 Samuel 14–15, where Saul loses his kingship over a failure to obey ritual regulations with respect to captives), and that the Egyptians, at least at the Last Judgment, were every bit as aware of common social and personal decencies that we label morality as the Hebrews or, later, Christians and Muslims.

Reading the Confession carefully, we see that even the elites are still living in an agricultural world: many protestations deal with not mistreating animals, damming up running waters, or taking more from irrigation canals than one is allotted. The mummy states that he or she has not committed evil, lied, killed, caused weeping, or commanded to kill. The latter act, causing death, tells us that the writers and speakers understood notions of causality and collusion. Common features of ancient Near Eastern wisdom literature's view of the duties of a good person are found: the mummy has dealt fairly with orphans, has not taken milk out of the baby's mouth, has not made anyone suffer, taken more wealth than his own lands, committed usury, stolen, been lascivious or committed adultery. Likewise, a series of oaths concern not having perverted measuring standards used in daily commerce or sacrifices, a wisdom theme, and the mummy claims other wisdom virtues, too: he has not been sullen, or a loud-mouth, a tale-bearer, a busy-body, or a nay-sayer.[53]

If the *Book of the Dead* has been at all understood properly by modern scholars, then it presents us with a self-conscious reflection of the values and concerns of its writers and makers, for they were the very persons for whose use the scroll was intended. The local communal ethic so strong at the village levels and made functional and embodied there in the local tribunal had its corollary in scribal ethics of the elites who formed the infrastructure of the state, temple, school, or economic foundation. Just as the tribunal used the views of others to shame the losing litigant because they had no enforcement abilities, the divine tribunal of the Hall of Double Ma'at insures that the elite scribe, ruler, or priest, male or female, would be held accountable for their deeds during life. Ritually, everything hinges on this legal ritual of judgment after death, liberally spritzed as it is with magical elements *just in case*. The outcome of the judgment (perhaps with a little magical nudging) had direct impact on the future of the mummy. In other words, the body would both present the evidence for the trial in the form of its heart (mind), and the body would show forth the verdict: total annihilation of body and personality, or real, bodily life in the Field of Reeds.

Overtones of the Egyptian scribal ethics are found in Hebrew wisdom literature, particularly Proverbs and Job. Proverbs 16.11, 17.3, 20.9-10, 24.10-12 all play off the visual imagery and content of the scene of judgment of the heart. As with other adopted texts, Yahweh plays all the roles normally parceled out to a number of gods. The same imagery appears in the Psalms (62.8-10) and Daniel (5.27), and in Revelation too one of the four horsemen carries a set of scales (Rev. 6). Job takes a key legal-ritual oath of innocence in chapter 31 which brings him to a judgment scene with the Lord just when the dialogue with his friends has broken down. That passage follows a pattern similar to the Egyptian

---

53. Robert K. Ritner, 'Book of the Dead 125: "The Negative Confession"', in Simpson, *LAE*, pp. 267-77 (269-77).

Negative Confession, and is notable for its use of the full curse formula.[54] The curses Job wills upon himself if lying are reminiscent of the *Book of the Dead*'s grisly fascination with the body.

3. *The Book of Job: A 'Humanitarian Narrative'?*

If the *Book of the Dead* gives us a view into scribal consciousness in imperial New Kingdom Egypt, then we can compare it to a scribal creation in the Hebrew Bible, if not with impunity, at least with some success. Generally dated to the postexilic period, anywhere from the time of the Exile down through Persian home rule, the author of Job chooses a foreign chieftain from the despised Edomites as God's test case on human disinterest in divine reward. Job is chosen, not because he is bad, but because he is *good*—a strange case where reward does *not* follow good action. Since God allows the District Attorney for Planet Earth, the Satan, to put Job to the test, it is hard to come away with a sense of the divine realm as 'fair' by any human standards of measurement. The best that can be said of this wager that sets up the plot of Job's unfolding suffering is that Yahweh, at least, seems to be torturing Job for information. The 'test' is real and the outcome not known;[55] the only way out of it for Job is through it. God might be either a 'professional' (who only tortures until he finds out what he needs to know) or a zealot on the subject of retribution. It should be noted, too, that Yahweh orders the Satan to spare Job's life, another sign of God's professional approach. Whether he or the Satan are also sadistic torturers the reader must decide. Certainly, Job seems to think so at points, though he does not know that the Satan carries out the experiment, filling the slot of secondary causality.

The Book of Job might well be thought of as *The Book of Wishing You Were Dead*, given its focus on the dreadful bodily conditions that have befallen its hero. Only in a few psalms of individual lament and a parable on old age in Qoheleth does the Hebrew Bible come anywhere close to describing the horrors of embodiment when it all goes horribly wrong. At least the dangers in the *Book of the Dead* were lurking to overtake a *corpse*; in the Book of Job, we have an account of *lived* suffering. Because Job thinks of himself as nearly dead, hopefully dead, and soon to be gladly dead at God's hands, and gives *so* much detail of what has been

---

54. Usually, in an 'if...then' oath, the 'then' clause is suppressed, since naming it would make it magically active, with potential negative outcomes.

55. So, too, with other examples of God testing humans: God actually wants to know how humans will respond in various circumstances (James Crenshaw, *A Whirlpool of Torment: Israelite Traditions of God as an Oppressive Presence* [OBT, 12; Philadelphia: Fortress Press, 1984]). The Experimenter is at least interested in the information gained and not simply in torturing for pleasure.

done to his body, it is not too far a stretch to compare this aspect of the book to the modern genre known as the 'humanitarian narrative' in Human Rights research.

The Humanitarian Narrative
The Humanitarian Narrative, so named by cultural historian Thomas W. Laqueur,[56] began in the eighteenth and nineteenth centuries and ultimately formed part of the impetus for the development of European humanitarianism, an early sibling of Human Rights discourse. These narratives focused on the physical body, rather than some ideal or philosophical concept of the body, and marshaled large amounts of detail about how the body had suffered, especially those bodies never previously considered of interest to writing elites—the abandoned baby, the slave, the prisoner, the war captive, the coal miner, the prostitute. Of course, the simple exposure of the fates of such bodies was not considered an end in and of itself: by delineating the sympathetic connections between the observer and the body observed, the narratives hoped to excite compassion, change the vision of who 'counted' in society, and ultimately, disclose a solution to end such future sufferings.

Laqueur characterizes narratives having these elements in common not simply by their goal, but by their method and content, uncovering three basic features: (1) a reliance on detail to prove the truth of the account; (2) focus on the individual, personal body as the site of pain but also commonality between the victim, the writer, and the reader, and (3) exposure of the role of human causality and agency in perpetuating unacceptable suffering.[57] By showing that humanity had caused the suffering, it was hoped that the reader would be moved to ask how humans might act to end it. Such writings proposed, implicitly or openly, that failure to act would constitute a grave breach of human solidarity and be morally unacceptable. Whether as novel, medical, or autopsy report, the clinical narrative gives pride of place to the suffering body at its very last point, death, and lets it speak for itself, because its narrator '…has the authority to expose for scrutiny the subjective consciousness of others and to do so more effectively than they could themselves'.[58] It is the 'icy language of science' which finally gives a voice to the anonymous sufferer in death, with profound consequences for the reader-now-turned-bystander.[59] Because 'the body, almost by convention, is recognizable as a shared

56. 'Bodies, Details, and the Humanitarian Narrative', in Lynn Hunt (ed.), *The New Cultural History: Studies on the History of Society and Culture* (Berkeley: University of California, 1989), pp. 176-204.
57. Laqueur, 'Bodies', pp. 176-204 (177-78).
58. Laqueur, 'Bodies', p. 185.
59. Laqueur, 'Bodies', p. 196.

locus of sympathy binding reader to text, and both to social context', failure to respond to a narrative of the suffering body may indicate a kind of moral pathology, or at least, a deep detachment from experiences of *any* body.[60]

By all three of Laqueur's features of the humanitarian narrative, the Book of Job seems to fit the description, even if Job's suffering is 'fictional', fabricated, folkloric, or foreign. The sheer bulk of Job's detail of his bodily distress draws the reader in as a horrified witness, a bystander, to the great theological drama being enacted on one man's flesh without his knowledge or consent. The body is the canvas on which Job's spiritual and physical drama unfolds, and its contours are extreme: God is the Divine Warrior and Job is his helpless captive.

> For the arrows of the Almighty are in me;
> my spirit drinks their poison;
> the terrors of God are arrayed against me (6.4).

The image of Nergal and Resheph, the plague gods who strike down armies with their arrows of sunstroke and poisons, has replaced the more normal meanings of Almighty, *Shaddai*. Normally found in contexts of generative blessing (cf. Gen. 17, 28, 35, 49, etc.), that which normally is source of life is now the image of terror. No wonder Job's skin—the eye of the soul, says modern medicine—reflects his torment: open sores close up, harden, only to reopen again (7.5). All Job's bodily boundaries betray what is happening to him: he is being deconstructed by God just as the bodies of victims are taken apart by the warrior in order to inscribe new boundaries under his own complete control. The process is iterative.

It is the predicament of the person whose embodiment has become a source of perpetual pain that causes Job to call out this aspect of human life for God's consideration of justice. God is peeling Job like an onion, skin after skin, removing each of his social and physical boundaries. How *can* God know what is happening to Job?

> Do you have eyes of flesh?
> Do you see as humans see?
> Are your days like the days of mortals,
> or your years like human years,
> that you seek out my iniquity
> and search for my sin,
> although you know that I am not guilty,
> and there is no one to deliver out of your hand?
> Your hands fashioned and made me;
> and now you turn and destroy me.
> Remember that you fashioned me like clay;
> and will you turn me to dust again? (10.4-9).

---

60. Laqueur, 'Bodies', pp. 176-204 (195).

Mortality, the final condition of the body, places a full stop to the possibility of any interchange between Accuser and Victim. Others have suffered, too, but Job knows that the origin of his distress is that Divine Watcher who torments him with awful presence. Again, as Scarry noted, God's presence is manifested in the body's physical pain. Even venting his emotions brings Job no relief:

> 'If I speak, my pain is not assuaged,
>   and if I forbear, how much of it leaves me?
> Surely now God has worn me out;
>   he has made desolate all my company.
> And he has shriveled me up,
>   which is a witness against me;
> my leanness has risen up against me,
>   and it testifies to my face.
> He has torn me in his wrath, and hated me;
>   he has gnashed his teeth at me;
> my adversary sharpens his eyes against me...
> God gives me up to the ungodly,
>   and casts me into the hands of the wicked.
> I was at ease, and he broke me in two;
>   he seized me by the neck and dashed me to pieces;
> he set me up as his target;
>   his archers surround me.
> He slashes open my kidneys, and shows no mercy;
>   he pours out my gall on the ground.
> He bursts upon me again and again;
>   he rushes at me like a warrior.
> I have sewed sackcloth upon my skin,
>   and have laid my strength in the dust.
> My face is red with weeping,
>   and deep darkness is on my eyelids,
> though there is no violence in my hands,
>   and my prayer is pure (16.6-9, 11-17).

The Cosmic Combatant makes war on Job's body, and that very fact, in a society where the mechanisms of illness are not well understood, acts to confirm Job's sin—why would he be punished if not for some grave, hidden transgression? Job images himself both as the city being battered (raped?) and besieged, and as the hunter's prey who is torn, shaken, thrown, targeted, and slashed. He continues his lament using images reminiscent of the surviving Sumerian citizens of demolished Ur, gasping like fish out of water or huddled in their pond in fear, wandering in the rubble of their city gates as they try to flee the conquered city. Images from city-laments like the lost treasures (economic), the looted crown (political), and the uprooted tree (environmental) appear:

> He has walled up my way so that I cannot pass,
>> and he has set darkness upon my paths.
> He has stripped my glory from me,
>> and taken the crown from my head.
> He breaks me down on every side, and I am gone,
>> he has uprooted my hope like a tree.
> He has kindled his wrath against me,
>> and counts me as his adversary.
> His troops come on together;
>> they have thrown up siegeworks against me,
>> and encamp around my tent (19.8-12).

Like the worst positioned prisoner in the 'torture game', Job has been weakened and is innocent. Only giving up immediately can stop his physical torment, but since he has nothing to confess, will this strategy work? Must he make up some plausible tale for his tormenter? He is sure his own lips will condemn him simply out of dread and terror.

> How then can I answer him,
>> choosing my words with him?
> Though I am innocent, I cannot answer him;
>> I must appeal for mercy to my accuser.
> If I summoned him and he answered me,
>> I do not believe that he would listen to my voice.
> For he crushes me with a tempest,
>> and multiplies my wounds without cause;
> he will not let me get my breath,
>> but fills me with bitterness.
> If it is a contest of strength, he is the strong one!
>> If it is a matter of justice, who can summon him?
> Though I am innocent, my own mouth would condemn me;
>> though I am blameless, he would prove me perverse.
> I am blameless; I do not know myself;
>> I loathe my life.
> It is all one; therefore I say,
>> he destroys both the blameless and the wicked.
> When disaster brings sudden death,
>> he mocks at the calamity of the innocent.
> The earth is given into the hand of the wicked;
>> he covers the eyes of its judges—
>> if it is not he, who then is it? (9.14-24).

Confession will not end this game of torture for Job; better to stand by what he knows to be true, however tiny that embodied truth may seem to the Divine Interlocutor. If it causes negative consequences, so be it.

> As God lives, who has taken away my right,
> and the Almighty, who has made my soul bitter,
> as long as my breath is in me
> and the spirit of God is in my nostrils,
> my lips will not speak falsehood,
> and my tongue will not utter deceit.
> Far be it from me to say that you are right;
> until I die I will not put away my integrity from me.
> I hold fast my righteousness, and will not let it go;
> my heart does not reproach me for any of my days (27.2-6).

Job's longing for death must be seen as a positive, pro-active 'last decent choice' of the tortured: he is not choosing death; he is choosing to end his pain. Deprived of human solidarity (30.28-29, *et passim*), one of the only things which can strengthen prisoners in their determination to resist or choose death, his fixation on the attempt to get justice from his captor is reminiscent of the way captives are taught to endorse the world-view of their torturers.

Others have noted that the plight Job experiences is similar to that of the abused child or political prisoner.[61] However, the addition of a divine player in the game of torture, whether for information or fun, adds an impressive dimension to the enormity of Job's despair:

> Therefore I am terrified at his presence;
> when I consider, I am in dread of him.
> God has made my heart faint;
> the Almighty has terrified me;
> If only I could vanish in darkness,
> and thick darkness would cover my face! (23.15-17).

The inexplicable torment that has visited Job is combined with a malevolent watchfulness on God's part, a repeated breaching of Job's physical boundaries that make him want to disappear into the darkness of his metaphorical cell, his body. Skin, tongue, eyes, flesh—all these are loci of Job's integrity, which is embodied not just in his acts, but apparently in his flesh as well.

Eventually, the 'friendly' dialogue in Job breaks down entirely, even at the textual level: one speech is truncated (Chapter 25) and another lost

---

61. Kimberly Parsons Chastain, 'The Dying Art of Demon-Recognition: Victims, Systems, and the Book of Job', in Cynthia L. Rigby (ed.), *Power, Powerlessness, and the Divine: New Inquiries in Bible and Theology* (Scholars Press Studies in Theological Education; Atlanta: Scholars Press, 1997), pp. 161-78; Carol Newsom, 'The Character of Pain: Job in Light of Elaine Scarry's *The Body in Pain*' (paper presented at the Annual Meeting of the SBL, Orlando, FL, 23 November 1998); F. Rachel Magdalene, 'Job's Wife as Hero: A Feminist-Forensic Reading of the Book of Job', *Biblical Interpretation* 14 (2006), pp. 209-49.

(Zophar has no reply to Job's third speech). Job directs his words to the oppressor rather than his comforters. Has God succeeded in 'breaking' Job in the *Book of Wishing You Were Dead*? Job's own Negative Confession tells a different and remarkable story.

Lost and Found: Intrinsic Human Worth and Dignity in the Hebrew Bible
Most scholars agree that the legal metaphor is fully at work in the plotting of Job's story, and that it represents a moment of 'imaginative outreach' by Job.[62] He envisions a level playing field of sorts: meeting God in a law court where testimony is given and judged. Yet, Job upends the lawsuit genre of the Hebrew Bible: it is God who is brought to trial, not just Job. Whether one views Job's final repentance and the Epilogue's 'happy ending' as ironic or misguided, the fact that God pays double restitution for all of Job's losses underlines the power of this legal fiction to shape the narrative. If we compare Exod. 22.4, 7, 9 to Job 42.10, we are left with two possibilities, both favorable to Job in his lawsuit. Either God has made double restitution because the goods taken from him were found alive and returned, or God pays a fine for losing his lawsuit against Job. Either way, Job must indeed have 'spoken rightly' of God and his own predicament, as evidenced by the narrative outcome of the legal fiction.

Just after the dialogue with friends terminates and before Elihu suddenly breaks in to summarize the preceding arguments of earlier chapters, Job takes an Oath of Innocence in Chapter 31. Like the *Book of the Dead*, this self-judgment ritual is efficacious and customary: swearing an oath before the divine is a common feature of the legal proceedings of all the cultures we have surveyed. While this is not Job's first oath, it is certainly his terminal one, as it provokes the outcome about which he has been fantasizing for chapters: the *Deus absconditus* finally puts in an appearance, coming to Job from the 'midst of the whirlwind' (38.1). While commonly associated with the theophanies of weather gods in the Near East, in fact this wild wind may be more likely to be an association with the violent 'bitter storm' metaphor used in Mesopotamian city-laments to describe the destruction of the beloved city by a god.[63] Since Job has repeatedly compared himself to a raped and besieged city whom God attacks, we must take this whirlwind quite seriously. It refers not simply to a weather phenomenon's conventional explanation, but to the *whole* of Job's suffering and God's role in the midst of it.

---

62. J. Gerald Janzen, *Job* (Interpretation, a Bible Commentary for Teaching and Preaching; Atlanta: John Knox Press, 1985).

63. The vicious storm in Mesopotamian city-laments is usually associated with the god Enlil, 'Lord Wind' (Dobbs-Allsopp, *Weep, O Daughter*, pp. 56-57).

In fact, it is the prayers of Job, the wise man and leader, which restores right order and lures the Hidden One to return to Job's habitation (signified by the restoration of all Job's goods and children). From the ruined sanctuary of his body, Job has offered a lament that has finally induced God's return. The Book of Job is not the only place, of course, where the violent storm refers to Yahweh's destruction of life. In Lamentations 2.1a, we read:

> How Yahweh in his anger engulfed the Daughter of Zion in storm clouds!
> He threw down from heaven to earth the splendor of Israel.[64]

Like the Judgment Scene in chapter 125 of the *Book of the Dead*, Job's frenzied oath is the highpoint of Job's willingness to defend his integrity. While not an Israelite himself, nevertheless the ethical and ritual violations Job professes not to have done show a full knowledge of the legal traditions of the Hebrew Bible. Compare excerpts from the Covenant Code in Exodus 22 with Job 31:

> Whoever sacrifices to any god, other than the LORD alone, shall be devoted to destruction. You shall not wrong or oppress a resident alien, for you were aliens in the land of Egypt. You shall not abuse any widow or orphan. If you do abuse them, when they cry out to me, I will surely heed their cry; my wrath will burn, and I will kill you with the sword, and your wives shall become widows and your children orphans (Exod. 22.20-24).

> If my heart has been enticed by a woman,
>   and I have lain in wait at my neighbor's door;
> then let my wife grind for another,
>   and let other men kneel over her (Job 31.9-10).

> If I have withheld anything that the poor desired,
>   or have caused the eyes of the widow to fail,
> or have eaten my morsel alone,
>   and the orphan has not eaten from it—
> for from my youth I reared the orphan like a father,
>   and from my mother's womb I guided the widow—
> if I have seen anyone perish for lack of clothing,
>   or a poor person without covering,
> whose loins have not blessed me,
>   and who was not warmed with the fleece of my sheep;
> if I have raised my hand against the orphan,
>   because I saw I had supporters at the gate;
> then let my shoulder blade fall from my shoulder,
>   and let my arm be broken from its socket (Job 31.16-22).

---

64. Dobbs-Allsopp makes this translation of *yā'ib*, occurring only here in Lam. 2.1a on the basis of Yahweh's traditional connection with clouds in his divine warrior aspect (cf. 2 Sam. 22; Ps. 68, 97, 104, Isa. 19); *Weep, O Daughter*, pp.64; so too Claus Westermann, *Die Klagelieder* (Neukirchen–Vluyn: Neukirchener Verlag, 1990), p. 125.

> ...if I have looked at the sun when it shone,
>> or the moon moving in splendor,
> and my heart has been secretly enticed,
>> and my mouth has kissed my hand;
> this also would be an iniquity to be punished by the judges,
>> for I should have been false to God above (Job 31.26-28).

Other sections of the oath echo the Covenant Code in subject matter, tone, and outcome: the land is to be cared for (Exod. 23.11; Job 31.38-40); the resident alien and stranger are to be cared for and not oppressed (Exod. 22.21, 23.9; Job 31.32), justice is not to be perverted (Exod. 23.1-2, Job 31.5), and even the rights of those who are enemies must be taken into account (Exod. 23.4-5, Job 31.29-30). Even Job's less than salutary use of his wife's rape, enslavement, and shame as a punishment should he have lusted after another woman has its echoes in the legal traditions: repayment in kind in Exod. 22.22-25 and neighboring legal traditions means that family members, thought of as an extension of the metaphorical boundaries of the patriarch's own body, are a 'legal' mechanism through which an offender might be punished, just as they are the father's to dispose of in order to pay his own debts.

While we cannot charge Job with wrong in not raising his wife to the level of an equally-suffering Subject (she has lost children, economic resources, and reputation as well) because his use of her in this way is a customary, culturally informed mechanism of 'justice', we do take leave to comment that suffering's enlargement of Job's moral universe is not *quite* complete in all respects. While he *did* finally notice that hedging his bets on progeny by giving his daughters an inheritance along with sons was probably a Good Thing, his treatment of his wife, so wise in her understanding of the true issues underlying his torment,[65] leaves much to be desired.

Job's consciousness has definitely undergone a change, interpreters agree. Whether he has come to see himself as a member of the most wretched class, as Gutierrez suggests, or has had a vision of different sort of God practicing a different kind of justice as Buber thinks, Job has moved from the position of silenced sufferer to that of legal challenger of oppression. Often, Job is held up as a paradigm of all human suffering and abasement, often to make his alleged 'patience' even more glorious than all those contentious dialogues might suggest. However, these views, grand and poetic though they are, lack a full social analysis of Job's suffering compared to that of captives, slaves, and women. Job has not been permanently mutilated, so his shame is not eternal. He has not been beheaded, displayed, flayed, or impaled. Neither has he

---

65. Magdalene, 'Job's Wife', pp. 209-49 (231-34).

been the object of rape, beatings, or forced marriage with an abductor. Job suffers in the 'male register': no one tries to uncover *him*, use him physically, or toss him away empty when done. If his loss of honor, so poignantly set out in chapters 29–30 is a major blow to him, that must be considered the consequence of his having had the male option of honor and glory of leadership in the first place. Job imagines he is being treated as a hireling, but he does not know the half of it—the female half.

> Has not man a hard service upon earth,
>   and are not his days like the days of a hireling?
> Like a slave who longs for the shadow,
>   and like a hireling who looks for his wages,
> so I am allotted months of emptiness,
>   and nights of misery are apportioned to me.
> When I lie down I say, 'When shall I arise?'
>   But the night is long,
>   and I am full of tossing till the dawn (7.1-4 RSV).

The RSV translation is preferred here because, as this study has shown, the lives of female captives and slaves are *not* the same as men's in the same situation. Domestic slaves only *wish* their months were filled with emptiness, and that they might get real wages. Tossing until dawn and sleepless nights would be a considerable improvement over the sexual exploitation that is common for women in such circumstances. Job does not know what he is talking about. Job can be restored to his former glory; women cannot, for such glory is absent from the outset of being born female.

Still, such criticisms notwithstanding—and even the *United Nations Declaration of Universal Human Rights (UNDUHR)* had to be supplemented with subsequent statements covering women and children, since those 'universal human rights' turned out to be, in fact, the 'rights of Man'—we may still locate Job's oath as a major victory and step forward. Job *has* suffered dreadfully for one in his originally blessed position, and he *has* enlarged his theology beyond the retribution theory he inherited. He *has* placed his experience of embodied suffering at the core of his 'confession', rather than following the majority in claiming that all was well in the system of acts and their consequences. He *does* stand up to God, even if only to immediately fall into the dust repenting. All of these things, imputed to a foreigner from a group held in deep hatred for their role in aftermath of the Babylonian conquest of Judah, speak of a recognition of intrinsic morality in the Other, a basic decency supposedly known to all. Compared to the war reports of Mesopotamia and Egypt with their contempt and demonization of the wretched enemy at war with cosmic order, the oath that Job takes is far-reaching in its implications. Job has discovered worth and dignity in *all* those around him:

> If I have rejected the cause of my male or female slaves, when they brought
> a complaint against me; what then shall I do when God rises up?
> When he makes inquiry, what shall I answer him?
> Did not he who made me in the womb make them?
> And did not one fashion us in the womb? (31.13-15).

Looking through the eyes of the suffering flesh, Job's vision has expanded dramatically, *and* it gives him hope for his own situation. Even female slaves have the right of appeal to Job the Household Judge and Community Elder, and God is viewed as the Guarantor of those rights to fair and decent treatment. Social distinctions are made, not born. Job knows that simply being here is enough to confer rights on everyone, and he commits in both past and present to being a duty-holder who enforces those rights. His hope inheres in the fact that Job knows his own fair principles when *he* was the honored judge; he daydreams that he might have a similar outcome in facing God. If a slave can challenge the master, then Job can challenge his Creator with some hope of a hearing.

Here, finally, our long meander through the history of rights begins to overlap in a significant way with the trajectories of modern dialogues. My humanitarian narrative of Job's suffering hopes to excite the passions, and press toward redress, past, present and future. The body represented is not the same as the body itself, but they influence each other mutually, and must be the simplest starting point for ethical concerns.

Chapman had noted that the only places where female gendered tropes intersect with those of military tropes is around the area of weakness, terror, incapacity, vulnerability, and inability to take protective action.[66] Perhaps that was so in the texts and practice of the past, but in our world, new connections have been forged. Post-traumatic stress disorder in soldiers who bravely carried out their duties during combat (rather than being 'sissies' who deserve to be sickened by their own cowardice) made the 'hysteria' seen in female victims of incest and sexual abuse respectable. Having a womb turned out *not* to be the source of the psychological problems; being abused *was*. Soldiers and women have a great deal in common when we consider the impact of patriarchal ideology upon their experiences.

Next, it should be noted that the legal idiom, which is the main way in which modern Human Rights discourse founds itself and seeks remedies, is the format in which the ancient writers of the Bible sought

---

66. Cynthia R. Chapman, *The Gendered Language of Warfare in the Israelite–Assyrian Encounter* (HSM, 62; Winona Lake, IN: Eisenbrauns, 2004).

to resolve issues of rights and duties. From prophets to wise men to women captives, all in theory had recourse to the law. So, too, have military tribunals and local governments found that the issues of returning soldiers and women at risk must seek legal remedy, and perpetrators of crimes of war on the battlefield or in the home must be held accountable. This is critical for fostering a dialogue between men and women, believers and secularists, all of whom might make common cause for human rights if they could find more common ground than agreeing that the other party is part of the problem.

From the high to the low, from the male chieftain to the female slave, from the human being to furrows in the earth, all have rights and duties. The 'august cattle' of ancient Egypt have found themselves a livable habitation in the Scriptures of Synagogue and Church, even though they may often be interpreted as a warrant for slaughter or exclusion. Despite the legal disabilities of slaves and women, the presence of mutilation and capital punishment in the Bible's legal practices, the overall aim of biblical law is the restoration to wholeness through fine, restitution, or some other sanction. The helpless should not suffer and the wicked should not prosper. The use of the death penalty for sexual crimes must be challenged, because it goes against that standard of restoration, and imputes to males an authority to end life which is theologically questionable unless we consider patriarchy itself to be *the* crucial content of the biblical faith.[67] Death puts an end to everything. The practice owes more to expediency of restoring male honor quickly and decisively, and the purity fetish which inspires the community to rid itself of the contaminating offender. So while we may dispute individual examples of the application of biblical law, we may take our ethical warrants from the overall trajectory of restoration...as the traditions of rabbinic Judaism did and do. One will look in vain in ancient Near Eastern law codes for *any legal protections* of slaves, captive women, or compassion for prisoners. Here the Hebrew Bible stands head and shoulders above all the nations,[68] and *this* should be the fulcrum on which we turn our reflections on the role of a biblically informed praxis of universal ethics, pressing to extend the same enhanced legal considerations to members of groups the Bible did *not* place among their classes of protected persons. Universal rights are fully implied in the Hebrew Bible, just as they are in strands of Egyptian

---

67. Some fundamentalist extremists do indeed think that the elevation of male to the level of idolatry is the whole point of Scripture; obviously, I disagree vehemently.

68. While this argument does not proceed entirely from silence, I am quite aware that the vagaries of preservation may militate against my claim. By all means, let us have more law codes from people and sites as yet uncovered, and comparison and revision can ensue. But at present, Jews, Christians, and Muslims have something in their textual heritage of which they may rightfully feel very proud.

thinking, but they are partially implemented in legal practice in the textual form of law codes only in the Scripture to which all three Peoples of the Book turn as their resource text. The Torah converts Bystanders into Duty-bearers who must restore justice; even God rejects the role of Bystander by appearing to Job and making restitution. Those seeking to model their actions on a faithful response to the teachings of the Bible had better take notice: let everyone listening pay attention!

Job's oath makes clear that justice does not simply involve refraining from evil deeds, but that proactive behavior on the behalf of right-bearers is also required. Failure to participate in the making of justice is the hallmark of the bystander, and the Hebrew Bible rejects this stance. God's legal engagement with Job and justification of him in the Epilogue show that even the Deity cannot long exist in the role of Watcher and Bystander. When God finally shows up, the Almighty is driven to speak of the value of all life from the very midst of the whirlwind of its suffering. Even where we may disagree substantially and materially with the details or values embodied in ancient legal traditions in the Hebrew Bible[69]—and we must—we may confidently endorse their view of human decency in response to human worth.

4. 'I died there': Hearing the Silenced

My review of legal traditions around brutality and torture has tried to bring to consciousness those very things that torturing states and bodies try to suppress. Burying our traumatic past and the deep flaws in our religious traditions is no way to integrate that knowledge for the purpose of changing the future. We do *not* have access to the testimonies of ancient survivors of torture and captivity, slavery and sexual abuse. The ancient world preferred them out of sight and out of mind; we cannot take that path today.

> My young driver took one look at my cane and said, 'Ah, you are the one who goes up front', and hustled me carefully into the front seat of the organization's van. 'We will wait here for the other ladies; they are taking longer than you.' As we chatted, I was aware once more of the Terra Incognita of polite conversation in a mixed group of activists, survivors, bereaved families, spies and government flunkies keeping track. When I asked what sort of work the driver did normally, he looked around and then said quietly – we were alone – 'I work for Them. But I fix cars'. Did he have his own

---

69. Genocide, patriarchy, xenophobia, and homophobia are all things which ought not to be repeated despite their appearance in any group's sacred texts, since all these violate the scriptural principle that all are to be valued because all stem from the same Source.

business in D.C.? Oh, indeed. 'Well, that must make your family very proud. How old are you?' There was a long silence.

'I have two birthdays', he said. 'The person I was...I died there, in Evin Prison. I broke. I was dead for a long time, I thought forever. But then I had a birthday on the day when I met X.[70] So I say, 'I am only 17 in real years, because that is how long I've been back from the dead'.

Like the barbaric Western feminist that I am, I reached out to touch his hand as he said 'I died there' and he recoiled as though SAVAK[71] had just burst in on us. 'Ah, now', I told him. 'There is no shame in this; I am old enough to be your mother. If she were here, she would have done the same.' He nodded, and even found a small smile for my embarrassment and apology.

And then we went on.

---

70. Insert martyr's name here.
71. Acronym for Iran's National Information and Security Organization, in control from 1957 to the time of the Revolution in 1979, and notorious for brutality and torture under Shah Pahlevi.

Chapter 4

READING FOR THE BEST:
TOWARD DIVERSITY IN INTERPRETATION

1. *Standard Feminist Statement of Disclosure*

It is common among my branch of biblical studies that commentators 'come clean' about their social location and personal expectations or biases, since feminist biblical hermeneutics rightly notes that no one is 'objective' and that such specific, personal elements figure strongly in our subconscious desires to create and collate meanings in the text and of the text. I am a 57-year-old white woman who has been married to the same man for over thirty-five years; I am not a mother. Though white, I was raised in close contact with poverty and especially the oppression in the African American, Jewish, and Caribbean communities of the South I remember from my youth. At present, I am employed in a 'freestanding' (no associated university) Protestant seminary whose fiscal lifeblood is the support of individual churches and founding denominations. My students do not want to hear 'bad' things about the Bible, any part of it. Their churches do not want them to preach on such topics, and their ordination papers do not regularly feature their skills in critiquing the biblical text, though our seminary doggedly teaches the methods.

Although I was raised Southern Baptist, I parted ways with conservative and fundamentalist theologies as a teen working on civil rights in the 60s in Project Head Start in a black southern ghetto. Recognizing that I could not (and did not want to) pass the conservative litmus test so routinely administered by those who style themselves as the 'real' Christians, my journey into theological honesty continued, with many way stations offering respite from time to time. If forced to pick a label that is something other than Late Bronze wise woman, I would list myself as a progressive with a deep passion for the ancient world, and an abiding compassion for the one we inhabit now.

Out of the Past: Reading as a Member of a Professional Guild
As a visual artist, somehow translated into biblical studies by a whimsical cosmos, I have struggled for many years to find a satisfying, reliable

hermeneutic I could call my own. We all began as historical critics in the olden days, but the confidence in that method's ability to produce stable meanings collectively waned. I experimented with all the tried-and-true approaches for teaching, knowing my students were more interested in 'living' by the Bible than studying where and how it came into being. The original intent of the author—ah, we were taught to be *so* confident that we could know that and proclaim it objectively—was the Holy Grail for interpreters. Find that meaning and you're done, which is fine for the *Journal of Biblical Literature*, but what about the world beyond? Ah, 'dynamic analogy' rode in on a white (yes, white) charger to help us battle the dragons of the world—find a similar social setting in the modern world that 'matches' or is at least moderately congruent with the original context and intent of the author, and take a flying 'leap of faith' from 'then' to 'now'. By insisting on congruence in social settings, we were able to teach students to critique rich white churches with prophetic texts, and support struggling minority communities with messianic or Exodus-oriented traditions.[1] So far, so good.

However, the naiveté of this position was becoming increasingly transparent to some critics. Many feminist interpreters began to agree that there was no *one* pristine reading of a text which pointed us in the direction of an unproblematic code of morality. The polyvalence of the text was a blessing to the dissatisfied interpreter, but a curse to churches and denominations looking for those Ten Words that would always and everywhere be correct when applied faithfully to the world of the believer. Critical awareness of competing readings only egged on competing readers, and the stakes were high. Not only were we less sanguine that we could know the past objectively or that there was only *one* past to be known, the readings inscribed within the text itself were becoming problems themselves.[2] Are women or homosexuals really *people* (suitable for ordaining), not failed males or moral deviants? Why do we follow only the *sexual* regulations of the Bible (not that they are all *that* explicit and straightforward) while simultaneously ignoring the Bible's fairly clear witness on the topic of wealth and poverty? Slavery,

---

1. Two standard statements on these theological developments can be found in Krister Stendahl's 'Biblical Theology, Contemporary', in George A. Buttrick (ed.), *The Interpreter's Dictionary of the Bible: An Illustrated Encyclopedia*, I (Nashville: Abingdon Press, 1962), pp. 418-32, and Elizabeth Achtemeier, *The Old Testament and the Proclamation of the Gospel* (Philadelphia: Westminster Press, 1973), especially pp. 144-59.

2. See, for example, Itumelang J. Mosala, 'The Use of the Bible in Black Theology', in Itumelang J. Mosala and Buti Tlhagale (eds.), *The Unquestionable Right to Be Free: Black Theology from South Africa* (Maryknoll, NY: Orbis Books, 1986), pp. 175-99; R.S. Sugirtharajah (ed.), *The Postcolonial Bible* (The Bible and Postcolonialism Series, 1; Sheffield: Sheffield Academic Press, 1998).

roundly reported and supported everywhere in the Bible, is judged by critics to be a 'cultural' contaminant from the time and place of the biblical authors. Why is slavery discarded by theologians as a betrayal of the Gospel when patriarchal hierarchy and androcentrism are *not*? The lack of logical coherence in the application of the Bible to the world of believers was exacerbated by the purported postmodern position of 'anything goes'.

One problem, it seems to me, is that biblical scholarship was not necessarily developed as a wing of constructive theological inquiry; if anything, we were glad to be 'scientific' in our descriptive study of the Bible and the *theological meaning* of 'what really happened' was beyond the scope of our research. If, in the early years of biblical criticism, historical critics had been the enemies of believers for casting doubt on the 'historicity' of biblical miracles as revelations, now as born-again literary critics or postmodernists we were friend to all, proclaiming 'your reading is as good as mine.' Everybody is invited to the interpretive task, and all efforts are welcome and equal, to be negotiated with civility and appreciation.

All Readings Created Equal?
But all readings are *not* equal. Some are uninformed, uncontextualized, selective, or downright manipulative. We may have taught ourselves to look suspiciously upon coherence as some winning editor's attempt to silence divergent opinions buried below the surface of the text, but we have had nothing to put in its place. In current construals of textual meaning, it sometimes seems that there are more 'gaps' in the text (empty spaces in which some critics adjure us to insert ourselves midrashically) than stable pathways. In fact, we are searching for a 'meta-hermeneutic' to guide us from grammar-and-lexicon to city hall and Congress. Who *says* that the Book of Joshua should outweigh the books of Ruth and Esther in shaping our understanding of what to do with that pesky Other in our midst? It behooves interpreters to make clear how and why they interpret as they do, and to keep a rigorous eye on one's own interpretive biases and outcomes. On what grounds does one say *No!* to white supremacist readings of the text that casts the white race as God's eternal chosen, while saying *Yes!* to feminist or other liberationist readings which are aimed at deconstructing the whole parcel of dualistic and ideologically tainted ideas that suggest God loves some and not others?[3]

Many theologians throughout history have recognized the need to be able to 'update'[4] the text if it is to be applied fruitfully to their times and

---

3. This critique reflects a classically 'Universalist' position.
4. Or 'discard'?

communities.⁵ One method was based on using an appeal to 'tradition' to determine a group's 'canon-within-a-canon'; other options included adding 'reason' and/or a theology of ongoing revelation to the mix. But do such approaches *really* do the trick? Not only is 'reason' captive to socialization, teaching us *not* to see what needs to remain hidden for ideological purposes, but the so-called 'tradition' to which one appealed for answers was by no means inclusive or any less culturally captive than the biblical text itself. White supremacists have their own traditions of reading the texts to which they can appeal and feel justified, as does the male-exclusive Roman Catholic hierarchy in its failure to address the realities of human sexuality in all its variations. So, faith, reason, tradition, and revelation provide no sure yardstick—these will vary, because they are human constructs and humans are situated within a matrix of shifting values, authorities and experience. No wonder New Testament critic Daniel Patte argues so forcefully for the adoption of 'androcritical multidimensional exegesis', similar in nature to what is offered below.⁶

A Faith-Based Initiative: An Intertextual Hermeneutic
Perhaps the most successful meta-hermeneutic for the church has been the appeal to the Gospel and the person of Jesus of Nazareth whose story is narrated there. Evangelicals are always asking themselves, 'What would Jesus do?' Certainly, the story of a Palestinian Jew, a sage-healer-prophet-exorcist, going up against Imperial Rome with nothing but the Hebrew Bible and some great parables in his hand thrills us in the same way the tale of David toppling Goliath with some smooth stones does. Expect the unexpected, the content of the Gospels counsels us; look for God on the margins, and redraw the circle so that the despised Other ('sinners', 'gentiles', whatever) are within its boundaries of humanity. The ignominious death as a convicted criminal proclaimed as some kind of a *victory*? Well, *that's* unexpected, all right. But does it leave some of us wondering if the Osama bin Ladens of the world merit a bit more theological analysis than an angry government and its public are prepared to grant? If we construct the Bible as an overall story of the plucky underdogs whom God protects, nourishes and grants victory under unexpected circumstances, then are we willing to see ourselves as the rich stratified Canaanite city-states, the hard-hearted Pharaoh, or the Roman Empire? Can believers in the rich nations of the world see themselves as Job, a wealthy man suddenly encountering the underside

---

5. Clearly, the New Testament's 'Call no man your father' (Mt. 23.9, RSV) was *never* a big hit within some hierarchies.

6. *Ethics of Biblical Interpretation: A Reevaluation* (Louisville, KY: Westminster/John Knox Press, 1995).

of his society, when they would be so much more comfortable thinking of themselves as Suffering Servants carrying the White Man's Burden? We must de-colonize our own methods, identities and interests before we can ever expect to do justice to either the Bible or society.

Aside from the persistent problem of 'who's who' in mapping the Gospels onto the modern world, we have a few other kinks in using the Jesus of the Gospels as our measuring rod for all truth.[7] First, are we so *very* sure Jesus said this or that? Certainties are just as scarce in the study of the New Testament as they are in the world of the Hebrew Bible. Next, there are things upon which Jesus is never said to have pronounced a final position: *in vitro* fertilization, the ordination of women, homosexuality, and cloning are topics that immediately spring to this interpreter's mind. Finally, there are things that *are* attributed to Jesus or found in the New Testament writers that are worthy of critical dispute and whose ethics must be addressed. It's not fair making Jesus into a feminist, if the point of contrast is based on Christian constructions of alleged Jewish misogyny and legalism.[8] Should the Passion Narratives *ever* be read liturgically without some gesture toward the legacy of anti-Judaism they created and perpetuate, yea, even unto the death of Jewish communities throughout the Christian world in medieval and modern times? I think not.

2. *Toward a Multidimensional Aesthetic Theology*

Embracing the Gaps

The wonder of the disciplines of biblical studies and 'biblical theology' in such a time of critical uncertainty is that we are all invited to play along, alter the rules of game, or even find a new game board on which to play. While this may make zealots at either end of the continuum a bit queasy, it at least has the advantage of getting more people involved in the critical issues of how the Bible relates to a historical past, to the church and synagogue, to society and to a pluralistic world. *Perhaps* the meanings of our meanings are to be found in the *struggle* to create and live by them, as well as in the *content* of those meanings we choose. If we remember that the Sacred, as known through the Bible, is a dynamic Presence which is often marked by an absence—no idol in the Holy of Holies[9]—perhaps we may learn to take our gaps in certainty as pathways

---

7. 'Who would Jesus bomb?', 'What would Jesus drive?', have replaced the positivist question, 'What would Jesus do?' (WWJD, now popular as jewelry).

8. Katharina von Kellenbach, *Anti-Judaism in Feminist Religious Writings* (AAR Cultural Criticism Series, 1; Atlanta: Scholars Press, 1994), pp. 57-90.

9. This is very different from the ancient Egyptian view: there is no greater insult

in and of themselves, a well-traveled approach to understanding that the Bible itself endorses. The text is that 'gap' in the oppressive discourse of despair that piles up on either side of us[10] like mountains of water in the parting of the Sea of Reeds; we go through in the empty space the Redeemer creates. In this gap, we may discover that God is with us in our journey to something more whole-some. The gap itself should be treated as an invitation to redeem a text.

The Reality of the Text

I have always encountered the text, even those pericopes I hate, as a genuine *reality*—almost an 'entity'—over against which I am set (the Hebrew word for this is *neged*) as reader and artist.[11] As I would say of a piece of art I just *had* to purchase[12] or a new tool I *had* to learn to use, the text 'grabs' me. It's got 'carrying power'. Even from across the room, it captures the eye and engages the heart.[13] One is drawn, willy-nilly, to stand before it and gaze into a different reality from one's own. The text really exists. There are words in a certain order, and syntax, and content to be had from it. The text is, in my opinion, *not* entirely plastic, a shape-shifting entity that responds like a mood ring to its reader's present desires. Like it or not, it can't and doesn't say just *anything*, and it says *certain* things very forcefully indeed, for good or ill. The text is not the Presence itself, but it witnesses to it. We know we are in the presence of a Presence when the text takes us in its grasp—but as C.S. Lewis once wrote in *The Screwtape Letters*, this

---

to a god than to proclaim 'Your shrine is empty!' ('The Contendings of Horus and Seth', in W.K. Simpson (ed.), *The Literature of Ancient Egypt: An Anthology of Stories, Instructions, Stelae, Autobiographies, and Poetry* (New Haven: Yale University Press, 3rd edn, 2003), pp. 91-103 (94).

10. 'Nothing will ever change...nothing can be done...nothing *you* do will ever change anything...why even try?..why not just give up and enjoy your piece of the pie? ...'

11. All great art has the potential to engage its audience in a powerful, personal way. For some of us, life can be divided into 'before' and 'after' participating in such an event. For a ghetto teenager, it was the sculpture of Rodin, regardless of content (a nude Balzac), and Walt Whitman's *Leaves of Grass* that transformed me forever.

12. Glass—molten, shifting, light-made-concrete glass!

13. Jews reading the Talmud might conclude that the Torah is a Lover who beckons and fulfills, demanding complete allegiance. See Ari Elyon, 'The Torah as Love Goddess', in Michael Chernick (ed.), *Essential Papers on the Talmud* (New York: New York University Press, 1994), pp. 463-76. Talking about the text this way—as Person—in Christian feminist circles will get you labeled a Neo-Orthodox collaborator, however! See Elisabeth Schüssler Fiorenza, *In Memory of Her: A Feminist Theological Reconstruction of Christian Origins* (New York: Crossroad, 1983), pp. 14-21.

Presence cannot ravish; it can only woo.[14] We are not forced into submission; we are invited to 'turn aside' and see this great sight. We read the text and reread it, and it is not exhausted of meaning or surprise, or as the rabbis said of the Torah, 'Turn her and turn her; find everything in her' (*Pirqe Avot* 5).[15]

A Hermeneutic of Beauty and Useful Ugliness
For me, taught as a child to read the biblical text as a paean to white Christian privilege, my readings today stand in striking opposition to the meanings I inherited and now resist at every opportunity. Problems there are, but gifts and joy are found there, too. In asking questions of my own interpretive strategies, I have taught myself and my students to take experience of art and the drive to creativity[16] seriously as tools for meaning-making in interpretation. Paraphrasing William Morris of the Arts and Crafts movement, I tell students: Have nothing in your interpretation of the text that you do not know to be useful or believe to be beautiful. Ask of your reading: Is it large enough to express the surprises and ambiguity of the interaction of human and divine realities? Is it beautiful enough to capture something of the joyousness of a Creator who calls creation very good indeed, creates Leviathan for the fun of it, and yet hears the cries of the enslaved?[17]

As a feminist critic, I readily admit that parts of the text are both ugly in the original and devastating in later, real-world application.[18] If our texts have possessed us and expressed us, then even what is ugly and evil in them can be considered useful when employed critically in the service of justice. We *need* to question slavery, and sexual oppressions and our constructions of reality: *all* people do, anywhere and in every time. Yet, such difficult topics do not 'play' very well in a materialist, 'free' (rather than 'fair') market society which seeks moral and metaphysical

---

14. *The Screwtape Letters and Screwtape Proposes a Toast* (New York: Macmillan, 1966), p. 38.

15. I find the power of the text to be manifested in its ability to create communities charged with the quest of un-masking the powers of oppression. Hence, I argue based more on the *function* of the text for its communities, not its origin ('divine') or content (unique revelation).

16. I privilege these aspects not just because of an artist's personal preference (though that subject location certainly informs my textual sympathies), but because of the text's statement about the *imago dei* of the Creator in humanity, and our role as caretakers and co-creators of a good earth. The rationale for this is, however, beyond the scope of this essay.

17. I know of no other deity of the ancient Near East who holds regular conversation with those on society's margins.

18. See Carole R. Fontaine, '"Many Devices" ', Chapter 6 in this volume.

capsules of meaning as a medicine for despair.[19] You may hear the occasional sermon on the sufferings (but more likely, the 'patience') of Job, but you will seldom hear about the gang rape of a nameless woman in Judges 19. Yet those things happen to women everywhere around the world without much comment or public outrage. Our text 'authorizes' us to raise such painful topics—requires it, even when we feel that the text itself does not sufficiently critique the causes of suffering. The text invites us to make the ugly beautiful, transforming and redeeming it in the real world of experience by making us see what we would prefer to leave in shadow. This is very useful indeed.[20]

Transformational, Generative Content
Along with my notions of beauty as a hermeneutic and its correlate of 'useful ugliness', I find the Bible's thematic 'plot', if you will, to be one of transformation and generation. The text speaks of a Presence whose presence and absence[21] transforms the life of the world, and generates a new way of being.[22] Interpretations should strive to do the same. If the outcome of meaning-making is nothing more than reinforcement of the status quo, or self-congratulation, we would do well to be suspicious of our desires for such readings. Who or what are we trying to exclude, and how shall we transform our blindness into sight? Whether

19. Walter Brueggemann, 'A Text That Redescribes', *TToday* 58 (2002), pp. 526-40.
20. I learned the principle of beauty as a hermeneutic from the sages who wrote the Bible's wisdom literature (see 'Concluding Semi-Scientific Postscript', in Carole R. Fontaine, *Smooth Words: Women, Proverbs and Performance in Biblical Wisdom* [JSOTSup, 356; Sheffield: Sheffield Academic Press, 2002]), and from conversations with Claus Westermann, who knew a thing or two about beauty in the Bible ('Beauty in the Hebrew Bible', in Athalya Brenner and Carole R. Fontaine (eds.), *A Feminist Companion to Reading the Bible: Approaches, Methods, Strategies* [trans. Üte Oestringer and Carole R. Fontaine; Sheffield: Sheffield Academic Press, 1997], pp. 584-602). Beauty is an 'event' wherein the human becomes most fully human by encountering the Creator in the mode of 'blessing' (rather than 'saving'). Taking Westermann's view a little further, this artist finds that beauty can also be related to that 'redeeming' aspect also.
21. My close-reading publisher wonders here if a presence (capitalized or not) can really *be* present or absent. While the epistemology of religious experience and the nature of the universe is beyond the scope of my topic here, one may turn reliably to quantum physics, chaos theory, or human brain studies to adduce evidence of various sorts that more things exist in Heaven and Earth than can currently be explained. I do, however, base my statement on experience rather than faith, in its classic understandings.
22. I also endorse a theology which understands that the life of the world equally transforms the Presence, at least in the ways It makes Itself known to the world.

one says 'Exodus' or 'Resurrection', the story is one of possible *change* and growth of something new in the wake of that transformation.

Textual Transparency
I also counsel my students to observe closely the 'hows' of the text's delivery of its message, and to strive for an apprehension of the text which understands the limits and the possibilities of the internal textual aesthetic. What does it *mean* that so much of the Bible is poetry or story, and not simply historical documentation? Much is made of ambiguity and the open-ended nature of the ancient, alien text, but it seems to me that there is a suggestive *transparency* about that ambiguity. That is, in spots the text is pretty clear about *not* giving answers, driving us to come to terms with our lack of certainties. The ambiguities left for us to puzzle out are presented with the same aplomb that other texts (the much proclaimed 'Gospel Truth' of Deuteronomy or the New Testament) reiterate *exactly* what we are to take as True and Proved. Our hermeneutics should be likewise transparent; no one should be claiming the one, correct, inevitable meaning of any text. The best we can do is rule out some meanings on lack of textual markers that might support our reading. We cannot ever be certain we are wholly correct; nor should we speak as though we are. To achieve this, I juxtapose the regulations and creedal statements about the morality and necessity of something like 'holy war' with all those places in the text where the Other has become a blessing to the self-styled 'chosen'. Such a strategy demonstrates that even those things clearly and unanimously proclaimed as patently 'true' didn't seem quite so certain for the original communities or later faithful interpreters.[23]

3. Reading in Place: Reflections on Reading the Bible after Sept. 11, 2001

A Persistent Heresy: Anti-Judaism in Christian and Feminist Readings of the Bible
Why or how, you might ask, does reading the Bible after terrorist attacks on a 'Bible-believing' people bring us to a discussion of an old, *old* paradigm of reading that privileges one People of the Book over another? It is a commonplace in Human Rights work that during times of conflict and social stress, one must be particularly observant about the recurrence of old dysfunctions, of which Christian anti-Judaism is surely the most enduring in Christian theology. Further, the pattern

---

23. Hosea's reinterpretation of the incident in the valley of Jezreel, believed by the authors/editors of the Book of Kings to have been commanded by God, is a biblical example of reinterpretation *within* the text.

of how Christians have spoken of Jewish texts is being refracted in a new spectrum in the way many Muslims now speak of Christian and Jewish texts, which in theory they accept as normative. Has religious history taught our Islamic friends a well-hallowed, pernicious method by which to claim 'Our text is better than yours.'?[24] Studying the hermeneutical methods of the textual dismissal of the Other may teach us to spy out the next form of oppressive textual practices, especially now that the West has been so easily brought to think of Muslims as the 'true' enemy of the faith.

My theological education taught me that the proper way to read was as a 'pseudo-male', and not just as any male, but as a white Northern European Christian male, since they were the ones who had produced the theological methods and norms of my subject matter.[25] As a folklorist, I was trained to an objectivity that I now know cannot and does not exist: merely a collector and arranger of disparate materials of various peoples and epochs, I am in no position to comment on how such materials are interpreted by the folk who claim them. That is, I may document the various interpretations, but to call any one of them a '*mis*-reading' by the folk who made it? I may say it is an anti-Semitic, a misogynist, a white supremacist, or a classist reading, but a '*mis*-reading' I was taught that I may *not* say.[26] While I think it is fully warranted to make such politico-ethical evaluations, I tell you that some of us are transgressing some of our most fundamental training when we engage in such a practice. For me, the discipline of folklore allowed me considerable advantages in being able to hear both how my black ghetto used the Exodus as a text of future hope, while simultaneously maintaining the value and validity of the Jewish reading of the same book as a liberating past, now betrayed, or at least placed in question for many by the events of the Holocaust. As a folklorist and literary critic, I was not obliged to choose a correct reading; I gave myself permission to love them both. Yet, in a world where presidents use the Gospel of John to demonize an enemy or use the Bible as a 'wedge issue' in cynical political maneuverings, it is time for the experts to give their opinion as well. At least *we* are

---

24. One Muslim feminist of my acquaintance defends the Qur'anic creation stories by asking her audiences ironically, 'Have you been reading *Genesis*?'

25. Heather McKay, 'On the Future of Feminist Biblical Criticism', in Brenner and Fontaine (eds.), *Approaches, Methods, Strategies*, pp. 61-83.

26. Even the discipline of folklore has become political: folklorist Alan Dundes presents the view that 'evil folklore' can and does exist, and racist and sexist items of traditional culture ought to be labeled as such ('The Ritual Murder or Blood Libel Legend: A Study of Anti-Semitic Victimization through Projective Inversion', in Alan Dundes (ed.), *The Blood Libel Legend: A Casebook in Anti-Semitic Folklore* [Madison: University of Wisconsin, 1991], pp. 336-76 [335]).

informed by data as well as our ideologies. One point we need to make clear: Muslims are Semites, too. We must not simply replace one bad reading with another, substituting Islam for Judaism in our theological strivings to articulate confessional loyalties.

Readers of feminist theology know that 'location, location, location.' is the battle cry of interpreters, since we think that no such thing as a value-neutral or unbiased reading can exist. So we must ask: if we inhabit the region of Christian feminism, are we obliged to keep the anti-Semitism of the tradition that also informs our dearest theologies of liberation? Today I read in mostly white, mostly affluent Newton, Massachusetts, but I am fortunate to have sustained multicultural contact with Muslims and other world citizens through my work on Human Rights issues. We stand on the far edge of the millennial shift into a world of intifadas and terrors on every hand (or so we are told). Our theological world's supposedly seamless connection to the promises of both Testaments, Hebrew and Christian, has been violently torn asunder by the events of this new century — at least in the opinion of the present speaker. Others see the agonies of the world as sure sign that the Bible's predictions are *indeed* true, and believe that the end of the world is at hand. Religion, so often the province of the margins in technologically driven capitalist societies, has become central in all kinds of debates, and we have seen the worst of what it creates in Washington, Tehran, and Gaza. In no case do women profit from the upsurge of 'tradition' when the tradition is itself patriarchal and exclusive.

Never before has interfaith work been so difficult and so necessary, as politics have shown us. Christians have a way of reading their New Testament that is dismissive of the Scripture from which it originally came as a liberation movement for a people under brutal occupation. In our new climate, I believe Christians are coming to understand what it means when a 'new' group seemingly tries to usurp the sacred texts that have served so well. Muslims, in their acceptance of the Bible, but their insistence of Muhammed as the last and best prophet and the Qur'an as the uncreated word of Allah, present a direct challenge to Christian supersessionist theologies of Scripture. Now that Christendom has an upstart, younger sibling, the 'middle child' has the possibility for a better understanding of how Christian readings of the Hebrew text wound the children of the Elder sibling. Today, in the wake of the September 11, 2001 terrorist attacks, the entire world is affected by the way Christians, Muslims, and Jews read their holy books. In the global context in which we live secularists, humanistic or capitalist, read the Hebrew Bible also, and are affected by the kinds of interpretations we choose to make of it. If I usually find myself in the position of being a 'resistant reader' — that is, as a feminist woman

I must read with suspicion and critical clarity lest I be seduced by the categories the text presents to me as divinely fixed and ordained — now I find I am also a resisting writer, forced to speak. Quite frankly, most Christian 'readings' of the Hebrew Bible, feminist or otherwise, give me 'the willies', and Muslim knowledge of and attitudes toward the Torah are just heart-breaking.

My analysis here pertains to the ways Christian feminists and post-Christian feminists of various sorts read, not because they are the only readers, or even my favorite readers, but because I hold membership of sorts in these groups and I must be accountable should they repeat the errors of the past. I will necessarily present only partial surveys, piecemeal samples of Christian readings, since I cannot and should not speak for all Christians everywhere. The focus will be upon the presentation of Jews in biblical scholarship as performed by Christians, usually European or American, typically white, generally male. I will also take up similar questions in the realm of feminist Christian and post-Christian portrayals of the Hebrew Bible, its god and its people.

What Makes a Reading?
Now a good 'reading', just to review what we have all been taught in school since the onset of the historical and literary critical methods, is one that is *contextualized*, as we have said: a reading which deals with the social, historical and literary location of the text under consideration.[27] We may not take just the parts that are appealing, rip them out of their historical context and apply them, fast and loose, without making the principles of application and reuse clear.[28] Further, a good reading should be 'plausible' — that is, it cannot falsify its data, the text; it should be comprehensive, coherent and reproducible. If only an expert with a very particular set of tools and experiences can demonstrate the validity of a particular reading, then we have every right to be suspicious. Ordinary readers (those not especially trained in languages of the text or critical methodology) make plausible and coherent readings, too, and sometimes ones which are more faithful to the structures in the text than the ones put forth by the experts. A final criterion is that a good reading must be 'self-critical'; this means that elite men must be aware that they have been taught to read from a vantage point which privileges their readings as true, authentic, universal descriptions of reality

---

27. John Dominic Crossan, *Who Killed Jesus? Exposing the Roots of Anti-Semitism in the Gospel Story of the Death of Jesus* (San Francisco: HarperCollins, 1995); see his discussion of 'selective' and 'consistent' contextualization (38).

28. So much for the prophecies of Isaiah as used to 'predict' the coming of Jesus as Messiah.

to the exclusion of any other viewpoint.[29] Members of groups that are not part of the dominant elite (women, Jews, Muslims, racial minorities, gay and lesbian persons, children, the homeless, the handicapped, etc.) — all these are called upon to read in a self-critical way, too.[30] Today members, elite or ordinary, of any group that is *not* white, male European-American Christian need to realize that they have usually been excluded from the traditional horizon of concerns of elite Christian readers, and that this may well distort the meanings they take away both from the secondary literature and the text itself.

All this being the case, I find anti-Semitic and anti-Judaic readings of the Hebrew Bible *almost* inevitable when one reads through the polemics of the New Testament.[31] Such readings are context-sensitive and historically grounded: they place Jesus among his people who largely reject him and his message. Such readings are coherent: beginning with a world who knew him not, this light is assailed by shadows even unto death. Comprehensiveness and reproducibility are salient features of anti-Judaic readings, too. The fine treatises on the Hebrew Bible by Tertullian, Augustine, Jerome, Chrysostom, Aquinas, Luther, Calvin, Barth, and the rest of the theological elite meet most of the literary criteria I posed for adequate readings. I will also add that we will find such anti-Judaic readings in the writings of the sainted mothers as well (Mary Daly, Carol Christ, Rosemary Ruether, Gerda Lerner, Riane Eisler, Gerda Weiler, Elizabeth Moltmann-Wendell and others), though anti-Judaism usually appears there for different reasons. But because I am a feminist, raised in the midst of feisty women of ghettos, black and Jewish, I am quite capable of finding a way to reject *all* these readings of

---

29. For discussion of what makes a 'good' reading, see semiotician Mieke Bal, *Lethal Love: Feminist Literary Reading of Biblical Love Stories* (Bloomington: Indiana University Press, 1987), pp. 1-15; for ethical accountability in androcritical readings, see Daniel Patte, *Ethics of Biblical Interpretation: A Reevaluation* (Louisville, KY: Westminster/John Knox Press, 1995), pp. 1-36.

30. I assume children will require some guidance here: what I mean is that I rather expect a child to read *as a child*, and to cry out that the 'Emperor has no clothes' when that is how it seems to her. Children are excellent, attentive readers: they know if you miss a line of their favorite bed-time story. I suggest that we honor rather than dismiss the questions children ask about the text.

31. So, too, with Jon Levenson, 'Is There a Counterpart in the Hebrew Bible to New Testament AntiSemitism?', *JES* 22 (1985), pp. 242-60, and Krister Stendahl, 'Anti-Semitism', in Bruce M. Metzger and Michael D. Coogan (eds.), *Oxford Companion to the Bible* (New York: Oxford University Press, 1993), pp. 32-34 (34). I will also maintain the difference between the terms 'anti-Semitism', a nineteenth-century secular racial theory, and 'anti-Judaism', a theologically based rejection of Judaism, though I do find that anti-Judaic writings often display an anti-Semitic tenor as well.

the Hebrew Bible, its god and its meaning, even without labeling them as 'mis-readings'. Here is the reason why: most mainstream Christian and/or feminist readings fail to meet the criterion of self-criticism.

Anti-Judaism as Ideological Reading
New Testament scholar Krister Stendahl writes that anti-Semitism 'follows Christianity as its dark shadow', and is that faith's most persistent heresy.[32] Anti-Judaism is the theological backdrop of anti-Semitism, and consists of a kind of rhetoric and philosophical/theological approach to Judaism which renders that parent faith as a negative setting or outdated remnant to the new daughter religion. If classical anti-Semitism is, as Joshua Trachtenberg has styled it, a kind of medieval 'hang-over' afflicting the modern unconscious, then theological anti-Judaism is part of the 'intellectual camouflage' that allows the former to flourish largely unchecked by making it theologically respectable.[33]

Anti-Judaic readings miss the greater contexts of the formation of the Hebrew Bible, the Jewish context of Jesus' life and message, and the context of readers today who inherit a legacy of anti-Semitism and Christian violence against the Other which must be brought to any current reading. The Hebrew Bible, whether read by churchmen, scholars or feminists, is seldom the *primary* focus of interest; instead, it usually serves as an ideological counterpoint for the creation of readings which serve to create Christian and other identities for the readers. Over time, however, we *do* see a decided shift in the methods used to denigrate the First Testament in favor of the Second. These changes roughly coincide with the Enlightenment and the rise of biblical historical criticism as perhaps *the* lens through which biblical texts are read by modern elite readers. Prior to the growth, beginning in the Enlightenment, of a critical understanding of religion as a diverse *human* phenomenon, we find that the Church Fathers, the Roman Church and the great Protestant Reformers are of one mind. For them, the Hebrew Bible, like all 'Scripture', is true and authoritative for the Church. By this term, the pre-critical ecclesiastical elite readers mostly meant that the Hebrew Bible witnesses truthfully to

---

32. Stendahl, 'AntiSemitism', pp. 32-34 (33-34). The present writer objects here to the continued stereotypical use of metaphors of darkness for 'evil' in the work of European and American theologians. Even 'shadow', because of its psychological loading, may not be precise enough in indicating those things we desire to reject.

33. Joshua Trachtenberg, *The Devil and the Jews: The Medieval Conception of the Jew and its Relation to Modern AntiSemitism* (New Haven: Yale University Press, 1943), pp. 4-5. Crossan notes that 'They are equally despicable but differently so' (*Who Killed Jesus?*, p. 38).

the coming of Jesus of Nazareth as the Christ. For pre-critical readers, Jews who rejected their own messiah then added to their calumny by perverting the 'plain sense' of Scripture, in refusing to read the 'new' Christian message as the basic meaning of the 'old' text.[34] That Jews should continue to deny the 'plain sense' of their own book makes perfect sense for these theologians, since the coming of Christ causes a new people to be elected, effectively displacing the Jews. To these basic charges against the Jews, others may be added, especially that of 'deicide'—that Jews are the killers of Christ and have freely accepted 'blood-guilt' for this act throughout all their generations. In this scenario, hatred and persecution of Jews almost became a matter of faith for Christian believers.[35] Elite readers within the Christian hierarchy had, from time to time, attempted to ameliorate the effects of such a polemic on living Jewish communities, but minor clergy, through preaching and liturgical passion plays, routinely continued to incite laypeople to violence with virtual impunity.[36]

With the rise of biblical criticism, we discern a turn away from the earlier forms found in Christian anti-Judaism. Once all Scripture had come to be understood in relationship to new paradigms—historicity, science, evolution, psychology—the negative role of Judaism and its Bible continued, but with a markedly changed emphasis. For the most part, only conservative traditionalists, trying to live flat in a world newly rounded, argued that the Hebrew Bible's prophetic claims were to be understood as a witness to the coming of Jesus. Instead, the Hebrew Bible now becomes a remnant of a superstitious, legalistic, petty way of relating to God which has been refurbished, reformed and reissued under a new covenant. Whence this need to paint Judaism into the theological shadows? Jon Levenson writes:

> A prime objective of interreligious polemics is to make the competitor look...ridiculous... [A] religion centered on a Torah given in love and able to increase in love, on a Torah through which the Holy Spirit still speaks, on a Torah which holds out the possibility of reconciliation through repentance by the grace of God but without an innocent victim or other intermediation, on a Torah open to Jew and gentile alike, if only the latter will choose it—this is a religion too close to early Christianity not to threaten it.[37]

---

34. Rosemary Ruether, *Faith and Fratricide: The Theological Roots of Anti-Semitism* (New York: Seabury Press, 1974), pp. 117-82.

35. This erupts most especially during the period of the Crusades (Trachtenberg, *Devil*, 167-69), though not in every location.

36. Trachtenberg, *Devil*, pp. 7, 168. See, especially, the role of the cult of the Flagellants in inciting anti-Jewish riots during the outbreak of the Black Plague, p. 105.

37. Levenson, 'Counterpart', pp. 242-60 (254).

4. *Reading for the Best*

Charlotte Klein, in *Anti-Judaism in Christian Theology*,[38] makes a compelling study of how anti-Judaism in New Testament theology makes its presence felt in Christian readings of the Bible, even when many of the elite scholarly readers are far from anti-Semitic in their regular thought or conduct. Pointing out that German Christian theology still proceeds in the absence of a vigorous Jewish community and in the midst of massive repression of the history of German anti-Semitism, its practitioners generally make use of dated and biased material on Judaism which they continue to reproduce uncritically. In her analysis, she points to key features which define modern theological anti-Judaism in the age of biblical criticism. These are:

1. Judaism has been superseded and replaced by Christianity.
2. Consequently—this is rarely expressed so brutally today—Judaism has scarcely any right to continue to exist.
3. In any case its teachings and ethical values are inferior to those of Christianity.
4. The Christian theologian continues to assume that he has the right to pass judgment on Judaism, its destiny, and its task in the world—even to be permitted to dictate this task.
5. Only some few real specialists in the departments of Jewish studies make a fresh examination of authentically Jewish sources. In most cases the material collected in certain works about the turn of the century is taken over as a matter of course and quoted, without bothering about the Jewish interpretation of the sources or considering how the Jews see themselves.
6. We often find that the same author when he expressly speaks of Judaism in an ecumenical context has a strikingly different approach from that which he adopts when he is dealing mainly with the Christian religion and mentions Judaism more or less incidentally.[39]

That remarks that directly smack of anti-Judaism or worse, anti-Semitism, are made as off-hand comments by Christian New Testament and Old Testament theologians is of particular interest to this literary critic. In such unguarded, less-than-careful statements by writers, one is likely to see evidence of deeply-held beliefs, normally subject to self-censorship, surfacing in 'throw-away' lines or asides. Consider some of the following on this topic, written by our respected fathers of the discipline of Biblical Studies.

In Joachim Jeremias' theology of the New Testament we read:

---

38. Trans. Edward Quinn (Philadelphia: Fortress Press, 1978).
39. Klein, *Anti-Judaism*, p. 7.

'*Children*. Closely connected with the new position which Jesus accords to women in the sphere of the approaching *basileia* is a view of children. In the world of Jesus, children, like women, were counted as things of little value. Jesus, on the other hand…promises salvation to children as such… As a result, he brings children nearer to God than adults'.[40]

Now, to anyone who has read the Book of Lamentations or who knows anything about Judaism—or even the other patriarchies of antiquity for that matter—this is theological tripe of the most pernicious kind. As Klein notes, if Midrash Rabbah on Lamentations tells us that the Shekinah goes into exile not with the Sanhedrin, but rather with the little children, this hardly argues for a climate in which children were held as valueless.[41]

E.P. Sanders writes in his *Paul and Palestinian Judaism*:

> The frequent Christian charge against Judaism, it must be recalled, is not that some individual Jews misunderstood, misapplied and abused their religion, but that *Judaism necessarily tends* towards petty legalism, self-serving and self-deceiving casuistry, and a mixture of arrogance and lack of confidence in God. But the surviving Jewish literature is as free of these characteristics as any I have ever read.[42]

In surveying the work of European and American scholars on Rabbinic Judaism, Sanders comments trenchantly that 'what is striking about all these works is that the authors feel no need to *defend* their view of Rabbinic Judaism or even to turn to the sources to verify it'.[43] Though outstanding Christian Judaicists like George Foot Moore called New Testament scholarship to account for this bias early in this century,[44] such work, while cited by theologians, makes no noticeable impact on their bias as they paint Jesus against a degraded backdrop, all the better to make him shine. It is—perhaps—these lopsided and debased views of Second Temple and Rabbinic Judaism which allow the theologies of New Testament scholars to proceed on 'seamlessly', as Emile Fackenheim has put it,[45] after the events of the Holocaust became widely known. Jews had already been theoretically disposed of in Christian theology; secular anti-Semitism's rush to finish up the task was apparently worth little discussion as far as the Christian eschatology and hermeneutical programs were concerned.

40. Joachim Jeremias, *New Testament: The Proclamation of Jesus* (New York: Scribner, 1971), cited in Klein, *Anti-Judaism*, pp. 8-9.
41. Jeremias, *Theology of the New Testament*.
42. Philadelphia: Fortress Press, 1977, p. 427.
43. Sanders, *Paul*, p. 54.
44. 'Christian Writers on Judaism', HTR 14 (1921), pp. 197-254.
45. *The Jewish Bible after the Holocaust: A Re-reading* (Bloomington: Indiana University Press, 1990), pp. 19-23.

We might think that it is the continued exposure of New Testament scholarship to the bitter polemics against the Jews found in their texts which make these scholars especially susceptible to anti-Judaic readings, especially in a Europe largely made free of Jews. But while I am sure that is true, we find that 'Old Testament' scholars often share the same biases as their brothers.[46] Speaking of Jesus, Martin Noth writes in *The History of Israel*:

> In him the history of Israel had come, rather, to its real end. What did belong to the history of Israel was the process of his rejection and condemnation by the Jerusalem religious community. It had not discerned in him the goal to which the history of Israel had secretly been leading... Only a few had joined him, and from them something new had proceeded. The Jerusalem religious community...kept aloof from this new movement. Hereafter the history of Israel moved quickly to its end.[47]

That a Jewish state now existed at the time of the second edition of this work had no impact on this particular Christian view of Jewish history.

On the whole, 'Old Testament' scholars proceed differently from their New Testament colleagues when they read their subject text as 'Christian Scripture'. One is allowed, nay, almost *required*, to paint a glowing portrait of the 'uniqueness of Israel', that old slogan of the Neo-Orthodox Biblical Theology movement which flourished in the post-war period. This is especially so with reference to ancient Israel's alleged philosophical and moral superiority to the 'pagan' cultures surrounding it. This theological purity of 'our' heritage is vigorously maintained while simultaneously pushing any unpleasant (i.e., not leading directly to Christianity) or syncretistic practices into the realm of degraded 'popular religion'. While this *does* require scholars to ignore both archaeological and inscriptional evidence that muddies up their reconstructions, it proves to be a useful skill for maintaining Israel's superiority when things like the Moabite Stone or the Hittite archives from Late Bronze Age Anatolia turn up. In those materials, we find that the supposed uniqueness of Israel in its understanding of a god not bounded by 'nature' (as pagan deities are purported to be), its view of history as linear (rather than pagan 'cyclical' time tied to nature), with an interactive deity whose will is felt in real lives and historical events (including holy war) is matched, point by point, with similar perspectives by 'pagan' theologians, historiographers, and royal writers. As Levenson has pointed out, not only does the anti-Semitism of the New Testament have its parallel in the Hebrew Bible in that text's polemical treatment of

---

46. At that point in biblical scholarship, 'sisters' had yet to raise their voices.
47. Martin Noth, *The History of Israel* (New York: HarperCollins College Division, 2nd edn, 1960); cited in Klein, *Anti-Judaism*, pp. 7-8.

pagan neighbors and indigenous peoples of Canaan, but the New Testament scholarly paradigm of ignoring the parallel culture or distorting it as a foil to one's own finds its parallel in Old Testament studies as well.[48] Once the Babylonian Captivity draws to a close, 'Old Testament' scholars reach an impasse in their lavish descriptions of superiority; now that prophecy (the road to Christ, and hence highly valued) has dried up, Judaism is portrayed as a moribund, decaying edifice which must naturally degenerate into legalism so that Jesus can arrive to assert superiority over it. As we near the New Testament period, we find that Christian scholarly interest in the religious history and thought of the Jews is, as George Foot Moore wrote over a century ago, either 'apologetic or polemic'.[49]

I am sorry to say that it would be easy to multiply the examples of such theological judgments rendered by Christian theologians. But we are speaking here of elite readers—that is, critically trained scholarly readers using 'modern' methodologies. Perhaps ordinary Christian readers read their Bibles differently on the subject of Judaism?

Ordinary Readers of the 'Old Testament'

William L. Holladay's introductory comments in *Long Ago God Spoke: How Christians May Hear the Old Testament Today*[50] are instructive on the subject of how ordinary Christians read their Old Testament. In his list of *barriers*, we find:

1. 'If Jesus is the full revelation of God, why bother with what has come before?' (Marcion's view)
2. The Old Testament is just so darn long; who can be expected to read it all?
3. 'Much of the Old Testament is only of antiquarian interest'. What do Christians need all those genealogies for?

In his list of 'more substantial objections' he notes:

4. 'There is so much of the Old Testament that requires us to suspend our disbelief', its stories leaving us 'puzzled and dubious'.
5. 'Long, long ago in a galaxy far, far away': the Old Testament is from a largely unrecoverable time and place, and 'The world of the Old Testament, being even older [than the New Testament], and being bereft of Jesus, is really an alien landscape' which seems to have little of relevant guidance for the modern Christian.

48. Levenson, 'Counterpart', pp. 242-60 (248-50, 255-60).
49. Moore, 'Christian Writers', pp. 197-254 (197).
50. William L. Holladay, *Long Ago God Spoke: How Christians May Hear the Old Testament Today* (Minneapolis: Augsburg Fortress, 1995).

4. *Reading for the Best* 137

6. 'There are so many battles and so many instances of cruelty in the Old Testament...and the worst of it is that God seems to sponsor these battles. What kind of God is this?'
7. 'How can we believe that god chose one people, Israel?... IF God has created all humankind and loves the whole of creation, how can we take seriously the Old Testament claim that God chose a single nation, Israel?' Holladay goes on to liken this claim to the kind of racism that had German World War I army belt-buckles read *'Gott mit uns'*.
8. 'Some of the Psalms are so self-righteous...and this holier-than-thou attitude is often linked to prayers against one's enemies.'
9. 'From time to time, we notice real contradictions between given passages in the Old Testament'.
10. 'In the Old Testament women are subordinate in a world dominated by men'.[51]

While Holladay does not answer these questions directly in his introductory chapter, he takes up their trajectory throughout the chapters that follow. He does not aim to take up the issue of whether these objections occur when reading the New Testament, but the implication lingers—what do puzzled and doubting readers of the Bible make of resurrection from the dead, if they have problems with sweet honey from the rock? What immediately follows his laundry list of objections is in fact a discussion of historical criticism, but lest we think we have finally found salvific answers there, instead the reader finds appropriate caveats about thinking we can ever get fully accurate reconstructions of history, or that any method is infallible.[52] He understands that these methodological limitations may destabilize our certainty and expectations of finding a 'dependable voice of God'[53] in the pages of this long, boring, Jesus-free, irrelevant, racist, male supremacist relict of an age gone by and a people passed over (my words, not his). Concluding with a nice discussion of the metaphorical nature of theological language, we are intrigued into reading more, in hopes that this old, used-up half of the Bible can indeed be saved for Christian believers.

I find much trouble in this introduction, because the trenchant profile of most mainstream Christians' view of the Hebrew Bible is basically accurate. I discover, like the Queen of Sheba (though hopefully not the demonic figure of medieval midrash and Islamic folklore), that I must test this conventional academic wisdom with some 'hard questions' of my own. The first problem is one with which I am all too familiar:

51. Holladay, *Long Ago*, pp. 11-16.
52. Holladay, *Long Ago*, pp. 20-21.
53. As though this were any easier in the New Testament!

Christians seem to think they are performing some kind of penance, doing some kind of favor, when they read the Hebrew Bible. That they must be cajoled and coaxed, have Jesus waved under their nose as an incentive for reading part of their Scripture strikes me as a direct legacy of the New Testament's and Christian Church's anti-Judaism. Martin Luther at least thought there actually *was* a 'plain sense' to Scripture, although he, like Christian theologians before him, alleged that Jews willfully perverted that plain sense.[54] Most of the Christian objections that Holladay cites could be and have been lodged against the New Testament as well, but *there* such issues do not seem to trouble most Christian readers. But beyond that caveat, could it be that there are *two* standards for reading Scripture, one marked 'theirs' and another labeled 'ours'?

Modern Christians, having been asked to read the Hebrew Bible critically and on its own terms before 'jumping to Jesus' to solve their textual difficulties, become suddenly offended and outraged, straining at gnats in one Testament while they routinely swallow camels in the other. By casting the Hebrew Bible in the role of antithesis and a 'prologue' to the really 'important' material found in the New Testament, Christians create a shadow and a foil on which to project the elements of the biblical world-view they find unacceptable or unbelievable.[55] Miracles are a problem in the 'Old Testament' but usually become evidence of God's fidelity and power in the New.[56] Male dominance, which is as nicely displayed in the New Testament as anywhere else in antiquity, becomes a major objection in the 'Old'. Jesus never said a recorded word about the laws of *Sotah*, or *Niddah*,[57] and neither challenges nor dismantles the teachings on slavery or female inferiority in any overt, direct way beyond preventing an Honor Killing. We may draw life-giving implications from his interactions with women,[58] but how do we know that these are not typical portraits of a first-century

---

54. So, too, much earlier Tertullian, Justin Martyr, Jerome, *et al*. See discussion above and Trachtenberg, *Devil*, p. 15.

55. Von Kellenbach, *Anti-Judaism*, pp. 42-56.

56. And this may not even touch the 'real' problem for most ordinary readers: where are these miracles, now? As my 'ordinary reader' husband commented, 'God seems to be in a much less proactive phase these days: I don't see anyone making fish out of baskets recently'.

57. Von Kellenbach, *Anti-Judaism*, pp. 59, 112.

58. Or we may not, as it is quite possible that female figures appear as 'literary props' which highlight the inclusivity of Jesus. See the present writer's 'Disabilities and Chronic Illness in the Bible: A Feminist Perspective', in Athalya Brenner (ed.), *A Feminist Companion to the Hebrew Bible in the New Testament* (FCB, 10; Series 1; Sheffield: Sheffield Academic Press, 1996), pp. 286-301.

4. Reading for the Best 139

healer and prophet living in Roman Judea? We mutter about the exclusive, clannishness of 'those Jews' and their racist nerve in claiming an election which excludes, all the while cheerfully displacing them with our own covenant as the 'New Israel'. Of course, we invite the whole world into our universal covenant, and if they don't want to join, we have a remedy for them: the Inquisition or some other wing of Christian jihadis will find time to prosecute their heresies, for their own good (of course). Christian elite theologians and ordinary readers alike cast Judaism and its Scripture as the legal strait-jacket from which Jesus then liberates 'us'. We have 'grace' which is better than 'law', at least in part because we are the ones who have got it.

But how can an attentive reader think grace came out of nowhere? Ask the newly freed slaves standing at the foot of Sinai what they think about this false dichotomy...and then ask the women, who are apparently standing elsewhere. Further, there is no first-century Messiah without a Second Isaiah, not because we use the prophets of the Hebrew Bible to proof-text the appearance of Jesus, but because *what he does* when he does appear is conceived and understood through the dynamics of a pattern of redemption already developed in the First Testament. To quote another German father, Claus Westermann:

> Looking back again over the relation of the message of Old Testament prophecy to Jesus Christ, we conclude that the most substantial part of it does not lie in salvation prophecy, but in the prophecy of judgment. This means that the prophets' task of announcing God's judgment to the people, which was important in all their activities, also linked them most closely with Christ. This task had made suffering an increasingly important part of the prophets' service, and their suffering, in an apparently fruitless task, is directly linked to the suffering of the servant of God. This, in turn, points ahead to the suffering of Jesus Christ. The prophets' message of salvation, on the other hand, has only an indirect relation to the coming of Christ. Nor do the messianic prophecies in the prophetic books have more than a remote relation to what the New Testament Gospels say about Jesus, the Christ.[59]

To put it plainly, one can have a Judaism without the New Testament, but there can be no New Testament, much less a Christianity, without the Hebrew Bible.

One of the traits of theological anti-Judaism is the continued need to 'set up' the 'Old' in such a way that it can be superseded or answered by the 'New' (sometimes the literary device of 'typology' or the theological concept of 'promise and fulfillment' is used to construct this binary opposition). Can Christianity exist without a Fall? Who will buy the

---

59. Claus Westermann, *The Old Testament and Jesus Christ* (trans. Omar Kaste; Minneapolis: Augsburg Press, 1970), pp. 34-35.

'cure' of redemption/salvation in Christ, unless first convinced of an 'illness' which must be remedied? This entire Messiah business makes a whole lot less sense when ripped out of the national history of the Jews and grafted onto the needs of Gentile pagans. Judaism can and does exist without a 'fall' from original blessedness: the divine image is not irrevocably blurred or broken in humanity, the earth is not to be tossed aside for a home in heaven, and salvation must make itself known on this side of the grave. This is not to say that Judaism is naïve on the subject of human nature; far from it, but 'grace', even in the First Testament, has the last word. In the New Testament, however, it seems only a lost Eden can make Gethsemane understandable or bearable.

Can Christianity exist without Christ-killers? Oddly enough, the natural group to be cast in this role, the Romans, receives precious little attention in Christian theology, perhaps because of the Church's triumph over and assimilation to the Roman Empire in the fourth century of the Common Era.[60] When the Passion narratives, 'the seedbed for Christian anti-Judaism',[61] are read closely, we find that *all Jewish persons* through time are supposed to bear the stigma of rejecting and burdening Jesus with the sins for which his death atones. In most readings, though, this collective guilt is nicely shifted onto the Jews filling the role of 'sacred executioners', now violent oppressors and knowing god-killers, thus relieving Christians of the need for substantive self-examination.[62] This totally ignores the political situation of the Jews with respect to the first century, as well as any consideration of whether or not the Passion accounts can, in fact, function as an accurate historical record of the events they narrate.[63] But such readings *do* offer considerable balm to the Christian conscience, allowing readers to identify with the innocent, persecuted victim, the spotless lamb, when, in fact, centuries of Christian domination are the substance of our history.[64] We are hardly fearful *Jewish* Galileans, forced to hide our faith in a hostile world; we are, in fact, the conquerors and the perpetrators. But with the ever ready presence of Christ-killers in our midst—and that's the incredible thing

---

60. Rosemary Ruether, *Faith and Fratricide* (New York: Seabury, 1974), p. 88.
61. Crossan, *Who Killed Jesus?*, p. 35.
62. Von Kellenbach, *Anti-Judaism*, pp. 47-49.
63. S.G.F. Brandon, 'History or Theology? The Basic Problems of the Evidence of the Trial of Jesus', in Jeremy Cohen (ed.), *Essential Papers on Judaism and Christianity in Conflict: From Late Antiquity to the Reformation* (New York: New York University Press, 1991), pp. 114-30; see also Crossan, who considers the Passion Narratives to be 'prophecy historicized', as opposed to 'history remembered' (*Who Killed Jesus*, pp. 1-38).
64. So, too, with Crossan, on the ethics of reading in the Passion Narratives (*Who Killed Jesus*, p. 35).

about anti-Semitism: despite so many cultural changes and variants, it just keeps going and going and going—with Jewish Christ-killers in our midst, Gentiles can always invite themselves to feel innocent.

This relief from guilt is why most white European-American male scholars of Bible and the history of 'ancient Israel' (notice how well we like to avoid the idea of an ancient 'Jewish' state, by the way) seek to end Jewish history with the New Testament and the destruction of the Second Temple by the Romans in 70 CE. Jewish history *must* end then, since we require the guilty Jews to be punished for their condemnation and rejection of the Jesus as Messiah. For this same reason, the folklore of the 'Wandering Jew' is another requirement of Christian anti-Judaic readings: having failed to find their spiritual home in Jesus, the Jewish community must ever be denied a rightful place, a safe place of their own.[65] A rooted Jew might remind us that the Tree of Life existed before the Tree of the Cross and that the one has not been uprooted on account of the other. For more of the particulars of Christian theological anti-Judaism, I refer you to the bibliographical materials made available here.

4. *Aryan Christ or Matriarchal Jesus:*
On the Theology of 'Same-Old, Same-Old'

Attempts to read either Testament as a unified, monolithic text containing only one voice, from one time and place, with only one meaning and one implication for the communities that read them are simply wrong. We must thank the assaults of postmodern and feminist literary criticism for many of the cracks we now find in our customary certainties. One voice? Ha. Even the Torah gives the Decalogue twice, and there *are* variations. In addition, there are two Talmuds, one from the Diaspora community in Babylon, and the other from the land of Israel, and they do show significant variations.[66] That there are four *official* gospels, two heretical ones from Nag Hammadi (one of which, the *Gospel of Thomas*, may actually be the earliest of them all) and more being reconstructed all the time, should suggest to us immediately that there are varieties of perspectives and interpretations preserved in both Testaments.

---

65. Galit Hasan-Rokem and Alan Dundes (eds.), *The Wandering Jew* (Bloomington: Indiana University Press, 1986). Assessment of this motif and its historical appearance with a Jew (rather than a Gentile) as the one cursed to live until the Second Coming shows just how well anti-Judaism serves its masters: when Jews are expelled from Christian lands, this motif surfaces to legitimate their 'wandering' as the form of the 'curse', whereas in previous ages the longevity of the main character was seen in far more neutral terms.

66. Daniel Boyarin, *Carnal Israel: Reading Sex in Talmudic Culture* (Berkeley: University of California, 1993), pp. 48-49 *et passim*.

Yet even as we try our best to read in context, an act for which we have argued strongly, modern critics wonder if we *can ever* know, *how* we know, *why* we think it is so important to know and know how we know: we the readers have come to understand ourselves as an integral part of the meaning-making process in any reading. This is because any text consists of intersections of different sets of semantic codes, systems of meaning-making.67 Read one way (that is, privileging one code instead of another) a text means one thing; turn it and emphasize a different, but equally valid, code and our reading yields a different outcome.68 This is why readerly hermeneutics has become such a subject of study in literary criticism of the Hebrew Bible: we *must* wonder why readers choose the codes they do, because obviously a *choice has been made*. For myself, as a thing which does not exist in nature—a rooted feminist who loves the book of Leviticus—I am obliged to ask *why* that is so: my Israeli, American Jewish, and Christian friends certainly find no such anthropological lyricism in the ritual direction for dealing with mold and mildew (but perhaps they are not from the American South?).

We have learned, then, as critics of our own reading strategies, that the methods we use to question our texts set up and define the answers we allow the text to give us; now we are trying to integrate the fact that those methods always reside in a particular person's hands, used for a particular end. In this new framework of readerly hermeneutics, 'coherence', which was previously cited as a hallmark of a 'good' reading, now becomes the act of repression of textual inconsistencies which witness against the text's own fraudulent portrayal of a unified reality where no voices dissent. 'Comprehensiveness', under these same new rubrics, is an arrogant claim made by modern critics, feminists included, and 'reproducibility', when what is reproduced is abhorrent to justice-loving readers,69 is not all that counts. 'Plausibility' is nothing to write home about, as we have seen in this century where every horror committed by humans can now seem terribly, fearfully plausible.

Given these enlarged sets of considerations for reading endorsed by feminist literary criticism of the Bible, I wish that I could report that feminists had succeeded in avoiding the anti-Judaic biases which have been criticized in earlier biblical scholars' writing. I am sorry to report that such is not the case, although acknowledgment and repentance seem to be at hand. Whether Christian reformer or post-Christian theologian,

---

67. Terence Hawkes, *Structuralism and Semiotics* (Berkeley: University of California, 1977), pp. 59-122.

68. Patte, *Ethics*, pp. 27-29. This is also the reason why oppressed persons can read genuinely liberating meanings out of a patriarchal text.

69. Athalya Brenner's 'Identifying the Speaker in the Text: Isaiah 50', in Brenner and Fontaine (eds.), *Approaches, Methods, Strategies*, pp. 136-50.

feminists have drunk from the same poisoned wells as their brothers and their writings display the same tendencies, though sometimes to a lesser extent. While no one is arguing for an 'Aryan Christ', the fictive creation of Nazi theologians, a 'matriarchal Jesus' makes his appearance in some feminist writings, once again allowing Christians to feel they have re-covered or un-covered a truth obscured by the rigidity of Jewish legalism. Add to this the unfounded claim that it was Hebrew monotheism which 'killed the goddess', and the charge of Jewish deicide surfaces under a new guise. Katharina von Kellenbach details the new polemics against Judaism.

For Christian feminists, seeking to reform a female-unfriendly church hierarchy and body of literature, Jesus becomes the feminist *par excellence* in their bid for equality for women believers. Part of the way this goal is achieved is by the strategy of contrasting Jesus to the purported Judaism of his time.

Judaism is, like all the recorded religions of antiquity, highly patriarchal in its structure and affect, but no more so than the goddess-filled religions that surrounded it. Nor is it proper to speak of Judaism as though it were only one, normative entity. Indeed, in many cases, later Judaism's reflections on the state of woman, her abilities and her destiny, are highly varied within different streams of the tradition, and are decidedly *better* than what is found in comparable pagan religions or, *in many cases, Christianity*, but the reader of Christian feminist works rarely sees this point made.[70] Instead, Jesus, is considered strikingly 'un-Jewish', and interpreted as one who specifically breaks Jewish law to highlight his opposition to the treatment of women.

The same interpretation is meted out to the apostle Paul, who, in some feminist writings, turns out to have a kind of Jewish-Christian multiple personality disorder: when he is good, he is very, very good—and a Christian, and when he is bad, he's Jewish. Restrictions of women promulgated by the early Church are routinely attributed to 'Jewish Christian' elements among the Church, or to the legacy of that awful Hebrew Bible. Where Christianity incorporates female imagery drawn from goddess cults, it is interpreted as 'openness' to reform of patriarchy; where Judaism does the same, it is judged to be 'co-option' of woman-friendly pagan practices. Passages from the Mishnah and the Babylonian Talmud, both of which are considerably later than the New

---

70. Phyllis Trible, for example, in her *Texts of Terror: Literary-Feminist Readings of Biblical Narratives* (OBT; Philadelphia: Fortress Press, 1984) can only make the portrait of the conflict between Sarah and Hagar as bad as possible by ignoring relevant sections of the Code of Hammurabi as well as other legislative sections of the Torah. She refracts the Hebrew Bible's ambiguous treatment of Hagar through Christian liturgical language, assaulting the reader at a subconscious level.

Testament materials, are used uncritically in reconstructing a version of first-century Judaism that shows 'the Christian' Jesus, to advantage in the struggles of women. That Jesus might be a typical example of Palestinian Judaism that routinely affords women greater opportunities than the Babylonian version, or pagan religions, has only recently begun to be considered, largely due to the protest of Jewish feminists over the anti-Jewish biases kept alive by their Christian sisters.[71]

The ready absorption of Jewish materials for use in Christian apologetics is another place where Christian feminists have followed the lead of earlier scholarship. Early modern European learned Christian males 'discovered' the Kabbalah, and found in it not a rich source of Jewish theology done by particular communities confronting their own world, but rather evidence for the coming of Christ.[72] So, too, modern feminists have read their Hebrew Bibles with an eye toward salvaging that other Testament for feminist purposes. Personified Lady or Woman Wisdom, who began her biblical career as Hebrew is readily swallowed up by reformist Christologies seeking to ameliorate the scandal of Jesus' maleness: now Hebrew Wisdom is Greek Sophia. On the basis of a statement made by Paul, Jesus is given an alternative female messianic identity as the living Sophia of God—as though he didn't already have enough 'natures' to contend with. Seldom is mention made that the world-view of the sages for whom Lady Wisdom was a scribal patron was, in many ways, *far* from 'both-genders-friendly' and that the kind of 'life' offered by Lady Wisdom was *not* the sort of salvation of which New Testament writers are speaking.[73] No matter what the current vogue is in describing 'Judaism the foil', Christianity or some recovered matriarchy turns out to be its opposite and superior tradition.[74]

---

71. Judith Plaskow, 'Blaming Jews for Inventing Patriarchy', *Lilith* 7 (1979): pp. 9-11, 14-17; 'Feminist Anti-Judaism and the Christian God', *JFS* 7 (1991), pp. 99-109. The problems raised here for Christian feminist Christologies are manifold: as Susan Brooks Thistlethwaite points out, even 'relational' Christologies rely on a perceived 'difference' between Jesus and the Other (*Sex, Race, and God: Christian Feminism in Black and White* [New York: Crossroad, 1989], pp. 94-95).

72. Trachtenberg, *Devil*, p. 77.

73. Susan Cady, Hal Taussig and Marian Ronan, *Wisdom's Feast* (San Francisco: Harper Row, 1989); while the work of New Testament feminist Elisabeth Schüssler Fiorenza is considerably more nuanced in appropriation of a 'wisdom Christology', nevertheless the Hebrew Bible's unique formulation of woman Wisdom's engagement with the world is pressed into Christian service in support of a feminist advocacy position.

74. In earlier malestream scholarship, Judaism was the irrational ritual of an emotional people, and Christianity its rational and logical successor. For feminist reformers, Judaism loses all its 'emotional' qualities and is associated with 'left-brain' thinking (= bad), for which 'right-brained' (= good) feminist Christian or matriarchal

Elsewhere, Christian Feminists have relied heavily on Christian biblical reference materials, largely German and pre-war in origin, which are blatantly anti-Semitic, and so biases of these works are reproduced, undigested and uncritiqued, in many feminist writings. It is worth giving an example of this problem. A major reference resource that falls into this category is *The Theological Dictionary of the New Testament*, a translation of *Theologisches Wörterbuch zum Neuen Testament*, ed. Gerhard Kittel.[75] One might particularly note the entry under 'woman' (*gyne*) by George Oepke. This is a reworking of his 'Der Dienst der Frau in der urchristlichen Gemeinde'[76] article which was first published in 1939. He writes in *TDNT* that 'the general rule is that the further west we go the greater the freedom of woman'.[77] This statement would occasion major surprise to the numerous women who were victims of ritual murder in Celtic Europe during the same periods Oepke discusses.[78] That the intensely patriarchal Roman family should be favorably contrasted with Talmudic promulgations, which include among other things the first-ever recognition and condemnation of marital rape, along with regulations to provide for harmony, intimacy, female desire and affection in conjugal relations,[79] is both astonishing and deeply disturbing. Only by distortion and selective use of sources is this view of first-century Judaism sustained, and the areas in which this occurs—divorce, education of women, head-covering, submission, role in public, obligation to fulfill commandments—are ones that are often the crux of feminist Christian challenges to biblical sexism. Worst of all, as von Kellenbach writes, this kind of distortion 'denies the possibility that the Christian vision of egalitarianism and liberation has its roots in Judaism, leaving the impression that Judaism stands for racism, sexism, classism and Christianity for egalitarianism and inclusiveness'.[80]

---

religion is the cure. This is similar to Nazi propaganda where Jews are *both* members of an international capitalist conspiracy *and simultaneously* members of a communist conspiracy. The structural rule at work is that Jews and Judaism are invariably associated with the negative half of the binary opposition (hence, the symbolic identity between Jews and femaleness or Jews and nature).

75. Stuttgart: W. Kohlhammer, 1957; Grand Rapids, MI: Eerdmann Publishing, 1964. For discussion, see Robert P. Ericksen, *Theologians Under Hitler: Gerhard Kittel, Paul Althaus and Emanuel Hirsch* (New Haven: Yale University Press, 1985), pp. 28-78.

76. *Neue allgemeine Missionszeitschrift* 16 (1939), pp. 39-53.

77. *TDNT*, p. 777.

78. Miranda Green, *Celtic Goddesses: Warriors, Virgins and Mothers* (London: British Museum Press, 1995), pp. 151-59. Green suggests that the preponderance of women victims may be related to their high status as wise women and healers, which suggests that high status may not be all it is cracked up to be.

79. Boyarin, *Carnal*, pp. 114, 129-33.

80. Von Kellenbach, *Anti-Judaism*, p. 72.

When we move outside of the Christian feminist community, we find that things are no better in the presentations of Judaism made by Neo-Pagan writers like Charlene Spretnak, Merlin Stone, Gerda Lerner, Riane Eisler, Mary Daly, Starhawk, Carol Christ and others—though once again, to varying degrees and for different reasons. While there is no need to castigate Jews for being Christ-killers since the reference point for these theologians is no longer New Testament claims about Jesus, the Hebrew Bible's monotheism is held responsible for most of the social and psychic ills besetting women under patriarchy. Monotheism is reinterpreted as *monolatry*, the idolization of deity in the form of a *male*—which is not *quite* what the Hebrew Bible is saying. (It is interesting to note, however, that while the Hebrew Bible's god is demonized and his priests denounced, Jesus, reinterpreted as the child-consort of a matriarchal goddess, once again comes off looking like a fairly hopeful option in limited ways.) Most of these writers cast Judaism as a foil, but now it stands opposite the supposedly peaceful matriarchal cultures which predated its monotheistic conquest of the known world. This is the theology of 'Same-old, same-old': it uses the same strategies of Christian feminist and mainstream writers to achieve similar goals. Murderers of either Jesus or the Goddess, Jews remain the designated victims and the ones to be held responsible for current social, psychological and religious dysfunctions.[81]

Now given that such writers are usually *not* trying to defend Christianity, we might ask, as von Kellenbach does, what is at work in such feminist readings. Much as Martin Luther used the Hebrew Bible and his description of Judaism as a 'cover symbol' for the real target of much of his critique, the Roman Catholic Church of his day, so, too, modern feminists single out Jewish patriarchy as the sexist culprit when they are actually criticizing Christian patriarchy.[82] But the Christian majority, with its institutions in which many feminists are employed and its history of witch-hunts and persecutions of women who did not fit its pattern of submission, is too formidable and dangerous a target for the beleaguered feminists who are trying to create (or less successfully, retrieve) a more woman-friendly metaphysics and spirituality. Jews, on the other hand are much safer objects of disdain, ones hallowed by long use in Christian theological circles. Since both Jews and women have shared so many negative characterizations and so much persecution[83] at

---

81. Von Kellenbach, *Anti-Judaism*, pp. 91-122.
82. So with von Kellenbach, *Anti-Judaism*, pp. 43-44. Zeus, for example, is a *much* more unpleasant deity in his treatment of women than is the Hebrew Bible's god, but no one is using Zeus to attack and harass women's search for equality.
83. For the feminization of male Jews, see Daniel Boyarin, 'Torah Study and the

the hands of the Christian hierarchies of Europe,[84] this gap in solidarity is especially ironic and painful. A sign of hope is emerging, however: as anti-Judaic biases are uncovered in feminist writings, writers seem able to repent of it, and move forward—another tribute to the effectiveness to interreligious dialogue.

5. What Is to Be Done?

We are doing it here today, as I write and you read: we must, as the inheritors of bias in our theological paradigms, face up to the fact of anti-Semitism (and increasingly, anti-Islamic rhetoric) squarely, without flinching, and repent. First, Christians must learn to articulate their continuities and differences from Judaism in ways that allow Judaism and Jews, in all their diversities, to retain and maintain full 'subjectivity'[85] rather than being annexed as plot devices in a universal Christian drama. Jews must be valued as subjects of their own Scripture, and partners with God in their own covenant. It should be recognized that they are not present in theological discussion so that Gentiles may gather new theological data about the nature and purpose of the biblical god.

Second, interfaith dialogue, as well as elite and ordinary collaborations, must continue, and should do so along several lines. We need to learn each other's histories if we are to understand each other's passions. I suggest we continue this by learning to read together, reading separately.[86] That is, let Christians and Jews, and everyone outside and in

---

Making of Jewish Gender', in Brenner and Fontaine (eds.), *Approaches, Methods, Strategies*, pp. 585-621. Compare, also, the language used to describe witches and their acts in the Papal Bull of Innocent VIII (1484) with that used of Jews in the 1569 Bull of Pius V explaining the expulsion of the Jews from the Papal states (Trachtenberg, *Devil*, pp. 76-77; Montague Summers (trans.), *The Malleus Maleficarum* [New York: Dover Publications, 1971], pp. xliii-slv).

84. Steven T. Katz, *The Holocaust in Historical Context*. I. *The Holocaust and Mass Death before the Modern Age* (New York: Oxford University Press, 1994), pp. 401-505. While I agree with Katz's negative evaluation of Mary Daly's position (anti-Semitism as a minor subset of gynocide), his use of percentages of women persecuted during the Burning Times to minimize the terror experience by (largely) Christian women during this historical period distorts the existential dilemma in which they found themselves.

85. 'Subjectivity', as defined in poststructuralist feminist theory, is 'an effect of language which is the site of conflicting and contradictory discourses, located in social and institutional practices' (Chris Weedon, 'Post-structuralist Feminist Practice', in Donald Morton and Mas'ud Zavarzadeh (eds.), *Theory/Pedagogy/Politics: Texts for Change* [Chicago: University of Illinois Press, 1991], pp. 47-63 [53]).

86. A literary guideline for this initiative may be derived from a theory of intertextuality which sees the composite text ('Old' and 'New' Testaments together) as a new

between, read together—I suggest the Books of Esther and Paul's letter to the Romans—fully acknowledging that we come with and depart with differences. Those differences are the stuff of celebration and enlarged meaning for both communities. Let Christians study Talmud; let Jews read Origen; let everyone read the Qur'an, and provide feminists on call to offer metaphysical first-aid.

We have a great advantage in the United States in that we do not carry the full burden of Europe's history of centuries of hate between these two communities. We have vital and articulate Jewish communities here, so a dialogue is actually possible. We must make it happen. We will.

Third, we must invite the third and final People of this Book, Muslims, into the circle of readers for whom justice matters and issues of faith are taken seriously. Given the resurgence of fundamentalist, extremist interpretations of all three Scriptures, nothing could be more important than probing the gaps and weaving connections between people of good will belonging to all three traditions—and *no* traditions. After all, the United Nations Declaration of Universal Human Rights does not just grant the full freedom to practice one's religion; it also recognizes and protects freedom *from* religion. If religions do not find ways to reform and reformulate their basic tenets for a diverse and interconnected world, we will *all* need to make use of that provision in international Human Rights law.

Results of Opening the Circle of Readers
In recent days as I have become swept up in interfaith struggles to make a more just and peaceful world, I find that I have added a new question that I must ask of my interpretations: have I read this text 'Other'-ly? What happens when you read alongside and make meaning in the presence of the Radical Other, the one who does not and will not *ever* agree with your notion of the text or its meanings? If we read along and interpret only with others *inside* Christendom or our professional guild, we will never surmount the death struggles caused by the sometimes mutually exclusive claims of the other Peoples of the Book. So one must ask, how do Jews read this text? (Which Jews? When?) How do Muslims do it? Which ones? Where? Native Americans? People from the Southern Hemisphere? Reading with the Radical Other is no easy thing, but it is a necessary task if we do not want to be unwitting contributors to the sorrows of the planet. For she who would stand between Jerusalem and

entity of mingled Signifiers, rather than viewing the younger text as supplanting the Signifiers and Signified of the Old with their own 'new', true meaning. Daniel Boyarin's work on gender is most instructive on this point (see above).

Jenin and defend the basic human rights of both, the ability to 'read around' with many partners is critical. For myself, reading midrash with Jewish lesbians or studying Hebrew with Guatemalan immigrants is an ethical discipline. Studying with Jewish colleagues teaches one to add new questions: 'What does the Talmud say?' needs to appear alongside of 'What would Jesus do?' so that we are not left with the feeling that we are uniquely alone and un-partnered in our attempts to read the text for livable meaning in later times. The very shape of a rabbinic Bible or page of Talmud provides an 'eyeful' for Christians, offering a visual lexicon of the plethora of voices, often disagreeing, which surround any text's interpretation.

Reading the Qur'an with Muslim feminists, joining them in their struggles to transform the place of women in popular Islamic practice, requires more from me than the discipline of History of Religions ever suggested. I can only be grateful that such contact has turned my scholarship upside down, ripping the self-imposed critical veils from my face,[87] leaving me exposed for all to see. I am a better and more responsible reader because I read Other-ly. If, by nature of my expertise, I am to be a 'sentinel' charged with watching out for the integrity of interpretation with an eye to both scholarship and faith, then it is only fair that Others ought to be watching out for *me!*[88]

---

87. I use the term 'veil' with extreme care, as it has been clearly demonstrated that the veil functions as a symbol of Islamic inferiority to the West within colonial discourse. As such, it is a powerful ideological tool of colonialism for perpetuating all sorts of oppressions. Homa Hoodfar explores this dynamic in her 'The Veil in their Minds and on our Heads: Veiling Practices and Muslim Women', in Elizabeth A. Castelli (ed.), *Women, Gender, Religion: A Reader* (New York: Palgrave, 2001), pp. 420-46, where she points out that 'veiling is a lived experience full of contradictions and multiple meanings'. She continues: 'While it has clearly been a mechanism in the service of patriarchy, a means of regulating and controlling women's lives, women have used the same social institution to free themselves from the bonds of patriarchy' (p. 412).

88. As with any dropped garment, whether this loss spells freedom, dishonor, or enhanced political options for its wearer remains to be seen!

Chapter 5

THE ABUSIVE BIBLE:
ON THE USE OF FEMINIST METHOD IN PASTORAL CONTEXTS

A trusting child is bound for sacrifice and placed by his father upon an altar waiting to receive his blood. It is God's will, we are told, and the father's willingness to kill his son is reckoned to the father as 'righteousness' (Gen. 22).

A lone wife is shoved out of the door of safety to satisfy the desires of a lustful crowd seeking to 'know' her husband and master. After a night of rape and abuse, she is found with her hands stretched across the threshold of the house that offered her no sanctuary. To announce the results of the deed, her husband dismembers her body and sends the pieces as tokens to the males of the surrounding tribes (Judg. 19).

A royal princess is raped by her half-brother, who goes unpunished by their father. The full brother who takes up her cause does so for his own political ends, which leads in turn to the tragic end of his quest for power. The innocent victim dwells 'desolate' in her brother's house. The father says nothing (2 Sam. 13).

A queen is commanded to appear before her husband's feasting nobles and satisfy their lust. When she refuses, she is 'disappeared' from the story and replaced with a more appropriately submissive beauty (Est. 1).

A neglected wife questions her husband's behavior. When she does, she is narratively 'disappeared' from his story. She is replaced with a more docile female, another man's wife (2 Sam. 6.20-23).[1]

An unknown woman raises her voice in blessing of the Messiah who is passing by. 'Blessed is the womb that bore you', she says, 'and the breasts that you sucked'. She is silenced immediately and her blessing nullified, as the Messiah replies 'Blessed rather are those who hear the word of God and keep it!' (Lk. 11.27-28).[2]

---

1. For a discussion of this text and the fate of Michal, daughter of Saul and sometime wife of David, see J. Cheryl Exum, *Fragmented Women: Feminist (Sub)versions of Biblical Narratives* (JSOTSup, 163; Sheffield: Sheffield Academic Press, 1993), pp. 42-60.

2. This text is beautifully interpreted in Kerry M. Craig and Margaret A.

5. *The Abusive Bible*   151

When students in the Jewish and Christian traditions turn to their heritage in search of answers to the questions and problems that beset them today, it is natural and not at all surprising that the Bible should occupy a central position in their struggles. It is a formative complex of texts and traditions, treasured and revered for centuries. In many respects, the Bible has performed its function well: generation after generation, it has told the story, 'kept the faith', and enlightened the human journey by continuously indoctrinating each successive generation into the 'faith of the fathers'. Communities created the Bible and proclaimed it 'Sacred Scripture'; now that Scripture creates communities, by serving as an ongoing resource on faith and practice.

Within the seminary, church, or synagogue setting, the pastoral engagement of such issues as domestic and sexual violence within society most typically might take the form of 'bible studies', sermons, or topics dealt with in prayer or study groups. These are not, however, the only contexts in which such topics might legitimately be studied, although such questions posed by a community of faith may well offer the most poignant settings for this type of inquiry. The discussion presented here seeks to ask how such subjects may be handled in teaching for pastoral contexts, especially Christian seminary settings where the Bible is taught as course subject matter. In fact, the Hebrew Bible may be taught in many different ways: in secular settings it may be seen as literature, as a (semi- or pseudo-) historical document, or as a source for sociological and anthropological reconstructions of early 'historical' religions (as opposed to archaic and primitive religions which, it is usually supposed, biblical religions supersede in a more or less orderly evolutionary development).[3] In seminaries, Jewish or Christian, in contrast to departments of 'Religious Studies' which contain 'Biblical Studies', the starting point for the consideration of the biblical text also (typically) includes some notion of its 'inspiration' and/or 'authority' as a foundational text for the communities which accord it the status of 'Sacred Scripture'. In these settings, how does existing methodology handle the evidence of abuse, first found in stories told by the text, and then perpetuated by the commitments of the text itself, as interpreted by its believing communities?

One of the basic assumptions with which Christians and Jews seem to operate is that the Bible is a document which stands wholeheartedly and unreservedly on the side of human dignity. The faithful assume

Kristjansson, 'Women Reading as Men/Women Reading as Women: A Structural Analysis for the Historical Project', *Semeia* 51 (1990), pp. 119-36.

3. Robert Bellah, 'Religious Evolution', in William A. Lessa and Evon Z. Vogt (eds.), *Reader in Comparative Religion: An Anthropological Approach* (New York: Harper & Row, 3rd edn, 1965), pp. 36-50.

that the Bible has words of comfort for the victims—mostly women and children—of sexual and domestic violence; that the Bible is clearly against such violence; that it is a major resource on such questions for people of faith, a friend and not an enemy. Critical feminist biblical scholarship which attends to the consideration of what the Bible is and how it does what it does, does not, however, automatically endorse these basic, positive assumptions.[4] The brief synopses of biblical stories with which this essay began should raise at least the suggestion that something may be terribly wrong with the uses made of the Bible by its communities of faith, if not also with the Bible itself.

The objection might be raised that the feminist biblical scholar's view of the role of the Bible in shaping the thoughts of society and believers on these issues is a rarefied, academic perspective not applicable to the world-views of the contemporary sufferers themselves. Perhaps. But let us turn to some case studies of how victims of abuse interpret the biblical God's role—and by implication, the Bible's role—in their distress:

A 55-year-old woman was raped by a stranger who broke into her home during the night. Her explanation for why this had happened to her was that God was punishing her for having divorced her husband ten years earlier.

A 19-year old woman had been sexually abused by her older brother since she was 10 years old. Her explanation was that the incestuous abuse was God's punishment for her being a bad person. In addition, at age 15 she had an abortion because she had been impregnated by her brother. The incestuous abuse continued and then she was convinced that God was punishing her for having had the abortion.

A battering husband, in addition to physically beating his wife, also regularly raped her. She interpreted this pattern of abuse as God's way of correcting her tendency to rebel against the authority of her husband.

A gay man who had just begun to be more open about his sexual orientation was kidnapped and brutally raped by three men. 'He…concluded that God was punishing him for his positive feelings about his homosexuality'.[5]

These case studies are taken from Christian pastor Marie Fortune's groundbreaking work, *Sexual Violence: The Unmentionable Sin*, which

---

4. See, for example, essays in Athalya Brenner and Carole R. Fontaine (eds.), *A Feminist Companion to the Latter Prophets* (FCB, 8; Sheffield: Sheffield Academic Press, 1995); and Kwok Pui-Lan, 'Racism and Ethnocentrism in Feminist Biblical Interpretation', in Elisabeth Schüssler Fiorenza (ed.), *Searching the Scriptures: A Feminist Introduction*, I (New York: Crossroad, 1993), pp. 101-16.

5. Marie Fortune, *Sexual Violence: The Unmentionable Sin* (New York: Pilgrim Press, 1983), p. 194.

has become a standard text in the field of Christian pastoral response to sexual and domestic violence. Anyone who counsels parishioners or students, or listens closely to stories of friends and family, could add other stories: the 20-year old rape victim who was told by a clergyman that the event had been God's will because she was not a virgin; the devastated 24-year old victim of three separate attacks of rape who concluded that she didn't even deserve to be alive, since such violence against her could only be a sign that God's love had been forever withdrawn from her; the 34-year old incest survivor who recalls being sexually active from the age of two, now an outcast to her family because she would not visit her abuser as he lay dying in a hospital.[6]

We all know these stories; if they are not our own, then they might belong to people we love. In some sense, even those of us who are lucky enough not to have been physically or sexually abused have shared, through love and empathy, in the emotional wreckage wrought on survivors as we have reached out to our broken friends, relatives, students, and parishioners. No doubt those who love their god, cherish their religious traditions, and are in some sense the propagators of those traditions, regularly cringe as they hear victims voice their understanding of how God was present or absent in the midst of that suffering. Clearly, those suffering from this sort of trauma may be prone to shaping their theologies of suffering in ways that echo the reality of their experience of abuse.[7] Most pastors and rabbis have tried hard to assist the survivors of violence and their families and friends in moving from what Joy M.K. Bussert has characterized as a 'theology of suffering' to an 'ethic of empowerment'.[8]

But there comes a point when one must wonder whether we are all reading the same Bible, since the interpretations made in these situations seem to be so divergent. Are the survivors all crazy, suffering from well-earned paranoid delusions and post-traumatic stress, when they express their belief that somehow God was 'out to get them' and that the betrayal and abuse they endured were a manifestation of that divine enmity?

While most feminists do not believe in a God who punishes in such a fashion, I do *not* think the survivors who speak in these terms do

---

6. These examples are drawn from pastoral counseling sessions with my white, middle-class seminary students.

7. Judith L. Herman, *Trauma and Recovery: The Aftermath of Violence from Domestic Abuse to Political Terror* (New York: Basic Books, 1992).

8. Joy M.K. Bussert, *Battered Women: From a Theology of Suffering to an Ethic of Empowerment* (New York: Lutheran Church in America, 1986), pp. 65-66. On the Jewish side of the aisle, see David R. Blumenthal's excellent work in *Facing the Abusing God: A Theology of Protest* (Louisville, KY: Westminster/John Knox Press, 1993).

so without justification. They have read their Bibles, and in doing so inhaled the toxic fumes of the patriarchal ethos of the Biblical tradition, especially where it deals with the topic of bodies. The 'theological' problems raised by the fact of human embodiment are played out differently in each Testament. The Hebrew Bible, while it maintains a more wholesome view of the entire body 'complex' (i.e., it does not divide persons into 'soul' and 'body', but sees them as a unity), is deeply fearful of women's bodies and the powers of procreation and blood which they hold.[9] The New Testament's apocalyptic worldview and affirmation of a Savior embodied in *male* (*not* female) form caused its writers to place a low valuation on female embodiment, and its anthropology does see a 'soul/body' split. The position taken by the New Testament has traditionally worked to disadvantage women in theological discussions, since women are associated with 'body' (because they are the vehicle for the production of new ones), and body is clearly inferior to spirit in such theological thinking.[10] Paradoxically, however, it is through their bodily states that Christian women receive salvation, either as humble, consecrated virgins[11] or as devoted mothers (1 Tim. 2.14-15). Given the dysfunctions that survivors of sexual violence often face in the area of their sexuality, it is worth hearing the reformer Martin Luther's words on this text in Timothy, as he envisions the spiritual well-being Christian salvation offers to Protestant women believers:

> *She will be saved.* That subjection of woman and domination of men have not been taken away, have they? No. The penalty remains. The blame passed over. The pain and tribulation of childbearing continue. Those penalties will continue until judgment. So also the dominion of men and the subjection of women continue. You must endure them. You will also be saved if you have also subjected yourselves and bear your children with pain. *Through bearing children.* It is a very great comfort that a woman can be saved by bearing children, etc. That is, she has an honorable and

---

9. Alice Bach, 'Good to the Last Drop: Viewing the Sotah (Numbers 5:11-31) as the Glass Half Empty and Wondering How to View it Half Full', in J. Cheryl Exum and David J.A. Clines (eds.), *The New Literary Criticism and the Hebrew Bible* (JSOTSup, 143; Sheffield: Sheffield Academic Press, 1993), pp. 26-54; Mieke Bal, *Lethal Love: Feminist Literary Readings of Biblical Love Stories* (Bloomington: Indiana University Press, 1987), pp. 1-8, 65-67.

10. For further discussion see Carole R. Fontaine, 'Disabilities and Chronic Illness in the Bible: A Feminist Perspective', in Athalya Brenner (ed.), *A Feminist Companion to the Hebrew Bible in the New Testament* (FCB, 10; Sheffield: Sheffield Academic Press, 1996), pp. 286-301.

11. Bernard of Clairvaux, *Magnificat: Homilies in Praise of the Blessed Virgin Mary* (trans. Marie-Bernard Saïd and Grace Perigo; *Cistercian Fathers Series*, 18; Kalamazoo, MI: Cistercian Publications, 1979), pp. 9-13.

salutary status in life if she keeps busy having children. We ought to recommend this passage to them, etc. She is described as 'saved' not for freedom, for license, but for bearing and rearing children.[12]

It is no wonder, then, that survivors of sexual and domestic violence have devised the explanations that we saw above: they have read the stories of Genesis, Judges, Samuel, and Job; they have heard the discourses on sexuality by Paul and those who spoke in his name; they have heard their clergy send them submissively home to abuse in order to protect the 'sanctity' of the family and 'traditional family values'. They are *not* crazy. On bad days, I tend to think that those of us who seek to use the Bible in a liberating, empowering way are the crazy ones. To turn again to Marie Fortune's work, she writes in *Keeping the Faith*, in the Appendix 'Suggestions for Clergy and Laypersons': 'The Bible has often been misinterpreted and misused in response to the Christian battered woman by those who have wanted to help her. This has been sometimes due to ignorance, sometimes due to denial of the seriousness of wife abuse, sometimes due to a desire to control the battered woman and limit her options'.[13]

While deeply appreciative of Fortune's desire to make the Bible part of the solution instead of part of the problem, I cannot second the analysis quoted here. I only wish that it were so simple as a case of misinterpretation which could be solved with better translations and more thorough historical-critical research. Unfortunately, the problem goes deeper than that, into the core of the Bible itself.

It is important, then, to take a closer look at what is going on in the way communities of faith, as well as academic communities, view the Bible, and the uses made of it. Most of my remarks will be illustrated from the Hebrew Bible since that is my area of major competence, but the critique offered here applies to the New Testament as well, and is in no way meant to imply that the Hebrew Bible is theologically or morally inferior to the New Testament, or incomplete without it. Things do not become instantly better with the appearance of Jesus. This is due to the thoroughgoing underlying patriarchal assumptions of the New Testament writers and communities, as well as to the apocalyptic world-view which caused them to think rather differently about sexual and domestic issues than they might have otherwise, had they not been expecting the imminent end of the world (and hence, the

---

12. Martin Luther, *Luther's Works* XXVIII (ed. Jaroslav Pelikan; 30 vols.; St Louis: Concordia, 1955–1971), p. 279.

13. Marie Fortune, 'Appendix B: Suggestions for Clergy and Laypersons', in *Keeping the Faith: Questions and Answers for the Abused Woman* (San Francisco: Harper & Row Publishers, 1987), pp. 81-85 (81).

end of sexuality altogether).[14] Even after the appearance of the Christian Church, Judaism continued to be a viable and vital tradition to which its women adhered. In fact, differences between Jewish, Christian, and pagan women in the early centuries of Christianity may well have been exaggerated by Christian triumphalist readings.[15]

It is also important to emphasize here that there is no one 'Christian', 'Jewish', 'academic', or even 'feminist' way to understand the Bible; there is a broad range of variation in how different Christian and Jewish communities deal with the issues of interpretation, and the disagreements among feminists are legion. Further, I am asking questions of the text and making interpretations which clearly reveal my philosophical and social location as a Caucasian woman born in the United States, raised in poverty in the American South, and baptized as a Protestant Christian, now a feminist seminary professor in a new century which seems to be marked by a rise in religious authoritarianism, climatic hostilities, and global collapse of infrastructure. My allegiances are with the abused. The whole notion of 'individual rights' is a fairly modern one and has little support in the texts of antiquity, nor does the idea that the destiny of women is or should be anything other than the role of mother and wife receive much attention there.[16] I honestly do not know if ancient women ever asked themselves the questions raised here; the classically trained biblical scholar in me believes that probably they did not, but the feminist is not so sure.[17] Bearing in mind these qualifications in the way texts will

---

14. The role of the New Testament and Christianity in perpetuating such abuse as discussed here is amply reviewed in Joanne Carlson Brown and Carole R. Bohn (eds.), *Christianity, Patriarchy, and Abuse: A Feminist Critique* (Cleveland: Pilgrim Press, 1989). On the role of New Testament theology, see especially Joanne Carlson Brown and Rebecca Parker, 'For God So Loved the World?', pp. 1-30 in that volume. For a critique of the implicit anti-Judaism inherent in Christian feminist interpretations which make Jews responsible for patriarchy and the death of the Goddess, see Judith Plaskow, 'Anti-Judaism in Feminist Christian Interpretation', in Schüssler Fiorenza (ed.), *Searching the Scriptures*, I, pp. 117-29. The tendency on the part of some Christian feminists to make the 'Jewish' heritage of Jesus and Paul responsible for any anti-female elements of the text, while ascribing any liberatory properties to the 'new' Gospel, is as unhelpful as it is unhistorical.

15. Barbara Geller Nathanson, 'Toward a Multicultural Ecumenical History of Women in the First Century/ies C.E.', in Schüssler Fiorenza (ed.), *Searching the Scriptures*, I, pp. 272-89.

16. The exceptions here are Mesopotamian creation epics which suggest that certain classes of females (she-demons who prey on children, priestesses, and naditu-women) were created by the gods for human population control. 'Story of the Flood' (Atrahasis Epic), in *From Distant Days: Myths, Tales and Poetry of Ancient Mesopotamia* (trans. Benjamin R. Foster; Bethesda, MD: CDL Press, 1995), pp. 76-77.

17. The fact that wives and slaves run away (for which we have textual indicators)

5. The Abusive Bible 157

be handled here, let us turn to the primary materials. The Bible contributes to the past and present exploitation of women, children, and gay, lesbian and bisexual persons in three areas: by its *nature*, by its *content*, and by its *function*. We will examine each of these in turn.

1. *The Nature of the Bible*

What exactly is the Bible anyway? Is it the direct, literal words of God? The words of humanity *about* God? God's word back to humanity's word? An imaginative record of humanity's musings about the nature of human life and the deity? A factual, historical account? The record of a people? A great and compelling work of literary artistry? A recipebook that can teach anyone, anywhere, anytime how to cook up a successful, rewarding life? There are communities which endorse each of these views, and do so in good faith according to their best understanding of these complex questions. While I suspect that many who attend Christian seminaries—as well as those who teach there—might opt for some version of the progressive 'middle' view that the Bible is a divinely inspired *human* product, we must not forget that the literal interpretation (i.e., the view that the Bible is the *actual* Word of God) holds sway for a large number of the faithful in United States and around the world. And for those subscribing to that view, 'biblical' theology's stranglehold on the lives of women and children is felt most keenly and with its most deadly and deadening effects. For some, 'bibliolatry', that is, turning the Bible into an idol whose authority is worshipped *instead* of God, is a reality. Further, by any progressive reading, the reality of literalism is one that can rob sufferers of abuse of the comfort of a faith in a real God: not the punishing patriarchal tyrant who sexually humiliates the female Israel (so with Hosea, the so-called 'prophet of love')—but the one who bends low to comfort the abused and humiliated (Jn 8.1-11), the one who could no more forget humanity than a mother could forget her nursing child (Isa. 49.15), the one who is *god* and *not* man, who does not come to destroy (Hos. 11.9).[18]

It is precisely because religious communities have held a privileged view of the Bible's nature as some sort of divine product with

---

is a sure indication that they were not happy with their individual lots; whether or not they questioned the existence of structures that caused their conditions is difficult to assess from extant records available to us.

18. For a discussion of the imagery in Hosea see T. Drorah Setel, 'Prophets and Pornography: Female Sexual Imagery in Hosea', in Letty M. Russell (ed.), *Feminist Interpretation of the Bible* (Philadelphia: Westminster Press, 1985), pp. 86-95; and Carole R. Fontaine, 'Response to the Book of Hosea', in Brenner and Fontaine (eds.), *Latter Prophets*, pp. 60-69, as well as other essays in that volume.

divine content and purpose that it has been so difficult to analyze the ways in which the Bible might be contributing to the various oppressions visited upon different groups—women, children, foreigners of other faiths, homosexuals, and the created universe. Those engaged in scholarly research on the Bible have also been blinded by inherited religious sensibilities about the nature of the Bible, refusing to ask some of the common-sense questions which they would put to any other ancient document as a matter of course. This may be seen particularly in the ways the *character of God* has been exempted from the rigorous critical study that is usually applied to human characters.[19] One could read the Hebrew Bible for years using the 'value-neutral' mainstream/ malestream scholarly methodology developed in historical criticism, without ever asking the kinds of questions about character and action, human and divine, raised by feminist scholarship.[20] Given the problematic behavior displayed by the Father God of the Bible in both Hebrew and Christian Scriptures,[21] the careful reader is certainly entitled to some serious doubts when being asked to affirm the standard Christian theological metaphor 'God is Love', for the truth of that claim is by no means clear. If the patriarchal God is *really* an impartial and loving Redeemer, then let him redeem: we the readers should not be forced to make humanity 'guilty' in order to preserve the innocence of a god who does not act.[22] If the combined impact of historical-critical scholarship allied with the feminist method has worked to erode some of the Bible's traditional authority as the Word of God and branded it for what it is—the words of elite males projected onto deity to protect and legitimate the powers of patriarchy[23]—then we are truly living in a time of signs and wonders. The god of the text is a composite literary figure, woven by male authors from many times and places. At best,

---

19. Danna Nolan Fewell and David Gunn, *Gender, Power and Promise: The Subject of the Bible's First Story* (Nashville, TN: Abingdon Press, 1993), pp. 18-19.

20. Phyllis Trible, *Texts of Terror: Literary-Feminist Readings of Biblical Narratives* (OBT; Philadelphia: Fortress Press, 1984). While flawed methodologically in various ways, this work represents one of the first fruits of feminist literary analysis of abusive texts.

21. Male deities from the ancient Near East share in the abusive tendencies seen in the Bible, especially Enki, Marduk, Chemosh/Molech, Ba'al, and so on, but jealous rage is more associated with goddesses, such as Inanna/Ishtar and Anat.

22. So, too, with the Book of Lamentations and *Lamentations Rabbah*. For modern perspectives, see Blumenthal, *Abusing God*; James L. Crenshaw, *A Whirlpool of Torment: Israelite Traditions of God as an Oppressive Presence* (OBT, 12; Philadelphia: Fortress Press, 1984).

23. Edwin M. Good, 'Deception and Women: A Response', *Semeia* 42 (1988), pp. 117-32 (132).

this figure can be seen as the depository for many ideas about divinity, some common to the Bible's world, some different; at worst, we have an ideological portrait that has little or nothing to do with the experiential reality of most humans through the ages: the good are *not* protected; the weak are *not* preserved. History provides us with ample evidence that cheap theological answers to the problem of undeserved human suffering simply do not serve. Yet, one need not endorse a Divine Big Brother keeping score up in the sky in order to read the Bible profitably or in honest faith. There is much we do not, and will probably never know, but that does not mean that Meaning is absent from the cosmos or the human experience of making it, 'finding' it, living it. Furthermore, those who prefer a literal interpretation must make room somewhere for the human element in the production of the actual manuscripts of the Bible, and there we find a wedge for enlightenment. Perhaps God *did* whisper the words of the Torah in Moses' ear or sent Living Word into the world, but between the ear and the hand there is tremendous room for 'sin' and error to slip in. Acknowledgment of the Bible as a human product is the first step in undercutting its seeming authorization of the exploitation of any who are not in-group, elite males.[24]

In saying that the Bible is the human product of elite males, I do not mean to suggest that flashes of divine compassion and purpose may not be found within the Bible's covers, nor that the voice of marginalized persons is absent from its pages. The majority of those who composed and edited the Bible simply do not 'see' women, children, and gay or lesbian persons as true 'subjects' and in this, they usually are only following the reigning world-view of the cultures to which they belonged.[25] The Bible is the *heir* of patriarchy, not its originator. Ancient Near Eastern culture had made patriarchy its response to historical and socioeconomic changes long before Jews and Christians ever appeared on the historical scene, and pagan communities of the Greco-Roman world were thoroughly patriarchal as well.[26]

It is common for liberation theologians to suggest that the Bible is a manifesto of divinely authorized freedom for the oppressed.[27] It can be

---

24. Kwok Pui-Lan, 'Racism', pp.101-116 (102-103); Monika Fander, 'Historical Critical Methods', in Schüssler Fiorenza (ed.), *Searching the Scriptures*, I, pp. 205-24.

25. Fewell and Gunn, *Gender, Power and Promise*, pp. 9-21.

26. For example, Gerda Lerner's analysis of ancient Near East culture in *The Creation of Patriarchy* (New York: Oxford University Press, 1986), pp. 54-160.

27. See Susan Brooks Thistlethwaite's presuppositions in 'Every Two Minutes: Battered Women and Feminist Interpretation', in Russell (ed.), *Feminist Interpretation*, pp. 96-110; and also Elsa Tamez, *Bible of the Oppressed* (Maryknoll, NY: Orbis Books, 1982), where the author is unable to come to terms with the content of the Book of Joshua and leaves it out of her survey entirely.

read as such, certainly, but only by ignoring major portions of the work and burying any consideration of compositional factors. As New Testament theologian Elisabeth Schüssler Fiorenza has pointed out admirably, the Bible was written and edited by those who won the theological struggles of their day. It is the legacy of the 'winners', and shows little or no interest in promoting the perspectives of the losers.[28] One prominent black South African biblical theologian, Itumeleng Jeremiah Mosala, has stated that failure to identify the oppressor *within* the text is the single most pressing issue in Biblical liberation studies. Until we understand that injustice has been coded into the very text itself as it pursues the class interests of its authors and protagonists, progressive believers will be dumbfounded by the Bible's ability to support oppression. Even when the Bible falls into liberating hands, it can still provide the catalyst for domination and submission because, as a human product, it is not free from finitude, particularized vision, and sin.[29] I would add to Mosala's strictures that we must also foreground the *gender*, *class*, and *race* interests of the biblical authors when we seek to construct liberating interpretations.

These interpretations will naturally vary, depending on the communities making them. Some Jewish feminists may see their Christian sisters as having something of an advantage in the New Testament's (supposed) portrayal of a gospel of liberation against which all non-liberating traditions may be measured, judged, and reformed—while Jewish texts, reflecting Jewish life and practice over centuries, may lack such a unifying theme to press into feminist service.[30] Others, like Judith Plaskow, may rightly point to subliminal and inchoate anti-Judaic propositions buried within the Christian feminist appropriation of the Hebrew Bible and understandings of Jesus which highlight his opposition to Judaism, rather than the manifold continuities which the New Testament also preserves.[31] Some Christian feminists may find Jewish feminists more empowered by the wealth of Jewish traditions about El-Shaddai, the suckling God, or God's Shekinah, the indwelling, feminine

28. *In Memory of Her: A Feminist Theological Reconstruction of Christian Origins* (New York: Crossroad, 1983), pp. 3-91.

29. Itumeleng J. Mosala, 'The Use of the Bible in Black Theology', in Itumeleng J. Mosala and Buti Tlhagale (eds.), *The Unquestionable Right to Be Free: Black Theology from South Africa* (Maryknoll, NY: Orbis, 1986), pp. 175-99; Katie Cannon, 'Womanist Interpretation and Preaching in the Black Church', in Schüssler Fiorenza (ed.), *Searching the Scriptures*, I, pp. 326-38.

30. Ellen M. Umansky, 'Creating a Jewish Feminist Theology: Possibilities and Problems', in Judith Plaskow and Carol P. Christ (eds.), *Weaving the Visions: New Patterns in Feminist Spirituality* (San Francisco: Harper, 1989), pp. 187-98 (189).

31. Fortune, *Keeping the Faith*, pp. 81-85 (81).

presence of God.³² Clearly, the grass sometimes seems greener on patriarchy's other side, and each group may have something to learn from the other.³³

To most of the Christian and Jewish scholarly world, even those seminary outposts of the scholarly guild, the Bible is in some part a human product which pursues the interests of its authors and authorizing patriarchal communities. We should not be surprised, then, when the agendas of the Bible's male authors seem to be working at cross-purposes to the establishment of a baseline of personal dignity for women, children, and non-heterosexuals. Even where women or children are allowed to speak they are almost always shown as carrying out the patriarchal imperatives of their culture, and gay men are translated right out of existence.³⁴ The Songs of Miriam, Deborah, Hannah, and even that meek and mild Virgin Mary speak glowingly of the vindicating violence of their male god and judge, simply reversing the roles of oppressor and oppressed through divine intervention.

> I will sing to the Lord, for he has triumphed gloriously;
>   the horse and his rider he has thrown into the sea.
> The Lord is my strength and my song,
>   and he has become my salvation;
> this is my God, and I will praise him,
>   my father's God and I will exalt him.
> The Lord is a man of war;
>   Yahweh is his name (Exod. 15.1b-3).

> Those who were full have hired themselves out for bread,
>   but those who were hungry have ceased to hunger.
> The barren has borne seven,
>   but she who has many children is forlorn.
> The Lord kills and brings to life;
>   he brings down to Sheol and raises up… (1 Sam. 2.5-6).

> He has put down the mighty from their thrones,
>   and exalted those of low degree;
> he has filled the hungry with good things,
>   and the rich he has sent empty away… (Lk. 1.52-53).

---

32. For example, M.T. Winter's *Woman Prayer, Woman Song: Resources for Ritual* (Oak Park, IL: Meyer-Stone Books, 1987), pp. 5-10, 17-21, 51-57; Susan Cady, Marian Ronan and Hal Taussig, *Wisdom's Feast: Sophia in Study and Celebration* (San Francisco: Harper & Row, 1989). For a philological discussion see David Biale, 'The God with Breasts: El Shaddai in the Bible', *History of Religions* 21 (1981-82), pp. 240-56.

33. For difficulties raised by Christian feminist appropriation of Jewish theological motifs, see Chapter 4 in this volume.

34. Fewell and Gunn, *Gender, Power, and Promise*, pp. 148-51.

Now, even if we were to be able to prove that these psalms of thanksgiving were authored by the women to whom they are attributed—to be sure, no easy task, though research on women as authors of victory and other songs continues to inform our inquiries[35]—have we gained very much by being able to point proudly to these passages as if they were written by women? Miriam's exultation in her war-god easily glosses over the fate of the Egyptians; Hannah's joy in her pregnancy expresses itself in the gleeful observation of the wicked getting their 'just desserts'; and this same theme dominates Mary's Magnificat. Once contextualized,[36] we can see liberating reasons why the text might have been shaped in such a way—the wonder of proto-Israelite slaves escaping from the might of an imperial empire, the vindication of the humiliated barren woman (a stock character representing social failure), the acceptance of the Annunciation. But even so, are the sentiments expressed, however human and understandable, actually sentiments we want to flourish and grow? Is the answer to the violence visited on women and children to mete out the same treatment to little boys and men? An uncritical reading of these 'liberation' passages certainly leaves the answer to such questions in doubt. When the Bible (or the Midrash, or the Church Fathers, and so on) fails us, we should feel no hesitation in saying so. Were we to apply the same code of behavior encapsulated in these psalms to modern situations of domestic and sexual violence, we would do nothing more than contribute to the creation of another generation of abusers. Only by ending the cycle of violence once and for all, and not by perpetuating it through role reversal, can we have hope of bringing to a halt the reign of terror under which so many lives are lived.

---

35. Jonneke Bekkenkamp and Fokkelien van Dijk-Hemmes, 'The Canon of the Old Testament and Women's Cultural Traditions', in Athalya Brenner (ed.), *A Feminist Companion to the Song of Songs* (FCB, 1; Sheffield: Sheffield Academic Press, 1993), pp. 67-85; Athalya Brenner and Fokkelien van Dijk-Hemmes, *On Gendering Texts: Female and Male Voices in the Hebrew Bible* (BIS, 1; Leiden: E.J. Brill, 1993).

36. Social location and literary context are powerful forces which shape our reception of any motif. To give a personal example, most middle class white children in the United States are taught in kindergarten to identify 'our friend the policeman' as a person of safety and protection from whom they should not hesitate to seek help. As a child raised in a black ghetto in the South, I was taught, both by adults and personal observation, to classify 'policemen' as sources of danger and external coercive force. However, servicemen in the Armed Forces, who might have been thought to conform to the category 'men in uniform', were *not* identified by ghetto-dwellers as dangerous, since it was our own population group which filled the lower ranks of the military: in this case, '*they*' were also '*us*'.

5. *The Abusive Bible*

The very nature of the Bible, then—human words in fancy divine dress—has worked to undercut critique of its violence,[37] and most Christian readers have taken the easy way out by displacing objectionable material onto the Old Testament with its God of Wrath in order to exempt their New Testament with its God of Love. But there are other ways in which the believing communities' views of the Bible's divine nature have empowered the abuser as well. The male programs which guided the writing, selection and final editing of sacred texts decreed what would be of interest and what would be left out. In real terms, this means that merely on the basis of these texts we can know very little about the actual living conditions and thoughts of those who were outside the mainstream of the writer/editor's interests. Too much has been left out, and not all the power and glory of feminist biblical studies can write us back in, though many are trying. We are left arguing from silence or heretical texts, as Schüssler Fiorenza does in her *In Memory of Her*, but how binding will such arguments be to those who do not share her hermeneutic? It is a wonderful hermeneutic, this judging of the authenticity of revelation by measuring how far it goes *against* patriarchal expectations; I use it myself. But I also know from personal experience that it holds very little credibility with some of the 'old school' of biblicists and even less with conservative believers.

The Bible's assumption that male traditions and words are adequate expressions of female experience of the divine will continue to mutilate women's souls as long as certain literalistic interpretations hold sway. Let us consider the Psalms as an illustration of what is meant here. Students are often told, far too often in my opinion, that the Psalter is the prayer book of the peoples of God, that it is one of the most complete and finest expressions of all the seasons in the life of prayer. Is it really? I find no psalms that express despair over miscarriage, or seek vindication for the rape or incest survivor. My Psalter contains no thanksgiving psalms specifically aimed at the celebration of the survival of childbirth, no lyric praise for the miracle that takes place with menarche, no attention at all to the various phases of growth and biological change that mark a woman's life—unless we wish to count the royal wedding psalm, Psalm 45. This psalm addresses a few lines to the lucky bride, assuring her that her kin and the protection they offer are to be replaced by the king's desire for her (vv. 10-11) and ending with a line any abuser would cheerfully second: 'Since he is your lord, bow to him'. Despite recent admirable attempts to reconsider the possibility of women's author-

---

37. For a powerful analysis of this tendency in prophetic works, see Athalya Brenner, 'Introduction', in Brenner and Fontaine (eds.), *Latter Prophets*, pp. 21-37.

ship of some of the psalms,[38] the Psalter I read is about the seasons and yearnings of men's lives; and that is fine, as far as it goes. Men need poetry and prayer, too. It is only with much rewriting that women's voices and concerns are heard in these prayers. We may write ourselves in—we do and we should—but not all the feminine pronouns in the world, bracketed into the original text, can produce a book that cared from its inception about women and girls as central *subjects*.[39] I don't believe that the Psalmists left women out deliberately; I doubt that it ever occurred to them to put them in as anything other than bit players in the drama of the male quest for meaning, hegemony, and progeny.

With such a legacy of support for the male author's unconscious tendency to place himself at the center of God's concerns, it is no wonder that the Bible can make laws which sentence a virgin who is the survivor of sexual violence to death if she was assaulted in the city, since she must have not screamed loudly enough to bring help (Deut. 22.23-29). The men who wrote those laws either did not understand or did not care to acknowledge all the methods of coercion and terror employed upon a woman in such circumstances. As if this law were not bad enough, its corollary is in some ways even worse: if the survivor is *not* a betrothed virgin, her father receives financial compensation from the aggressor for the damage done to the woman's market value as 'untouched', and the victim receives the unenviable compensation of being forced to marry her attacker. The New Testament presses its patriarchal vision even into the metaphysical realm: presumably, the survivor is forever joined in spirit and flesh to the one who violated her (1 Cor. 6.15-16). Those who can worship a god portrayed as authorizing such conditions for survivors are welcome to him.

These comments should not be taken to mean that the Bible is any *worse* than most of the literature of its kind from the rest of the ancient Near East, though I have found texts from Mesopotamia, Egypt, Canaan, and Anatolia that are empowering in the extreme. The Bible is not as bad as some, and certainly better than many, parallel texts from the neighboring cultures—particularly in its treatment of in-group slaves, the powerful role of mothers and those not favored by being the privileged first-born.[40] But the more or less overt exclusion of the female voice from

---

38. Patrick D. Miller, *They Cried to the Lord: The Form and Theology of Biblical Prayer* (Minneapolis: Fortress Press, 1994), pp. 233-43.

39. There are, of course, wonderful exceptions to be found in both Hebrew and Christian Scriptures.

40. By 'in-group' slaves, I mean slaves (usually debt-slaves) who belong to the same ethnic group as their masters. The Hebrew Bible's positive treatment of the second born is sometimes referred to as 'the success of the unsuccessful' motif.

the Bible's pages[41] was possible in part because the canonical Bible was missing an important element found in other ancient Near East religious texts: the presence of goddesses. When a culture engaged in goddess-worship, women—though, to be sure, usually drawn from the elite classes—were sometimes necessary to officiate in the cult, and hence were not so easy to exclude as citizens of the moral universe.[42] It may be, however, that our usual dismissal of pagan cults containing goddesses on the basis of their presumed elitism and moral inferiority[43] must be reevaluated. Recent evidence from the Late Bronze Age Temple of the Storm God at Emar (Tell Meskéné on the Euphrates in Syria) suggests once again how the vagaries of the survival of evidence may have skewed our interpretations. The ritual (Emar 369) for the installation of the Storm God's High Priestess (NIN.DINGIR), who is clearly understood as a human surrogate for and devotee of the Mother Goddess consort of the Storm God, says that the new priestess is chosen by lots from among the daughters of 'any son of Emar'. While it may be that betrothal customs caused some noble daughters to be designated for this applicant pool at birth (thereby ruling out candidates from less exalted families), we cannot ignore the fact that we may well have a sort of egalitarian cultic job-opening presented here, in a ritual where kings and royal family play very limited roles in contrast to the city elders. While the NIN.DINGIR was related primarily to the Storm God, it is clear from the ritual that her relationship to his consort Hebat, the ancient Syrian mother goddess of the Hurrian/Hittite pantheon, forms a major part of the symbol system which authorizes the NIN.DINGIR's role. What is also clear from the ritual is the assumption that the enhanced status of High Priestess of the Storm God is viewed as a result of the transfer of the woman in question from the sphere of control by her father to that of her divine 'husband'. The other high priestess installation text from Emar, dealing with the *mašartu* of the military goddess Aštart (Emar 370), while sharing many characteristics with the installation of the NIN.DINGIR, also contains significant differences which are possibly to be attributed to the martial character of the goddess in question.[44] Some

---

41. But for an intriguing reassessment of the presence of the female voice in the Hebrew Bible, see Brenner and van Dijk-Hemmes, *On Gendering Texts*.

42. H.G. Güterbock, 'An Outline of the Hittite AN.TA.ŠUM Festival', *JNES* 19 (1960), pp. 80-86 (86). For an overview of the relation of women to goddess-cults, see Carole R. Fontaine, ' "A Heifer from thy Stable": On Goddesses and the Status of Women in the Ancient Near East', in Alice Bach (ed.), *Women in the Hebrew Bible: A Reader* (New York: Routledge, 1999), pp. 159-78.

43. For example, cultic practices in which women (allegedly) have more than one sexual partner, or a partner to whom they are not legally married.

44. See D.E. Fleming, *The Installation of Baal's High Priestess at Emar: A Window*

of these goddesses whom the Bible so skillfully propagandized as some sort of an 'abomination' were believed to protect women in childbed, stand as the protector of prostitutes[45] (surely one of the most marginalized classes of women in the ancient world), and serve as the focus of prayer for real women whose words have been found on clay tablets across the Fertile Crescent.

The words and deeds of these ancient females, human and divine, speak specifically to the matters here before us. When Inanna, the Queen of Heaven and Earth from ancient Sumer (modern Shi'a Iraq), is raped by a gardener who comes across her while she sleeps beneath a tree, she hunts him into the cities of Sumer. When she cannot find him in the midst of the populace that shelters him, she turns all the wells of the land to blood—a motif repeated, with slight variation, by the Hebrew God in defense of the enslaved children of Israel (Exod. 4.9; 7.17-21). When Ninhursag, the mother-goddess, discovers that her mate Enki, the god of sweet water/wisdom, has impregnated successive generations of her daughters, she intervenes, telling the latest object of his desire how to turn the deed to her own benefit (i.e., how to become a desiring subject), and has a part in the later punishment of the god.

Moving from the cosmic to the earthly domain, when Enheduanna, a priestess of Sumer and devotee of Inanna, is ousted from her temple by a male usurper, her psalm of lament is specific and to the point: 'O my divine impetuous wild cow', she cries to her goddess, 'drive out this man, capture this man!' When a royal princess of Mari, a city on the Euphrates during the Old Babylonian period, is abused emotionally and physically by her husband and then threatened with death, she writes home, 'If he (the king) does not bring me back, I shall die; I will not live'; and again, 'If my lord does not bring me back, I will head toward Mari (and there) jump (fall) from the roof'. The determination of that one real, flesh and blood woman to reach safe haven—which she

---

on *Ancient Syrian Religion* (Atlanta: Scholars Press, 1992), pp. 49-59, 174-75, 188-92, 209-211 and 'More Help from Syria: Introducing Emar to Biblical Study', *BA* 58 (1995), pp. 139-47.

45. This motif of 'goddess functions' needs to be contextualized, since it is clear that goddess temples benefited economically (as did private owners) from the use of female slaves hired out to brothels for prostitution: Amélie Kuhrt, 'Non-Royal Women in the Late Babylonian Period: A Survey', in Barbara S. Lesco (ed.), *Women's Earliest Records: From Ancient Egypt and Western Asia* (BJS, 166; Atlanta: Scholars Press, 1989), pp. 232-37 (232-33, 235-37). In cultures where women's status and fulfillment come through legal marriage and childbearing, the closing off of these options to certain groups of women must be viewed as negatively impacting their self-esteem and life circumstances.

eventually did—is more of a tribute to women's will to survive than all the historicized wails for the dutiful daughter of Jephthah.[46] It may be noted from this brief citation of parallel texts that the sentiments expressed in them are *no less violent* in some respects than those mentioned above in the Bible, nor are they necessarily any more 'moral' by modern standards. But these parallel texts *do* express the depth of emotional reaction by women suffering abuse, rather than the pious words of women characters whose real-life responses have been edited out of existence, or subsumed under a nationalistic epic.[47] Such ancient Near East texts point to the need for a divine advocate who is unambiguously ranged on the side of female sufferers and with whom women might reasonably identify. This brings us to the actual content of the Bible. As bad as the supposed nature of the Bible has been and is in authorizing and perpetuating a unified view of existence which excludes the voices of women and children and the identification of a deity who really protects them,[48] often the *content*—what the stories and laws actually *say*—is much, much worse.

2. *The Content of the Bible*

I have suggested how what has been *left out* of the Bible—the unedited voices of real women and children and a deity who saves them, regardless of their gender—works to the disadvantage members of those groups. Now we must consider the effects of what has been *put in*. Here, I would like to address some trends in certain aspects of the patriarchal world-view which many modern readings of the Bible work to sustain.[49] I divide some of these trends into three categories and will deal with each in turn: establishment of gendered authority, role reversal, and the commodification of fertility.

---

46. Fontaine, 'Heifer', pp. 159-78 (168-69). For translations of the mythological texts see James B. Pritchard, *Ancient Near Eastern Texts Relating to the Old Testament* (Princeton, NJ: Princeton University Press, 3rd edn, 1969), pp. 38-41. For discussion of Inanna, see Carole R. Fontaine, 'The Deceptive Goddess in Ancient Near Eastern Myth: Inanna and Inaras', *Semeia* 42 (1988), pp. 84-102.

47. Bekkenkamp and van Dijk-Hemmes, 'Women's Cultural Traditions', pp. 67-85 (69). Metaphorization of female experience into a signifier of more important *male, national* themes is a defining trait of androcentric biblical narrative.

48. All the deities and human rulers of the ancient Near East had a special obligation to protect widows and orphans, so we cannot attribute any special concern for these groups to Yahweh (contrary to popular interpretive practice), since this is a standard motif. See Charles Fensham, 'Widow, Orphan and the Poor in Ancient Near Eastern Legal and Wisdom Literature', *JNES* 21 (1962), pp. 129-39.

49. Bussert, *Battered Women*, pp. 55-66.

Gendered Authority

The critical role that gender plays in the establishment of coercive and exclusive authority may be seen exerted in arguments from antiquity (e.g. 1 Tim. 2.11-14), right down to present-day pronouncements by the Vatican on the fitness of womanpersons for the priesthood. Men's fear of women's power is everywhere in evidence (cf. Gen. 38.11; Est. 1.13-22; 1 Esd. 4.13-32; and many more). The almost absolute authority of the father in the patriarchal society is empowered by the choice of male pronouns to refer to the god who is the source of the father's authority. This works to create a vicious little circle in the construction of gendered authority: because God is male—not *really*, we are always told; the referential language for God just *happens* (sic) to be male—obviously the elder male in the household *ought* to be the one to hold the most authority. The contrary is then true: because the eldest male holds the most power in the household (which is the basic unit of production in antiquity and hence usually the model for larger social units), obviously the divine being who holds the most authority *must* be the Father-god. Within strict monotheism, the goddesses are officially 'disappeared'. They are polemicized out of the pages of Scripture even though they remain alive and well, though sometimes reshaped, in Aggadic legend, popular worship, the portraits of the New Testament Marys, and Sophia theology.[50] This official disappearance makes the reinforcing bond between deity and maleness so much easier to view as 'normative', as does the direct transfer of the activities of goddesses to the Israelite Father-god. It may be, too, that this very transfer of 'goddess functions' to the biblical god has allowed women over the centuries to find comfort and concern in a Scripture which otherwise tends to exclude them. It must be pointed out, however, that even when the protective goddesses are present as in other ancient Near East societies, we do not always see a marked improvement in the economic or power circumstances of women and children.[51] Surviving texts, while suggestive, do not usually allow for a full reconstruction of their spiritual lives.

---

50. There is currently considerable debate about whether or not Yahweh had a consort. Whatever the proper translation for 'Asherah' turns out to be, Yahweh certainly had one! See Ze'ev Meshel, 'Did Yahweh Have a Consort?', *BARev* 5 (1979), pp. 24-35; Walter A. Maier, III, *'Ašerah: Extrabiblical Evidence* (HSM, 37; Atlanta: Scholars Press, 1986); and Saul M. Olyan, *Asherah and the Cult of Yahweh in Israel* (SBLMS, 34; Atlanta: Scholars Press, 1988). See also Steve Davies, 'The Canaanite-Hebrew Goddess', in Carl Olson (ed.), *The Book of the Goddess: Past and Present* (New York: Crossroad, 1985), pp. 68-79, and other articles in that volume. For a strikingly negative assessment of the presence of goddesses in ancient Near East culture, pressed into a defense of the Hebrew Bible's monotheism, see Tikva Frymer-Kensky, *In the Wake of the Goddesses* (New York: Fawcett Columbine, 1992).

51. The effects of the presence of goddesses are analyzed in Gerda Lerner's

We see now how this all works: if the Divine Father has absolute power over the lives of his worshippers, it must have seemed very natural that men should have similar powers over their dependents. Now the Bible itself sees such authority and power as good and stabilizing, and tends to view any sort of challenge to the father's authority as an attempt to rend the very fabric of society—and rightly so. An attack on the patriarchal family wherein women and children and the rights to their unpaid labor are viewed as the exclusive property of the father *is* an assault on the fundamental locus of patriarchal power.

Now, common sense tells us that a father who routinely sacrifices his children and murders his wives is not going to be very successful in maintaining a problem-free base of power, and so we do see limitations on the father's absolute right to do as he pleases with the lives of his 'dependents'. Still, this image of God as a patriarchal father has had a nasty, deforming effect on our theological portrait of the deity; and its legitimation of male power has had drastic and tragic effects on the lives of real women and children, even unto this very day.[52] The father-god portrayed in Hosea is an ambivalent, mean-spirited father who is jealous of the attempts of his 'son' Israel to individuate and grow into a mature, self-directed adult; the Christian Father-god who shows his love by sacrificing his innocent son continues this disturbing paradigm.[53] We should not be shocked then to discover that the human fathers of the Bible are as apt to sacrifice their children for the fulfillment of pious vows as they are to cradle them with tender love. One of my men students, after a course on feminist critical hermeneutics, pointed out that the gender roles decreed for men in the Bible are just as oppressive and terrorizing as the ones laid out for women—imagine being condemned to live out one's family life playing out the roles authorized by the stories of Abraham, Jephthah, David, or Job. If the Bible has sometimes worked to slay women's bodies, it has also had the effect of killing men's souls.[54] If the role of the pastor, rabbi or priest has been

---

Creation of Patriarchy, pp. 141-60; for a more textually based and methodologically nuanced discussion of the meaning of goddesses in women's religious lives, see my 'Heifer'.

52. One of my women seminary students remarked that she knew an upcoming event in her life must be 'God's will', because she felt such revulsion when she thought of the dreaded and disliked duty. I commented that perhaps there might be other images of God than that of commanding father, and suggested that God was a Clown who wanted to take her to the circus, ply her with all the fat-free chocolate ice cream she could eat, and then tickle her until she collapsed in laughter.

53. Fontaine, 'Response to Hosea'.

54. The 'maleness' of God is certainly not without problems for men; see Howard Eilberg-Schwartz, *God's Phallus and Other Problems for Men and Monotheism* (Boston:

modeled on that of the Father-god or the human father, as presented by patriarchy, are we still surprised that opportunities for abuse routinely occur? If the 'root metaphor' is flawed, then the fruits of praxis drawn from it usually carry and replicate that same flaw. I personally doubt if a wholesome theology can be built using the models of dominance and submission that are the real 'message' carried by the structure of patriarchal family. If we are to call humanity into greater responsibility toward the planet and those who populate it, we need models of mutuality and common respect, not gods who sacrifice their children. Rita Nakashima Brock takes the first step for Christians in reinventing the meaning of Incarnation from a feminist perspective in *Journeys by Heart: A Christology of Erotic Power*; whether this re-imagining of the faith can be tolerated, much less embraced, by the Christian Church remains to be seen.[55]

Role Reversal

That the content of the Bible can often be understood as patriarchal propaganda is attested by the number of times the text engages in overt role reversals. Powers that have to do with women's 'biological creativity' are transferred wholesale to the Father-god, who is now considered to be the one who opens and closes the womb[56] and brings healthy children to birth. This may be because Israel's God bears the marks of goddess mythology and roles which have been transferred to him, but the effect has *not* been the creation of an androgynous god who is authentically 'there' for most women; at least, we haven't read it that way so far. The pragmatic effect has been a lessening of women's visible role in the creation of life. Think of the Genesis narratives where the first humans are created: what a shocking reversal. Instead of the natural order of men (and women) emerging from the bodies of women, a fact verified by simple observation, we are told as a religious datum of the highest order that the first woman emerged from the body of a male—assisted, of course, by the Father-god.[57] Yes, we *can* read that

Beacon Press, 1994); Daniel Boyarin, *Unheroic Conduct: The Rise of Heterosexuality and the Invention of the Jewish Man* (Contraversions – Critical Studies in Jewish Literature, Culture, and Society, 8; Berkeley: University of California Press, 1997).

55. Rita Nakashima Brock, *Journeys by Heart: A Christology of Erotic Power* (New York: Crossroad, 1991).

56. Hence, the Father-god is the one who determines a woman's status among her patriarchal folk group, since her evaluation as a success or failure is based on her ability to produce sons. See Jacob's reply to Rachel in Gen. 30.2.

57. This feature of the Genesis account was first pointed out to me by Judith Plaskow. For a textually based, psychoanalytic interpretation of these reversals in the area of fertility see David Bakan, *And They Took for Themselves Wives: The Emergence of Patriarchy in Western Civilization* (New York: Harper & Row, 1979), pp. 103-34.

first earth-creature as androgynous, as do various Jewish traditions and many feminist biblical scholars; but this has seldom been the dominant reading in religious circles, and the reason for that is that the existing role reversal functions to privilege men over women.

Another example of role reversal occurs in places where the questionable actions of men are given a new twist that conveniently allows the survivor to be blamed. Incestuous relations are usually instituted by the parent, primarily the father, not by the children; but in Gen. 19.30-38 we are told that Lot's daughters instigated the incestuous unions that resulted in the birth of the eponymous ancestors of Israel's disliked neighbors, Moab and Ammon. Of course the story serves a complex etiological function in its literary context, but the plain reading of it—which is what most people in the Church are doing with the text—excuses Lot and leaves a false impression about the gender of those who usually initiate such forbidden contacts within the family unit. It is Judah who begins the questionable coupling with a supposed hierodule in Gen. 38.16, an act allowed by a full-functioning 'double standard'; but Tamar is the one blamed for 'playing the harlot' (v. 24).[58] It is the disreputable judge Jephthah who makes the unnecessary vow to safeguard his victory in Judg. 11.30-31; but it is his innocent daughter who is blamed for the outcome in v. 35. The mighty hero chastises the unarmed girl with his reply to her expected greeting at his return, 'Alas, my daughter! You have brought me very low, and you have become the cause of great trouble to me; for I have opened my mouth to the Lord, and I cannot take back my vow'.[59] Samson initiates the 'dangerous liaisons' with foreign women in Judges but the text implicitly blames the foreign women (Judg. 14–16). David's lustful eye falls upon a married woman as she bathes in 2 Sam. 11.2, but it is Bathsheba and David's other children who suffer the consequences for the deaths that follow from the illicit union. When Prince Amnon sexually violates his half-sister Tamar in 2 Samuel 13, we hear that after the act, 'he hated her with a very great hate' (v.15). Rabbinic exegetes supplied here a motivation that astonishes the modern reader: one of Tamar's pubic hairs mutilated Amnon during intercourse. Clearly, the blame is *hers*.[60] In 1 Kgs 5.13-18, Solomon exerts

---

58. This example is somewhat unusual since Judah allows that Tamar was 'more righteous' than he, since he refused to obey the law of the levirate marriage with regard to his daughter-in-law.

59. Trible, *Texts of Terror*, pp. 93-118.

60. *B. Sanh.* 21a. The passage continues by attributing a patriarchal value lesson in submission to all women on-lookers: 'It was taught in the name of R. Joshua b. Kora, In that hour Tamar set up a great fence [about chastity]. They (all other women) said: If this could happen to kings' daughters, how much more to the daughters of ordinary men; if this could happen to the chaste, how much more to the wanton?

more coercive power over his subjects than any who have gone before; but it is his foreign wives who are held responsible for any troubles in his reign in 1 Kgs. 11.1-6. And so it goes: if a woman so much as allows herself to be *seen* by the male protagonist, much less possessed by him, she can be blamed for anything that ensues, or so it would seem.[61]

The Commodification of Fertility
I have alluded to aspects of this phenomenon earlier, by suggesting the ways in which attributions of fertility to the Father-god and his human stand-ins lessens the role of women in this realm. The male usurpation of the primary symbolic roles in the production of new life—otherwise known as paternity—also had concrete effects in restricting the lives of women. Once the male role in conception was properly understood, probably through contact with animal husbandry, the patriarchal control of women's sexuality was set in train. If a father was to transfer his property and power to his own offspring, he had to have some way of feeling relatively certain that the inheritor was *indeed* his son.[62] The most convenient way of safeguarding the paternity of a woman's child was to restrict her movements and, hence, the opportunity for some other male to 'poach' on the husband's private territory. Here is born the double-standard: while men are permitted a variety of sexual contacts, the woman's reproductivity is to be regarded as belonging exclusively to her husband, for it is a valuable commodity to which the owner has exclusive rights.

Once a woman's body is rhetorically 'owned' in such a way,[63] rather than given freely in an atmosphere of mutual consent as in the Song of Songs (but note that the lovers there have yet to marry), the step toward the abuse of that body has already been taken—who has the authority

(I. Epstein [ed.], *The Babylonian Talmud* XXIII: *Tractate Sanhedrin* [trans. J. Shachter and H. Freedman; London: Soncino Press, 1935], p. 115). One wonders what kinds of evaluation would have been applied to Tamar, had she refused to obey an order of the king her father in order to guard a potential threat to her chastity. A traditional saying covers very well the sort of net which ensnares women trapped in patriarchal power politics: 'Damned if you do; damned if you don't'.

61. The same problems obtain in modern genres which treat women primarily as objectifications of the desiring male subject. See Ann E. Kaplan, 'Is the Gaze Male?', in Ann Snitow, Christine Stansell and Sharon Thompson (eds.), *Powers of Desire: The Politics of Sexuality* (New York: Monthly Review Press, 1983), pp. 309-27.

62. We might think here of the old joke which differentiates 'belief' from 'knowledge': a father may *believe* that his wife's child is his own, but the mother *knows*—at least, we trust that she does.

63. Said one feminist poet from Algeria of the gender jihad in her country, 'What began in words ended in crimes'.

to interfere in the way one man chooses to treat his own property? And if that ownership has been handed over as part of the divine plan (the typical reading of Gen. 3.16b),[64] in what court, human or divine, will the voice of the one so owned be raised with any real effect? Granted, the Bible and the traditions that interpret it try to nuance all these laws of ownership of women, children, slaves and animals so that humane treatment is the rule and not the exception; the occasions presented for abuse and betrayal out of such a way of thinking and being cannot be so easily swept away. It is no surprise that the Women's Rights Movement in the United States was born out of women's participation in the Slavery Abolition movement. Once women learned through their anti-slavery efforts where they *really* stood as persons and citizens, they realized that they must improve their own condition and achieve the vote if they were ever to be of any potent political use to slaves. It is a great sorrow to see the way white women and peoples of color in the United States today have allowed a wedge to be inserted between their struggles against racism and sexism, for the two are bound together in their real-life expressions, if not always in theory. Minorities will discover eventually that most elite white men are willing enough to give them the same kind of 'equality' that they have extended to white women, and newcomers to the power structure will learn in bitterness just how *little* such equality really means. White feminists who think no further than advancing the class interests of themselves and their sisters will discover too that unless they address issues of race and class, the freedoms and dignity they achieve will remain hollow and partial. When feminist criticism in the Christian churches and their seminaries addresses itself primarily to the equality of (white, educated) women and their vocational quest to break through the 'stained glass ceiling' which keeps them from holding real power positions in the structures of authority in the Church, it fails to uphold its multi-cultural origins and rightly fails to interest womanist, Mujerista, and Asian women theologians in its agenda. As complex and difficult as these challenges are, they must be addressed together if progress is to be made.

3. *We the Readers: The Function of the Bible, Revisited*

I have already touched on some of the functions of the Bible in its original settings and traditional theological interpretations: preserving a perspective on the history of the community that accepts it as its own, and serving as a template upon which new members of the communities

---

64. For a markedly different reading, see J.J. Schmitt, 'Like Eve, like Adam: *mšl* in Gen 3, 16', *Biblica* 72 (1991), pp. 1-22.

might shape their behaviors and beliefs. Within this matrix of remembrance and education, texts could serve as many different purposes as there are genres; that is, wisdom texts teach, laws regulate community life, prophecy calls the community to account, gospels bear witness, and so on. Scholars often tend to assume implicitly that a text usually pursues and propagates the meaning intended in it by the author, but the recent flowering of literary and aesthetic theory in biblical studies has brought other analyses to bear. What I want to mention here in particular is the fact that, as religious[65] art—and since the Bible is a literary composition, it can certainly lay claim to some of what we mean when we speak of art—the Bible is capable of carrying a range of meanings and interpretations all *at the same time*. This view of the Bible's multivalence is perhaps *the* basic tenet of the literary critical approach. We are beginning to understand better *how* texts make meaning, and to press our questions into the realm of reader response. By what rules do readers select the meaning they will take away from a text? As readers, how do we do what we do, and *why* do we do it? These are the sorts of questions troubling the literary branch of biblical studies these days. Another great question is waiting in the wings once the issue of reception of a text is taken up: What relationship does an artistic text bear to social reality? For instance, if a prophet raves on and on about Israel 'playing the harlot', what inferences, if any, does that text allow us to make about harlotry in general, Israel's behavior in particular, and how society thought about women whose sexual behavior was viewed as improperly regulated by men?[66]

The issue of how the Bible functioned in ancient days and at present is not an easy one, and simple answers will fail to express the complexity embodied in our questions. Reading communities have always made interpretations with their own needs and circumstances in mind: slaveholders in the nineteenth-century Southern Confederacy had no trouble in justifying their practices from biblical teachings; slaves and those who acknowledged them as persons rejected those interpretations and supplied ones more conducive to their eventual liberation.[67] African

---

65. By 'religious' I do not mean the context of institutional religions, but the more broad human concern with questions of ultimate meaning.

66. Compare, for example, Robert P. Carroll, 'Desire under the Terebinths: On Pornographic Representation in the Prophets—A Response', in Brenner and Fontaine (eds.), *Latter Prophets*, pp. 275-307, with Renita J. Weems, *Battered Love: Marriage, Sex, and Violence in the Hebrew Prophets* (OBT ; Minneapolis: Fortress Press, 1995). See also Claudia V. Camp, 'Metaphor in Feminist Biblical Interpretation: Theoretical Perspectives', *Semeia* 61 (1993), pp. 3-38; and Mieke Bal, 'Metaphors He Lives By', pp. 185-208 in that volume.

67. Justice and full freedom for women, children, ethnic minorities, non-

American poet Paul Dunbar (1872-1906) demonstrates the liberating power of a Scripture reinterpreted by readers in distress in his 'An Ante-Bellum Sermon' which re-reads the Exodus of the Hebrew Bible for the slaves of the American South:

> But I tell you, fellah christuns,
> > Things'll happen mighty strange;
> Now, de Lawd done dis fu' Isrul,
> > An' his ways don't nevah change,
> An' de love he showed to Isrul
> > Was n't all on Isrul spent;
> Now don't run an' tell yo' mastahs
> > Dat I's preachin' discontent.
>
> 'Cause I is n't; I'se a-judgin'
> > Bible people by deir ac's;
> I'se a-givin' you de Scriptuah,
> > I'se a-handin' you de fac's.
> Cose ole Pher'oh b'lieved in slav'ry,
> > But de Lawd he let him see,
> Dat de people he put bref in,—
> > Evah mothah's son was free.[68]

4. *The Plain Sense of Abuse*

The readings presented in this essay have used the Bible in the most critical way possible, focusing on the 'plain sense' of the passages that authorize abuse and the hidden assumptions that motivate and sustain such texts and their readings. Since the principle of multivalence operates even in noxious texts, it is quite plausible that many alternative meanings might be given for the texts which I have used as examples. I stand by the readings presented here, for we have enough evidence to show that even if texts did not *set out* to marginalize women and children, such an interpretive move *did and still does* take place. No one should be surprised when someone for whom the Bible's divine authority (and hence, the preservation of patriarchy) is the highest value affirms that, no, it doesn't mean *that* at all. There *are* many legitimate readings of a single text, but for Christians I suggest the use of Jesus' measuring stick: *by their fruits you shall know them* (Mt. 7). Does a way of reading produce shame, terror, helplessness and self-hatred; or does it empower survivors to action, peace, love and self-acceptance? Why have we read the Bible traditionally in such a way as to support God's

---

heterosexuals, the disabled, and others in the United States remains an unfinished program as of this writing.

68. Dudley Randall (ed.), *The Black Poets* (New York: Bantam, 1971), p. 45.

and men's right to own and abuse instead of reading it as liberation, post-Holocaust Jewish, and feminist theologians now do?[69] We have done so because we have been taught to read in ways that limited our willingness or ability to challenge the status quo, but in some circles that is changing. If the Bible's function in past societies has been to socialize its people into an acceptance of the patriarchal world-view, for many people now, its current function is to serve as a locus for our critique of that very system. That is as it should be: we are entering a promised land where we the readers increasingly recognize our role in the making of meaning, and refuse to submit to the old rules that made us passive receivers of the eternal 'truths' supposedly contained in the text. Denial of the widespread abuse experienced by women, children, and others is still a feature of the religious communities' day-to-day existence. A Bible filled with abuse offers us a legitimate tool for foregrounding these issues that are so readily repressed by leaders and laypeople alike.

5. *Accounting for Hope: The Four 'R's*

I have come full circle back to the question raised by my title: the abusive Bible—how shall it be used in teaching for pastoral settings? Gentle Reader, you may now be wondering at this point why anyone in her or his right mind would have anything to do with the Bible at all. Good question. Fortunately, there are two solid answers: we deal with the Bible because we *must* and because it is *ours* to deal with.

First, we must take the Bible into account as long as women, children, and non-heterosexuals sitting in church or synagogue are exposed to the damage that a patriarchal Scripture can wreak on their self-understanding and sense of the world. As long as government officials in the United States Senate use the Bible as a resource for denying civil rights to homosexuals or launching pre-emptive wars against 'evil-doers', while at the same time ignoring the Bible's teachings about responsibility toward the poor, we must continue to be vocal and engaged *critical* readers.[70] As long as survivors of abuse turn to the Bible for comfort, or locate the God of the Bible as an actor in their history of suffering, then we must be prepared to talk openly and seriously about the nature of the Bible and the problems in its uncritical use.[71]

---

69. There have always been significant exceptions, even in mainstream scholarship. See, for example, C. Westermann's discussion of God's treatment of Cain in *Genesis 1–11: A Commentary* (trans. John J. Scullion; Minneapolis: Augsburg Publishing, 1984), pp. 281-320.

70. The so-called 'Defense of the Family' Act of 1996.

71. In fact, those who seek to provide pastoral care for survivors of abuse from

5. *The Abusive Bible*

Second, we must continue to deal with the Bible because it is ours and we are engaged with it, shaped by it, and can decide whether or not that should include a positive theology of abuse. That may sound too self-evident to be meaningful, but restated: the Bible is part of the religious and literary heritage of Jews and Christians. To jettison it because we see it with all its pits and valleys, all its byways into oppression, is to lessen our understanding of how we got where we are and what we are up against on the paths that we now choose to travel. Give up the loving intimacy and restored paradise of the Song of Songs? Do without the active, compassionate women of the Book of Exodus? Throw aside the first successful slaves' rebellion in recorded history? Live without the creation celebrated in Proverbs 8 or Job 38–42? Give up a Jesus, the Jew who envisions a new humanity, demonstrating that there may be another paradigm of maleness, another way to be human, perhaps even another way to understand God than by the traditional means of structures of domination and submission?[72] Never.

The canon must be made to serve the abused instead. This can be done by attending to the 'Four Rs': Re-opening, Re-assessing, Resisting, and Re-appropriating. We must *reopen* the canon to include other texts which help us understand the religious experience of the text's non-subjects. We must *reassess* what is presently there within its pages. Then we must decide: content, form, and function must be either *resisted* or *reaffirmed*, based on our best contextualizations and analysis. In all of this, we must covenant (as feminists do) to read *together*, even while fully acknowledging the manifold differences wrought by class, race, sex, nationality, and religious commitments, as well as our separate and differing approaches to reading as Christians, Jews, feminists, Third World persons, Neo-pagans, and so on. Only by including many points of view can we then expect to walk with integrity the fine line between a particularity that obscures and a universalism that blurs.

The Bible can be abusive, it is true. Its nature masquerades as divine and universal when it is not; the content contains assumptions and

---

conservative religious backgrounds must be prepared to enter into that world-view of the counsellee, and manipulate it for a positive outcome (which will, ideally, include critique of that world-view and its wholesome revision in the final stages of recovery). Holocaust survivor and psychiatrist Viktor Frankl makes the same point: '...when a patient stands on the firm ground of religious belief, there can be no objection to making use of the therapeutic effect of his religious convictions and thereby drawing upon his spiritual resources. In order to do so, the psychiatrist may put himself in the place of the patient...' (*Man's Search for Meaning* [New York: Pocket Books, rev. and updated, 1984], pp. 141-42). Admittedly, this process is far more difficult when the religious system of ideas is itself permeated by abusive concepts.

72. This is, of course, a feminist liberationist reading of the 'message' of the Gospels.

prescriptions that are downright harmful to the health of some of us; the function has too often been that of keeping the survivors quiet and submissive. Students entering ministry in the United States face an epidemic of domestic and sexual abuse which their mainstream, historical-critical study of the Bible leaves them ill-equipped to address. But in the midst of all that, it is also the record of the suffering of many who never saw redemption. We must keep faith with their memory for their sake, and because we do not wish to endlessly replicate their fate. Whose side is the Bible on? It can be on *our* side, the side of hope, the side of survival, if we choose ways of reading that neither deny the truth of abuse nor seek to normalize it in order to safeguard male authority, cultural heritage, or divine innocence and prerogatives. I suggest that we read with eyes wide open. Perhaps in reading together across time, space, and social location, believers can find in it a spirit of survival, and reason to give account for the hope that is in them (1 Pet. 3.15).

6. *Afterword: The Bible Abused in the Wake of September 11, 2001*

The United States, one of the most religious countries in the world, is in the midst of a 'culture war', we are told, with true Americans (always white Christians) pitted against godless secularists who do not seem to understand that God *wants* America to have all the world's resources on account of our exceptional goodness. Anyone who would care to dissent is neither truly American in a patriotic sense, nor a true believer of a 'Bible-based' faith. God even has his own president, we understand.[73] Nuance and history are both submerged beneath bleak apocalyptic theologies of election and punishment.

Since the early days of the new empire's attempt to spread *Pax americana* to the globe, things have come a long way. Public political figures are challenging the media and government propaganda that used religion in divisive ways to support anti-democratic programs of social change.[74] Blogs allow anyone with an opinion to make it known to the

---

73. Colin Campbell and Bert A. Rockman (eds.), *The George W. Bush Presidency: Appraisals and Prospects* (Washington, DC: CQ Press, 2003).

74. Raymond G. Helmick, SJ, and Rodney Petersen (eds.), *Forgiveness and Reconciliation: Religion, Public Policy, and Conflict Transformation, with a Foreword by Desmond Tutu* (Philadelphia and London: Templeton Foundation, 2001); Mark S. Burrows, ' "Peering into the Abyss of the Future": Empire in the Age of Globalization and the Call for a New Ecumenism', *Theologies and Cultures: Church and Empire* 2 (2005), pp. 26-55; Guy D. Nave, Jr, 'No Pax Romana: A Lukan Rejection of Imperial Peace', *Theologies and Cultures: Church and Empire* 2 (2005), pp. 56-72; Jimmy Carter, *Endangered Values: America's Moral Crisis* (New York: Simon & Schuster, 2006), especially pp. 30-46; John W. Dean, *Conservatives without Conscience* (New York: Viking, 2006), pp. 73-116.

world (even though the average blog has only one or two readers a day); Wikipedia, the on-line encyclopedia, gives everyone a chance to join in on the creation of knowledge. Even a feminist theologian of minor visibility can become a public target for the crimes of truth-telling about history and text. In particular, feminists have come in for their own weird experience of being bandied about in an ideological conflict in which they have little stake. We feminists, one learns from a *google* of blogs, have proven that the Bible is human, flawed, pornographic, and abusive. Hence, our work is flaunted as a tool to prove the superiority of Islamic Scripture.

Having been labeled a traitor for taking leave to doubt American exceptionalism, a pornographer (for writing on the Song of Songs), a person of no faith who perverts the righteous congregations trying to rid the world of the polluting stain of homosexuals in our midst, and a teacher who asks good US believing citizens to take a look at parallel literature or textual reception or…whatever, I confess that our brave new world is getting a little old at this point.[75] Naturally, I expect literalists to disagree with me (but I also expect them to learn Hebrew and Greek if they would like to have a serious conversation on issues), but some of the secular responses to a critical position on Bible are just as amazing.

The world's view of American religiosity is such that very few outside the shores of the US think that a believer can be thoughtful, well-educated, committed, or dedicated to global peace and justice. Our leaders and their politicized Christianity have abused the Bible so badly by making it a tool of our drive for world domination that anyone wishing to speak of the Bible is viewed with skepticism or outright contempt. 'Why do you even care?', one Muslim woman activist asked me. 'What does it matter to all of you if we are being slaughtered just for being women?'

It matters because we are all children of one planet, globally connected whether we like it or not. The female body as the site of abuse and the culturally-designated victim is a global condition. If my Muslim sisters are not safe, I am not safe either. If they are allowed no choice in whether or not to wear a head scarf as part of their daily routine of devotion, then all women's choices are at risk.

Thinking critically about the Bible is all the more important in the wake of terrorism and the conservative religious climate that manipulates responses to it away from the Gospels and toward apocalyptic holy wars. Many theologians, even evangelical ones who supposedly belong

---

75. Jack Cafferty, *It's Getting Ugly Out There: The Frauds, Bunglers, Liars, and Losers Who Are Hurting America* (Hoboken, NJ: Wiley Publishers, 2007).

to the groups so aggressively propagating their agendas, are speaking up.[76] Our goal is neither to abuse the Bible, nor to be abused *by* it, but to know it and use it for universal good.

I think we had better stay the course.

---

76. Jim Wallis, *God's Politics: Why the Right Gets It Wrong and the Left Doesn't Get It* (San Francisco HarperOne, 2005), especially pp. 137-58 on 'Dangerous Religion: The Theology of Empire'; Tony Campolo, *Speaking my Mind: The Radical Evangelical Prophet Tackles the Tough Issues Christians Are Afraid to Face* (Nashville, TN: Thomas Nelson, 2004). This book you are reading is an entry in the feminist category.

Chapter 6

'MANY DEVICES' (QOHELETH 7.23–8.1): QOHELETH, MISOGYNY, AND THE *MALLEUS MALEFICARUM*

1. *Foreword*

This paper, in its new form, is dedicated to the Reverend George Burroughs, of Salem, Massachusetts and Wells, Maine, hanged for a witch in 1692 by the town fathers of Salem who owed him money for past services. He was the first person in the jurisprudence of the New World to be convicted on 'spectral evidence' (a ghost gave information concerning him in a dream had by a local woman). Further, he was hanged despite his successful passing of the popular 'witches' test' (if a person could recite the Lord's Prayer completely and without stuttering, in local view it was believed that that person could not be a witch). Although Burroughs recited the Lord's Prayer in its entirety without error while standing on the gallows platform, the town fathers used the opportunity of the town's people's uproar in the pastor's favor to hang him quickly. Only short decades later, his descendants were compensated monetarily for wrongful death, a clear admission of George's innocence.

Evidence of similar transparent ('spectral') quality and reliability is now being used by the United States government to detain 'terrorists', designate US citizens as 'enemy combatants', and torture both groups in Guantanamo Bay, in Iraq, and in shadow prisons in Europe and elsewhere.

2. *When Readers Respond...*

As the present writer was conducting a training session on the topic of 'Women in the Biblical Wisdom Traditions' for lay Sunday school teachers, male and female, of the United Church of Christ, the following interchange, termed 'proverb performance'[1] in paroemiological studies,

---

1. The meaningful transmission of a 'proverbial' statement in a social interaction to provide an evaluation or reinterpretation of a situation, especially one involving conflict by persons or groups of different status. The 'proverb' acts as a traditional authority which shields its lower status user from the implications of the point of view just raised. For a discussion of this linguistic interaction in the Hebrew Bible,

occurred. The subject was a 'hot' one: not only had biblical scholars been rediscovering the implications of the female personification of Woman/ Lady Wisdom and her wicked twin, Woman Stranger/Lady Folly for the study of women's roles in 'ancient Israel', but significant leakage of such inquiries into the area of New Testament theology had begun to occur.[2] Not only was 'Sophia' Christology coming to the forefront as a feminist re-reading of the early traditions of the Jesus-movement, but that very fact had begun to spawn counter-groups within several Christian denominations, including the UCC, claiming that such Christologies constituted a modern heresy to be put down at all costs. Hence, into such a mixture, it seemed good to place some actual reflection on the foundational texts themselves before jumping to any ecclesial conclusions about their meaning for modern followers of the New Testament.

The Interaction Situation: Why Quote a Folk Saying?
After a general background on the multiple origins of the wisdom tradition—from concrete tribal problem-solving to the elite, abstract productions of bureaucracies and schools of scribes—we began to delve into a close reading of Proverbs 1–9 and Proverbs 31, texts which contain both positive and negative stereotypical reflections on the subject of the female, cosmic and human. Moving from there to texts which had received less attention by the Sophia-Christology groups, we began looking at the distinctively unflattering passages to be found in Qoheleth and Ben Sira, where it seemed that the dignity and value of Cosmic Woman Wisdom was inversely proportional to that of real, human women. In general, we agreed with scholars like Camp and others that while negative evaluations of females in Proverbs were usually limited to certain kinds of females (the loose, garrulous, nagging, adulterous, idolatrous, foreign, seductive females who give content to the characterization of Woman Stranger), by the time of the later sages, it appeared as though all females were being lumped into a single, negative category. This trend might be explained by reference to the strong influence of classical Hellenistic and Greco-Roman dualism, or to the changing social circumstances of Judah under Persian home-rule, or later domination

see Carole R. Fontaine, 'Proverb Performance in the Hebrew Bible', in David J.A. Clines (ed.), *The Poetical Books: A Sheffield Reader* (The Biblical Seminar, 41; Sheffield: Sheffield Academic Press, 1997), pp. 316-32.

2. Susan Cady, Marian Ronan and Hal Taussig, *Wisdom's Feast: Sophia in Study and Celebration* (San Francisco: Harper & Row, 1989); Robert Wilckens (ed.), *Aspects of Wisdom in Judaism and Early Christianity* (Notre Dame: Notre Dame University Press, 1975); Claudia Camp, *Wisdom and the Feminine in the Book of Proverbs* (Bible and Literature, 11; Sheffield: Almond Press, 1985). For an extensive bibliography on Sophia and Christology, see Cady, *Wisdom's Feast*, p. 215 n. 5.

6. *'Many Devices' (Qoheleth 7.23–8.1)*   183

by harsh invading groups bent on imperialist expansion in first Hellenistic and finally Roman Judea.

Under such circumstances, two impulses might be discerned in the literature produced. The first is an apologetic desire to respond to the challenges of Greek philosophy by recasting Hebrew Wisdom into the categories and discourse of one's supposedly culturally 'advanced' conquerors. This could be done either by showing that Wisdom (equivalent to Torah in Ben Sira) was superior to that of one's conquerors (Ben Sira), or by suggesting that Hebrew Wisdom was sufficiently similar to classical philosophy, that it could naturally and suitably be reframed as a concurrent rather than competing tradition (Wisdom of Solomon). In the former case, it was a natural move to bring the 'category' of 'woman' into harmony with the surrounding philosophical traditions, which were largely negative in tone, although paradoxically, elite women were achieving more social prominence and power in the later periods (Hellenistic through Roman). These social gains may have spurred on the conservatism and misogyny of the classical and biblical writers of late antiquity.[3] Add to this the later effects of Roman misogyny propagated throughout its empire during the very time from which some of our texts come and the recipe for the symbolic and literal exclusion of women from consideration as full human beings is complete.[4]

The second impulse behind the learned misogyny of the sages under political domination grew up more as a survival strategy. While the ancestor stories of Genesis and 'early' Israel are notable for their positive evaluations of the crucial roles women might play in Salvation History, during the later time of foreign domination, our sages may have been anxious to differentiate the conduct of their women from those of the surrounding cultures, as yet another way to reinscribe 'difference' and social control.[5] When exercise of control in the political, 'public' domain

---

3. Sarah B. Pomeroy, *Goddesses, Whores, Wives, and Slaves: Women in Classical Antiquity* (New York: Schocken Books, 1975), pp. 92-189; *Women in Hellenistic Egypt from Alexander to Cleopatra* (New York: Schocken Books, 1984). As always, possibilities open to women in the 'public domain' varied by social class and status. For selections of classical and clerical misogynist texts, see Alcuin Blamires (ed.), *Woman Defamed and Woman Defended: An Anthology of Medieval Texts* (Oxford: Clarendon Press, 1992), pp. 17-98.

4. Luise Schottroff, *Lydia's Impatient Sisters: A Feminist Social History of Early Christianity* (trans. Barbara and Martin Rumscheidt; Louisville, KY: Westminster/ John Knox Press, 1991), p. 77.

5. Warren Trenchard concludes that Ben Sira is 'personally negative' towards women, since he reworks positive traditional material from Proverbs in such a way as to render it negative in tone (*Ben Sira's View of Women: A Literary Analysis* [BJS, 38; Chico, CA: Scholars Press, 1982], pp. 167-73); see also Claudia V. Camp,

is denied the patriarchal male, a compensatory mechanism is required. In the case of the later wisdom period and the postexilic period in general, this took the form of close control of the household and its residents.[6] Growing concern in this area leads to a fixation on mixed marriages, dietary practices, ritual observance, and inheritance laws, all of which provide an enhanced sense of control over one's life, at least at the private level. Clearly, since females are required in the process of getting sons for inheritance of land critical to family survival, in the preparation of foods, the performance of household religious observances, and were key players in interracial/'interfaith' marriages, the compulsive need to control their sexuality becomes part of the male response to a specific social predicament.[7] Male honor required no less than an obsessive preoccupation with the sources of female shame, that is, sexuality.[8] It was against this background of shifting cultural paradigms for 'faithfulness' to one's tradition that the vicious evaluations of womankind were to be understood, suggested this writer. Always grateful for a 'way out' of having to disagree with or challenge the Bible's views, the readers/hearers responded positively...until we actually opened to Qoh. 7.23–8.1a[9]:

'Understanding a Patriarchy: Women in Second Century Jerusalem through the Eyes of Ben Sira', in A.-J. Levine (ed.), *'Women like This': New Perspectives on Jewish Women in the Greco-Roman World* (SBL Early Judaism and its Literature, I; Atlanta: Scholars Press, 1991), pp. 3-39; 'Honor and Shame in Ben Sira: Anthropological and Theological Reflections', a paper read at the First International Conference on Ben Sira (Soesterberg, the Netherlands, July 28-31, 1996); and 'Honor, Shame and the Hermeneutics of Ben Sira's Ms C', in Michael Barré (ed.), *"Wisdom, You are My Sister!": Studies in Honor of Roland E. Murphy, O. Carm., on the Occasion of his 80th Birthday* (CBQMS, 29; Washington, DC: Catholic Biblical Association, 1997), pp. 157-71.

6. Tamara C. Eskenazi, 'Out from the Shadows: Biblical Women in the Post-Exilic Era', in Athalya Brenner (ed.), *A Feminist Companion to Samuel and Kings* (FCB, 5; Sheffield: Sheffield Academic Press, 1994), pp. 252-71.

7. It may also have been the case that females were at special risk of sexual exploitation by the various overlords of Judah and Judea. For a grisly example, examine a coin minted in the region about three years before the fall of Masada (70 CE): a Roman soldier looms over a prone Jewess, while the legend reads 'Judea capta'. Rape is often a 'symbol' for imperialist conquest, suggesting that the actual practice of rape under such circumstances was, if not customary, at least commonplace (Susan Brooks Thistlethwaite, '"You May Enjoy the Spoil of your Enemies": Rape as a Biblical Metaphor for War', *Semeia* 61, [1993], pp. 59-78).

8. For a general introduction to the categories of honor and shame in biblical literature, see Victor H. Matthews, Don C. Benjamin and Claudia V. Camp (eds.), 'Honor and Shame in the World of the Bible', *Semeia* 68 (1994).

9. I use the RSV translation here as that was the text to which our young reader responded. Some scholars begin this passage at v. 25; we choose to add in vv. 23-24, since the identity of the referent there is included in some modern readers' attempts

6. 'Many Devices' (Qoheleth 7.23–8.1) 185

All this I have tested by wisdom; I said, 'I will be wise'; but it was far from me. That which is, is far off, and deep, very deep; who can find it out? I turned my mind to know and to search out and to seek wisdom and the sum of things, and to know the wickedness of folly and the foolishness which is madness. And I found more bitter than death the woman whose heart is snares and nets, and whose hands are fetters; he who pleases God escapes her, but the sinner is taken by her. Behold, this is what I found, says the Preacher, adding one thing to another to find the sum, which my mind has sought repeatedly, but I have not found. One man among a thousand I found, but a woman among all these I have not found. Behold, this alone I found, that God made man upright, but they have sought out many devices. Who is like the wise man? And who knows the interpretation of a thing? (RSV).

Before she could be 'shushed' by her elders, a young woman in her twenties called out from the back of the room, 'Them's fightin' words!!'

This was a classic occasion of proverb performance by the young woman.[10] Although she disagreed with both the text and the validity of my scholarly attempts to nuance it, she herself did not have the specialized training or the social power needed to challenge the 'expert'. Further, though relations are often strained, it may be that she had no wish to discomfit the learned speaker out of bonds of common sisterhood—how often does a woman expert speak on the Bible in the world of the Church, after all? In such a multifaceted interaction, she chose to let 'tradition' speak and offer the challenge.[11] As it happened, I agreed

to mitigate the misogyny of Qoheleth's great findings (Thomas Krüger, ' "Frau Weisheit" in Koh 7, 26?" ', *Biblica* 73 (1992), pp. 394-403.

10. In an interaction, X (female Sunday School teacher, low status) says to Y (female Bible 'expert', high status), 'Just as A equals B in this proverb ('them's', A = 'fightin' words', B), so C (Qoheleth 7:23–8:1) equals D ('fightin' words') in this context!' The user of the proverb is concealed behind its traditional authority; the correlation of terms A, C = B, D with a negative evaluation associated with Y (and not X!) is typical of twentieth-century proverb performance. In modern contexts, proverb users almost always apply positive proverbs to themselves or their own evaluations of a situation, whereas negatives are applied to their opponents in the interaction.

11. The verbal context which usually evokes this proverbial response might be characterized as gendered 'trash talk', often in the form of shaming remarks about one's female relatives. These ritualized exchanges are still frequent and customary in military and sporting contexts (e.g. between offensive and defensive linemen before the snap of a football in order to lure the opponent 'offsides'). Similar 'fightin' words" may also be used *by* men to shame other men into acting in accordance with male codes: see the statements by the Philistine army in 1 Sam. 4.9, before the battle of Shiloh, which they win after originally losing heart: 'Take courage, and be men, O Philistines, in order not to become slaves to the Hebrews as they have been to you; be men and fight!' Similar men-to-men proverbial usages in war are recorded in Hittite

whole-heartedly with her proverbial assessment of this piece of traditional wisdom, enshrined as 'authoritative' due to its inclusion in 'Holy Scripture'. Though I might offer many ways of understanding the background of these misogynist passages, I could not displace the 'plain sense' being conveyed by the anti-female sentiments expressed. Further, I began to wonder how the Christian community had heard such texts in the past, and the impact of those responses on the lives of actual women (e.g. had Qoheleth's words always been perceived as 'fightin' words'?, were they 'performed' by the community on behalf of women and their dignity, or used to denigrate the female sex?, were/are they perceived as generalities which may not apply in specific situations, or as universals which always hold true?). The following study is in many ways a response to that young woman, and takes her characterization seriously in choice of method: we will fight these passages with words...

3. *Establishing the 'Plain Sense' in Qoheleth 7.25–8.1a*

The Context Investigated
The passage under discussion is in many ways typical of Qoheleth's preferred style of discourse (experiential 'tests'; citation and contradiction;[12] tallying up of examples and statement of conclusions) and is linked by key words to many of the catch-phrases already encountered in the book (seek/find; wisdom/folly; straight, wicked, 'see', etc.). There is, however, no denying that the text bristles with grammatical difficulties and/or ambiguities which render the search for its 'plain sense' almost as difficult as Qoheleth's search for deep Wisdom.[13] Referents and antecedents are not always clear (what or who exactly is 'far off and deep' in v. 24?, to what does the 'this' in v. 27 refer?), nor are the connections between some clauses and main verbs;[14] a piling up of double accusatives in v. 25b ('wickedness of folly' or 'wickedness and folly'; 'foolishness and madness' or 'foolishness which is madness'?) leads to a variety of difficulties and translation possibilities. Syntactic obscurity routinely

---

texts from Late Bronze Age Anatolia (O.R. Gurney, *The Hittites* [London: Penguin Books, rev. edn, 1981]).

12. Even the acceptance of this penchant in interpretation still leaves the reader to puzzle out what is being cited and whether it is being affirmed or disputed.

13. As one commentator wryly notes, 'Our difficulties are many' (Graham Ogden, *Qoheleth* [Readings; Sheffield: JSOT Press, 1987], p. 120).

14. Is the woman more bitter than death *because* she is snares and nets, or is it 'the woman *whose* heart is snares and nets...', that is, only women of that type? The relative clause may be interpreted either way (M.V. Fox, *Qoheleth and his Contradictions* [JSOTSup, 71; Bible and Literature, 18; Sheffield: Almond Press, 1989], p. 241).

6. 'Many Devices' (Qoheleth 7.23–8.1)

leads modern scholars to redivide consonants,[15] reconstruct from Syriac and the LXX, and repoint the vowels as needed, as well as adopting others stratagems (positing Aramaisms in v. 29 or new Hebrew roots like *mrr* for 'strong' instead of 'bitter' in v. 26) to render meaning from the sage's musings.[16]

Even where syntax is not peculiar, it is often difficult to know just what the writer is referring to: what kind of wisdom did the sage achieve, if he also says it was beyond him? What, then, is supposed to be the great finding (Hebrew, *ḥešbōn*, or the sum of one's calculations) of this sage who is not wise[17] (and if the latter is really the case, then why are we listening?)? That women are, at worst, dangerous; at best, ambivalent, from the point of view of men? All women, or just a certain type? Or is this what he has *not* found? No wonder this sage begins and ends his essays on the meaning of life by characterizing all as 'vanity'—evanescent, insubstantial, an exhalation of hot air, gone in a moment![18]

Grammatical difficulties and their limits to our understanding of the 'plain sense' of the text may not be the only ambiguity a responding reader is up against, as is suggested by the many devices employed in translations by critical commentators. In fact, what we may have in Qoheleth's digressions, uneasy juxtapositions, dangling clauses, and hanging rhetorical questions is not simply, or even primarily, a disorganized text or compilation of competing traditional teachings, but a deliberate use of the 'dialogue' genre to convey content and method.[19] Commentators have long posited at least two voices in Qoheleth: that of the sage himself (pretending to be a king in his use of 'royal fiction'), and a pious editor who introduces and ends the book on a note of orthodoxy (12.8-14); others have seen as many as nine different hands adding

---

15. Based on supposed *content*?

16. For a summary of linguistic and grammatical considerations, see Fox, *Contradictions*, pp. 236-44; Roland E. Murphy, *Ecclesiastes* (WBC, 23A; Dallas, TX: Word Books, 1992), pp. 74-75.

17. Michael V. Fox and Bezalel Porten, 'Unsought Discoveries: Qoheleth 7:23–8:1a', *Hebrew Studies* 19 (1978), pp. 26-38 (32, 34).

18. Unfortunately, the standard effect of Qoheleth's words, whatever the reason for them, has had a longer impact than the male vanity which might be responsible for them, as will be seen in the discussion below.

19. See T.A. Perry, *Dialogues with Koheleth: The Book of Ecclesiastes* (University Park, PA: Pennsylvania State University Press, 1993), pp. 3-50 for a compelling solution to the problem of 'voices', contradictions, and pessimistic content in Qoheleth. Perry's contribution to the standard 'quotation and argument' interpretive tradition is his view that this is not just a matter of style or content, but a method of pedagogy of the sage who uses it.

glosses to resolve contradictions.[20] Beyond that, it has been the fashion to understand that in many sites of contradiction in the text, Qoheleth is deliberately citing a proverb or saying encapsulating traditional wisdom, with which he then argues.[21]

In one of the more ingenious solutions to the problem of contradictions in Qoheleth, T.A. Perry proposes that the sage here allows two sides, 'voices' if you will, of a dialogue on the meaning of life to emerge by letting each position 'have its say'. Thus, we hear the words of K, a voice in Koheleth which Perry identifies as a 'seeker of experiential knowledge', a greedy Collector of people, things, and experiences (Qoheleth 2.4-10), King, Pedagogue, and Pessimist. The counterpoint to this voice, 'differentiated by tone and style', intentionally adopted to provide a 'second opinion' before judging life totally worthless, is that of the 'Presenter', 'Antagonist', or 'Arguer'. Perry writes of this literary *pas de deux* in 1.4-7 (where K's words are presented in italics and 4b, 5b-6a; 6c; 7b belong to the Presenter):

> *A generation goes forth, only to die!*
> But the earth endures forever.
> *The sun rises, only to set!*
> Yet it pants to return to its starting point, where it rises again. Moreover, it goes southward but returns northward.
> *The wind goes forth around and around!*
> Yet it can reverse its direction.
> *All rivers flow to the sea!*
> But the sea is not filled. And the rivers must return to their source, since they continue to flow to their destination.
>
> ...K the Pessimist, tends to poetic assertion, uses the enchantments of rhythm and generalizations to support an otherwise weak argument, namely everything in nature dies and therefore humans have no hope. By contrast, the Presenter's reply is cool, deliberately prosaic, unwilling to skip to hasty conclusions, and perhaps joyously contradictory. To configure this scene as a dialogue not only makes perfect sense but is consistent with the dialogic nature of both the wisdom genre and the essay...[22]

The very contradictions which caused the book's canonicity to be questioned in antiquity[23] have now become the interpretive key to the

---

20. R.N. Whybray, *Ecclesiastes* (Old Testament Guides; Sheffield: JSOT Press, 1989), pp. 23-24.

21. The so-called '*zwar-aber Aussage*'. See Murphy, *Ecclesiastes*, pp. xxxii-xli, for a full discussion of critical theories regarding integrity and authorship of the book.

22. Perry, *Dialogues*, p.10.

23. See discussion in Murphy's 'History of Interpretation' section, *Ecclesiastes*, pp. xlviii-lvi.

text's meaning for modern readers whose experience of history may have spawned something of the same pessimistic world view and paralysis that afflicts the K voice. In Perry's translation of our 'fightin' words' of 7.23-29 we then read:

> All of these things I tested for the sake of wisdom. I said:
> 'I shall grow wise, even though it is far from me',
> What has always been is far and deep indeed.
> And what is deep who can find!
> (I and my heart turned repetitively to know and explore and seek wisdom and strategies, and to know the wickedness of folly.
> But foolishness is insane!)
> For example, I personally find woman more bitter than death, for her heart is full of traps and snares and her hands are chains.
> He who is good in God's eyes will escape from her, but the wicked will be entrapped.
> Said Koheleth:
> Look, I have found this, as I set out step by step to discover a strategy, and anything beyond this I did not find: I found one good man in a thousand, but not even one good woman in the same number.
> Except that I have found this, and note it well: At the outset God made all human beings righteous.
> But they have invented many stratagems.[24]

The Arguer continues to present the basic tenet of the 'goodness of creation' — a basic wisdom theme — which Perry feels that K only questions indirectly. The 'they' of 7.29 refers to humanity as a whole, and the 'stratagems' refer back with irony to their cognates in 7.25, where the 'devices', 'calculations', 'plans' of great wisdom thinkers lead to so few results in the end. The Snarehearted Woman is a symbol for all of the worldly pleasures which the king found so worthless. The 'thousand' is also understood through the vehicle of the royal fiction: in all of Solomon's extraordinary harem, not one good woman was to be found.[25]

For Perry, the recognition that K is in fact *not* referencing the wisdom tradition's full, typical stance on women is heightened by the assumption and identification of a counter-voice that brings the grandiose claims of the sage K back to the bar of experience. Still, this pedagogical literary device is sufficiently obscure that readers through the ages largely have been unaware of it, and have heard the content of this text quite differently (see below).

---

24. Perry, *Dialogues*, pp. 125-26.
25. Perry, *Dialogues*, pp. 131-32. Perhaps the one who got away (the Queen of Sheba in 1 Kgs. 11) was the virtuous one and had good reason to flee (cf. the Ethiopic version of this legend in the *Kebra Nagast*).

Typically, Qoheleth contradicts himself later (cf. 9.9, 'Enjoy life with the wife whom you love, all the days of your vain life which he has given you under the sun, because that is your portion in life and in your toil at which you toil under the sun'). Elsewhere, in Proverbs, 'traditionally' ascribed to the same 'King' who speaks in 7.23–8.1, we read a broader range of men's experiences of women finding their way into proverbial forms:

> Let your fountain be blessed,
> and rejoice in the wife of your youth... (Prov. 5.18 RSV).

> A gracious woman gets honor,
> and violent men get riches (Prov. 11.16 RSV).

> A good wife is the crown of her husband,
> but she who brings shame is like rottenness in his bones (Prov. 12.4 RSV).

> He who finds a wife finds a good thing,
> and obtains favor from the LORD (Prov. 18.22 RSV).

> House and wealth are inherited from fathers,
> but a prudent wife is from the LORD (Prov. 19.14 RSV).

> A good wife who can find?
> She is far more precious than jewels... (Prov. 31.10 RSV).

Further, the acrostic poem begun in Prov. 31.10 continues in a paean of praise to the dutiful, industrious, wise, gracious, compassionate female who is the one who, in the words of the modern saying, 'makes a house a home'.[26] Exemplary wife, eager mother, thoughtful household manager, business woman, speaker of Torah, Proverbs gives us a biblical portrait of a veritable 'SuperMom', a picture of efficiency and approved domestic values[27] to which few real human women are able to live up—at least, not without her staff of servants or willingness to stay up until all hours to get everything done.[28] As 'off the scale' as this figure

---

26. The full citation in folkspeech is 'It takes a heap o' livin''/ to make a house a home'; the literary version is 'It takes a heap o' livin' in a house t' make it home/ A heap o' sun an' shadder, an' ye sometimes have t' roam/ Afore ye really 'preciate the things ye lef' behind,/ An' hunger fer 'em somehow, with 'em allus on yer mind' (Edgar Guest, 'Home', in John Bartlett, *Bartlett's Familiar Quotations: A Collection of Passages, Phrases and Proverbs* (Boston: Little, Brown & Company, 14th edn and rev., 1968), p. 963.

27. Barbara H. Geller Nathanson, 'Reflections on the Silent Woman of Ancient Judaism and her Pagan Roman Counterpart', in Kenneth Hoglund *et al.* (eds.), *The Listening Heart: Essays in Wisdom and the Psalms in Honor of Roland E. Murphy, O. Carm.* (JSOTSup, 58; Sheffield: Sheffield Academic Press, 1987), pp. 259-80.

28. Is this a virtue or a symptom of dysfunction? Does she, like the Hebrew god

might be, she provides a necessary counterweight to all the nagging, jealous, adulterous females that also frequent the pages of wisdom literature. Indeed, this may, in fact, be the reason why she is there in the 'last' place: to answer former charges of frivolity lodged against most or all of womankind.

> For the lips of a loose woman drip honey,
> and her speech is smoother than oil... (Prov. 5.3 RSV).

> And lo, a woman meets him,
> dressed as a harlot, wily of heart.
> She is loud and wayward,
> her feet do not stay at home
> ...Her house is the way to Sheol,
> going down to the chambers of death (Prov. 7.10-11, 27 RSV).

> Like a gold ring in a swine's snout
> is a beautiful woman without discretion (Prov. 11.22 RSV).

> It is better to live in a corner of the housetop
> than in a house shared with a contentious woman (Prov. 21.9, 25.24 RSV).

> It is better to live in a desert land
> than with a contentious and fretful woman (Prov. 21.19 RSV).[29]

> The mouth of a loose woman is a deep pit;
> he with whom the LORD is angry will fall into it (Prov. 22.14 RSV).

> For a harlot is a deep pit;
> an adventuress is a narrow well.
> She lies in wait like a robber
> and increases the faithless among men (Prov. 23.27-28 RSV).

> A continual dripping on a rainy day
> and a contentious woman are alike;
> to restrain her is to restrain the wind
> or to grasp oil in his right hand (Prov. 27.15-16 RSV).

> This is the way of an adulteress:
> she eats, and wipes her mouth,
> and says, 'I have done no wrong' (Prov. 30.20 RSV).

> Under three things the earth trembles;
> under four it cannot bear up:

(Ps. 121.4), suffer from sleep deprivation? Is her sleeplessness a sign of something to which we should be paying more attention?

29. We might add to this list Prov. 22.10, 'Drive out a scoffer, and strife will go out, and quarreling and abuse will cease', which rabbinic Judaism interprets as referring to a contentious wife who should be divorced, although the term 'scoffer' (*lēṣ*) is masc. singular as it appears in Proverbs.

>   a slave when he becomes king,
>   and a fool when he is filled with food;
>   an unloved woman when she gets a husband,
>   and a maid when she succeeds her mistress (Prov. 30.21-23 RSV).

Seen from the perspective of the earlier voices of tradition, Qoheleth's reflections in chapter 7 are not so out of line with what is said elsewhere; what is new is that the K voice may be translated in such a way that it fails to note that not *all* women fall into the category of 'snare'. That young male students should be warned of the 'wiles' of females for whom the only hope of status and fulfillment offered them by patriarchal culture is in the capture, acquisition and annexation of the unwary male who cannot escape their machinations: this is surely the stock in trade of patriarchal pedagogy.[30] It recognizes the trap into which women are forced by the limitations placed upon them, though of course, it condemns them for acting in accordance with the messages their culture has sent. Even the Queen Mother of King Lemuel says as much in her instruction to her son ('What, my son? What, son of my womb? What, son of my vows? Give not your strength to women, your ways to those who destroy kings', Prov. 31.2-3). The Egyptian *Instruction of Ptahhotep* gives even clearer warnings to young men entering court service:

> If you want friendship to endure
> In a house you enter
> As master, brother or friend,
> In whatever place you enter,
> Beware of approaching the women!
> Unhappy is the place where it is done,
> Unwelcome is he who intrudes on them.
> A thousand men are turned away from their good.
> A short moment like a dream,
> Then death comes for having known them.[31]

That wisdom tradents should reflect on the tricky matter of dealings with 'work-related' females, or finding a woman worthy of becoming the wife of a man 'on the way up' should occasion no surprise, and we find here that once more, men by the thousands are endangered by their interest in women who are 'off-limits'.[32] This is simply another area in which scribal goddess Wisdom seeks to equip her male followers with

---

30. Carol A. Newsom, 'Woman and the Discourse of Patriarchal Wisdom: A Study of Proverbs 1–9', in Peggy L. Day (ed.), *Gender and Difference in Ancient Israel* (Minneapolis: Fortress Press, 1989), pp. 142-60.

31. Miriam Lichtheim, *Ancient Egyptian Literature: A Book of Readings*. I. *The Old and Middle Kingdoms* (Berkeley: University of California, 1975), p. 68.

32. These characterizations are certainly not flattering to males: they seem more like lemmings in the grip of ineluctable instinct than rational humanoids.

6. 'Many Devices' (Qoheleth 7.23–8.1)

the survival skills needed for success in an ambiguous world. Since the phrase 'to find a woman' (*māṣā' 'iššā*) also means 'to take a wife', it may be that Qoheleth, who is not known for his celebration of family life,[33] is simply announcing in 7.28b that he never found a female who could meet his high standards for the mate of a sage.

There are, of course, other possibilities: his statement may be meant literally. Following the 'royal fiction' that makes our speaker into Solomon, the author of Proverbs and Song of Songs, we might conclude that his harem relations were singularly unsatisfying. Perhaps K may even be telling us not to take what he says too rigidly! He does not comment specifically on the nature of the one man who escapes from the Snarehearted Woman,[34] and one can hardly conclude that his opinion of males is much higher than his estimation of women. But there is more: the adjective 'bitter' (*mar*) used to describe the Snarehearted Woman is masculine, and K's verb in 7.27's 'said Qoheleth' is feminine in gender![35] Does he mean that he too is no more reliable than the woman/wife he could not find?

Beyond the intertextual links to proverbial thoughts about woman and her place, our text displays other connections which help us understand the sage in his test of wisdom and folly. Genesis 1–11, with its depiction of the original human couple's exit from Eden and humanity's descent into sinful nations, may have influenced the thoughts expressed in 7.29: Qoheleth's plaintive questions about 'what is good' (for a person) is a cynical reversal of the Creator's pronouncements of goodness on creation.[36] As in the Eden story, both human quests for knowledge end in frustration, and women are implicated in men's stymied desires to grasp and know. For some commentators, this explains the unusual use of *hā'ādām*, the generic term for human, in v. 28 in opposition to 'woman/wife', *'iššâ* (the more usual choice would be *'îš*, 'adult male human').[37]

---

33. More Egyptian advice makes clear the link between a woman at home and founding a family: 'When you prosper, found your household, take a hearty wife, a son will be born you. It is for the son you build a house, when you make a place for yourself' (*The Instruction of Prince Hardjedef*, in Lichtheim, *AEL*, I, p. 58). Since Qoheleth has no use for his successors, he has little incentive to acquire a woman/wife.

34. So with Murphy, *Ecclesiastes*, pp. 75-76; Fox, *Contradictions*, p. 241; Ogden, *Qoheleth*, p. 123. If we take *'ādām* as generic in this verse, we might even say that women could be counted among those who please God and escape the snare.

35. Elsewhere, the word *Qoheleth*, presumably a title or job description takes a masculine verb (1.12; 12.8, 10). Most commentators redivide the consonants to create 'says (masc.) *the* Qoheleth'.

36. So with Midrash and Targum (Whybray, *Ecclesiastes*, pp. 60-61; Fox and Porten, 'Unsought Discoveries', pp. 26-38 [33]).

37. Fox and Porten, 'Unsought Discoveries', pp. 26-38 (27, 33). In v. 29, the meaning of *hā'ādām* reverts to its more typical meaning, 'human being'.

Some critics have argued that this passage should also be heard against the intertextual backdrop of the Song of Songs—yet another play on the Solomonic royal fiction. In Song of Songs 3.1-5, the same word-pair, 'seek/find',[38] from our 7.27-28, is used to describe one of the sequences in which the Beloved searches for her lover, in order to bring him to a secure, private trysting place. More fortunate than Qoheleth, our pursuing 'Bride' finds what she seeks, but not without an initial setback. This theme is reduplicated in the dream sequence of Song of Songs 5.2-8, with a further venture into the territory of honor and shame: this time when the watchmen find the Beloved, they mistake her for a less savory person on a similar errand (a prostitute?) and commit violence against her for her boldness. Here, her quest is defeated as she transgresses the boundaries of female honor, is shamed by the watchmen, and forced to enlist the help of the daughters of Jerusalem in her pilgrimage to love.[39] If we take the Beloved's case as a paradigm for Qoheleth's search for a wife/woman, a dialogue between the two voices of these texts suggests that Qoheleth might have succeeded had he tried harder (left his usual habitat to search in all sorts of places, however unlikely), looked more eagerly and insistently, showed a willingness to be shamed as a test of the worthiness of his quest, or enlisted aid in his investigation. Even though our text suggests that his search was repetitive, exhaustive, and relentless ('adding one to one to find an answer'; 'repeatedly'), and is discussed with terms used to denote physical 'motion', it is clear from the outcome that Qoheleth—and his personified 'heart' which accompanies him[40]—have not gone very far.

4. *Qoheleth among the Commentators: A Selective Sampling*

It is beyond the scope of this essay to present an exhaustive treatment of this passage as it occurs in the history of the Synagogue's and Church's exegesis; bibliography for such studies is readily available, but many Christian sources are known only through later references to them in other works, or are unpublished, or survive only in fragmentary form.[41]

---

38. Fox and Porten, 'Unsought Discoveries', pp. 26-38 (34-37). See also Gen. 27 and 1 Sam. 9 for other examples of intensive use of this word-pair to build plot.

39. *Contra* Dianne Bergant, ' "My Beloved is Mine and I Am His" (Song 2:16): The Song of Songs and Honor and Shame', *Semeia* 68 (1994), pp. 23-40, who reads the Beloved as displacing the honor/shame paradigms of the brothers and watchmen by means of her own unmediated speech.

40. This may represent Egyptian influence; at any rate, it is a peculiarity of Qoheleth's speech. It should be remembered that the heart in Hebrew *and* Egyptian is the perceiving, rather than the feeling, organ (Fox, *Qoheleth*, pp. 86-88; 241).

41. See Murphy, *Ecclesiastes*, xlviii-lv for extensive references on patristic, medieval

We will, however, dip our feminist ladle into the waters of interpretation as they flowed from the world of the Jewish Diaspora into late medieval and modern Europe. Nowhere does it become more clear that 'time and chance' (9.11) affect the interpretations given a passage, even though the text translated has not changed its original words. Clearly, the 'plain sense' of our passage from Qoheleth, K, the Arguer, King Solomon or later masquerader is to be found in the eye of its beholder!⁴²

The Babylonian Talmud, Targum of Qoheleth, and Qoheleth Rabbah
In most of the places where this passage is quoted in the Babylonian Talmud, it is routinely paired with Prov. 18.22, 'He who finds a wife finds a good thing, and obtains favor from the LORD', whose Hebrew forms a word-play on Qoheleth's Hebrew, 'and I found'.⁴³ The word 'woman' is clearly taken to mean 'wife' instead of all women, or as a metaphor for something else. The rabbinic authors sublate the negative implications of Qoheleth's statement by contrasting it to an earlier saying of 'Solomon's', giving a view which is exactly opposite of Qoheleth's in 7.23–8.1: the blessing of a (good) wife is indeed a Good Thing, and comes directly from the Hebrew God. Apparently in the matter of seeking and finding a mate, for these Rabbis, things can go either way; it is in the hand of the Lord. Thus, by finding a contrast to the text's (purported) view, it casts into doubt the universal validity of the K's statement.⁴⁴ In this interpretive move we clearly see a *zwar-aber* ('to be sure', 'however') construction composed by juxtaposing two contrary statements attributed to the same author: a mode of discourse worthy of Qoheleth himself.

It is worth noting that when our passage appears in the *BT* without its sublating partner from Proverbs, the interpretation and context do not go well for women. In *Sotah* 8b, where v. 27's 'adding one to one to find the sum' is quoted, it is used to heap punishment on the wife suspected of adultery: just as she schemed by her acts, one upon one, to do that which would bring her to her lover's bed, so the judges should place like punishments upon her, one by one.⁴⁵ In *Gittin* 45a, the citation of 'no

and Jewish exegesis of the book; cf. also Beryl Smalley, *Medieval Exegesis of Wisdom Literature* (ed. Roland E. Murphy; Atlanta: Scholars Press, 1986).

42. The eye is not satisfied with seeing (1.9).

43. *BT Yebamot* 63a, 63b; *Berakhot* 8a (*The Soncino Talmud: Yebamot*, I [trans. Israel W. Slotki; London: Soncino Press, 1936], pp. 422-23); *Berakhot* (trans. Maurice Simon; London: Soncino Press, 1948), p. 40.

44. *Well done!* The process of sublating patriarchal texts through the juxtaposition of contrary authoritative statements is a useful tool for feminist interpretation which seeks to stay in dialogue with traditional texts.

45. *The Soncino Talmud: Sotah* (trans. Ada Cohen; London: Soncino Press, 1936), p. 38.

woman in a thousand' of v. 28 is used to render sense out of the experiences of the righteous daughters of R. Nahman. These females were so pious that they could stir a boiling cauldron with their bare hands and not be burned. When they are later taken captive and placed into forced marriages with their captors, they are overheard talking in the privy. They reject the option of escaping to return to their former Jewish husbands, in order to remain with their captors. The Jew who overheard them returns to tell the tale, much to the chagrin of the community. The passage concludes with the view that they must have been protected by witchcraft rather than righteousness in their former culinary feats. If even such righteous women as these could fall so far from the ideal, is it any wonder that the Sage says he could not find even one woman who was better than she should be![46]

The *Targum of Qoheleth*, of Palestinian provenance and provisionally dated to a time after the Babylonian Talmud (based on *Targ. Q*'s use of that text) but before the Islamic conquest of the region, and the *Midrash Qoheleth Rabbah* (similarly difficult to date) struggle to understand the 'plain sense' of our ambiguous text.[47] Both follow the rabbinic interpretive scheme which posits Qoheleth as King Solomon, and both make use of interpolations based on Genesis 1–11. But King Solomon for rabbinic readers is now more than simply the king of Israel's 'glory days': he is the wonder-full king with knowledge of demons, magic, and the deep things of the world.[48] He has gone from King to Beggar to King once again, as part of his dealings with the demon Ashmodai (Ashmodeus of Tobit) whom he took captive.[49] Magician, lover and sinner with many foreign women (one thousand in all!), folklore hero punished by God for his arrogance and sent into exile, who would know better than this man about what is more bitter than death?[50] For the Targum, Qoheleth

---

46. *The Soncino Talmud: Gittin* (trans. Maurice Simon; London: Soncino Press, 1936), pp. 197-98.

47. Peter S. Knobel, *The Targum of Qohelet, translated with a Critical Introduction, Apparatus and Notes* (The Aramaic Bible, 15; Collegeville, MN: Liturgical Press, 1991), pp. 12-15; for a discussion of the history of texts and interpretations, see Murphy, *Ecclesiastes*, xxiv-xxvi; xlviii-lvi.

48. Solomon's mastery of demons and magic is based on the Babylonian Jewish interpretation of '*šād*' (root *šd*) in 2.8 to mean 'male and female demons' rather than 'carriages' (*Talmud Yerushalami*), 'concubines' (preferred by modern translators) or 'cupbearers' (preferred by ancient versions), *BT Gittin* 68a.

49. At one point, Ashmodeus masquerades as Solomon, whom he has exiled, and rules in his place. Is the passage in question a typical demonic trick played on humanity?

50. *BT Gittin* 68a; *contra* Murphy, *Ecclesiastes*, p. liv, Ashmodai does *not* 'depose Solomon'; this is rather a consequence of his seeking to be free of enslavement. It should be noted that Solomon is restored to his throne after three years of exile

the king has become a sage of the 'rabbinic' sort,[51] for whom Wisdom is best known as Torah:

> All that, I said, I have tested with wisdom. I said to myself, 'I will be wise also in all the wisdom of the Torah, but it eluded me. Behold, already it eluded man to know everything which was from the days of old and the secret of the day of death and the secret of the day when King Messiah will come. Who will find it out by his wisdom? I turned to reckon in my mind and to know how to examine and to seek wisdom and the reckoning of the reward of the deeds of the righteous and to know the punishment of the sin of the fool and folly and the intrigues of government. I found a thing which is more bitter to man than the bitterness of the day of death (that is), the woman who causes her husband many sorrows and in whose heart is nets and snares. Her hands are tied so that she cannot work with them. Upright before the Lord is the man who divorces her with a bill of divorcement and escapes from her, but guilty before the Lord is the man who marries her and is caught in her harlotry.' See, this is the matter I found, said Qoheleth who is called Solomon the king of Israel. I determined the relationship of the planets one to the other to find the reckoning of men what will be at their end. There is another thing which my soul still sought but I have not found; (namely) a perfect and innocent man without blemish from the days of Adam until Abraham the Righteous was born, who was found faithful and innocent among the one thousand kings who were assembled to make the Tower of Babel but I did not find a worthy woman among all the wives of those kings. Only see this, I have found that the Lord made the first man upright and pure before him, but the serpent and Eve seduced him to eat from the fruit of the tree whose fruit enables those who eat it to know the difference between good and evil, and they caused the day of death to be imposed upon him and upon all the inhabitants of the world and they tried to find many calculations in order to bring a plague upon the inhabitants of the earth.[52]

We see here not only the glossing of the 'hidden' things of vv. 23-24, 28 with the coming of the Messiah and the day of death (things sought out by the 'prophet' Solomon looking ahead at Israel's future), but the addition of other elements to explicate the ellipses of the original Hebrew text. The 'one thousand' which will become important in modern

---

through the offices of a good woman. In one version, the beggar Solomon is taken in by a kindly old lady who shows him a fish she bought which turns out to contain his very own signet ring (formerly thrown in the sea [or: swallowed] by Ashmodai). When he puts it on, he is transformed and returned to the throne; in a different version, it is his wife, Naamah, daughter of the King of Ammon, who guts the fish, finds the ring and brings about the beggar's return to kingship (Angelo S. Rappoport, *Myth and Legend of Ancient Israel*, III [New York: Ktav, 1966], pp. 131-39). These legends, perhaps of Indic or Iranian origin (as is Ashmodai) find their way to medieval Europe, probably via Byzantine transmission.

51. Murphy, *Ecclesiastes*, p. liv.
52. Knobel, *Targum*, pp. 40-41.

attempts to save Qoheleth from the charge of misogyny (see below) now refers to the builders of the Tower of Babel and their unworthy wives. The woman more bitter than death is the noxious and lazy wife who ought, by Talmudic law, to be divorced speedily (*b. Yeb.* 63b) and shunned for purposes of remarriage. This is something of an improvement since it acquits all women of being guilty as charged. This slight gain is balanced, however, by the imputation of guilt to womankind through Eve's conspiracy with the Serpent: now v. 29 is read to mean that 'Man' (the male creature, not humanity in its generic form) was created upright. He—and they do mean 'he'!—was then corrupted by Eve and Company, the referents of the cryptic 'they' who seek devices, bringing many plagues upon the earth (and not just the plague of a bad wife, as in Prov. 22.10). In the same place, *Qoheleth Rabbah* reads:

> He (Adam) was upright, as it is said: 'That God made Adam upright' (7.29) and it is written, 'Behold Adam was one of us' (Gen. 3.22) one of the ministering angels. When however he became two then 'They sought out many inventions' (7.29).[53]

From a feminist perspective, the Midrash is somewhat better than the Targum—but only somewhat—in its general implications: in the latter, Eve and the Serpent were the seekers of many devices against the noble Adam (and presumably, his god); in the Midrash, however, both humans bear the responsibility for those machinations. The impetus which causes the move from being upright, however, is clearly to be found in the creation of the female gender as a 'free-standing' entity. The alternative traditions of Gen. 1.27 where both humans, male and female, are created simultaneously and both in the divine image offer no apparent challenge to the male interpreters of womankind in these reworkings of the Hebrew text.

5. *Qoheleth among the Christians:* *Literary Proverb Performance in the* Malleus maleficarum

Long before Talmud, Targum, or Midrash sought to inscribe a patriarchal ethic of female guilt in Qoheleth's puzzling words, the New Testament entered the lists in favor of a Fall to be attributed primarily to women. Ironically, without the falling women of the world, men would have had no need for a savior; Woman's deception by the Serpent (now attributed to all women throughout all history) is a critical element which brings about the drama of Salvation History. However, She receives no particular reward for this key role in helping God fulfill his plans for humanity. Instead, we hear in 1 Tim. 2.12-14:

---

53. Quoted in Knobel, *Targum*, p. 41.

6. 'Many Devices' (Qoheleth 7.23–8.1)   199

> I permit no woman to teach or to have authority over men; she is to keep silent. For Adam was formed first, then Eve; and Adam was not deceived, but the woman was deceived and became a transgressor.[54]

The text continues by telling us that women may be saved by the bearing of children, with 'modesty' as their watchword in all things. Despite some arguments which try to make the early Jesus Movement into a sort of 'women's liberation' event, at present two things are clear: (1) we do not know what attracted Jewish and pagan women to the Jesus Movement in the early days, or if they were attracted as women to the movement; and (2) whatever egalitarian impulses toward women and slaves which may have existed in the Jesus Movement at its inception, by the time of the formulation of the 'doctrines' of the Church Fathers and Councils, women had been put firmly in their place as inferior, misbegotten males defined by Aristotle, less-than-fully-human creatures whose duty was to be submissive to the men who rule over them.[55]

Within this philosophical and social matrix of female inferiority, Qoheleth's words on Woman, read with the customary negative slant, were scarcely perceived to be out of place among the teachings of the learned doctors of the Church.[56] This is not to say that Churchmen did not have other problems with Qoheleth (such as the pessimistic statements suggesting that all activity is more or less futile, unacceptable to a world redeemed by Christ), but his purported views on women were not among them. Commentator James Crenshaw notes, 'Qoheleth added his voice to the choir that sang about the weaknesses of women, but he

---

54. See Schottroff, *Lydia's*, pp. 69-78. Cf. Sir. 25.24; for discussion of the 'sexual' nature of Eve's seduction by the Serpent, see John A. Phillips, *Eve: The History of an Idea* (San Francisco: Harper & Row, 1984), pp. 38-51. Speculation about the origins and nature of evil remained fairly fluid in the early centuries before and during the rise of Christianity; it is by no means clear that this passage attributed to Paul can be 'blamed' on any sort of normative position of the Judaisms of the time.

55. A.-J. Levine, 'Second Temple Judaism, Jesus, and Women: Yeast of Eden', in Athalya Brenner (ed.), *A Feminist Companion to the Hebrew Bible in the New Testament* (FCB, 10; Sheffield: Sheffield Academic Press, 1996), pp. 302-31 (306-308, 326-28); see also Schottroff, *Lydia's*, pp. 3-42; Elizabeth A. Clark, *Women in the Early Church* (Message of the Fathers of the Church, 13; Wilmington, DE: Michael Glazier, 1983); Karen Jo Torjesen, *When Women Were Priests: Women's Leadership in the Early Church and the Scandal of their Subordination in the Rise of Christianity* (San Francisco: Harper, 1993), esp. pp. 118-20; 136-49; 203-41. All of these writers attempt to trace the legacy and impact of classical misogyny on Jewish and Christian traditions, as well as delve into the social circumstances of the increasing restrictions placed upon women during the rise of Christianity.

56. In fact, Qoheleth's words in this passage are 'obsessively quoted in the Middle Ages' (Blamires, *Woman*, p. 34 n. 56).

viewed men as only slightly better...'⁵⁷ Qoheleth's surly estimation of his own sex, however, never similarly contributed to a doctrinal stance which had direct and dire impact on the lives of those so evaluated. And how could Qoheleth's words be disbelieved, when it was the wise and experienced 'King Solomon' who uttered them? If some women were driven to look to a different, heavenly King, a kind of 'knight in shining armor',⁵⁸ who defended prostitutes and healed women in their bloody 'impurity', we will not dispute with them here the emotional validity of that interpretative move, given their time and place. We will only note that, unfortunately, such allegiances did nothing to protect observant Christian women when they fell into the hands of the Church's all-male inquisitors.⁵⁹

Many factors came together in early modern Europe to create the several centuries' long reign of terror for Christian⁶⁰ and pagan women. These governmental and social shifts include but are not limited to: the rise of the modern state and its use of coercive power against its citizens, the ceding of witchcraft prosecutions to secular courts as the capital crime of 'treason' rather than ecclesiastical courts who had previously treated such charges as 'heresy', changes in jurisprudence,⁶¹ the Roman church's attempts to curb the nascent Protestant Reformation which ensued in almost continuous 'wars of religion'. At the same time the First World saw continent-wide inflation caused by the influx of gold from the exploited 'New World', modernization of economies which moved

57. James L. Crenshaw, *Ecclesiastes: A Commentary* (OTL; Philadelphia: Westminster Press, 1987), p. 147.

58. Schottroff, *Lydia's*, p. 14-15.

59. Trial transcripts from torture sessions indicate that Christian women routinely called to God the Father, Jesus Christ, Mary, and Our Lady of Guadeloupe to bear witness to their innocence and stop the torture. They received no recorded reply (Claudia Lewis, 'Requiem for a Jew', *Tikkun* 11 [1996], pp. 77-79). Although this particular case concerns a *converso*, many others could be cited.

60. Both Protestant and Catholic women were at risk. The outbreaks of the witch-craze were worst in Scotland, Germany, and France. England, which refused to sanction the use of torture to obtain confessions, had a rather different experience because of this fact. See Anne Llewellyn Barstow, *Witchcraze: A New History of the European Witch Hunts* (San Francisco: Pandora/Harper Row, 1994), and H.C. Erik Midelfort, 'Witchcraft and Religion in Sixteenth-Century Germany: The Formation and Consequences of an Orthodoxy', *Archiv für Reformationsgeschichte* 62 (1971), pp. 266-78.

61. The first occurrence ever of large numbers of women in the penal system; the admission of 'spectral' evidence in trials and other changes in the understanding of what constituted 'proof' of the crime; the accused having no right to counsel nor to confront their accusers; the use of torture to obtain confessions with no cessation of the torture even after confession (Barstow, *Witchcraze*, pp. 15-55).

peasant workers out of the agrarian feudal system into cities, resulting in record numbers of unemployed causing the average age of marrying couples to soar and the size of families to decrease. Added to this was the collapse of medieval medical paradigms which had failed miserably to respond to the Black Plague, the transmission of syphilis from the New World to the First World through soldier 'carriers' infecting prostitutes,[62] and the rise of the university-trained male-exclusive medical profession now in direct competition with village folk healers (wise women). A large group of unmarried or widowed older women was created by the confluence of these factors. These were women past the age of bearing children, without means of self-support, and hence, of no use to the patriarchal state but deserving of 'alms' by traditional church teachings.

Theologies of demonic 'conspiracy theories', each with an appropriate ideological 'twist' as required by Protestants or Catholics, held sway as the Church's general explanation for disruptive social change, especially once most heretical groups, lepers, homosexuals, and Jews had been either wiped out or expelled. These theories were quickly made available across the continents, along with lurid descriptions of the proceedings of witchcraft trials, by the invention of Gutenberg's printing press. Indeed, the *Malleus maleficarum*, or 'Hammer of Witches' was an immediate best-seller in the fifteenth century, second only to the Bible. As is often typical, women of the under classes were some of the first casualties of technological advances. It is no wonder that modern students of medicine, law, government, colonialism, psychopathology, anthropology, sociology of the modern era, heresy, and feminist theology all turn a fascinated—if horrified—gaze upon this period as they try to discern the mechanisms that caused the people of Europe to go stark, raving mad, almost in unison. This period left the modern world with a legacy of intolerance and public cruelty that it has yet to successfully renounce.[63]

While the *Malleus maleficarum* was not the first nor the last treatise on witchcraft, its origins, abilities, and remedies for it, it is arguably the most important (with Jean Bodin's *Demonomanie* perhaps taking second place) in its impact.[64] Certainly it was accorded a status which

---

62. Advanced symptoms of syphilis created many of the dreaded effects of the 'witches' disease' (impairment of fertility, changes in male genitalia, dementia, and 'cold spots' with no sensation on the body), Brian P. Levack (ed.), *Articles on Witchcraft, Magic and Demonology: A Twelve Volume Anthology of Scholarly Articles*. X. *Witchcraft, Women and Society* (New York: Garland Publishing, 1992), pp. 273-306.

63. Barstow, *Witchcraze*; Levack (ed.), *Witchcraft, Women and Society*.

64. Sydney Anglo, 'Evident Authority and Authoritative Evidence: The *Malleus Maleficarum*', in S. Anglo (ed.), *The Damned Art: Essays in the Literature of Witchcraft* (London: Routledge & Kegan Paul, 1977), pp. 1-31 (14).

its opponents never obtained with their fierce denunciations or carefully argued legal or medical insights. The *Malleus maleficarum* remained 'the' text which any detractor of the witchcraze must confute. Penned by two Dominicans, Henrich 'Institoris' Kramer and Jacob Sprenger, with the blessing of the conspiracy-minded Pope Innocent VIII in his Bull, *Summis desiderantes affectibus* (December 9, 1484), directed specifically toward his beloved Inquisitors.[65] Composed shortly after this, the work was approved—though not without some hostility—by the Doctors of the Theological Faculty at the University of Cologne in 1487.[66]

Truly a 'child of its time', this treatise is marked by the full use of the rhetorical devices of its age: citation of 'classical' references piled up in circular fashion, analogical reasoning,[67] arguments from silence, all deployed with an entirely cavalier attitude toward what might constitute 'proof' of such activities as alleged by its authors. Modern readers—though not all![68]—might take particular note of the 'enthusiastic sadism'[69] of the Inquisitors as they give directions for the dehumanization and torture of their unfortunate captives. This reader can imagine no scenario short of direct, divine intervention with a host of 'special effects' which could have convinced these talented theological torturers of the innocence of their prisoners. As one later medical detractor, Johann Weyer, commented sourly in his own refutation of the *Malleus maleficarum*, the only evidence of demonic possessions and pacts with the Devil were to be found in the behavior of the Inquisitors and civil authorities.[70]

---

65. Heinrich Kramer and James Sprenger, *The Malleus maleficarum* (trans. with an introduction bibliography and notes by Montague Summers; New York: Dover, 1971), p. xxv.

66. Kramer and Sprenger, *Malleus*, p. xxxvii.

67. For example, the evidence of naturally caused sickness is used to 'prove' the occurrence of demonically induced illness.

68. The modern translator Montague Summers turns his attention to the usefulness of the purported misogyny of the text: 'Possibly what will seem even more amazing to modern readers is the misogynic trend of various passages… However, …I am not altogether certain that they will not prove a *wholesome and needful antidote* (italics mine) in this feministic age when the sexes seem confounded, and it appears to be the chief object of many females to ape the man, an indecorum by which they not only divest themselves of such charm as they might boast, but lay themselves open to the sternest reprobation in the name of *sanity and common-sense*' (Kramer and Sprenger, *Malleus*, p. xxxix).

69. Anglo, 'Authority', pp. 1-31 (27).

70. Gregory Zilboorg, *The Medical Man and the Witch during the Renaissance* (The Hideyo Noguchi Lectures; Publications of the Institute of the History of Medicine, The Johns Hopkins University Press, 3/2, 1935; repr., New York: Cooper Square Publishers, 1969), pp. 111, 131-2, 141.

6. 'Many Devices' (Qoheleth 7.23–8.1)

Naturally, for men of the cloth, the Bible must be seen to both prove their claims and sustain their arguments for speedy legal redress of the heinous crimes of old women. The Bible was not entirely on their side, however: for every 'Witch of En-dor', one could put forward an universalistic statement about the ultimate power of God and the triumph of good over evil. The problem of God's participation in the witches' evil deeds, by allowing them to occur, was readily solved by deferring to doctrines of 'free will'. Certainly, the Satan's behavior in the Book of Job might suggest to some that no evil is done to a good man unless the Lord wills it, but such considerations do not trouble our authors. Nor do they look to the preaching of the prophets, as did other writers arguing for and against the existence of witchcraft, which identified cosmic, natural and personal misfortunes *not* as a deed done by an enemy, but as the natural and just retribution for one's sins at the hands of the Lord.[71] Our text on Qoheleth 7 commences in answer to Question 6 of Part One, 'Why it is that Women are chiefly addicted to Evil Superstitions':

> It is this which is lamented in Ecclesiastes vii, and which the Church even now laments on account of the great multitude of witches. And I have found a woman more bitter than death, who is the hunter's snare, and her heart is a net, and her hands are bands. He that pleaseth God shall escape from her; but he that is a sinner shall be caught by her. More bitter than death, that is, than the devil: Apocalypse vi, 8, His name was Death. For though the devil tempted Eve to sin, yet Eve seduced Adam. And as the sin of Eve would not have brought death to our soul and body unless the sin had afterwards passed on to Adam, to which he was tempted by Eve, not by the devil, therefore she is more bitter than death.
>
> More bitter than death, again, because that is natural and destroys only the body; but the sin which arose from woman destroys the soul by depriving it of grace, and delivers the body up to the punishment for sin.
>
> More bitter than death, again, because bodily death is an open and terrible enemy, but woman is a wheedling and secret enemy.
>
> And that she is more perilous than a snare does not speak of the snare of hunters, but of devils. For men are caught not only through their carnal desires, when they see and hear women: for S. Bernard says: Their face is a burning wind and their voice the hissing of serpents: but they also cast wicked spells on countless men and animals. And when it is said that her heart is a net, it speaks of the inscrutable malice which reigns in their hearts. And her hands are as bands for binding; for when they place

---

71. Weyer writes caustically 'It is fortunate that [Job and Nebuchadnezzar] are not among us today, for if they were hereabouts some old woman would have to shoulder the responsibility for their distress, and the brains of these old women are so inflamed that under torture they would confess to having caused all these terrors' (Zilboorg, *Medical Man*, p. 152).

> their hands on a creature to bewitch it, then with the help of the devil they perform their design.
>
> To conclude. All witchcraft comes from carnal lust, which is in women insatiable. See Proverbs xxx: There are three things that are never satisfied, yea, a fourth thing which says not, It is enough; that is, the mouth of the womb. Wherefore for the sake of fulfilling their lusts they consort even with devils. More such reasons could be brought forward, but to the understanding it is sufficiently clear that it is no matter for wonder that there are more women than men found infected with the heresy of witchcraft. And in consequence of this, it is better called the heresy of witches than of wizards, since the name is taken from the more powerful party. And blessed be the Highest Who has so far preserved the male sex from so great a crime: for since He was willing to be born and to suffer for us, therefore He has granted to men this privilege.[72]

The theological methods of these exemplars of the privileged, preserved male sex are clear enough: the eternally valid biblical text which must be at all times true and applicable is freely used to give meanings to the passage which, while certainly inherent in previous interpretations, were held in check to some degree by the contrary contours of Qoheleth's own text. Now, the Preacher's words delineate a collective character for women which, were it true, should leave men frightened indeed.[73] Along with classical authors, Augustine and Thomas Aquinas are trotted out in force to bolster the claims made concerning woman. Even Proverbs with its praise of the Woman of Worth and continued affirmation that a good wife is a gift from the great God is turned to the witchmonger's needs by piecemeal readings interpreted with extreme prejudice.

Several elements are of particular interest in the inquisitors' use of the passage from Qoheleth. First, it is rather interesting that Qoheleth's dictum about not even 'one in a million' does not appear here, though it was much quoted by male authors during the period. Is it perhaps the case that such inclusion might cast some doubt upon the theologically and morally privileged status of males as a gender? Further, Solomon, the all-knowing king and great enemy of demons who supposedly authored our text, is not invoked, though it would have been natural, given the context, to do so.

Most telling of all, beyond generalizations and late medieval/early modern eisegesis is the uncanny transfer of the traits of the witch hunters

---

72. Kramer and Sprenger, *Malleus*, p. 47.
73. We might note here that the witch's malevolent control of both male and female fertility, as well as her preoccupation with damage to the male genitals, are salaciously narrated by our theologians. Cf. *Malleus*, Part 1, Question x; Part 2, Question i, chs vi-vii, xiii, *et passim*.

which they project onto their victims. Their torture was more bitter than death or devil, for the accused were suffering at the hands of their own duly authorized 'saviors'; similarly, the trauma of captives went far beyond the torment of the body, leaving captives destroyed in soul and betrayed by a faith that had no deliverance for them. The 'wheedling' of the 'secret enemy' more aptly describes the procedures of the inquisitors than the behavior of the women they sought to destroy. The 'bands' and 'nets' of the churchmen's 'inscrutable malice' found their manifestation in the shackles that manacled the wrists of the accused, supposedly the 'more powerful party' against whom any extreme measures of cruelty were warranted. It would appear that Weyer and others were correct after all: the crimes against humanity committed during this age must be attributed largely to those in power.[74] We disagree with the good friars: the male sex has been preserved from nothing in this matter; any devils in evidence during these centuries wore the guise of Adam. Following the reasoning of Sprenger and Kramer, we must name this movement for the more powerful party and proclaim it a heresy of male hierarchy.

6. *Many Devices of the Modern Commentators*

We have seen in our discussion above that critical commentators are of many minds about how to translate, resolve, or make palatable the sentiments expressed in one of Qoheleth's most famous passages — and one of his few mentions of women.[75] The trend by modern critics, as noted by Christianson, is to find a way to excuse Qoheleth for the views on women he expresses, either by deferring to the 'quotation' model which has him citing, then rejecting, the attitudes that most moderns find repellent, or using grammatical ambiguities to nuance the passage, or both.[76] We will take up two interpretations which return us to our original metaphor: the 'plain sense' of this passage to many hearers and interpreters alike is one which invites conflict, rather than settling it (more typical of the way of Wisdom, even when

---

74. Such opinions caused Weyer's work refuting the *Malleus* to be dubbed 'Weyer's Poison' by the Church (Zilboorg, *Medical Man*, p.201).

75. For further discussion, see Eric S. Christianson, 'Qoheleth the "Old Boy" and Qoheleth the "New Man": Misogynism, the Womb and a Paradox in Ecclesiastes', in Athalya Brenner and Carole Fontaine (eds.), *A Feminist Companion to Wisdom and Psalms (Second Series)* (FCB, 2; Sheffield: Sheffield Academic Press, 1998), pp. 109-36, and the present writer's 'The Proof of the Pudding: Proverbs and Gender in the Performance Arena', *JSOT* 29 (2004), pp. 179-204.

76. So Murphy, *Ecclesiastes*, pp. 75-77; T. Krüger, ' "Frau Weisheit" ', pp. 394-403 (394-95); Klaus Baltzer, 'Women and War in Qoheleth 7:23-8:1a', *HTR* 80 (1987), pp. 127-32; see Christianson's discussion, ' "Old Boy" ', pp. 109-36.

Fightin' Words, One More Time

One approach to sanitizing Qoheleth 7 is taken by critics who note that the Tanak, from time to time, cites women as exemplars of strength.[77] In the wisdom tradition, this is also true of the rhetoric used to warn young men against the foreign, strange or adulterous woman.[78] But it is not only wicked women, or their mother Eve who brought death to all men, who are associated with the moral, physical and emotional strength that is the hallmark of the 'coping' female: the 'Woman of Worth' of Proverbs 31 is designated by the term '*ḥayil*', used of men to designate their champion-like natures as (primarily) warriors. Further, such critics read in the Song of Songs that 'love' — surely the province of women and their mates — is 'stronger than the grave' (8.6). Could it be that Qoheleth is really lauding women, experts in the realm of emotions and relationships, perhaps claiming they are 'as strong as' death, rather than more bitter than death?! Baltzer makes a case for this reading by pointing out that the 'thousand', 'nets' and 'devices' (e.g. 'siege-works') are typical of military vocabulary. The point would be then that when Qoheleth examined the brigades composed of a thousand soldiers, replete with their technologies of death, he found no woman among them, for this is not the way of women. That is, women may be 'death machines' through their 'original' sins and their come-hither biological differences from men, but at least they have no part in the official killing machines of the Persian or Hellenistic state.[79] The critic has indeed located words about fighting in our passage, but his device is to relocate their referents in order to deflect their impact on the biblical theory of womankind evinced here. It is interesting to note that the post-biblical Jewish and Christian male readers of Qoheleth, who must surely have been more familiar with the 'true' military meaning of these words, should have never before put forward this interpretation — until they started reading in the company of learned women. Previously, the only war intuited from this text prior to our century was the 'gender war' which women, by nature (through means of their carnal lust, weakness of intellect and propensity toward witchcraft),[80] wage against helpless males. The views of Sprenger and Kramer stand as the rule, and not the exception.

---

77. Claudia Camp and Carole R. Fontaine, 'The Words of the Wise and Their Riddles', in Susan Niditch (ed.), *Text and Tradition: The Hebrew Bible and Folklore* (Semeia Studies; Atlanta: Scholars Press, 1990), pp. 127-52.
78. Krüger, ' "Frau Weisheit" ', pp. 394-403 (395).
79. Baltzer, 'Women', pp. 127-32 (131).
80. Note, too, the use of such language of extremes during the witchcraze: Judge

One final modern interpretation is of interest for its different tack on freeing Qoheleth from the charge of misogyny: Krüger suggests that, given the passage's emphasis on seeking and (not) finding, perhaps the one woman in a thousand Qoheleth could not find was Woman Wisdom herself![81] Certainly, one might support this from Qoheleth's own musings: he says that he made a test of wisdom, but it ended in the puzzle of the grave ('How can the sage die like the fool?', Qoh. 2.16). Later he claims that Wisdom remained far off and very deep, despite all his struggles to know her and grasp her (7.23-24). That this is true we cannot deny: the content of his words on women reveals how little he found out about the nature of women's ways, or relationships in general. Perhaps he shakes his fist angrily at an indifferent cosmos which gave him no reason to think differently, hoping to provoke a better answer than any he could devise by himself. The many devices of those who interpret him cannot disguise the man's ambivalence about human-to-human contact, and his 'more bitter than death' disappointment with women in particular. Though we may explicate all the various meanings of his grammatical ambiguities and put forth gentler readings, interpreters should not and cannot ignore the very real, negative effects on the lives of actual women that the 'plain sense' of this text, read over the centuries, created. Here are words from tradition which must be fought; to do otherwise would be only more vanity, and a striving after wind.[82]

Afterword: Proverbs and Women on the Border of Iran

Reader, much has happened since this essay first appeared: the author received tenure, despite doing television, having a female body, and a certain tendency to be too tolerant of 'other' religions. Study into the use of the genre of proverbs, gender and genre has proceeded apace, too.[83] *Professor Niam Kamaal has shown that women use proverbs more often than men in Iraqi society, and more often amongst themselves than in gender mixed groups. Kamaal speculates that proverbs are perceived as 'home' wisdom from the world of family and tradition; in the secular society that was Iraq before*

Boquet of Burgundy writes to Henry IV that 'the Sorcerers reach everywhere by the thousands; they multiply on this earth like the caterpillars in our gardens' (Zilboorg, *Medical Man*, pp. 73-74).

81. Krüger, ' "Frau Weisheit" ', pp. 394-403 (398).

82. My special thanks to Brian Noonan, Margaret Tabor, Mary Jane Jenson, and Nancy Citro, for their help in the preparation of this manuscript.

83. Peter Seitel, *The Powers of Genre: Interpreting Haya Oral Literature* (Oxford Studies in Anthropological Linguistics 22; New York: Oxford University Press, 1999), pp. 35-48; Fontaine, 'Proof of the Pudding', pp. 179-204.

the imperial wars, men had no wish to be associated with a tradition that was…well, traditional, and from women's worlds, to boot! [84]

Human Rights work with women from traditional societies, or modernized societies with strong traditional ties has proved a fertile field to observe real women in actual contexts drawing upon proverbial wisdom to educate and evaluate the actions of those in their care. One Muslim reporter for the Toronto Star *told an international women's group in her introduction of the role of religion and human rights, 'We always say, "Trust in Allah – but tie up your camel!"' Nods of heads came from everyone, and not just those who were wearing traditional head gear: everyone immediately took up our context (how can we be effective against so much suffering with so few financial resources?) and used it to exegete the proverb: yes, be faithful and pray, but don't forget to do the leg-work, home-work, and piece/peace work! One must operate at both the local and the meta-level to effect real changes in the lives of women.* [85]

An even more deliberate strategy in proverb use occurs with Muslim women who have used their marginalization as a fulcrum for radical change, both personal and social. On the edge of the Iran–Iraq border, Iranian political refugees, led by women, form an enclave of résistance to the fundamentalist regime of the Mullahs in Iran. In Ashraf City, a population of about four thousand Iranians and supporters has provided the decades-long serious opposition to the human rights abuses inside Iran. Since 2004, this group has been classed as Protected Persons by Coalition Forces and the UN Assistance Mission for Iraq under the Fourth Geneva Convention, and the Iraqi populace have signed numerous petitions stating their support for the women with the dangerous name – The People's Mojahedin Organization in Iran (PMOI). Depending on whom one listens to – the law courts of the European Union, the US State Department, the US Military, Iranian monarchists or the Mullah's Shi'ite loyalists, these women are either a legitimate resistance movement, the most gallant, astonishing group of freedom fighters the world has seen since the Amazons of antiquity, or they are murderous, lying, anti-Islamic terrorists constantly threatening legitimate theocracies, [86] *and supporting Israel. They have been considered clannish, Marxist, feminist, man-hating betrayers of Islam, hell bent on destroying the traditional family by bombing the government (an odd approach for that goal, certainly). By the Iranian diaspora, they are considered something akin to revelatory: leadership by and for women has transformed a whole generation of*

---

84. Niam Kamaal, 'Sociolinguistic Study of the role of Occupation in Women's Use of Proverbs' (PhD dissertation, University of Mosul, Iraq, 2001).

85. Read more about this Canadian Muslim Woman of the Year, Raheel Raza, in her recent book, *Their Jihad is Not my Jihad: A Muslim Canadian Woman Speaks out* (Ingersoll, ON: Basileia Books, 2005).

86. If a group refers to Camp Ashraf as the *Mujahedin-e-Kalq* (MeK), then they are usually Islamic extremist detractors.

Muslim men from Iran, and they are not likely to forget what they have learned working shoulder to shoulder with their sisters.

The PMOI existed as a legitimate political party during the time of the Shah, whose rule they opposed forcefully, and briefly after the Khomeini regime took power. At a peaceful rally in 1981 the government turned their guns on the political group, and the many who were simply bystanders. Afterwards, the arrests and executions started. More than one hundred-twenty thousand of their citizens have been executed so far. Remaining leaders fled the country to spearhead an indigenous movement to depose the fundamentalist opportunists who were busily demolishing the economy and infrastructure of Iran for their own financial gain.

The women and girls of the PMOI at Ashraf City constituted the only so-called 'terrorist' camp in Iraq at the time of the illegal invasion of that country by the Bush regime in 2003. It was fortunate that these survivors of rape, torture and political massacres of their families had only recently been named terrorists by Madeleine Albright under President Clinton – a move designed to appease the Iranian government (while still providing the US with intelligence on the ground from the only ones to give the Mullahs pause in their scheme of world domination). Had the United States not so thoughtfully made these women into a terrorist threat, there would have been no activity worth misrepresenting as terrorism in Iraq in the run-up to the Second Gulf war, and no terrorists to bomb. Even now, assorted members of the Bush regime, Congress and Senate routinely support the PMOI in Washington's invasion fantasies, working with intelligence provided by those in Ashraf City, while at the same time maintaining them on the State Department's list of terrorist organizations.[87] During times when Osama bin Laden is considered to be hiding in the eastern provinces of Iran, there is low level 'chatter' that the United States is willing to trade all the residents of Ashraf City to the Iranian regime in return for bin Laden's seizure. Such is the nature of being a 'female' organizational ally of the United States: the PMOI is a 'designated expendable' of the current regional struggle, just as average women are the expendables in all patriarchal systems of value. Woman is just a tradable commodity.

What makes the women of Ashraf City and their leader in exile, Maryam Rajavi, so threatening to the Mullahs in Tehran? As a political party, they won large shares of votes when allowed to run in elections, so their credibility is certainly high in that respect. On the other hand, their long stay as refugees in Iraq has not earned them the love of the Iranian populace remembering the bitter war between neighbors in the 1980s. Under a campaign of disinformation, any public disruption or atrocity in Iran is attributed by that

---

87. Mohammad Mohaddessin, *Enemies of the Ayatollahs: The Iranian Opposition's War on Islamic Fundamentalism* (London: Zed Books, Ltd, 2004).

government to the PMOI. But it is the symbolic and material roles taken up by the women Mojahedin that outrage the misogynist fundamentalism preached by the Mullahs as the only acceptable form of Islam.

I use the term 'fundamentalist' advisedly in the Islamic context, not because I am unaware of the unsuitability of comparing a Muslim movement to a modern Christian one in the West, but for the sake of convenience. In essence, we are speaking of a form of any religion that uses literal and exclusive interpretations of ancient texts to abridge the religious rights and freedoms of others. While there are many structural features of fundamentalisms that reach across the three Religions of the Book, one marked feature is the anti-woman stance and social program these movements promote, as well as their hatred of all diversity and 'secular' cultural values. Copious study of fundamentalisms before and after 9/11 suggests (at least to this author) that this rejection of modernity may be a form of (male) 'group' personality disorder to deal with the dissonance and changing values in a globalized world competing for scarce resources.

That most women internalize such dreadful teachings with their views of the body, female sin and breeding destiny is no surprise: so it has always been. On the other hand, the testimony of the PMOI concerning women living under Muslim laws in Iran suggests that women have excellent abilities to feign acquiescence while maintaining their own views with considerable strength. A literary immersion in this context of the Other Woman can be found in Persepolis *and* Reading Lolita in Tehran,[88] *for those unfamiliar with women's subtle ways of resisting oppression.*

'Meetavaan va baayad – We can – and we should!'

On a Human Rights trip to Paris in celebration of International Women's Day in 2005, I found myself sitting next to a new activist acquaintance. I first met Jila via the internet where I lurked on her site as part of my work for the Women's United Nations Report Network, which highlights gender issues in the Human Rights arena. The news coming out of Iran and Iraq via families and refugees was appalling, as only a pogrom against women and children can be. Subsequently, Jila was invited to speak to a local Human Rights group in Newton, MA, consisting of members of the Andover Newton Theological School and Hebrew College community, along

---

88. Marjane Satrapi, *Persepolis: The Story of a Childhood* (New York: Pantheon Books, 2003); *Persepolis 2: The Story of a Return* (New York: Pantheon Books, 2004); Azar Nafisi, *Reading Lolita in Tehran: A Memoir in Books* (New York: Random House, 2003). For other perspectives on Muslim women's struggles against oppressive regimes, see Betsey Reed (ed.), *Nothing Sacred: Women Respond to Religious Fundamentalism and Terror* (New York: Thunder's Mouth Press, 2002).

6. 'Many Devices' (Qoheleth 7.23–8.1)

with local pastors, rabbis, activists, and legal professionals. Again, her presentation seemed to lift the veil that had covered the real inside stories in Iran since the Revolution of 1979.

On our way to the event which featured the leaders of the National Council of Resistance of Iran (the diplomatic and governmental side of the push for reform in Iran) and their President-Elect, Maryam Rajavi, my companion shared her own personal story of being trapped in the United States as a student during the 1979 upheaval. In the years that followed, she had to come to terms with the wholesale disappearance of many of her family, friends and school companions: the joyous Revolution had quickly given way to brutal repression. What was one to do, but support the only viable political challengers, even though they might be across the border in a refugee camp?

Jila shared as well how timorous she had first felt in moving into national activism on behalf of her country of origin. No stranger to power, competence, and the special ways women must negotiate them (she manages the information system at a university), she nevertheless found it difficult to be the 'point person', the public speaker on a topic about which she felt passionately. But, she said, none of us started out thinking that we would be political leaders…we were just engineers, writers, students, mothers, scientists, computer specialists. We didn't know how to do any of this at first, but we knew we had to. Mrs Rajavi led the way for us: she always says 'We can and we should', and I try to remember that.

Naturally, I was eager to hear Rajavi speak, having the scholar's natural interest in a modern example of her special area, proverbs. Indeed, Rajavi's speech to over a thousand women and men was peppered with proverbs, and she prefaced them all with the traditional prolegomenon, 'We have a saying…'. Some proverbs were extant in the Iranian culture: 'A knife cannot cut its own handle' was quoted to discuss and summarize the reasons why one should not expect reformist policies toward women and children under a fundamentalist leader, even if the West touts him as 'not a hardliner'. Beauty in the eye of the beholder takes a different turn when the eyes are from the East: 'it is because your eyes are beautiful that you can behold beauty'. This she said to many Westerners who praised her words in the receiving line; that we could 'hear' and 'see' beyond the terrorist label was proof enough of our vision, and it was beautiful to those who had been so repeatedly slandered.

Most interesting, however, was Rajavi's use of the saying, 'We can and we should!' Using it to introduce her narration of the particular struggles faced by women in learning to un-learn sexist expectations, she noted that women literally had to start 'from scratch' to cook up a recipe for female confidence and effectiveness. She spoke of the role of support groups of women who gave feedback to one another, and their leaders; she spoke of 'positive discrimination' when the PMOI deliberately decided to use women in leadership positions as a teaching tool for men and women in the movement.

An engineer by training before politics swept her family away in a storm of killing and imprisonment,[89] *she described the young people of Iran, especially the women, as similar to a compressed spring — too long denied any movement, they were poised to spring forward with great leaps and bounds the moment the pressure restraining them could be lifted. Yes, it was hard; yes, the work of relearning personhood is tedious and ongoing, but…'we can and we should'. Serenity, reason, and power endowed the delivery of this saying to an eager audience.*

As the fates would have it, not every speaker at a feminist Human Rights conference finds governments on her side. Some expected to be presenters had been denied visas or run into other 'security' problems at the last minute, so never made it to the event. One of the organizers quickly button-holed Jila to perform a trinity of public speaking tasks: chairing a session, translating from Farsi, and giving a report on the progress of her own NGO. 'I was trembling!' she told me. 'I have nothing with me, nothing! Not a word written, no materials. But then I told myself, Remember what Mrs Rajavi says: we can and we should. Then I knew I could do it.'

And she did.

What I did not know until later was that she had spent the night in flashbacks, nightmares and tears. Thumbing through a new publication by the National Council of Resistance of Iran on those tortured and disappeared by the government, she had suddenly come across the picture of a dear high school friend with whom she had lost touch after the Revolution. One always wonders and it is terrible, she told me. Sometimes one knows, and that is terrible, too. She knew from family that her friend had simply been handing out pamphlets on the street during a demonstration when she was arrested and taken to Evin prison. For this crime, her life — and that of her unborn child — was taken under torture and all word of her lost. Jila's quotation of 'We can, and we should' clearly took on the quality of 'We MUST; how else could we live with ourselves if we ignore this?'

Observing the citation of proverbs in feminist groups from a technical point of view offers a wonderful living laboratory of rhetorical styles. The behaviors noted in a variety of contexts of proverb use hold true in feminist groups (though these have certainly been under-observed by folklorists). Positive proverbs are most likely to be used in reference to oneself or allies; negative proverbs are used for the opponent, and cast them in the light of traditional disapproval, even when the opponents are supposed to be the arbiters of the tradition!

---

89. Rajavi has trained herself as a first-rate pastoral feminist theologian of Islam, and speaks passionately about the need for a 'progressive democratic' Islam in her *Islamic Fundamentalism and the Question of Women* (Auvers-sur-Oise: Women's Committee of the National Conference of Resistance of Iran, 2004).

6. 'Many Devices' (Qoheleth 7.23–8.1)

On a follow-up trip in 2008 to attend briefings concerning the Iranian assaults on the Diyala province in Iraq, I had occasion at dinner to have a 'modern' proverb quoted to me by the men of the NCRI. I had teased them, first, for eating all at their own table with no women seated there: 'I'm telling Tehran on you!' I said. No, no, they replied laughing: 'We were too hungry to wait for the women; now that you are all finally here, see, we serve you!' After new introductions and greetings, I sat with a couple of men from the Washington office, and asked if Ashraf City had a gift shop yet, as I was admiring the new PMOI scarves. No, said one man, but do you know that old television show, 'Leave it to Beaver'? Yes, of course, I replied. 'Well, you are sitting on its true "set": around here, all we say is "Leave it to Sarvi" (the head of the Women's Committee), and all will be arranged as it should be!'

As a proverb specialist, I was delighted with the transgressive quality of this interchange. First, my informants were non-native users of English, so their use of an American TV series title as a proverb was a tribute to the new global culture spawned by broadcast media. A re-applied, Hollywood-authored statement had passed into common usage as what might be called a 'traditional sentence' (rather like, 'Where's the beef?!'). Next, it was interesting to hear the men speaking in proverbial terms at all, given my readings on proverb use in modern Iraq which suggested that in public roles, men avoided invoking any traditional female images or styles of leadership to apply to themselves. Further, I was interested in hearing 'the Beaver' cross-gendered as female, and positively so: I had always taken 'Leave it to Beaver' as a statement that one could count on the baby of the television family to cause an upheaval of some sort, not necessarily positive. Finally, the NCRI men's use of all of the above to laud their female factotum was a delightful move from simple sentence to metaphorical insight: the real 'baby' of the human family, the female as imaged by patriarchy, has grown into a Woman of Power, openly acknowledged and celebrated by the men she leads.

Those who know this movement often comment that the men of the NCRI are as extraordinary as the women. This can be verified by things as simple as observing patterns of speech, choice of pronouns, tone of voice, and willingness to transgress gender boundaries by gladly performing work usually classed as 'female' or 'service'. Put another way, one cannot 'fake' the inner meanings or intent of application of proverbs terms to contextual situations: critical attention to rhetoric in use will always betray discrepancies to the expert observer between what is said and what is meant. Confidence in female leadership and pride in it as well has become a standard mode of operation for the men of the NCRI. Herein lays the symbolic threat posed by realized female equality: that men will call themselves happy to have a woman leader of strength, character and courage. Indeed, the Mullahs of Tehran are correct: the heavens do tremble at the example set by those resisting misogynist theocracy in Iran!

> That empowering proverbs pass between mother and daughter, leader and follower, women and men, is a potent anecdote to killing discourse of Qoheleth, the witch hunters, and their modern inheritors, the Mullahs. That believing women stand on the borders between warring countries, sects, and worldviews, guided by the wisdom of ancient voices — and many modern ones — is a matter for much hope: we can — and we should.[90]

---

90. As of May 7, 2008, the British courts have directed the government, finally and definitively, to remove the PMOI from its list of terrorist organizations. Iranian missile strikes against refugee camp at Ashraf City have increased dramatically in intensity and frequency.

Chapter 7

'COME, LIE WITH ME!':
THE MYTHOLOGY OF HONOR KILLINGS AND FEMALE DESIRE
IN BIBLICAL ISRAEL AND THE ANCIENT NEAR EAST

1. *What's All the Fuss About?*

A student wondered once, 'How can it make sense to study the Hebrew Bible from the point of view of women when it's not about women!' Aside from lamenting the student's lack of 'Bible knowledge', so clearly displayed in the question for all to see, I took this question seriously. I asked if the assorted regulations about sexuality in Leviticus or Deuteronomy, which concern women, don't make the subject a bit more legitimate as a topic of genuine interest within the text itself. 'Oh, families!', he said, 'if it's the man who makes all the decisions, why should we study the women?' Ah, families, I replied. Did the student notice that whenever a documentary on wild creatures appears, almost half of the time is spent on the subject of mating, reproduction, and rearing the new generation? How odd that when *homo sapiens* is the species in question, studying the exact same topics is considered a bore. (No reply was forthcoming.)

So, in answer to my student and others who wonder what the fuss is about, I simply point to the world of natural sciences at large and global politics among the species which thinks it runs things. As I write, a scenario which puts Judges 19–21 into context is occurring in the United States's disastrous imperial adventures in Iraq. In April 2007, a seventeen-year old girl, Du'a Aswad Dekhil, of the Nineveh province of Iraq, converted to Islam from her Yazidi sect (a mixture of the religions of the Book, but primarily a Christian sect with some Zoroastrianism and Gnosticism added into the mix) so that she could marry a Sunni Kurd. When she arrived home on the seventh of the month, she was greeted by a crowd of relatives, townsfolk, and on-lookers who proceeded to stone her to death for betraying their view of religion and ethnicity by choosing a man outside her immediate circle of preferred mates. Cell phone cameras caught the vicious attack on the girl, and soon, the whole world knew of it. Du'a was dead and the videos clearly showed local police standing back, watching as she was tortured to death by her brother and uncle, cheered by the mob. The world had its first taste of a broadcast 'Christian honor killing'.[1]

The story, brutal though it is, is not atypical for those who work in women's rights in Middle Eastern and other societies where male honor takes precedent over Qur'anic injunctions, Talmudic due process, the Sermon on the Mount, international law, and plain human decency. What is *not* typical is that in the current bizarre conditions of a civil war in which *no* authority can be trusted to look out for the interests of anyone considered Other by that authority, we can see the full range of violence enacted in a community of tribal organization and a history of persecution by the Muslim majority. Since Du'a was a Yazidi who wanted to marry a Sunni Kurd, the stoning was quickly appropriated as a *cause célèbre* for the religiously motivated civil war. On April 23, a bus carrying elderly factory workers home to Du'a's village was stopped, and Christians were ordered off the bus. The rest of the old men, all 23 of them, were lined up against a wall and shot by the Sunni faction who hijacked them.[2] Writes Bill Weinberg of the *World War 4 Report*:

> Islamist groups active in the area have sought to capitalise on this crime and are urging revenge attacks upon all Yezidis, claiming that she [Du'a] had converted to Islam and characterising the murder as a 'martyrdom' rather than an 'honour' killing. Women in the Middle East face patriarchal oppression and violence whether they are Muslim, Druze, Yezidi or Christian. 'Honour' killings are common amongst Kurds (the UN has recorded 40 honor killings in Kurdistan in 3 months in 2007) and public murders like this have been noted before: for example in the case of Semse Allak in the Kurdish region of Turkey. Islamists throughout Iraq seek to exploit the racial and religious divisions in the country; one mosque has declared a *'fatwa'* against the Yezidi and twenty-three have been murdered. For this reason, prompt action to locate the relatives of the young woman and the police who failed to act is essential to restore peace and allow the Yezidi community to feel safe again.[3]

---

1. Patrick Cockburn, 'A Wave of Revenge Killers: The Horrific Stoning Death of a Yazidi Girl', cited May 8, 2007 <http://www.counterpunch.org/patrick05082007.html>. Sadly, other Christian honor killings have occurred in Syria and Palestine (Chris McGreal, 'Murdered in the Name of Family Honour' [June 23, 2005], cited March 5, 2008 <http://www.guardian.co.uk/world/2005/jun/23/israel>), but this is the first to garner widespread attention. The video of the stoning may be viewed at <http://farkous.blog.ca/2007/05/17/stoning~2289644>, as well as many other sites; cited August 21, 2007.

2. WorldWar4Report, 'Iraq: Yazidi Workers Massacred in Mosul', cited September 27, 2007 <http://ww4report.com/node/3681>.

3. 'Another Account from Issam Shukri', World War 4 Report, posted May 3, 2007; cited September 27, 2007 <http://ww4report.com/node/3681>. You may also

7. 'Come, Lie with Me!' 217

Du'a's story is not *quite* so neat as has usually been reported on the web and world news, however. She had run away to convert to Islam a full five weeks before the stoning occurred. Police held the couple, kept the man in jail but released Du'a. Another local version of the story omits the police detention, but claims Du'a was rejected by her suitor after her conversion (it is not clear why). Desperately frightened and afraid to return home, Du'a stayed for several days with a Yazidi tribal leader, who assured her that her family had forgiven her and that it was safe to return to her village. Once there, she was abducted out of her home, and stoned. Desire meant death for Du'a.

But, of course, as in Judges 19–21, it does not end there. Over 200 Yazidi village residents protested the revenge killings over the next two days, causing all members of the village—Muslim, Christian and Yazidi—to remain indoors for fear of violence on the streets. Now, much to the dismay (or secret delight) of US authorities in Iraq, al Qaeda has joined the fray to honor Du'a as a fallen martyr to Sunni Islam. On August 15, 2007, al Qaeda took credit for an attack on Yazidi villages Qataniyah and Adnaniyah (Du'a was from Bashiqa) where four trucks carrying bombs were blown up by suicide bombers, killing over 250. This is the deadliest 'terrorist' attack since September 11, 2001.[4]

Alert US citizens must marvel at the strange effectiveness of Muslim militants—women avenged? Medicine found and brought in to a war zone for the elderly in Lebanon in 2006? Creative yet crude plans made and brought to conclusion? This is certainly nothing we are used to in our *own* experience of government during the Everlasting War on Terror.[5] But before we praise al Qaeda for its striking feminist position with respect to Du'a's suffering, let us recall that the same group would have been happy to see her dead in an honor killing had she been a Sunni girl who defected to the Yazidi sect, all in the name of love. Just as in the Hebrew Bible, the plain sense of the story of a woman's death is hijacked to talk about something *really* important: the stories of the male heroes, their states, and their gods. The gang rape and murder of the Levite's patrilocal wife in Judges 19 becomes linked to a much more critical story of tribal marriages and wars; Hannah's victory thanksgiving psalm in response to her longed-for baby is symbol for the whole

---

sign a petition to the regional authorities in Kurdistan calling upon them to protect the lives and safety of all women in their territories.

4. Al Jazeera.net, 'Al-Qaeda blamed in Iraq sect attack', cited September 27, 2007 <http://english.aljazeera.net/NR/exeres/EED9104C-42E5-4DD8-9B6A-6C92B5B32C43.htm?FRAMELESS=true&NRNODEGUID=%7bEED9104C-42E5-4DD8-9B6A-6C92B5B32C43%7d>.

5. Organizational Behavior Professor Craig Fontaine says that this efficacy is a result of a 'flat' decentralized organizational structure.

tribal nation yearning for a king. And so it goes: even in death or the making of life, the real events in the life of a woman's body are erased in favor of the patriarchal agenda of the moment.

2. *The Wages of Sin: Women's Desire in the Ancient World*

Given the very real and disturbing story just related, it seems almost jejune to move into a feminist discussion of desire, female or otherwise, in an ancient text. Yet, the texts we will consider form a backdrop to the dramas of desire today in which real women are really dying. There can be no question here of 'is it history?' or 'does it matter?' In order to deconstruct the abuses of the present, we must dismantle the oppressive texts, interpretations and practices of the past which helped create our current 'gender jihad' by religious extremists of all types. By showing that the patriarchal construction of women's desire as negative and in need of strict and brutal control in fact represents a common cultural practice of the ancient past, we provide direct assistance to those persons working inside the religions to bring reform. In particular for Christians and Jews, why should the violence of the text be perpetuated when the interpretive experts of those groups often work relentlessly to restrict the violence that the text permits? Likewise, from the point of view of international law, a Scripture which provides for due process (whether patriarchal in nature or not) argues that any process that ends in death and did *not* include due process for the accused is in fact not justice, but murder. Knowing the origins of anti-female practices in Scriptures allows us to mount better challenges to the hegemony of patriarchal interpretation.

Desire is a hot topic in Western feminist theological studies and the psychology of women. Everyone seems to be thinking about desire these days: what is it, why is it, what is its role in thought and practice, its relationship to language? More pointedly, since desire requires the construction of a Subject, one who desires, and a target, the Other who is desired, is desire even something about which committed feminists ought to be concerned? Supposing we decide to keep desire and desiring, how shall a group silenced and indoctrinated for centuries into acceptance of patriarchal codes of behavior which require the suppression of desire now learn to know, speak and act on desires never acknowledged before now? Leaving the plethora of epistemological questions aside,[6] along with the naturalization of compulsory heterosexuality, compara-

---

6. For nuanced and substantive epistemological consideration of all these questions, Judith Butler's *Gender Trouble: Feminism and the Subversion of Identity* (New York: Routledge, 1990) presents a stirring introduction (in the sense of 'stirring up trouble').

tive explorations of the trope of the desiring female will show that for women, desire is dangerous but potentially transformative.

Female desire in the Bible seems to land itself in a critical blind spot with respect to the rest of the ancient Near East. There is a fairly standard cross cultural literary motif which demonstrates a negative valuing of female desire: the predatory female whose overtures are spurned. We will explore its appearance in texts about the divine world (the Gilgamesh Epic, the Egyptian Tale of Two Brothers, the Canaanite-Hittite myth of 'Elkunirsha, Asherah, and the Storm-God', and the Hittite myth of Illuyanka) which preceded its emergence in the Bible's treatment of this theme in the Joseph story and elsewhere. Because all of these forays into the now-written folklore of the ancient world will lead us to some inevitable and not very charming conclusions on the subject of female desire, it is only fair that we end our discussion with Song of Songs.

On Desire and Its Gendering
Aviva Zornberg begins her wonderful book, *The Beginning of Desire: Reflections on Genesis*, with a lovely quote from Wallace Stevens's 'Notes toward a Supreme Fiction': 'not to have is the beginning of desire'.[7] It is immediately apparent from this brief remark *why* desire might be a signal issue for the greater half of the world's population. If anything, we the women have been characterized consistently in religion, philosophy, and psychology by what we *do not have*: a penis, a rational brain, a choice, a right, a hope, a destiny beyond biology. By the very rules of masculinist discourse, women *ought* to be considered the clear experts on the implications of 'not having'. We do most of the starving and most of the scut work of the world, and things were not so very different prior to this century. When we look at the economic production of the ancient Israelite family so ably described by Carol Meyers,[8] we find similar social conditions with respect to women and their work. Women have been ruthlessly socialized to accept that they have no right to choose and *ought not* to have that right, since it is so dangerous to themselves and others. Women are targeted for duties as a 'helpmeet', whose job description requires that they should suppress all personal yearnings and needs for the good of the family, clan, tribe, nation, or religion. The lack of human rights for women has, more often than not, been given the *Imprimatur* of scripturally based religions. In folkloric terms, women of the historical religions have been trapped

---

7. Avivah Zornberg, *The Beginning of Desire: Reflections on Genesis* (New York: Doubleday, 1996), p. vi.
8. 'The Family in Early Israel', in Leo G. Perdue *et al.*, *Families in Ancient Israel* (Louisville, KY: Westminster/John Knox Press, 1997), pp. 1-47.

for centuries in the first half of a Native American folktale, whose pattern goes something like:

> Lack
> Difficult Task
> Solution
> Lack Liquidated.[9]

Experience and feminist critical methodology have allowed modern industrialized women to explore thoroughly the concepts of our 'Lack'. We have done so, and find ourselves in the next stage of narrative progress toward individuation and group evolution: Difficult Task (or, in V.I. Lenin's famous sentence, 'What is to be done?'). Yet, here we stay as a group, dead in the maternal waters, at least in most mainstream theological, human rights or even political discourse. We do not have a unified solution, or even common agreement on how alleged female Lack, the supposed justification for gender asymmetry, originated. Like the low status of women, I suspect that women's lack begins and ends in male self-definition of what is human and valuable. Butler describes this as 'the 'male signifying economy' which ineluctably requires a lesser Other in order to ground the illusion of male hegemony over personhood, a personhood which is presumed as a 'normative ideal' rather than a product of cultural practice and signification.[10] So as yet, our Lack in the male tales of culture cannot be liquidated, thereby moving women and their concerns to the next stage of evolving consciousness.

It is very natural to take up questions of just how the Bible has participated in inscribing into the religious traditions which helped shape the Western world the male view of female lack as *the* normative position, but if we study *only* the Bible on this topic we run risk of being handicapped by the very discursive ideologies we are challenging. Among 'ordinary readers' (believers), too often the Hebrew Bible turns out to be the 'Bad Guy', as noted earlier in Chapter Four. The mainstream defenders of the faith like to tell us that Jesus and Paul were feminists, so the New Testament, in much popular theology, is the supposed remedy for any of those nasty hangovers from that prior Other, the First Testament. The Hebrew Bible is the convenient scapegoat for much we abhor, but many of those elements were common to the ancient world. Patriarchal economics or phallogocentrism were no particular inventions of those proto-Israelites we love to hunt for in the Iron I highland settlements, but that is 'news' to many popular feminist thinkers and godly believers alike. The Tanak's scapegoat position of 'victim subjectivity' is one many

---

9. Alan Dundes, *The Morphology of North American Indian Folktales* (Helsinki: Folklore Fellows Communications, 1964).

10. Butler, *Gender Trouble*, pp. 11-18.

are glad to have as a fallback explanation, since it allows for a tried and true method of dealing with problems of scriptural content or authority. This allows one to both pity the writers of Scripture (poor, beset groups always in conflict with larger rivals) and yet permits the continued demonization of Judaism-the-Other as the source of error in Christian theology and practice. This leads to the notion that if people would *simply* accept the New Testament upgrade, all problems of gender, race, and class would be comfortably resolved. The subtle political play here is to call Christianity to repentance of gender sins by suggesting that to do so is just another example of the profound need to renounce the Jewish heritage of Bible: *real Christians* are feminists. Better to stand with your own women than with the Jews, after all.

But, as one Cole Porter song goes, 'It ain't necessarily so/ De t'ings dat yo li'ble/To read in de Bible—It ain't necessarily so.' The New Testament *does* give us comfortable answers to the challenges of exclusion, *if* we want slaves who obey their masters, and women silenced before God. Are there perhaps other options? The Hebrew Bible is *not* the culprit, even if many of its readers, past and present, may think so, and it has something to offer women that the other texts do not: a song of successful desire initiated by a woman. Ignoring the Hebrew Bible is not necessarily going to get believing women in the biblical traditions any further along on the topic of desire or anything else. Further, if deleting the Hebrew Bible in favor of the New Testament is not the answer, then the corollary of ignoring the ancient Near East in favor of the Hebrew Bible is also unworkable. All three bodies of texts share a common masculinist ideology, and we cannot deflect that by erasing one source in favor of another. Indeed, one could argue that, biblical or otherwise, the common functioning of the world as we know it *still* derives from that ideology of men's *right* to desire and the corresponding socially-proscribed lack of right to desire for women.[11] Yet, we find we want something else; we desire change for ourselves, our civilization, and our planet.

3. *Female Desire in the Bible and among the Neighbors*

As we turn to our exploration of mythology and narratives where female desire is clearly presented and evaluated, I would like to acknowledge that here I am much indebted to the work of many others: most especially, I commend the work of Susan Hollis, feminist Egyptologist

---

11. It *does* make perfect sense within its own discourse: how can a 'someone' incapable of being a true Subject possessed of agency in patriarchal discourse ever acquire the ability to desire, predicated as it is upon the very subjectivity denied women ontologically.

extraordinaire, on Potiphar's wife, and Athalya Brenner, the gendering power behind many of the best offerings on the topic of feminist biblical hermeneutics.

As Brenner so clearly points out in her *The Intercourse of Knowledge: On Gendering Desire and 'Sexuality' in the Hebrew Bible*, the concept of desire has been thoroughly gendered. To 'gender' a term, symbol or concept is to focus, use and understand it as more appropriate or representative of one sex rather than the other. An example of this might be drawn from a simple consideration of ancient Near Eastern symbols of masculinity and femininity: men are like oxen; women are like trees; men carry weapons, women carry spindles and mirrors. 'Gendering' as Brenner and van Dijk-Hemmes use the term occurs everywhere throughout the biblical text and in the societies which created it.[12]

In biblical concepts of desire, we find a thorough-going ideology of gender. Women are permitted only those desires that fit their ideologically constructed social roles. For example, matters are not so simple as the Bible would have us believe in its relentless portrayal of the ideology of motherhood, a primary field of reference in which desire has been 'gendered'.[13] Women do not just desire to become mothers; they want to become the mothers of *sons*, and *not* daughters. Likewise, despite the lack of specific and differentiated terms referring to male sexual physicality, almost all of the language of love and desire has been 'gendered' male.[14] These ideological mechanisms are also at work in the motif of the spurned woman and its assessment, moral or narratological, among the cultures which told and retold these tales.

4. *The Primary Texts*

We will explore here primarily the 'proposition' section of the spurned woman motif as we find it in earlier mythological formulations among Israel's neighbors. Our investigation of folktale motif K2111, Potiphar's Wife, will be confined to its mythic precursors which do *not* necessarily include the denouement of the K2111 type-scene (where the rejected female fabricates a tale of attempted rape to cover her own wrong-doing and punish the youngster who rebuffed her sexual overtures). Hollis divides the motif as it appears in the ancient Near East into the following components, which fall into the three phases of a typical rite of transition, Separation, Transition, Incorporation:

12. Athalya Brenner and Fokkelien van Dijk-Hemmes (eds.), *On Gendering Texts: Female and Male Voices in the Hebrew Bible* (BIS, 1; Leiden, E.J. Brill, 1993).
13. Athalya Brenner, *The Intercourse of Knowledge: On Gendering Desire and 'Sexuality' in the Hebrew Bible* (BIS, 26; Leiden: E.J. Brill, 1997), pp. 56-57.
14. Brenner, *Intercourse*, pp. 13-17.

1. A male, usually young and without exception virile, coexists with an older female in a position of authority;
2. The female, attracted by the male, attempts to seduce him or offer him marriage.
3. The male refuses for reasons appropriate to his culture and place.
4. The female falsely accuses him of attempting to seduce her.
5. Severe punishment is inflicted, usually administered by another male in an authority position.
6. Exile, analogous to death, results.
7. An exilic challenge is issued.
8. An exilic battle takes place.
9. The outcome, victory, brings about a return from exile to reconciliation.
10. The male assumes another status from that in which he was exiled.
11. The community benefits.[15]

As Hollis points out rightly, all of these episodes are 'embedded' ones, serving as a suspenseful plot device to set our gloriously gorgeous male heroes on their quests to adventure and transformation to a higher status.[16] Where a typical 'female' story stops with the 'happily ever after' of successful acquisition of a sexual partner as mate, a male hero's story is just beginning when he is sought as a sex partner.

The Gilgamesh Epic
We will begin with the Gilgamesh Epic (see Fig. 23). In a scene lodged within a larger epic cycle in Tablet VI, we find Ishtar looking with pleasure on the heroic and manly beauty of Gilgamesh, the part divine, part human king of Uruk. He has just washed demonic blood from his body, and put on fine garments so that he looks just like a bridegroom. Ishtar is straightforward in her offer: 'Come Gilgamesh, be thou my lover! Do but grant me of thy fruit. Thou shalt be my husband and I will be thy wife' (VI.7).[17] She goes on to enumerate all the wonderful things she will

---

15. Susan Tower Hollis, 'The Woman in Ancient Examples of the Potiphar's Wife Motif, K2111', in Peggy L. Day (ed.), *Gender and Difference in Ancient Israel* (Minneapolis: Fortress Press, 1989), pp. 28-42 (30-31).

16. Hollis, 'Woman in Ancient Examples', pp. 28-42 (30). She recognizes, however, that in many of the occurrences of K2111 (post-ANE, as it were), the hero is *not* necessarily moved to a higher status, suggesting that the use of the motif may vary by time or culture (p. 30; cf. p. 39 n. 20). Elements 1-6 represent Separation; 7-8, Transition; 9-11, (Re)incorporation.

17. E.A. Speiser, 'The Epic of Gilgamesh', in James B. Pritchard, *Ancient Near Eastern*

Chart 1. Chart of K2111 Variants

TEXT	GENRE & PROVENANCE	INITIAL SITUATION: ACTORS	OFFER; GENDER/ STATUS OF DESIRING SUBJECT	RESPONSE	COUNTEROFFER	OUTCOME	COMMENTS
Gilgamesh Epic (GE) Tablet VI	Epic: Old Babylonian (18th century), but motif may have originated in Akkadian version; known throughout ancient world	Ishtar, Gilgamesh, Anu, Enkidu, Bull of Heaven; Gilgamesh: human/divine king of Uruk, 3rd M; god of underworld by 24th century	female high status (divine); 'Come, Gilgamesh, be thou my lover' VI.7, p. 83 (ANET) Offer of marriage to a beautiful, high status male	3 responses: 1) what brideprice can he offer to a goddess; 2) her offers are deceptive 3) she transforms (kills) lovers	Rage: demands Bull of Heaven sent by ANU	G & E. kill Bull; insult Ishtar; gods convene to punish one of them and choose Enkidu, thereby setting Gilgamesh on his quest for immortality	Ishtar needs father god to carry out her revenge
The Myth of Illuyanka (MI) (Kbo III, 7; duplicates: KUB XII, 66; KUB XVII, 5, 6) Hattic: Extant copies from Hittite New Kingdom (1500-1190), but archaic linguistic elements from Old Kingdom (1750-1500).	Anatolian; 'Slaying the Dragon', Hattic (pre- Hittite) etiological myth for a local cult festival Two versions of myth recorded in the original tablets	Hupašiya & Inara; Storm God, the Dragon Illuyanka	low status (=human) male: 'Let me sleep with thee, and I will come and fulfill' p. 125; then Inara calls dragon 'come thou to eat and drink'; death of mortal p.126	she sleeps with him to acquire helper; she tells him not to violate interdiction	he looks out window, sees family, asks to go home;	Inara's quest is successful (dragon dies); perhaps mortal helper transfers power to human king who celebrates the festival	There are two versions of this etiological myth; this episode does not exist in the second telling

7. 'Come, Lie with Me!'

Source	Description	Characters	Approach	Response	Outcome	Notes
Tale of Two Brothers (TTB) (Papyrus D'Orbiney–BM 10183), written form: New Egyptian dialect in heiratic; c. 13th century?	Egyptian; mythological 'folk tale' Motif type K2111	Bata and brother's Wife, Anubis (god of Dead), animals, humans parallels to Osiris myth	related female: 'Come, let's spend an hour for ourselves sleeping together' p. 95	Bata says no, she is like a parent;	she accuses him to husband	Bata cast out, castrated, and eventually reborn as king	may reflect negative attitude to 18th dynasty queens by 19th dynasty due to problems of succession after Marneptah Bata's anxiety after castration: 'I am woman (like) you'
El, Ashertu, and the Storm God (EAS) various CTH fragments (for differing translations of our section, compare Goetze (p. 519 *ANET*) to Hoffner (*Hittite Myths*, p. 69)	Anatolian, found in Ugarit inversion of K2111	E, A, and SG, Anat-Astarte (ISHTAR ideogram) Standard relationship of El Kunirsha to Ba'al (Storm God); Ashertu is El's wife	high status female, "Come, sleep with me!" 'Give thyself to me' p. 519, *ANET*	Storm God goes to father El; who says to (?) her; SG 'goes' to Ashertu	Sleeps with her?; Humiliates her with story of death of her children; she mourns 7 years; she sleeps with El Kunirsha, (in exchange for right to punish Ba'al?)	broken text Ba'al eventually humiliated by the older couple; Anat-Astarte tells Ba'al of the plan, and in Hoffner's trans. eventually bring Ba'al back to life	This text is badly broken; Hoffner's recent translation reflects a new ordering and inclusion of fragments
Genesis 37.7, 12, 14	Hebrew Bible: latest version of motif K2111	Joseph & Potiphar's wife, Potiphar	high status female, 'Lie with me' 3x	refuses repeatedly; leaves garment	accuses slave to husband who believes wife; Joseph to prison, where elevated	leads to Joseph's elevation to Pharaoh's court	Strong afterlife in Jewish and Islamic folklore
Genesis 38.16	Hebrew Bible	Judah and Tamar, disguised as heirodule	high status male, 'come, let me come in to you'	she bargains for identification; accedes	pregnancy	Judah attempts punishment; she is 'more righteous'	Embedded within Joseph Story

TEXT	GENRE & PROVENANCE	INITIAL SITUATION: ACTORS	OFFER; GENDER/ STATUS OF DESIRING SUBJECT	RESPONSE	COUNTEROFFER	OUTCOME	COMMENTS
2 Samuel 13.11	Hebrew Bible: The Court History of David; narrates history of curse on David's family for sex and murder	Amnon, Tamar, Hushai, King David	high status male 'Come, lie with me'	Female gives moral reply: 'Ask king to give me to you properly'	rapes her; abandons her	brother of victim uses pretext to remove contender for kingship	
Song of Songs	Hebrew Bible	Beloved, Lover	female: come to garden and eat, 4.16; 7:11: come go forth give love; male: come away 2.10,13; 4.8: come with me			5.1: beloved comes to his garden, eats	
Lilith Myth	Late Judaism	Lilith, Adam	male Adam wants to dominate	Lilith says no	He tries to force her; she flees	Eve created	marital rape avoided
Genesis 19.32	Hebrew Bible	Lot's Daughters	'come...let us make drunk...lie with him'	sisters agree; make father drunk and rape	children born	neighbors disparaged	typical sex of instigators of incest reversed
Genesis 34.1-2	Hebrew Bible	Dinah & Shechem	'went out...he seized...lay with her'	male wants to marry her	deception	offending males killed	brothers use sister as pawn
Deuteronomy 22.23-29	Hebrew Bible	Casuistic legal text: 'a man'; different rules for 'a betrothed virgin'; 'unbetrothed virgin'	A man who: 'meets...seizes... lies with her'	If in the city, it is presumed the woman consented to sex; if she is outdoors, it is assumed that she cried out for help but none came	If betrothed virgin is in the city, both are executed; but if virgin is outdoors, only the man is punished	Marriage to unbetrothed virgin: No possibility of divorce of a virgin who was violated and then subject of 'forced marriage'	Assumption of betrothed virgin's consent in city tryst does not account for various forms of intimidation (cf. Amnon and Tamar)

give him: heroic and godly conveyances, expanded political hegemony, fertility in all its aspects (triplets of goats, and twinned sheep among other things). But Gilgamesh will have none of it, and gives a three part answer: (1) what brideprice can a mortal offer a goddess? (2) Ishtar's offers in the past have proved ambiguous, and (3) she has a history of transforming her lovers into dead men who rule the Underworld or shape-shifting them into animals.[18] With splendid Freudian clarity, the uppity mortal male tells the Queen of Heaven, 'Thou art...a shoe which pinches [the foot] of its owner!' (VI.41).[19] Abusch has offered a reading of this offer and response which suggests that Gilgamesh is refusing a practice of the Sacred Marriage Rite which inevitably leads to being crowned King of the Underworld by Ishtar, a fate which he achieved in historical legend by the twenty-fourth century BCE, well before the first written versions of the Epic began to appear.[20] Other than noting at this point that Gilgamesh's own speech to Ishtar raises the clear implication that crossing this goddess is a foolish thing to do, hence underscoring not only the folly of his refusal but also his deep antipathy, we will leave the question of his vehemence in rejecting Ishtar's offer open.

Ishtar, of course, need not go complain to a husband (after all, they keep dying on her, apparently) that the young male beauty has attempted seduction or rape; she is a goddess. She can act, and she does so with murderous rage that has social repercussions for her whole people. She demands that the high god, Father Anu, send the Bull of Heaven to punish Gilgamesh. Anu must seem on the point of taking sides with Gilgamesh, because Ishtar makes clear that she will open the Underworld and let the dead outnumber the living if Father Anu refuses her request. He tells her that letting loose the Bull will bring seven years of famine for Uruk, but she replies that she has saved up enough grain and fodder to survive the lean times. However, her plan is thwarted again by the Dynamic Duo of Gilgamesh and buddy Enkidu: they slay the Bull of Heaven, and offer its heart as sacrifice to the Sun-god.

When Ishtar cries out that this is yet another insult, Enkidu rips off the right thigh of the Bull and throws it in her face: he claims he would

Texts Relating to the Old Testament (Princeton: Princeton University Press, 3rd edn, 1969), pp. 72-99 (83). When God says this sort of thing to Israel, it's usually viewed as a 'Good Thing'; not so, with Ishtar!

18. Speiser, 'Gilgamesh', pp. 72-99 (84).

19. Alexander Heidel reads for this line, 'A sandal which [causes] its wearer to t[rip?]' (*The Gilgamesh Epic and Old Testament Parallels* [Chicago: University of Chicago Press, 1946], p. 50).

20. Tsvi Abusch, 'Ishtar's Proposal and Gilgamesh's Refusal: An Interpretation of the Gilgamesh Epic, Tablet 6, Lines 1-79', HR 26 (1986), pp. 143-87; Jeffrey Tigay, *The Evolution of the Gilgamesh Epic* (Philadelphia: University of Pennsylvania, 1982).

do the same to her if he could get to her, thereby reversing her plans for Gilgamesh. Ishtar's coterie of prostitutes and priestesses wail for the Bull, the craftsmen admire the raw material the Bull has provided for kingly crafts, the heroes embrace, the people bless the heroes; the girls of Uruk sing a victory ditty for them, and all ends well in this episode, for everyone but Ishtar and her dead Bull. The implication in the text is that the outcome 'serves her right' for all her stinking deeds. But later Enkidu dreams, and has a vision of the council of male gods (Anu, Enlil, Ea, and Shamash) who decree that someone must die in response to all this killing (even though some of it was permitted by a god), and it cannot be Gilgamesh. The resulting death of Enkidu, the wild man gone civilized, sets Gilgamesh off on a quest to discover the meaning of life and the potentials of immortality.

Observing this text from the perspective of the Spurned Woman motif, we note here that goddesses have a great deal more scope for enacting their response to refusals than do their human sisters. Yet, goddesses are endowed by their cultures with all the supposed wiles of mortal women, and analogous desires; like their mortal counterparts, they are as apt to be spurned as any human woman, and like it just as little. Further, it is through the vehicle of male power that Ishtar must seek her redress, even though she does not have to fabricate a story of attempted rape to instigate her revenge for losing honor. The dead apparently obey her wishes, as do her women followers, but what good is that to a goddess who is looking for 'a live one'? She still has to run to Daddy.

Tale of Two Brothers

This mythic motif proceeds in fairly standard fashion in the Egyptian Tale of Two Brothers and Genesis 39, allowing for cultural variations. The Egyptian tale,[21] written in hieratic New Egyptian dialect and tentatively dated to around the thirteenth century BCE, shows clear parallels to the Osiris myth in that it deals with two mortuary gods, Anubis, the older brother, and Bata, the studly young hero. Upon being propositioned by Anubis's wife with offers of an hour spent in bed, plus beautiful clothing afterwards, Bata becomes enraged, like an Upper Egyptian leopard, or so we hear, and replies that his sister-in-law is like a mother to him and his brother, her husband, like a father. He claims that he will never speak of the wicked proposition and departs back to his brother, but clearly, the wife is unconvinced and feels threatened. When Anubis returns home, she fakes the results of a violent beating and tells her husband the story in reversed form familiar from Genesis: Bata tried

---

21. Papyrus D'Orbiney (British Museum, Registration No. 10183).

to seduce her, she responded with the young man's own reply (violation of family ties), so he beat her to insure her silence. Anubis believes her, seeks to kill his brother, but Bata has been warned of the attack by friendly, loquacious cows. He is able to escape his brother's wrath with the help of the god Pre-Harakhty who places a crocodile-infested body of water between the two. When morning comes, Bata tells his brother his side of the story, berating his brother for taking the word of a 'filthy whore'[22] at face value. In order to underscore the truth of his account (apparently), he takes a reed knife, cuts off his own penis, and flings it into the water where a fish swallows it. Anubis returns home, kills his lying wife, and mourns for his brother. Bata proceeds to the Valley of Pine where he lives alone, having taken the thoughtful precaution of placing his heart at the top of a pine tree.

Bata's 'women troubles' do not end with his exile and castration, however. The tale proceeds with a new set of adventures in which the gods make a very beautiful woman to be his bride. A complicating scene familiar from folklore ensues: he tells his wife *not* to go out to the Sea which would seize her; he would be unable to save her because 'I am a woman [like] you'. Castration has made him weak. Also typical, she *does* violate this interdiction and the Sea takes one of her sweet-smelling braids of hair to the Pharaoh, who is then consumed with desire for her. Search parties find her eventually, and she tells them to cut down the pine tree (in which her husband's heart is lodged). She knows this will kill womanish husband Bata so that she will be free to be Great Lady of the Pharaoh in Egypt, and not coincidentally, acquire a husband with a functioning member. They do as she requests, but unknown to her, brother Anubis has been given a sign and a quest by Bata, telling him what to do for his brother's heart in event of such a disaster. Bata dies by yet another woman's treachery, but is revived by Anubis's successful action. Bata turns himself into a fabulous Bull which Anubis presents to the Pharaoh. But the Great Lady, upon chatting with the Bull, discovers it is her erstwhile betrayed husband and asks the Pharaoh to sacrifice the Bull and give her its liver to eat. The Pharaoh sadly complies, but two great drops of blood, from which bloom two Persea trees, fall on either side of the king's threshold during the sacrifice.

Bata, who seems never to learn, tells his wife that he is now the Persea tree, and she, in turn, asks the Pharaoh to have it cut down for furniture. When he does so, a splinter—yes, Bata again—flies into her mouth and she is made pregnant by it, eventually giving birth to—you guessed it, Bata! The Pharaoh loves his new son and elevates him, and eventually

---

22. The Egyptian here is quite graphic and derogatory: 'stinking cunt' would be a more accurate translation.

Bata rules after him, judging his mother-wife (upon whose final outcome the text is silent) and making Anubis his heir.[23]

Poor Bata! Castrated, alone, heart-less, he is clearly unable to find a trustworthy female with whom he can mate and give satisfaction, even when the gods make one up on special order. Given his track record of failing to provide sexual services to anyone,[24] it is no wonder that his tale abounds with images of male fantasies of lack: the castration scene, the seductive braid, the fallen pine, the dead Bull, the drops of blood, the cut Persea tree. Even pregnancy-by-splinter continues the image of Bata's sexual insufficiency.

We find a selection of elements which we came across in the earlier Gilgamesh Epic in this multi-episode myth with its nicely complete ending: an embedded incident of attempted seduction, a flirtation with death and revivification, a connection to mortuary deities, another lordly Bull brought low by sacrifice, a movement through a variety of locations, females who just can't be trusted.

As in the Gilgamesh version, the beauty of the youth signals trouble because it brings him to the attention of the predatory female. Mrs Anubis offers fit rewards for that beauty: beautiful garments. Since Anubis's wife cannot offer marriage in her proposition, we may have here the complicating factor which causes both her and Potiphar's wife to reverse the tale of seduction. Where Ishtar simply views Gilgamesh's refusal itself as an insult, the wives of the Tale of Two Brothers and Genesis are in inferior positions with respect to husbands whom they have now dishonored by their uncontained desire. Fearful, they cannot allow the real version of events to stand. In my readings, I see self-preservation from some version of the honor killing or violent punishment as the motivation for the reversed story of seduction, rather than a simple desire for revenge by the spurned female.

'Elkunirsha, Asherah, and the Storm-God'
Turning to Anatolia, a cross-roads culture whose surviving literature points to ties with the many cultures—Hurrian, Syro-Phoenician, Canaanite, Mesopotamian, Greek—we find two myths which place a twist on the standard motif just considered in the Gilgamesh Epic, the Egyptian Tale of Two Brothers, and Genesis 39. We will consider the direct variant of K2111, the myth of 'Elkunirsha, Asherah, and the Storm-God' (EAS) found in a badly broken state at Boghazköy.[25] The

---

23. Susan Tower Hollis, *The Ancient Egyptian 'Tale of Two Brothers': The Oldest Fairy Tale in the World* (Norman, OK: University of Oklahoma Press, 1990), pp. 5-15.
24. Fish don't count.
25. *CTH*, p. 342, translated by Goetze in *ANET*, and Harry A. Hoffner, Jr. in *Hittite Myths* (WAW, 2; Atlanta: Scholars Press, 2nd edn, 1998), pp. 69-70.

first attempt at placing the fragments in some kind of logical order was made by H. Otten in 1953,[26] and subsequent translators have tended to retain his order, with minor variations, though all are clear that the order is arbitrary.[27] The main players are the well-known Canaanite god, El-Kunirsha,[28] El, Creator of Earth, his wife, the biblically tree-ish Asherah (the Hebrew form; the original form of the name in West Semitic is Ashertu or Ashrata), Ba'al the Storm-God of Syro-Phoenicia, and Anat-Astarte.[29] It is fair to say that while this text is clearly based on K2111, form-critically speaking, all hell has broken loose here, and it's hard to judge the outcome for that very reason. We have no ending for this myth (naturally[30]), so must remain hopeful that one will turn up.

The background for the text's action seems, oddly enough, *not* to be the need for Ba'al to have adventures in death, but rather the aged El's *lack*: he has documented problems in sleeping with his wives, a mythic theme known from Ugaritic texts. The badly fragmented text becomes readable within the middle of Asherah's speech to Ba'al, where she seems to be speaking in parallel threats:

> You get behind me and I'll get behind you!
> With my word I will press you!
> With my spindle I will pierce you!
> With […] I will stir you up.[31]

Whatever Asherah is saying precisely, Ba'al takes it as a negative speech and proceeds to the Euphrates and the tent of Elkunirsha, telling him that his wife has sent maidens to Ba'al, with the message, 'Come sleep with me', and has propositioned him repeatedly. When Ba'al refused, she

---

26. 'Ein kanaanäischer Mythus aus Bogaszköy', *MIO*, 1 (1953), pp. 125-50.

27. Harry A. Hoffner, Jr's 1965 translation follows Otten's edition; his 1990 translation follows Laroche's ordering of the fragments and includes the final scene of exorcism.

28. Cf. Gen. 14.19, '*'ēl qōnēh šāmayim wa'āreṣ*'. See Patrick D. Miller, Jr, 'El, The Creator of Earth', *BASOR*, 239 (1980), pp. 43-46, for other inscriptional evidence. He argues, along with Frank Cross, that '*'ēl qōnēh 'ereṣ*' is an ancient title for the god of Jerusalem, later equated with YHWH.

29. All these names appear in their cuneiform Hittite versions, but translators routinely use the Levantine names since the myth is clearly of that origin.

30. Given that all the most interesting tales seem to have no endings, due to vicissitudes of survival of scrolls or tablets, it almost seems to beg for postmodern responses from the reader to fill the gaps.

31. Philological difficulties abound! I am using Hoffner's earlier translation ('The El Kunirsha Myth Reconsidered', *RHA* 23 [1965], pp. 5-16 [6-7]), where he follows Otten's restoration of 'spindle', although he simply indicates the broken text in his later translation (*Myths*, p. 69).

offered him the word-and-spindle threat, and he immediately tattled to El in person, rather than by messenger. Says the Storm God, 'Ashertu is rejecting you, her own husband', to which El replies, 'Go *something* her (threaten? sleep with? translators speculate differently) [...] my wife, and humble her'.[32]

Ba'al returns to Asherah but their exchange is only peripherally concerned with sexuality: Ba'al humiliates her by telling her that 77 of her children, yea, even 88, have been slain by him, causing her to become sad and appoint mourning women for a seven-year display of grief. If the next fragment of the text has been placed in proper order, the scene changes abruptly to a conversation between El and Asherah: we can't tell how it begins, but Asherah seems to be telling El that if he will hand over Ba'al to her, she will sleep with El. El concludes that this is an excellent deal, and tells her to do with Ba'al as it pleases her.

However, there is a friend of Ba'al at the ready: Anat-Astarte, hearing the conversation, turns herself into an owl (a *hapupi*-bird: other bird of prey, or a goblet?) on El's shoulder, and continues her eavesdropping as the divine couple consummates their bargain in the marriage bed. She flies off to the desert to warn Ba'al not to drink wine (a metaphor for sex?) with Ashertu, when the tablet breaks off. To this broken myth about Ba'al and Anat-Astarte more might be added to finish off the text with a cultic context: another badly broken text fragment mentioning Elkunirsha, Anat-Astarte and Ba'al has been added by translators Laroche and Hoffner. Ba'al seems to have been injured and sent to the netherworld, from which Anat-Astarte successfully revives him, penis and all. Ba'al's illnesses are exorcised and he is re-created from the Dark Earth, perhaps forming a paradigm for mortals who hope to be healed of similar dreadful conditions.

Due to the difficulties caused by the poor preservation of this myth, it is impossible to draw firm conclusions. We do not know if it is Ba'al's beauty and manly vigor that has attracted Asherah's interest, nor can anyone be certain that she inveigles El into allowing her to punish Ba'al by a reversed claim of seduction. As much as Asherah's spindle begs for psychoanalytic analysis, especially given the intersection of this symbol with the penis fetish displayed in Bata's story and Ba'al's penile revivification by Anat-Astarte, there are simply too many signifying gaps for the mythographer to claim dependence, cross-fertilization, deviance, or congruence. As appealing as the presence of wailing maidens, talking cows or seven years of grief may be in light of their occurrence in the

---

32. Hoffner ('Reconsidered', pp. 5-16 [8-9]) speculates here that the Hittite *luriyah-*, 'to humble' is probably a cognate of Hebrew *'nh* piel, which carries the notion of sexual dominance. His later translation leaves out the sexual connotation.

Gilgamesh Epic or the Bible, we must leave these elements where they are—greatly separated by time and theme.

However, some things *can* be said. If we had more of 'Elkunirsha, Asherah, and the Storm-God' myth, we might reflect with greater profit on the unusual behavior of the males. Ba'al seems to be in solidarity with El, worrying over the challenge to the father-god's virility and the peculiarity of the divine family's relationships (is El his father or not?); yet ultimately, Ba'al is turned over to Asherah at the promise of sex for El. Male bonding only goes so far, apparently, when sex is the matter at hand. But El is no more of a prize than Anubis or Potiphar: his desire for the humiliation of Asherah is simple tit-for-tat, and may even function as a death sentence for Asherah's many children whom Ba'al slays. Poor Asherah—trapped between El who is unable and Ba'al who is unwilling. No wonder she eventually turns into a tree who devotes herself to the children.

What seems to be unusual here is that Ba'al neither promises his silence to Asherah nor speaks of any sort of moral or pragmatic issue other than the challenge to El's sexuality, and by extension, his honor. Of our variants, this is the only one where the propositionee goes directly to the dishonored husband, and that husband seems to suggest a gentleman's agreement to humiliate the erring wife, perhaps even by means of sexual fulfillment. Among all the wives and goddesses making offers, so far Asherah is the only one 'getting any', but it is *not* from the one she wanted. Sex is viewed outright as part of the female bag of tricks and unfair advantage at the bargaining table with men. Desire might be fulfilled, but for the female the outcome is not particularly dazzling. At least Ba'al loses his penis briefly, which only serves him right for taking on so: it's not nice to fool Mother Asherah.

The Myth of Illuyanka

The 'Slaying of the Dragon' myth from Hittite Anatolia (*CTH* 321) offers some sister evidence to the ambiguous condition of divine female desire. The Myth of Illuyanka exists only in New Kingdom period texts, but its linguistic peculiarities make clear it emerged in the Hittite Old Kingdom and had been adapted from the indigenous peoples of Anatolia, the Hattic people.[33] The presence of powerful and effective goddesses who are active in all spheres, not just domestic ones, seems to be a repeated feature in the mythologies of these peoples, and so

---

33. Hoffner, *Myths*, pp. 9-10. Hoffner lists these myths in his first section, 'Old Anatolian Myths', though the text is in Hittite. For a more clear statement of the composite text as Old Hittite, see Gary Beckman, 'The Anatolian Myth of Illuyanka', *JANES* 14 (1982), pp. 11-25 (20).

provides a somewhat more positive platform for the consideration of female characterization.[34]

In brief, this dual-versioned myth relates the origin of the cult festival, the Purulli fall festival; this text is the ultimate demonstration of the validity of the so-called 'myth and ritual' approach to mythology, for it is clear that the myths are both the script for the ritual, and the reason the ritual is to be performed yearly. In the first version, the Storm God triumphs eventually over the Illuyanka snake and Company, serpent-style dragons who live in a hole and greedily drink up all the spring waters unless checked. In both versions, the Storm God only triumphs over the serpent with the help of a human male, suggesting at one level that achievement of ideal conditions requires both human and divine action.

We are concerned with the first version: after being defeated by the great snake, the Storm God invites all the gods to a feast, which his daughter, the goddess Inara, goddess of the steppe's wild animals, prepares. In food preparation for a party she excels, filling great vessels with intoxicating drink. Beyond such appropriately gendered duties allotted to females in the 'banquet' type-scene, she apparently feels the need of a big, strong mortal male to pitch in on the heroics to follow. She goes to a northern town Ziggarata and finds a mortal, one Ḫupašiya, whom she asks to join in with her plan. He replies, as mortal males are apt to do, 'If I may sleep with you, then I will come and perform your heart's desire'.[35] He gets *his* desire, and the goddess does, too: she acquires a Helper for her task.

Returning to the site of the feast, Inara adorns herself and calls the Dragon to come to the celebration to eat and drink. The dragons oblige and become drunk and unable or unwilling to descend into their hole, at which point Ḫupašiya materializes to truss them up. Apparently not trusting his own power this time around, the Storm God arrives and dispatches the incapacitated dragons while the gods look on. All is well and fertility is restored.

Immediately after this, we have another little fairy tale moment in which unwary characters *always* violate the interdiction given to them by someone who leaves them to their own devices; here it is entwined with the much loved biblical image of the wise house built upon rock.[36] Right after the destruction of the dragon, Inara magnanimously builds a

34. Carole R. Fontaine, 'The Deceptive Goddess in Ancient Near Eastern Myth: Inanna and Inaras', in J. Cheryl Exum and Johanna W.H. Bos (eds.), *Reasoning among the Foxes: Female Wit in a World of Male Power* (Semeia, 42; Atlanta: Scholars Press, 1988), pp. 84-102.

35. Hoffner, *Myths*, p. 12.

36. Vladimir Propp, *Morphology of the Folktale* (Publications of the American Folklore Society, 9; Austin: University of Texas Press, 1968).

house for Ḫupašiya on a *peruna*, a rock outcropping whose metaphorical associations are ones of permanence and joy.³⁷ She tells the mortal that he must not look out of the window while she is in the open country where she works with her animals, because he would see his wife and children and desire them. After twenty days of resisting, naturally Ḫupašiya looks out of the window, and of course, he sees his family for whom he begins to yearn. When Inara returns home, he whines about going home. Naturally the text becomes fragmentary at this juncture: early translations reconstruct the broken text to read that Inara kills the straying mortal, and the Storm God does something unpleasant to the meadow; Hoffner's recent reconstruction leaves the text broken with no indication of the final disposition of the randy Ḫupašiya. Gary Beckman's reconstruction of the myth from a variety of fragments is unable to resolve the issue, but he assumes the death of Ḫupašiya by Inara's agency, based on the clearly decipherable word 'anger' in the text.³⁸ When the text becomes clear again we are in the following episode: Inara returns to another northern Hittite town Kiškilušša where we hear of another house associated with this goddess and the festival:

> Inara [went] to (the town of) Kiškil[ušša] (and) set her house and the river (?) on the watery abyss (?) [into] the hand of the king because (in commemoration thereof) we are (re-) performing the first *purulli*-festival. The hand [of the king will hold? the house?] of Inara and the riv[er?] of the watery abyss(?).³⁹

In this myth, the spurning of the goddess takes place *after* and *not* before sexual intercourse has taken place, thereby separating the motif of the spurning from the proposition itself. The difference, compared to K2111, the Potiphar's wife motif, or Gilgamesh and Ishtar? Ah, it is a *male* who has made the first offer, and *not* the female, and outrageously, the male succeeds in obtaining sex in return for his future participation in divine plans. The successful consummation of his desires do not protect him from a 'bad end' (or at the very least, obscurity in the broken text), which is again caused by his desires, this time for his previous family whose loyalties he dispensed with so easily when he saw a chance to bed Inara.⁴⁰

37. Beckman, 'Anatolian Myth', pp. 11-25 (21), compares this outcropping to sites such as Gâvur Kalesa, Yenicekale and others at Boghazköy, and cites KUB 36, 110 rev., ll. 13-16: 'The house of Labarna is (one of) joy in his offspring to the third generation—it is built on rock!'
38. Beckman, 'Anatolian Myth', pp. 11-25 (19).
39. Beckman, pp. 11-25 (19); for philological commentary on the images of water, see pp. 21-23.
40. Perhaps he viewed sleeping with the goddess as a sort of promotion which would ultimately benefit his whole family.

There is much debate over whether or not Ḫupašiya is engaging in a Sacred Marriage Rite in order to become King-for-a-Day/Year, since the outcome of such putative arrangements is usually the final termination of that mortal. The skepticism about the applicability to this myth of a custom of selection of a *Jahreskönig* and celebration of the Sacred Marriage may be a subliminal factor for translators, determining their view of the death or life of the mortal Helper.[41] One might observe that while the two versions of the cult myth are very different, in the second version the mortal helper clearly dies because of his marriage ties, which may suggest this as the appropriate ending for the mortal in Version One.

It may simply be that once the mortal helper's job is done, he is 'exchanged' for a more powerful, readily visible mortal, the king whose role must be worked into the cult in some way or other. The text leaves us unsatisfied as to what the 'hand' of the king is actually doing for Inara's 'house'. Does she establish the king's house or does the king establish *her* house? While we cannot point to a clear answer, we do have some sort of successful reciprocity existing between goddess, king and house. Does 'house' here have the typical meaning of progeny and social unit, or is it a more pointed reference to the cult center where the festival is known to be held? We cannot say; we want more, but at present, more is not to be had.

A notable feature of this myth is that despite the bad outcome for the mortal sexual partner, sex was actually had, and both sexes' desires are fulfilled, though the goddess' desires were desires for help and *not* erotic play. Not coincidentally, fertility was restored to the land by Inara's tricky feast. It is a public 'lie' rather than a private one in the bedroom, with a successful result for the cult, which guarantees it is left under the firm hand of a king. Inara's activity is not viewed by the text as a 'stinking deed' as the Gilgamesh Epic characterized Ishtar's previous disposals of her lovers, but then, the *subject* of the sexual desire is a male who is allowed—nay, apparently *expected*—to have such desires and successfully act on them. If Inara *does* kill Ḫupašiya—and he certainly disappears from the text, no matter the means—it falls under the 'natural' female response of revenge against the male who would deny her continued sexual services by returning to his human family. The text would then conform nicely to the ideology of female desire, albeit with that Hittite *différence* of full-service goddesses. Inara does *not* express a sexual desire in the beginning—she only wants the mortal's help with heavy lifting, after all—but once she has acceded to male desire (accepted her position as his object of desire), she is given all

---

41. Hoffner, *Myths*, p. 11.

the jealousies of women's nature at the thought of his rejection—a kind of 'don't ask; *do* kill' variation.

5. *Concluding Remarks on the Mythology of Female Desire*

Much metaphorical ink has been spent on the subject of Potiphar's Wife and the type-scene of reverse accusations in the Bible and its later Jewish and Islamic interpretations. Less time has been spent on the mythic precursors of the episode, and I hope to remedy this oversight with a more detailed study of the motif of female desire, cosmic and human. Despite broken texts, philological problems and missing episodes, we *can* make some general observations.

The human wife in Genesis 39 is clearly based on earlier goddess characters, but as in the rest of the Hebrew Bible, we find that we have traded in all our goddesses for human women of a variety of status positions. The characterization, however, remains much the same, but in the human realm we need to take into account the loss of divine agency on the part of the goddess-gone-girl. On the motif of female desire and its outcomes, we can also speak of serious 'trouble' in the gendering of desire, so often considered the prerogative of the male subject alone. Judith Butler could have been speaking of our texts when she writes: 'for (the) masculine subject of desire, trouble became a scandal with the sudden intrusion, the unanticipated agency, of a female "object" who inexplicably returns the glance, reverses the gaze and contests the place and authority of the masculine position'.[42]

Characterization, Male and Female

Female characters are associated with the gendered motifs of their seniority over those they proposition, their kinship ties in the patriarchal family, their desire for sex, and their lies. Their activity takes place in the female zone of the private domain of the household, but they move with ease into cities as well—more reasons to fear them. In the home, they subvert male authority and break kinship ties; in the city, they carry out their revenge or are seen in powerful roles. They are attended by groups of maidens, young ones to act as servants and prostitutes, older ones to mourn. They are shown as liars, violators of interdictions, schemers, and ones who use adornment as a wile to lure dragons, men or gods. The females, cosmic and human, do not seem particularly motivated by a desire to conceive; as far as we know, only Asherah is especially noted for her motherhood, and even that ends in humiliation and death of her children.

42. Butler, *Gender Trouble*, p. ix.

Female predators are motivated by the sight of male beauty, and seem to view their offers to the younger male in the form of simple exchange: in return for sexual services, they promise gifts of clothes, pleasure, fertility, or snazzy modes of conveyance (the ancient equivalent of the flashy car?). These offers are not so very different from the standard situation when males solicit females for sex; when a male legitimately asks for a female as sexual partner, he pays brideprice. Perhaps our goddesses are simply trying to make the typical arrangements, as it were, and attribute no immorality to their offer since they are willing to make fair economic exchange, just as humans do. Egyptian wisdom literature comments on the woman's lot in the economics of marriage in advice to young men:

> Fill her belly, clothe her back... Make her happy while you are alive, for she is land profitable to her lord... Soothe her heart with what has accrued to you; it means that she will continue to dwell in your house... A vagina is what she gives for her condition...[43]

To use a modern proverb that sums up the way the goddesses seem to proceed in their search for fulfilled desire we might say, 'Fair exchange is no robbery'. Yet, none of the propositioned males seem to be able to view themselves in the same way females are asked to see themselves in the sexual economy of the ancient Near East. Inara does not respond to the mortal male's proposition with outrage that she should even be asked, while the young males, to a man, are scandalized by a woman seeking them out for sexual enjoyment, even when the females are willing to 'pay up'. Females are *expected* to trade their bodies for economic provisions or for matters of state (the temple harlot who 'civilizes' Enkidu with sex); when this gendered ideology of sex-for-hire is applied to males, human or divine, the tables turn, and kings and gods are called in to avenge the insult to male hegemony over penetration.

Male characters are marked by motifs of authority: they are kings, gods, fathers, elder brothers, determined avengers with agency to act. It is interesting to note the level of male anxiety about virility displayed in our texts; one wonders how that plays out in the focus on male bonding and beauty. Whether it is Bata without a penis, telling his new wife he cannot protect her because he is 'a woman', living Ba'al worried about the sexual slur on Father El, or dead Ba'al whose penis must get special attention from Anat-Ishtar, male fear of insufficient maleness is everywhere displayed. Given the high incidence of male bonding in our

---

43. Author's translation of 'The Maxims of Ptahhotep'; an alternative translation may be found in W.K. Simpson (ed.), *The Literature of Ancient Egypt: An Anthology of Stories, Instructions, Stelae, Autobiographies, and Poetry* (New Haven: Yale University Press, 3rd edn, 2003), pp. 129-48.

texts, we might also reasonably ask if we have uncovered a strain of masculinist sexual disdain for women and their bodies, that 'Other of their flesh' who must be conquered in order to preserve the illusion of male supremacy. The recounting of Ishtar's sexual deeds as well as the characterization of Mrs Anubis both use terms for 'stink', a lexical term which conjures up bodily shame, scent, and uncleanness. Further, the male protagonists tend to cite the female propositioner's lack of concern about male kinship ties, attitudes by which the females challenge the very social organization of patriarchy. No wonder kings are trotted out in these stories to invoke a kind of re-presentation of social order 'as it ought to be', with fathering males on top.

Another feature related to male characterization is the strong presence of killing and death in these stories. Gilgamesh, Anubis, Bata, and Ba'al all have connections to mortuary contexts, and most of them proceed by killing something in their stories: a bull, a straying wife, animals, divine children. The females do their fair share of slaughtering too: Bata's wife clearly holds the trophy in this realm, but even she can't keep a good god down. As often as Bata 'dies', he is also revivified. Desire and death seem to dance together in these stories, and it is by no means clear that life-affirming desire wins out in the mythology of female desire.

Interestingly, the motif of *race/ethnicity* appears only in the Joseph story, where Mrs Potiphar emphasizes that it is a *Hebrew* slave brought in by her husband who has insulted her. Elsewhere the conflict is characterized by generational violations, or human–divine struggles, which are not precisely the same as race, though they are a form of the same anxiety around the boundaries between Own and Other. The tale in Genesis has other features worth noting, as well: like the Gilgamesh Epic, it is the only story where 'blessing' is mentioned, though it is God blessing everything Joseph does, house or field—a sort of hyper-attenuated male bonding?—whereas it is the people of Uruk who bless the brotherly pair of Gilgamesh and Enkidu for killing the Bull of Heaven. Genesis also takes various motifs found in the other mythological texts and distributes them outside of the seduction scene: we get our dreams, cows, seven years, famines, tricky hosts at banquets, and nice clothing elsewhere in the Joseph story, suggesting a thorough familiarity with these bundles of oral motifs in the seduction mythologies of Israel's neighbors (see Fig. 24).

Desire, female or male—I am *not* forgetting Ḫupašiya—turns out to be, just as the Song of Songs told us, as strong as death, as jealous as the grave, and all too often under patriarchy, the one leads to the other in our stories. From the household to the steppe, wherever females reverse their subject positions from desired object to desiring subject, the whole order of the world, mythological, social, and literary is disarranged and

Chart 2. Chart of Distribution of K2111 Motifs by Variant

Motifs	Gilgamesh Epic	Tale of Two Brothers	Elkunirsha	Illuyanka	Genesis 39	Song of Songs
Genre						
Ritual Context			X	XX[2]		
Mortuary Gods	X	XX	X			
Humans	X			X	X	X
Interdiction		X		X		
Violation		X		X	X	
Reverse Accusations		X	?			
Action						
Offer of Marriage	X					?
Consummation			X	X		X
Gluttony/Drunkenness				X	X	X

7. 'Come, Lie with Me!' 241

Motifs		Gilgamesh Epic	Tale of Two Brothers	Elkunirsha	Illuyanka	Genesis 39	Song of Songs
	Hair Dressing		X	broken			?
	Adornment		X	broken	X		X
	Blessing					X	
	Fleeing		X		X	X	X
	Shapeshifting	X	X	X	X		X
	Dying	X	X	X	X		
	Killing	X	XXXXX	X	XX^2	X	
	Punishment	X	X	X	X		X
	Revivification		X	X	X^2		
Character							
	King	X	X		X	X	X
	Father	X		X	X^2		
	Brother		X				X

Motifs		Gilgamesh Epic	Tale of Two Brothers	Elkunirsha	Illuyanka	Genesis 39	Song of Songs
	Wife/Older Women	X	X	X	X²	X	
	Maidens (home)	X					X
	Female Redeemer			X	X		X
	Mourning Women	X		X			
	Male workers/overseer		X			X	X
	Children		X	X	X		
Marvelous Animals							
	Bull	X	X	Bull El'?		X	
	Cows	X	X				
	Snake/Dragon				X		
	Owl/Bird			X			X
					²Version 2		

7. 'Come, Lie with Me!'

Motifs		Gilgamesh Epic	Tale of Two Brothers	Elkunirsha	Illuyanka	Genesis 39	Song of Songs
Items							
	Sacrifice	x		broken	x		
	Clothing (gift/sign)	x	x	broken		x	x
	Hair (Braid)		x				x
	Seed		x				
	Window	x			x		x
	Famine	x		x	x	x	
	7 years		xx			x	
	Tree	x			x		x
	Race/ethnicity (own/other)		x	x			
	Phallus			X?			
	Spindle						

Motifs		Gilgamesh Epic	Tale of Two Brothers	Elkunirsha	Illuyanka	Genesis 39	Song of Songs
	Splinter		X				
	Feast/Jar		X		X		X
	Dream	X				X	X
Geographic	Field/Steppe		X		X	X	X
	City/City Wall	X			X	X	X
	House/Tent		X	X	X	X	X
	Rock				X		
	Body of Water		X	X	X	X	
	Underworld	X		X	X		X
Gender	Older Women	X	X	X		X	
	Kinswomen		X	X?	X		X

7. 'Come, Lie with Me!'

Motifs	Gilgamesh Epic	Tale of Two Brothers	Elkunirsha	Illuyanka	Genesis 39	Song of Songs
Divine Female	x	x	xx	x		
Predator, male/female	x	x	x		x	
Male Avenger	x	x	x	x	x	x
Honor Killing		x		x		
Lying Women	x	xxx	?	x	x	
Male Bonding	x	x	x		x	
Male Beauty	x	x	broken		x	x
Male Anxiety	x	x	x	x		
Male Elevation	x	x	broken		x	
Motherhood		x	x			
Marriage	x	x	x	xx[2]	x	?
				[2]Version 2		

threatened. Try as they might, neither gods nor men in the ancient Near East can slay the greedy dragon of female desire. We now turn to the Song of Songs, because when that female desire is met in partnership, freely chosen in the face of male avengers as in the Song, the Underworld yields up not the dead, but a wild testament to the shape-shifting power of female subject: 'My beloved is mine, and his *desire* is for *me*'.

In the Beloved's garden, no gods are needed; human love is all it should be and an equal match for death. Female choice is articulated, shared, and consummated—and the world of the home and the field manage to survive that fact. Nothing stinks here. Both sexes ask; both sexes receive: no wonder we speak of the Song as a mythical Paradise restored. We should not forget that when the rabbis (*Sotah* 11b; *Exodus Rabbah* 1:12) read the Song of Songs against the background of the oppression complex of the Exodus, they claim that Israel was preserved and delivered due to the righteousness of their women. It is clear that healthy desire for sexual congress with their dirty, tired, stinking slave-husbands was considered to be part of that righteousness. We could argue that once more the story of female desire has been appropriated to speak to the condition of the whole enslaved people—but perhaps that is a positive recognition that Woman and the Slave have much in common under patriarchy: neither can be their own agent.

6. *Watching Out for Watchmen in the Song of Songs*

It might seem odd to some that anyone wishing to address the general questions of competing readings and the ethics of hermeneutics would set out as their model text the little book of erotic poetry that is the Song of Songs, but like our fairy tale resolutions, the writer cannot let this go without a blessing, though you may think me blind like Isaac and fresh out of suitable words. However, it may not be so astonishing that I take the Song of Songs as my 'test case' blessing text because for centuries the Church and the Synagogue have advanced normative, but competing meanings for this wayward collage of love poems. These normative meanings have each resisted and redefined the 'plain sense' of the text.[44] With the growth of feminist interest in this text where a woman's voice dominates that of her male lover,[45] there are modern issues of libera-

---

44. Carole R. Fontaine, '"Go Forth into the Fields": An Earth-Centered Reading of the Song of Songs', in Norman C. Habel and Shirley Wurst, *The Earth Story in the Wisdom Traditions* (Earth Bible, 3; Sheffield: Sheffield Academic Press, 2001), pp. 126-42 (126-27).

45. André Lacocque, *Romance, She Wrote: A Hermeneutical Essay on Song of Songs* (Harrisburg, PA: Trinity Press International, 1998).

tionist interpretations being raised by the presence of the Song in our canons.[46] I will not be commenting here on the 'will-to-allegorize' a text whose content seems, at face value, to have little to do with the theological dicta of the Christian and Jewish theology. Instead, I want to reflect on the way that even seemingly *positive* texts carry along with them an inscription of violence and injustice that no commentator or believer can afford to ignore.

The Song is probably best understood as an anthology of love poems united by the presence of similar themes (seeking, finding, romantic love versus an ideology of male control of female sexuality, praise of the beloved's physical attributes, eroticization of the landscape of the lovers, etc.), none of which is grounded overtly in a 'covenant' theology or Christology that is anywhere explicit. God is not routinely invoked in the songs in any clear way, though euphemistic mediations of the Sacred Name may appear in Song 2.7, 3.5 and 8.6, thereby drawing a cloak of pious theology over the lovers' yearning bodies. We have love songs that praise the Other for their 'difference' (the so-called *waṣf* genre of 4.1-7; 5.10-16; 6.5a-7; 7.1-9), and dream sequences (3.1-5; 5.2-8), wedding songs for Solomon (3.6-11), and philosophical reflections on the nature of erotic love (8.6-7). With such a disparate collection of material from different times(?) and places (?),[47] it is almost certain that someone would find *something* about which to be concerned—that is the way of publication and career-building in our discipline, is it not? My concerns center around violence in the Song, especially as mediated by the character motifs of the 'watchmen' (RSV; 'sentinels', NRSV) and the 'brothers' of the Beloved, and the way commentators studiously ignore or trivialize these issues.

Now, overall it is hard for many of us *not* to love the Song. This is true despite warnings like those from Cheryl Exum[48] that the Song represents not a *real* female voice but one *constructed* by male authors, or worries about the theological gyrations involved in making theology

---

46. Alicia Ostriker, 'A Holy of Holies: The Song of Songs as Countertext', in Athalya Brenner and Carole R. Fontaine (eds.), *The Song of Songs: A Feminist Companion to the Bible (Second Series)* (FCB, 6; Sheffield: Sheffield Academic Press, 2000), pp. 36-54; and J. Cheryl Exum, 'Ten Things Every Feminist Should Know about the Song of Songs', in Brenner and Fontaine (eds.), *The Song of Songs*, pp. 24-35.

47. Scholars vary enormously in their conclusions on these topics; only compare the work of O. Keel, *The Song of Songs: A Continental Commentary* (trans. F.J. Gaiser; Minneapolis: Fortress Press, 1994); Roland E. Murphy, *The Song of Songs: A Commentary on the Book of Canticles or the Song of Songs* (Hermeneia; Minneapolis: Fortress Press 1990); and Marvin Pope, *Song of Songs* (AB; Garden City, NY: Doubleday, 1977) on these issues!

48. See n. 46 above.

out of poetic, erotic traditions rather than narratives of salvation history. Cary Ellen Walsh writes:

> ...this Song is affirming, even boldly so, of human sexuality. Given the taciturn nature of other biblical materials on sex, the Song is startling, refreshing, even flamboyant. Both the anticipation and the pleasure of sex are celebrated, lingered over, and nowhere decried. Sexuality and desire are not viewed as problems to repress or punish; nor are they sources of shame. More striking still, they are not areas to be legislated in any way or controlled through patriarchal customs such as the bride negotiation through the father, marriage dowries, bride prices and the like.[49]

While some critics might wonder if the world of erotic lyrics actually can be taken as an index of social practice or genuine female affect, for the most part even the inclusion of a *hypothetical* female voice that rejects patriarchal restrictions on her body and her choices is hailed as a bit of unlooked-for intertextual critique in support of the full agency of women as persons. We may not endorse every aspect of that hypothetical voice, but that some author could even *conceive* of a poem in which a woman spoke in such a way may be miracle enough. Those who find themselves in this camp[50] are usually quite impressed with the female voice's lack of 'shame' over her desire, her public searches for her lover, and her clear indication of enjoyment of sex with her lover without benefit of a formal marriage contract. At the same time, there may be a concomitant desire by those who love the Song and see it as hopeful to *downplay* what I see to be clear indications of social restraint imposed on the Beloved for the very behavior on her part that we praise.[51] These elements, along with much of the military imagery applied to the female, receive polite but scant attention from commentators who find the inclusion of these motifs outside of the Song's *Tendenz*. Hence, these textual markers seldom figure in theologies made from the Song.

A Walk Through History: Interpretations of the Song by Believers
Oddly, later allegorists, Jewish or Christian, have found no trouble acknowledging the violence in the Song, whether it be little foxes (Song 2.15), night terrors, beatings by the watchmen (3.2; 5.7), or brotherly 'love' (1.6; 8.8-9).[52] For most Jews, these textual markers represented

---

49. *Exquisite Desire: Religion, the Erotic, and the Song of Songs* (Minneapolis: Fortress Press, 2000), p. 136.

50. I would place myself in this group, with some minor variations and nuances.

51. So, too, Exum, 'Ten Things', pp. 24-35 (30-32); Fiona C. Black, 'Nocturnal Egression: Exploring Some Margins of the Song of Songs', in A.K.M. Adam (ed.), *Postmodern Interpretations of the Bible: A Reader* (St. Louis, MO: Chalice Press, 2001), pp. 93-104 (100-101).

52. Pope, *Song*, pp. 322-23, 678-82; Murphy, *Song*, pp. 12-18.

hostile surrounding nations and their attitudes towards God's chosen Beloved, Israel (the land) and its people (the Jews). For some Christians, those markers were clear indices of the existence of their *own* carping detractors within Christianity, or worldly enemies of Christendom in general. Wherever the allegorists found God as the Hidden Referent in a violent passage, the view immediately switched to something more positive—divine violence *for our own good*: those whom He loveth, he chasteneth (Heb. 12.6).[53] As noted elsewhere, in this theology, God beats us because (1) '*He*' loves us, and (2) we made '*Him*' do it. We know what we would say about these kinds of motivations for abuse if we were working in a Women's Shelter; why do we shy away from the same kind of critique when it is the Bible or theologies made from it that are being discussed?

While never specifically addressing the abuse of the watchmen in Song 5.7, Bernard of Clairvaux treats the parallel dream sequence with the watchmen in 3.3 in Sermons 77 and 78 on the Song. After first warning us that not *all* watchmen are guarding the church properly,[54] he goes on to ponder the Bride's peculiar statement that she was 'found' by those she did not seek, the 'apostolic men':

> And so it was; she sought the bridegroom, and this was not hidden from him, for he himself had urged her on to seek him, and given her the desire to fulfill his commands and follow his way of life. But there must be someone to instruct her and teach her the way of prudence. Therefore he sent out as it were, gardeners to cultivate and water his garden, to train and strengthen her in all truth, that is, to teach her and give her sure tidings of her beloved, since he is himself the truth which she seeks and which her soul truly loves…[55]

Bernard 'normalizes' the traditions of abuse on the part of the very ones set to guard over the woman's well-being by associating it with God's righteous work in the world on behalf of Woman (= the church). Indeed, it is the Groom who, by implication, sends physical abuse in

---

53. This kind of exegesis produces tragic results, and has been amply documented: Joanne Carlson Brown and Carole R. Bohn (eds.), *Christianity, Patriarchy and Abuse: A Feminist Critique* (Cleveland: Pilgrim Press, 1989); Renita J. Weems, *Battered Love: Marriage, Sex, and Violence in the Hebrew Prophets* (OBT; Minneapolis: Augsburg-Fortress, 1995); Athalya Brenner, 'Introduction', in Athalya Brenner and Carole R. Fontaine (eds.), *A Feminist Companion to the Latter Prophets* (FCB, 8; Sheffield: Sheffield Academic Press, 1995), pp. 21-37.

54. 'Now this (watching) is not to adorn the Bride but to despoil her; not to guard her but to destroy her. It is not to defend her but to expose her to danger; not to provide for her, but to prostitute her' (*On the Song of Songs*, IV [trans. Irene Edmonds; Kalamazoo, MI: Cistercian Publications, 1980], p.122).

55. Bernard of Clairvaux, *On the Song*, pp. 125-26.

order to 'teach' his Bride. With guardians and lovers like these, no woman needs enemies.

In interpreting the two searching episodes or dream sequences, feminist critic Fiona C. Black is neither willing to tell us that 'all attachment is suffering/love is pain', nor to allegorize as Bernard and other commentators do. Instead, she calls our attention to our repeated denials of the disturbing dimensions of this text, the diminution of its experiential authenticity by labeling it a 'dream', even though Hebrew knows words for 'to dream' and 'dreams', and they do not appear here. For her, the 'plain sense' of the text clearly includes the possibility of gang rape.[56] Speaking of the beating, she names it for what it is—'transgressive':

> As keepers of order and preventers of violence, they use disorder and violence to repress the actions of the woman. Their treatment of her is unexpected and inappropriate both to the amorous designs of the Song and to the 'right' sexual relation that the protagonist seeks with her lover. The woman's acts, however, are also transgressive, and this appears to be the reason for her treatment. In return for leaving her house (the 'proper' environ for women in the patriarchal order), she is 'reminded' by the keepers of patriarchy just where she should be at night. In return for her sexual license, she is reminded to stay covered, and she is reminded, painfully, to guard the boundaries of her own body and its desires. She is pushed from the center of the Song as a speaking, loving subject.[57]

It seems to me that Black's reading is clear-eyed and suggested by the text itself. She does not make the text say something other than what it says, and she is attentive to what the text does *not* say. Her methods are postmodern, depending heavily on the work of critic Julia Kristeva for their attempt to explore the 'counter-coherence' set up in the text by the actions of the watchmen. There is nothing to quarrel with here. Black has delineated the contours of a text of useful ugliness; she makes her method of interpretation transparent to her readers. One presumes that she hopes to generate questions in modern communities of readers that will change the way we read both the Bible and the world of future experience. By reading Other-ly, however, she could have gone even further.

7. Listening through the Textual Veils

Enlarging the Circle of Readers: Views from Muslim Women's Experience
What happens if we read our text alongside women who actually wear veils or other gendered, compulsory garments (whether over their face,

---

56. Black, 'Nocturnal', pp. 93-104 (101; see especially n. 27).
57. Black, 'Nocturnal', p. 102.

around their hair, or draped flowingly over the neck as a gesture toward custom), women for whom the seeking of a lover not chosen by their male relatives may be tantamount to a death sentence? In our own time reports of violence against women as forms of social control of female sexuality in traditional society can serve as a helpful referent for some of the troubling silences of the Song. If we have been willing to consider late-nineteenth- and twentieth-century wedding practices in Muslim Palestinian villages as likely analogues for the original social context of the Song (as some interpreters still do), then we should also look at the sexual practices of those villages in other venues besides the wedding feast.[58]

I refer here to the horrific vignette with which I began: the practice of so-called 'honor killings' in popular Middle Eastern religiosity, wherein the men of a family, often egged on or joined by their older female relatives, murder the allegedly offending female of their house. This is done in order to restore their own male 'honor', which can be destroyed by any female action deemed inappropriate.[59] While *never* prescribed in the Qur'an or considered normative Islamic teaching, such murders are wretchedly common nevertheless,[60] and most especially in tribal

---

58. In order not to add further fuel to the fire of odious comparisons, given the present ongoing crisis in Israel–Palestine, I will not use the phenomenon of honor killings in Palestine, where tribal women exist in conditions resembling the Iron Age when it comes to values, culture, health care and human rights. It should be noted, however, that honor killings are customary in the Palestine of the West Bank (in some statistics, second only to Pakistan), and that these common occurrences directly inform views that peace may be impossible because one side has 'no respect for life'. Not unpredictable but horrifying nevertheless is the drastic rise of honor killings in Gaza since the election of Hamas.

59. Some critics caution us that our 'feminist' outrage is insufficiently respectful of other cultural standards and inattentive to standards of cross-cultural methodology. See John J. Pilch, 'Family Violence in Cross-Cultural Perspective: An Approach for Feminist Interpreters of the Bible', in Brenner and Fontaine (eds.), *A Feminist Companion to Reading the Bible: Approaches, Methods, Strategies* (Second Series; Sheffield: Sheffield Academic Press, 1997), pp. 306-25. But for activists such a position of purported critical neutrality smacks of 'standing idly by in the presence of your neighbor's blood' (Lev. 19.16). See Hina Jilani's report for Amnesty International, 'Pakistan Women Killed in the Name of Honour' (September 21, 1999), <http://asiapacific.amnesty.org/library/Index/ENGASA330201999?open&of=ENG-325> , as well as their most recent report, 'Pakistan: Insufficient Protection of Women', available at <http://archive.amnesty.org/library/Index/ENGASA330062002?open&of=ENG-373>, both cited February 2008.

60. Riffat Hassan, *Women's Rights and Islam: From the I.C.P.D. to Beijing* (Louisville, KY: NISA Publications, 1995); 'Women in Muslim Culture', in M. Darrol Bryant (ed.), *Muslim–Christian Dialogue: Problems and Promise* (New York: Paragon Press, 1998), pp. 187-201; *idem*, 'The Issue of Woman–Man Equality in the Islamic Tradition',

settings. It is telling indeed that in Pakistan, the woman to be murdered is declared by her male relatives to be *kari* ('black' = evil), and so becomes a non-person whose life can be taken with impunity in front of witnesses. The male partner who supposedly had a hand in 'dishonoring' the *kari*-woman is punished, too: he is declared *karo*, 'black'. Typically the *karo* suffers only the punishment of paying a fine of money and supplying a 'replacement' female from his own family to restore the property of the outraged male—father, brother, uncle—who was 'forced' to murder his sister after she refused the mate chosen for her,[61] or spoke a *salaam* to her cousin, or bore a female child. Such murders usually go unreported to the police, and even when they are, investigation of the crime is treated with a casual or humorous disregard.[62] When challenged about these atrocities by human rights activists, the patriarchal system claims that it is *both* a religious and indigenous cultural practice, and as such, cannot be critiqued. Those who *do* offer such critique must expect to pay the price—the need to hire bodyguards in order to move from office to home, dismissal from access to power, exile, or other forms of harassment. In societies where rape is considered 'consensual', illegal sex on a woman's part,[63] reporting of which is likely to cause her death at the hands of her family, it is no wonder that the stories of the scant survivors of these practices do not afford much space to the emotional or narrative 'aftermath' of such events.[64] Not only do survivors have

in Kristen E. Kvam, Linda S. Schearing and Valarie H. Ziegler (eds.), *Eve and Adam: Jewish, Christian and Muslim Readings on Genesis and Gender* (Indianapolis: Indiana University Press, 1999), pp. 463-76.

61. The Qur'an requires women to be consulted and to give their consent to marriages arranged for them by family members, but the best and clearest statements of this right actually appear in *Ahadith*.

62. There are, of course, wonderful and brave men in official positions who provide an exception to the societies' prevalent failure to take such family violence against women seriously. Like women-identified imams, we fear for them.

63. The Zina laws, found in the Hodood Ordinances enacted under fascist dictator General Zia. Amnesty International writes, 'Legal scholar and secretary of the Pakistan Law Commission, Dr Faqir Hussain, said at a seminar in Islamabad in October 2000 that the Hudood Ordinances (which includes the Zina ordinance) had been enacted as a "political ploy" and not in fulfillment of a genuine mission aimed at enforcement of Islamic law... Enforcement of Zina Ordinance was contrary to Islamic injunctions, as had been agreed by many Islamic scholars' (cited February, 2008 <http://www.amnesty.org/en/library/info/ASA33/006/2002>).

64. The lack of any sustained discussion of the impact of the Beloved's violent experiences at the hands of the watchmen, along with the Song's failure to incorporate the outcome of this episode into its loose structure are routinely cited by critics as a reason to discredit the Beloved's report as a dream, fantasy, or trivial incident of no import for the reading of the text.

considerable difficulty articulating these deep, traumatic invasions of their bodies, often there is no audience willing to hear them when they do speak. Once a culture has silenced a woman on the subject of her oppression, it then uses her silence to presume that 'nothing happened' or that, if something *did* happen, it is not a matter of critical importance to the victim's self-understanding.

Reading with someone who knows these conditions to be true in feudal, tribal societies of the present time suggests, at least to this critic, that our interpretation of sexual customs in the ancient world against the background of a biblically idealized twelve-tribe structure of interrelated tribes needs to be wary of the gaps we find and how we choose to fill them. Violence against women is part and parcel of tribal control of the economics of marriage. We can see this clearly in well-documented modern contexts; our question must be whether such evidence is relevant for our reading of an ancient text. The Bible *does* speak of such practices directly in its stories of the tribal period, and the culture of violence against women does not substantially improve during monarchic times or in colonial times.[65] It is a violence so typical that it customarily goes unobserved by those who participate in it and unaddressed by the legal traditions of the societies that condone it.[66]

Contextualizing the Beloved's encounter with the watchmen Black characterizes as guardians of patriarchal gender ideology, we find that the nature of her 'veil/mantle' (*rdyd*) is actually indeterminate. Elsewhere in the Song, we hear her lover speak of her veil (*ṣmh*, 4.1, 3; 6.6, 7), from behind which at least her eyes are visible (6.5, 7). In Genesis, Rebekah and Tamar both present us with a mantle or veil (*ṣʿyp̄*, 24.65; 38.14, 19), yet its gendered usage is not clear. Rebekah puts *on* her veil to meet someone, as a good girl should, but Tamar puts *off* her garments of widowhood, putting on her veil to entrap her father-in-law Judah by posing as a prostitute. By that act, we assume her mantle/veil does not allow the man to recognize a woman who lived for years in his own

---

65. This dynamic has been explored by Mieke Bal, *Death and Dissymmetry: The Politics of Coherence in the Book of Judges* (Chicago: The University of Chicago Press, 1988).

66. The Bible knows all about the force of 'honor and shame' codes of justice in the treatment of its females. See Tikva Frymer-Kensky, 'Virginity in the Bible', in Victor H. Matthews, Bernard M. Levinson, and Tikva Frymer-Kensky (eds.), *Gender and Law in the Hebrew Bible and the Ancient Near East* (JSOTSup, 262; Sheffield: Sheffield Academic Press, 1998), pp. 79-96; in the same volume see also Victor H. Matthews, 'Honor and Shame in Gender-Related Legal Situations in the Hebrew Bible', pp. 97-112, and Carol L. Dempsey, 'The "Whore" of Ezekiel 16: The Impact and Ramifications of Gender-Specific Metaphors in Light of Biblical Law and Divine Judgment', pp. 57-78.

house. What precisely is being covered up here and in what circumstances? Our term (*rdyd*) occurs elsewhere only in Isa. 3.23, where it is found at the end of a long list of elite women's clothing, and is one of the things God will take away, putting shame and rottenness in its place. There it is distinguished from an 'over-tunic' (*m'tph*, 3.22), and a 'cloak' (*mtphh*). Loss of this garment is a sign of punishment in Isaiah, and fits in with all the 'stripping' motifs visited upon 'bride' Israel by God and his angry prophets. Any of these terms may also be found called a 'mantle' or a 'wrapper' by translators, as well as a veil, suggesting that it is an outer garment which signals the boundary between the woman inside it and the world outside. It is certainly not clear whether the wearing of the *rdyd* signals the status of a modest or married woman, while its absence marks the female as disreputable and an available target—just as prostitutes remain the favored victims of choice for serial killers. What *is* clear is that the item of the Beloved's garment is as variable in shape as any Muslim woman's: from a *burqa* or *hijab* to elegant silk scarf, a compulsory garment can be whatever a woman and her culture make of it—the ultimate answer to a bad hair day, or just a traditional item of clothing which symbolizes no special state of inferiority to the women who wear it. Further, any removal of a compulsory outer garment by force can only be taken as a move to intimidate and shame.

The brothers, the watchmen and the stripped garment[67]—these are all *real* features in the Song, just as they are in some women's lives today. When the brothers in the Song are angry at their sister, it has an impact on her life and marks her very skin with 'blackness' in 1.6. She represents an economic resource to them, one they intend to guard carefully and use flagrantly for their own financial purposes (8.8-9). They do not stop at placing their sister in a kind of *purdah*, a forced seclusion enlivened only by assigned drudgery and regulated by the family's desires. They hint at violent retribution should she prove to have eluded their control. The Beloved's repeated statements of a wish for privacy—taking her lover to her mother's inner chamber (8.2), going away into the fields with him (7.10-13)—these motifs are not motivated only by the simple desire for privacy. There is *fear* at work here, too. Given her brothers' fixation on control over her, she knows perfectly well that she is at risk when she steps outside of the constraints set for her.

67. Or perhaps 'mantle', which Pope explains as a light flowing garment covering head and shoulders and going almost down to the feet (*Song of Songs*, p. 527). For a discussion of sisters as an economic resource of brothers in the ancient world, see the present writer's *Smooth Words: Women, Proverbs and Performance in Biblical Wisdom* (JSOTSup 356; Sheffield: Sheffield Academic Press, 2002), pp. 22-23.

Having one's outer wrapper forcibly stripped away in the Beloved's social context is no little matter of dress or manners; it is a stunning humiliation designed to evoke terror and fear of further violence. It 'dishonors' her and her family by making publicly visible her shameful act of uncovering herself (for her lover), which she has supposedly done in private. Both the socio-cultural context of this act and the Beloved's report about it require something more than a simple hop, skip and jump to allegory. Only death-dealing allegories can be built from such episodes, and these in service of keeping the dirty little secrets of male anxiety over female sexuality well hidden from critical view. We must not overlook this startling incident just because our ugly text does not tell us that the Beloved went immediately into therapy for traumatic shock. This is one 'gap' we may not fill with hearts and flowers. Acquiring sensitivity to the power of the stolen veil for women in societies where veiling is the custom[68] adds a dimension of understanding to the Beloved's silence that we who are Western readers might otherwise overlook.

The 'Other-ly' reading of the loss of one's culturally assigned coverings has implications for other texts besides the Song, of course. We might think of Hos. 2.3, 9-10, as well as many other prophetic texts that strip the female 'Israel' publicly as a sign of God's displeasure with the people's idolatry.[69] Clearly, stripping in these texts is an ominous prelude to even more stringent punishments for the metaphorical adultery of the group, and has the added by-product of shaming men by forcing them to see themselves in the female 'subject' position.

Another text takes on new interpretive force when read in this light, though it does not explicitly mention the removal of a veil or clothing: the ritual ordeal of the Sotah found in Num. 5.11-13. When a husband 'suspects' his wife of adultery, his whole household and, by extension, his village are subjected to shame and conflict. Lacking witnesses to his wife's 'defilement' yet tormented by the specter of his own loss of honor ('spirit of jealousy', Num. 5.14 RSV), a husband may take recourse in the

---

68. 'Oh, it is a dreadful nuisance!', said one beautifully garbed Pakistani woman as I admired the sheer scarf around her neck. 'It gets into everything—the batter you are cooking, the children's toys, the flower arrangement—but you can't go out without it!' It is not unusual to find many fallen veils at the side of unmarked graves or in out-of-the-way groves where the bodies of *kari*-women have been left, since strangulation with one's own veil is a common form of honor killing. Though no one acknowledges these deaths with grave markers, occasionally women of the villages sometimes sneak out to leave memorials of flowers or prayers for the fallen at these sites.

69. Gerlinde Baumann, *Love and Violence* (trans. Linda M. Maloney; Collegeville, MN: Liturgical Press, 2003).

rite of the Sotah, a 'drinking ordeal', which is equivalent to the divine oracle of Egypt or the river ordeals of Mesopotamia. The suspected victim is brought before the priest (and God) who loosens her hair, prepares a cereal offering, and forces her to take an oath while drinking the 'waters of bitterness.' If she is guilty, the bitter waters and the oath will bring harmful physical results, public for all to see. If nothing happens, then she is justified and acquitted, and the husband, although proven to have harbored false suspicions, need not pay any damages to the woman's family, which has been dishonored by the husband's unfounded accusations against her. Because she has been 'cleared' of the slanders against her and her husband's fears have been dealt with in a ritual way, one could even imagine a basis in the ritual for a restoration of the marital relationship.

It is fair to say that the Sotah text has usually been despised by feminist interpreters, even as it is prized by those who study ritual and legal traditions.[70] Reading against the background of violence used to control female sexual infractions of traditional codes of conduct, we may note some features of the proceedings we might otherwise dismiss. First, the *unbinding* of the woman's hair by the priest is a shaming event on par with the stripping of the Beloved: the priest does in public what the lover has supposedly done in private. Although the woman is forced to participate in the ritual—and one can hardly think of her as eager to submit to a magically effective ordeal since these acts would have had real power in her world—the entire proceeding is left up to God as judge. Here it is helpful to remember a snippet from Hosea, a divine oracle in which God proclaims '…I am God and not man, the Holy One in your midst, and I will not come to destroy' (Hos. 11.9b RSV). In theory, a woman may expect a just God to give a more fair and empathetic hearing than she is likely to get from a man consumed by a spirit of jealousy or a priest called upon to resolve the matter in a way that enforces the status quo. As unpleasant as this ritual experience looks to moderns, it *does* have the effect of limiting both the husband's and the village's ability to enforce their sexual codes with terminal violence against the unfortunate accused. (I make the assumption here that the priest would not *a priori* poison the brew 'under the table', so to speak, since the table belongs to Yahweh and such an act might have serious repercussions; others would not agree.) Instead of a life of repeated private beatings to induce a confession or a public execution at the hands of those who would eliminate the source of potential shame, the woman has legal 'standing' before the Divine Assembly, and only God can pronounce

---

70. Alice Bach, 'A Case History: Numbers 5:11-31', in Alice Bach (ed.), *Women in the Hebrew Bible: A Reader* (New York: Routledge, 1999), pp. 459-522.

the sentence. It is no wonder that some rabbis noted that a woman with knowledge and understanding of the Torah would find protection from God even in the most dire of situations.

From There and Back: The Song Renewed by Reading
If one is forced to a new 'seeing' by reading with Others, the textual landscape now revealed is highlighted in both its glories of love and its depths of violence. With a sense of the real violence that many traditional societies exercise against their females, we hear the Beloved's yearning with a new accompaniment. We gain a sense of her astonishing bravery, and an appreciation of the unique qualities in her lover that inspire such devoted, dangerous actions on her part. My reading proceeds to a final understanding that her statements about love and desire are uttered not just as heated, romantic nonsense spoken by inflamed teenagers, but as a deliberate *choice* to confront death with the only power that can equal it—love (Song 8.6).

The Bible reminds me of beautiful things I have allowed to be forgotten in the overwhelming impact of the visions from the Pit that pervade my daily life as an activist against violence. It provides me with insights into motivation, cultural value and divine compassion that are often absent in a postmodern world that is sure of very little. It partners both my attempt to understand the past and to change the future. I have often wondered as I review the latest news reports sent to activists around the world by the faithful 'believing women' of Islam,[71] what on earth could drive these poor girls to such treacherous choices as defying their male relatives,[72] given the terminal consequences? When feudal lords and the tribes they control trade in prestige and power based on their ability to deploy female relatives in advantageous alliances, then a woman as a 'desiring subject' becomes a threat to the very infrastructure of society. She has no intrinsic value apart from the use her male relatives have for her. How did she *ever* even begin to desire, to choose? What is at work here in this day-to-day subversion of the will to control?

Only powerful, elemental forces can prevail against the hegemony of male violence toward women. Though the Song speaks of a kind

---

71. You, too, can have the casualty reports of the daily female gendercide delivered right to your computer, Gentle Reader (<www.wafe-women.org> or <http://www.rawa.org>). You can even help!

72. Very often, the *kari*-woman has done nothing whatsoever, shown no defiance, transgressed no custom—she is simply inconvenient, or her murder covers up another (reportable) crime, or the murderer was actually trying to obtain a desirable 'replacement' female from the *karo*-family, to whom he would not otherwise have access or could not have afforded.

of 'sisterhood' in the form of the Daughters of Jerusalem, it is not the approval or support of her girlfriends that motivates the Beloved and moves her from safety inside the home out into the dangerous world. It is the very Other-ness of her lover, male to her female, key to her lock,[73] that one who can be full companion to a whole person like the Song's Beloved. Male–female relations can be a source of *strength* for a woman, even as they can be the origin of much pain. Like fire and water, Love and Death are at war in the Song, and Love—though never quite fully experienced as total presence—wins (Song 8.6-7):

> ...for love is strong as death,
>   passion fierce as the grave.
> Its arrows are arrows of fire,
>   flames of the Divine.
> Many waters cannot quench love,
>   neither can floods drown it.
> If someone offered for love all the wealth of his house,
> it would be utterly scorned (RSV).

The economics of patriarchy are discarded in favor of acknowledgment of another kind of authority governing male–female relations: freely chosen partnership is the only proof against the powers of death. The text suggests this dynamic was implicit in the Song *then*; it is true for some of us *now*—and there inheres the authenticity of an interpretation which chooses to partner the text into a reading that affirms life and love in all their forms.

8. *Epilogue*

At the last, the biblical interpreters—the self-constituted 'watchfolk' who strive to guard against 'wrong' readings—make choices. I am well aware that in privileging the voice of the stripped woman against brothers, and watchmen, I make a rhetorical shift from semi-tolerant yet grounded critic (conscious of the ways in which the Song evades interpretive closure) to the passionate advocate. The movement to advocacy may *seem* as though it moves from 'passive' voice of the interpreter to the 'active' voice of the activist/preacher, but as I have tried to demonstrate, that passive interpreter isn't so very passive after all. Choices are being made in the very *desire* to interpret, and these come to fruition in that deceptively 'objective' presentation of any meaning.

---

73. I make no moral or essentialist judgments here concerning the authenticity, sanctity and complementarity of same-sex committed relationships. Other-hood may be constructed and understood in a variety of ways. In the Song, though, the erotic tension displayed in the celebration of the Other's body suggests a very intense heterosexual construction of erotic Otherliness.

Without choice, there can be no ethical action; without ethical action, the Bible cannot achieve relevance in a dying world. When I assert that the Beloved, the woman cloaked by culture, has embraced love as a deliberate choice in order to confront Death with the only power equal to it, I, too, am choosing. I make a deliberate hermeneutical choice, opting for one plausible interpretation against other plausible interpretations, including the reasonable interpretation that the Beloved does *not* choose love against patriarchy but is simply suffering an ordinary frustration in a patriarchal setting that frustrates her romantic pursuits.

Ironically, at least for the advocate in me, the one part of the Song that seems *least* susceptible to multiple interpretations is the brutal fact of the patriarchy itself. Apart from details, nothing strikes me as indeterminate about the brothers, the watchmen, or the stripped garment. The 'feminist former Southern Baptist' in me could wish that these signs of patriarchy were ambiguous—or at least that the suggestions of a woman's revolt against brothers, watchmen, and stripping were far more definite, incapable of being misread. But it is precisely the other way around. The signs of patriarchy appear unambiguous, while the suggestions of opposition to it are more fragile, variable signs, susceptible to other readings. And how could it be otherwise? For those fragile signs speak, if at all, only from behind the cloak that patriarchy imposes, obscuring the speaking woman.

None of this is to suggest that if we could tear away the outer garment of the text, a *single* perspective or reality would be exposed to us. Gender can be constructed as a site of conflicting codes about the meaning of biological 'difference', such that there is *no* one female *or* male 'subject' position. The Beloved *may* think that her brothers are nitwits whom she easily outsmarts time and again, the watchmen familiar family friends who take away her garment because it isn't flattering, or found impractical for evening wear. But her language, 'angry at me' (brothers, 1.6), 'they beat me, they wounded me' (watchmen, 5.7), statements in the text for which an interpreter must account, suggests to me that my readings have done a better job of trying to listen to the text, its nuances and omissions, than others have done in simply shooting past these disruptive verses in pursuit of a wonderful wedding song.

In the end, we choose. For me this hermeneutical decision between competing plausible interpretations can only be a choosing in solidarity with those who have no voice for their own choices, those who have been taught that they may not choose.[74] I cannot lift the veil of the text—at

---

74. This insight is one of the considerations that help us to distinguish between an interpretation in support of cloaked Muslim women, and one, say, in support of Ku Klux Klan-inspired readings (they too have a 'cloaking' device): the KKK has voice,

least not in a way that makes the face and voice behind the veil stand out unambiguously. But I can read with those whose lives are cloaked as a way of listening through the veils. I owe it to the text and the community of interpreters to be honest about the signal coming from behind that garment: honest about its uncertainty, its openness to a mundane (if romantically charming) or an extraordinary (and politically challenging) interpretation. I owe it to the woman in the 'cover-up'—and all women whose lives are enshrouded by gendered meanings—to advocate that extraordinary interpretive possibility, to partner the text into a reading that affirms life and love in all their forms against the tyrannies of domination and social death.

The Bible is full of 'near misses', situations where honor killings might have been the most efficient way of enacting community standards. Mrs Potiphar does not die; she becomes a model for all future mystics who fall in love with God in her Islamic afterlife. In Genesis, the pregnant Tamar is dragged to the gate of the elders to be judged and burnt to death. Only her cunning in preparing for such a moment spares Tamar One's life, though we will applaud Judah, the father of her child, for his one moment of compassionate honesty: 'She is more in the right than I...' (Gen. 38.26). Another ill-fated Tamar in 2 Samuel is raped and dishonored, but neither her brother Absalom nor David her father do anything to her or her half-brother rapist. Absalom's forbearance might come from the fact that it was a male relative, Jonadab, son of his father's brother Shimea, who cooked up the plan to help love-sick Amnon rape Tamar, thus leading to Absalom's later 'justified' revenge against the crown prince. That it takes violent use of a sister to get rid of a brother and take that step closer to the throne must have seemed a small price to pay. Later when Absalom, now a usurper, publically has intercourse with David's concubines to cement his position as the new king and dishonor his father into the bargain, a whole new group of women are put at risk through no fault of their own (2 Sam. 16.21-22). The use of the women as sexual pawns like sister Tamar is again presented as a 'wise' stratagem by a god-like counselor (v. 23), just as Jonadab's wily counsel is called out in the text for its cunning and wisdom (2 Sam. 13.3). Like Tamar Two, the royal harem are only doomed to live on shut up in a house; one presumes that motherhood, their only possible social justification for being female, has been placed out of their reach by the

---

access, power, technology. The veiled ones in fundamentalist societies do not, so this is one place where our Western ambiguity about support of the Other, so often tinged with a suspect cultural imperialism, can be put 'on hold'. In my opinion, we are absolutely required to support those without access, because they have no other entry into the dialogue at present.

same honor code that allowed their defilement. Since the biblical text construes all of this generational violence and maneuvering as a punishment by God on David for killing Uriah the Hittite and taking his wife Bath-sheba, God is shown as supporting and encouraging the use of females for male purposes. It is very hard to find a *genuine* male honor — the power to protect and preserve, globally practiced without reference to gender, ethnicity, or social status — among humans or the divine in the ancient world of patriarchies.

But the strange fact is that the women in the text *do* sometimes live on. The lustful wife in the Egypt of Genesis, the accused wife in the Sotah, the betrayed sister, the royal concubine in the courts of Jerusalem...we have seen such fates as other texts in other times might have meted out to them for being a source of man's desire, much less having desires themselves. Now, believing women must allow them to live on as examples where male rage to kill the dishonoring female found a different outcome, divinely inspired or not. The glass is half-empty *and* half-full; the only way out of that paradox for women is to refuse to drink the brew entirely, and trust themselves to the gentle mercies of the crowd.[75]

---

75. One must, however, take great care in choosing one's crowd.

Chapter 8

YOU SHALL NOT STAND IDLY BY

1. *Prologue: Jesus in the Human Rights Community*

I often tell my students that one of the things that makes teaching them delightful is the fact that I now talk with so many audiences that despise the Bible, or are, at the very least, deeply suspicious of it and all 'sacred texts'. Usually, I think my Human Rights colleagues are right on the money when they voice their critiques. Hence, I was shocked and surprised to find that Jesus of Nazareth holds pride of place, along with Gandhi, among religious figures who might just have something to offer us in our struggles for human decency.

But it goes far beyond that, this unsuspected 'Come to Jesus' stream running through the deep oceans of international laws, treaties and declarations. I was surprised but also glad of it, just as I had been as a small child in Southern Baptist Sunday School, when I heard Jesus say, 'Blessed are the poor.' (I knew the poor; 'they' were me.) Ever after, as the old Gospel hymn says,

I was glad when they said unto me,
Let us go unto the House of the Lord!

(They had cookies there in exchange for learning Bible verses, a fact not lost upon a child hungry in more than an intellectual way.)

In 2002, I was at a dinner with a foreign Human Rights delegation, to whom I had been recommended by the US State Department as a 'dissident' who could and would give a report on conditions for intellectual dissidents in the United States. Through our halting languages, I was questioned: Am I censored?[1] Am I safe? Do I think my country values civil society and human rights? How did it feel to be living in the world's most powerful empire in history? What did I think was the greatest, most basic human right? And…what about Jesus? Did he serve as a model or inspiration for me personally as the first religious leader to be executed by the state?

After my amazement at being asked a religious question by a secular team of investigators, I found myself turned around and upside down. Never, in the morass of academia and denominational struggles that serve as the context of my work, had I allowed myself to access the paradigm or archetype of what I would have called the

---

1. By the contents of this book, obviously not—but please note that only one of my publishers is a US Citizen, and lives abroad!

'Marxist Jesus' of the 1960s. 'Odd, that.', I thought as I pondered this lacuna. 'I wonder what happened to me and Jesus?'

Somewhere along the way, the concept that 'knowing' or 'following' Jesus should have some impact for the world had been bred right out of me. That confessional (and now I realize, perfectly logical) view is simply too, too far from the world of academic claims *or* the divisiveness of Christian denominations, each trying to assert its own 'brand' of the true Truth in order to maximize market share and expand their niche offerings. My world had turned white when I went away from my ghetto to college. The Jesus that had sustained the civil rights and anti-war communities in my youth was no longer part of the world to which I had been sent. Since no one is ever as spiritually hungry as a former Baptist, it was easy to see that I had gladly substituted academic studies of the Bible in place of the white churches I had left behind to stand in solidarity with my Haitian, African American, and Jewish neighbors.

It is with great amusement and surprise, then, that my own 'Come to Jesus' moment was spurred on by my peace and justice work, and that the subject of that metanoia came in the form of a Muslim woman from Peshawar, murdered in an 'honor killing'. Her family name was Ajeeban; the report did not give more. As you read you will see why it is a violation to name her on the basis of the family that murdered her, so we will refer to her as the Woman. A small domestic argument at the kitchen table had blown up into an assault with a firearm. In order to cover up their act, the husband and his brother decided to declare that the Woman had engaged in adultery, and finish her off rather than take her to the hospital for the initial, non-fatal gunshot wound. Dragging her outside, bleeding, they announced the situation to the village that stood by watching. They shot her several times more in the legs so she could not get away while they dug a grave in her sight. Hearing her baby cry, the Woman crawled to edge of the crowd where her sister held her baby. The Woman nursed her child one last time in the shadow of her own grave. She cried out for a drink of water, which her sister tried to provide, but was stopped by the mob. She continued nursing her baby until it was torn from her embrace. The men discharged their weapons into her. The Woman was riddled with bullets and dumped into her waiting grave. The police refused to investigate or question witnesses because it was deemed a 'domestic' matter.

After that, who could read John 7.53–8.11, the story of the Honor Killing That Wasn't, without tears in their eyes, and some fierce, persistent flame of hope?

Grounding Rights in the Gospel of John

As noted elsewhere, the Bible is a mixture of voices and concerns spanning space and time, and looking for modern concepts in it may be interesting but more often than not, such tasks are doomed to failure:

it's a long way from Galilee to Peshawar in Pakistan! The Gospel of John with its anti-Semitism and bickering, its more spiritual than synoptic telling of the story, hardly seems like a place to come out—were one reading without the eyes of female flesh.

I will not take up and try to solve the textual questions of this passage as other scholars have done so, but, Dear Reader, they abound.[2] If the woman was taken in adultery by witnesses, where is the male companion who also deserves a death sentence according to Leviticus 20?[3] Why are there no witnesses to the act in the crowd, which would normally require *them* to cast the first stone? Why is there no indication that the Sanhedrin has called for the death penalty after investigation? Why are the Pharisees presented as 'pro-capital punishment' when every other portrait of them from reliable historical references shows that they went out of their way to limit any executions?[4] If due process of the kind normally meted out to women who transgress the honor codes of their men has flown out the window, just *what* is the point of this passage?

Perhaps the woman brought to Jesus was a remarried, divorced woman, one whom Jesus' own statements would condemn as an adulteress (Mt. 5.31-32; 19.3-9; Mark 10.2-9). The law of Moses provided due process for the accused before capital punishment could be enacted, and a remarried divorced woman was *not* deemed to have transgressed any laws when she remarried. If the Pharisees actually are trying to 'test' Jesus and that narrative note is authentic to the earliest layer of the text tradition (Moses' law doesn't want to kill the remarried divorcee; Jesus' law holds her as adulteress, and Roman occupiers denied the right to execute anyone to those under their home-rule), maybe the Pharisees would simply like to know what 'the Teacher' (the only use of this term in John) has to say. Perhaps they want an oral *midrash* on a way to save the woman, not condemn her. Of course, Bible scholars being what they

---

2. A recent sampling of articles which might be of interest to Human Rights professionals as well as biblical enthusiasts are Gail R. O'Day, 'John 7.53–8.11: A Study in Misreading', *JBL* 111 (1992), pp. 631-40; Matthew Schneider, 'Writing in the Dust: Irony and Lynch-Law in the Gospel of John', *Anthropoetics* 3 (1997), cited June 8, 2007 <http://www.anthropoetics.ucla.edu/Ap0301/Dust.htm>; Alan Watson, 'Jesus and the Adulteress', *Biblica* 80 (1999), pp. 100-108; Barbara A. Holmes and Susan R. Holmes, 'Sex, Stones, and Power Games: A Woman Caught at the Intersection of Law and Religion (John 7.53–8.11)', in Cheryl A. Kirk-Duggan (ed.), *Pregnant Passion: Gender, Sex, and Violence in the Bible* (Semeia Studies, 44; Atlanta: Scholars Press, 2003), pp. 143-62.

3. As we would say 'down home' in the South, 'it takes two to tango!'

4. Brad H. Young, ' "Save the Adulteress!": Ancient Jewish *Responsa* in the Gospels?', *NTS* 41 (1995), pp. 59-70 (63-65).

are,[5] for them the great mystery of this text is the content and fact of Jesus writing in the dust, instead of giving a 'straight' answer. For the Human Rights defender, the mystery is something else yet again: you mean this appeal to decency and fairness actually *worked* in preventing violence against women? Where do we sign up for the 'how-to' workshop?

Putting all these intriguing questions aside, and willfully turning away from John's attempt to teach his readers to *always* suspect the Jews of nefarious plots, we will rely on the plain sense of this passage: in a case where the death penalty is called for, with or without due process, and where political dickering over jurisdiction was sure to accompany any choice, the Teacher[6] finds a way and the woman lives. Sitting in her circle of dust like Mrs Ajeeban, watched closely by onlookers who will make no move to assist, the Teacher does not turn to a written text to achieve his ends. Texts are writ on the shifting sands of ideology and interpretation. No; not this Human Rights Defender—he takes no chance on a contrary text and writes his own in the mortal dust that waits to receive the victim of this theological litmus 'test'. He turns the choices back on the crowd, which miraculously seems to be persuaded by the simple view that 'fair is fair'.

Whether this event is at all historical is certainly beside the point: yes, the story has been told to cast negative valuation upon Jewish leaders, and positive ones upon the Christian community. This *Tendenz* has caused what Albright called the *realia* of the jurisprudence and social customs of the day to be presented in a skewed fashion, in order to better make those points. But: all that being granted, the plain meaning of this text is the decriminalization of sexual sins, even though the Teacher's own view of the woman might be that she is indeed guilty. Since women are disproportionately affected and punished by sexual legislation under patriarchy, the pro-woman, *all women*, nature of this text is indisputable. Recalling that oral tradition often outranks written ones when it comes to matters of day-to-day interpretation of legal traditions, Jesus presents a principle which can be generalized beyond a hot, dusty day in ancient Judea. One scholar has called this a primary example of 'living Torah':

> If the Pharisees were looking for a way out, the *responsum*[7] of Jesus was just what they needed, because Jesus focused attention on the higher significance of Torah. The method is well known in the tradition of the Phar-

---

5. Characters in search of an Author? Afflicted with terminal textual yearnings? We *so* want to *know!*
6. 'Rabboni!' we were taught to say by King James, which then glosses it with the totally non-Jewish and unsatisfactory 'which is to say, "Master!"'.
7. This term is taken from the medieval period, when esteemed rabbis would give responses to community questions of interpretation which may have arisen,

isees and many of their followers in rabbinic literature. It is just such an approach to the diverse issues of religious faith and practice which made it possible for Jesus to give a response which saved this woman. She could not prove her innocence but the oral law made it possible to search for flexibility in such a case.[8]

The woman lives, not just because she has an advocate in the interpreter of the law, but *because* this Teacher knows the meanings toward which the Torah—more a 'way' than a 'law' as moderns understand it—presses in its slow progress through history. It is, needless to say, *Jewish* law practiced by a *Jewish* interpreter that saves the woman, and Christian and Muslim readers would do well to remember it. Jesus is who he is *precisely* because he stands fully in the traditions of his people, traditions too often demonized by Christians and Muslims. All those 'openings' toward liberation in the Gospels of which Christian theologians make so much all began in the Hebrew Bible—the same place where all too often scholars and believers lodge unacceptable violence, too.

2. *A Final Word on the Bible and Human Rights Abuses in its World and Ours*

The Narrative Power of Image

Like narratives, images tell a story, though they do so often without benefit of the written word. The art and artifacts we have seen have a story to tell as surely as any inscription or annal. Of course, their *real* story is usually *not* what we see—that is only what ancient makers and patrons wished us to know, set out in the ways they wished us to know it. Just as narrative has its typical markers that allow a plot to proceed—in biblical Hebrew, the so-called 'narrative tense', 'and it happened that'—so too images have their conventions to handle time, narrative flow, point of view, and guides to 'reading' the image properly. Like the Eskimo knife that shows all the phases of ice fishing in a single frame of reference, we found the same collapse of time in the Assyrian reliefs of the siege of Lachish. Women captives, lugging their belongings, stream from within the city while on their immediate right, Assyrian soldiers commit a range of crimes against the citizenry: impalements, flayings, and beheadings. To the right of this, we see the city under

---

and which needed an opinion. For example, R. Meier of Rothenburg allowed that 'even a poor Jew may have pictures in his book', when asked whether it was kosher to have drawings in prayerbooks (quoted by Carole R. Fontaine, 'Facing the Other: Ruth-The-Cat in Medieval Jewish Illuminations', in Athalya Brenner (ed.), *Ruth and Esther: A Feminist Companion to the Bible (Second Series)* (FCB, 3; Sheffield: Sheffield Academic Press, 1999), pp. 75-92 (78).

8. Young, 'Save the Adulteress', pp. 59-70 (68).

attack by siege-machines, and next to that, a line of humiliated captives crawls before the great king. Obviously, not all these events could have taken place at the same time, but their jumbled presentation accurately portrays the mayhem, the overwhelming horrific stimuli that are the stuff of war. Women and children are seen throughout as clear 'players' — or pawns — in this world gone wild.

Behind the image made durable are the intent, the decision, the medium, and the maker responding to the demands of the one for whom the image/artifact is ultimately destined. Put another way, the artistic image is *purposive*: it does not exist without a world of overlapping concerns, desires, and incidents all coming together in the final product. When we view the monumental or ritual art of empires, we are not viewing anything like the preference or virtuosity of artistic vision or craft; far from it. Instead, we have a tale as carefully crafted for the consumption of viewers as surely as any Deuteronomic text was composed to meet the political goals of the monarchy of its day. The image is no pristine reflection of reality, or even of cognition or perception. Like everything else human-made, it is an illusion which tantalizes with its false claim of representation. Flanked by enormous winged bulls designed to tower over the viewer and lead off into a dazzling tribute to the king's wars, the Lachish reliefs were presented in a way which displays their ideological function for all to see. Diplomatic visitors traversing the long hall of Sennacherib's Nineveh palace, with its optical illusions of great depth created by ever-smaller sized flanking colossi, are brought up short before the awful portrait of the consequences of defying the empire. As the viewers stand beneath the looming reliefs covering an entire wall, there is no doubt that the feelings of insignificance and horrified fascination are exactly what the designers of this scene had in mind.

The images of prisoner abuse at Abu Ghraib are as staged and ideological in intent as the videos of the beheadings of Western hostages by Islamic extremists, the palettes of Naqada-period Egypt, or the wall reliefs of Assyria. Only the method of recording and disseminating them has changed, as US military and Defense Department officials discovered to their disgust: those awful digital cameras and internets. Who knew? One had the feeling that their only problem with the crimes committed against prisoners of war was that the practices had become widely known.

What is amazing is that the 'script' of humiliation of male captives has changed so little over the millennia: there was in antiquity no worse fate for a male than being treated as a female, and so it remains. As long as male honor requires a female Other over which to define itself, the recipe for the exploitation of women and girls remains the same. Until male shame is re-defined as violence toward anyone weaker, smaller, younger, or of lesser status, and truly becomes viewed as *shame-full* by all, we will not see much diminution of male aggression and war.

The Hebrew Bible, and its daughters, the New Testament and the Qur'an, derives from a world in which broad individual human rights did not exist—only property rights are consistently protected in ancient law codes. Human Rights, as moderns think of them, would surely have been sacrificed to the survival needs of the ancient community if they *had* had them. Yet, we have seen in all sorts of texts and art that at least nascent ideas of human dignity, bodily integrity, and worth may be found, even if we discern their contours only in their violation. The ancient world was probably about the same in levels of brutality as that of the modern world, *mutatis mutandis*; it is impossible to measure such things accurately even now in our own time. Hence, the ancient materials on war still apply to the human condition as experienced by captives and slaves.

Consider, for example, two texts which both have significant ancient Near Eastern parallels: Proverbs 24.10-12 and Lamentations 3.34-36. Proverbs 24 continues a textual connection (if not outright dependence) on the Egyptian *sebayit*, or 'instruction', The Instruction of Amenemope, a New Kingdom wisdom text usually thought of as one of the most 'religious' or moral examples of the genre.

> If you faint in the day of adversity, your strength being small;
> if you hold back from rescuing those taken away to death,
>   those who go staggering to the slaughter;
> if you say, 'Look, we did not know this'—
>   does not he who weighs the heart perceive it?
> Does not he who keeps watch over your soul know it?
>   And will he not repay all according to their deeds? (Prov. 24.10-12 NRSV).

The 'Bible-believing' Christians of the United States have been markedly, shamefully silent on the subject of prisoner abuse at Abu Ghraib and Guantanamo Bay,[9] a position which their own Sacred Text does not excuse. Failure to know and act on behalf of the captive creates a kind of biblical act-consequence relationship, a state of disruption caused by inaction, which will certainly come back to haunt the believer. Being

---

9. Humiliating and degrading treatment like the type meted out to male prisoners in Guantanamo by female interrogators (sexual enticement or fake menstrual blood) once again invokes the paradigm of female-as-dishonored-by-nature. Only ingrained male fear of the feminine and horror of being feminized or made unclean by contact with it makes this type of treatment possible (Paisley Dodds, 'Gitmo Soldier Details Sexual Tactics' [January 27, 2005], cited March 5, 2008 <http://www.truthout.org/docs_05/012905A.shtml>).

a by-stander is not acceptable in circumstances of abuse. Amenemope imagined an after-death tribunal such as that in the *Book of the Dead*, but the writer in Proverbs not only recalls the image of the weighing of the heart, but also a day of distress when no one comes to offer aid to those who were indifferent to the plight of others. What goes around, comes around, says this wisdom text: when the rights of captives perish, the rights of all are placed in jeopardy in the name of 'Security'.

The Book of Lamentations, as we saw earlier in Chapter 3, relies in great measure upon the genre and imagery of Mesopotamian laments for the destruction of cities. The female city has become a mother in mourning, lamenting the (just, by the Hebrew Bible's reckoning) desolation of Jerusalem in the aftermath of conquest. Lamentations 3.34-36 is the only place in the Bible that mentions a term which might justifiably be translated as 'human rights', but we will give the gendered and more accurate translation here:

> To crush under foot all the prisoners of the earth,
> to turn aside the right of a man in the presence of the Most High,
> to subvert a man in his cause, the Lord does not approve (RSV).

This highly charged text bristles with legal terminology, and is especially notable for where it occurs in Lamentations. Although Jerusalem and its populace were thought by the authors to have 'deserved' their punishment, nevertheless the duty to accord justice and care to prisoners, any prisoners—even guilty ones—is fully inscribed at a narrative moment when we might expect to see another round of vengeful, venomous and well-earned cursing. Though the NRSV translates *mišpāṭ gāḇer*, as 'human rights', our analysis has shown that in fact, only the rights of men are referred to here, so we prefer the more literal rendering. Since we are arguing for extending the rights of elite males to all humanity,[10] we may feel certain that *some* form of a 'rights' concept was in operation for this text. That it is legal in nature is shown through the use of the term 'justice', *mišpāṭ*, which carries concrete as well as abstract meanings—it specifies certain actions rather than just an overall 'feeling' toward those who come for legal redress. Similarly, the terminology in v. 36, 'a man in his cause', also incorporates the verbal root *rîb*, 'lawsuit'. Once more, God is found to be on the side of people who stand both inside and outside the circle of community concerns and blessing. Alert readers will wonder that so much is made of these brief notices, given the plethora of contradictory passages. But it is powerful to know that

---

10. Actually, with many Human Rights philosophers, I see no legitimate, epistemological reason to draw the line at 'humanity' as the only living creatures having rights, but cannot develop that wisdom-based argument with respect to the whole biotic community here.

the Hebrew God has at least the same amount of compassionate care for prisoners that an aged Egyptian sage displayed in the Pharaoh's court.

The Power of the Text
The Hebrew Bible, of course, has left us no legacy of combat art in the form of monumental art or ritual items depicting successes (or failures). Yet, the epic traditions of biblical Israel's history form a narrative of words that are less open to misunderstanding than a mute image — usually. The Bible gives us its story in metaphors and verse, verbal artistry and storytelling, prophetic pejorative and wailing lament — and it does not shirk from a frank report of *all* the horrors that take place. One might complain that it takes a lot of chutzpah to turn the Weeping Goddess of ancient Sumer into the raped Daughter of Zion, stripped and abused for her 'sexual' sin of apostasy. This is no image to live by, and one could argue that the use of the female body to portray *male* dishonor and its just rewards reduces the female to yet another level of instrumentality. Yet, we must be sobered and grateful to have a text that speaks of what others do not, a text that does not scruple to describe it all despite our wish to look away.

No one looking for biblical sources for Human Rights should be surprised by the presence of something wholly antithetic to them like Psalm 137, the lament of the captives in Babylon, in our text. Noxious as this psalm is, it is nevertheless a way of keeping faith with the experience of the captive and adding it to the community's repertoire of experiences. As the Judeans are tormented by their oppressors, they indulge in fantasies of retribution that will dash their captors' babies against the wall, and certainly God is thought to have some part to play in all that longed-for death. The anger, hatred, despair, and longing in this text are as much a tribute to the history of deportation and enforced enslavement as any Assyrian relief from palace walls. Psalm 137 is the lament of the Losers.

But, consider the company the Bible keeps on topics of this kind. We find outright testimony of similar attitudes before ancient Israel was even a gleam in the Editor's eye. An Assyrian school boy's tablet images the king (Tiglath-Pileser I, perhaps?[11]) as a hunter when he goes to war:

> [The Hunter]: Assur is his ally, Adad is his help,
> Ninurta,[12] vanguard of the gods, [go]es before him...

---

11. A name so nice they used it thrice!
12. Assur is the national 'high god'; Adad is the classic storm-god who brings saving rain; Ninurta is an old Sumerian vegetation god who acquired an impressive 'warrior' portfolio and was known for his grisly war trophies and fractious nature.

He slashed the wombs of the pregnant, blinded the babies,
He cut the throats of the strong ones among them,
Their troops saw (?) the smoke of the (burning) land.
Whatever land is disloyal to Assur will turn into a ruin.[13]

Lest we be inclined to essentialism and feel like indulging in a fit of patriarchal generalizations, it is worth noting that it is not only male gods who are pro-death on behalf of their chosen constituencies. Goddesses are capable of blending their nurturing aspects with the 'warrior portfolio' in order to get things done for their state-appointed darlings. Ashurbanipal (c. 668–633 BCE) writes of the goddess Ninlil (Ninurta's mother):

> Ninlil, the lordly Wild-Cow, the most heroic among the goddesses who rivals in rank (only) with Anu and Enlil, was butting my enemies with her mighty horns; the Ishtar who dwells in Arbela, clad in (divine) fire (and) carrying the *melammu*-headwear, was raining flames upon Arabia...
>
> Upon an oracle-command of Ashur and Ninlil, I pierced his cheeks [the enemy king's] with the sharp-edged spear, my personal weapon, by laying the very hands on him which I had received to conquer opposition against me; I put the ring to his jaw, placed a dog collar around his neck and made him guard the bar of the east gate of Nineveh...[14]

Comparing this ancient account to the 'bad gay porn' photographs of prisoner abuse from Abu Ghraib, we can only note with Qoheleth that there is not much new under the sun.

Persons who accept my readings of the Bible as a 'mixed' book of authentic experiences of a particular people have every reason to condemn *all* human rights abuses, even where they may find that proclamation to be in conflict with the plain sense of the written text as it is usually pronounced. We have seen that often the plain sense of a text can spawn torture, violence, and exclusion, all for the sake of purity and right belief. Let us take that ugly aspect of the text as a useful and viable

---

He caused a cosmic eagle to drop the Tablets of Destiny into the Deep, and traveled there to get the god of Wisdom, Enki, to return the tablets. When he did not, Ninurta attacked Enki's vizier, causing Enki to send a great turtle to bite his toes. Eventually both god and turtle fall into a deep pit dug by Enki. Only Ninurta's mother, Ninlil, misses him (Gwendolyn Leick, *A Dictionary of Ancient Near Eastern Mythology* [London and New York: Routledge, 1991], pp. 135-37). Since Ninurta is patron of stones, and stones have much to answer for in Human Rights experience, good riddance to him!

13. Benjamin R. Foster, *Before the Muses: An Anthology of Akkadian Literature*, I. *Archaic, Classical, Mature* (Bethesda, MD: CDL Press, 1993), pp. 248-49.

14. A. Leo Oppenheim (trans.), 'Babylonian and Assyrian Historical Texts', in James B. Pritchard, *ANET* (Princeton, NJ: Princeton University Press, 3rd edn, 1969), pp. 265-317 (300).

opportunity to deconstruct the way idolatry of the Book displaces living knowledge of God, however that term may be understood. But there is An-Other Way. Oral interpretation that honors the gap, the vision, the prayer of the sufferer—these must be brought back to life among those communities which opt for obsessive (and highly selective) literalist readings. The rabbinic traditions of exegesis have already made this form of interpretation reasonable and customary for the Jewish community. For Christians, it will require a more nuanced presentation if our readings for universal dignity are not to posit Judaism as the restrictive tradition which exists only to be displaced. For Muslims, a revival of the Sunni practice of *Ijtihad*,[15] or critical interpretation, out of fashion since the tenth century of the Common Era, is already underway with the increasing number of moderate and progressive theological voices working within Islamic theological traditions. Asma Barlas writes in her important work, *'Believing Women' in Islam: Unreading Patriarchal Interpretations of the Qur'an*,

> ...there is a relationship between reading (sacred texts) and liberation... [I]f we wish to ensure Muslim women their rights, we not only need to contest readings of the Qur'an that justify the abuse and degradation of women, we also need to establish the legitimacy of liberatory meanings.[16]

Yes, we may understand the impulse behind the public honor killing and other abuses of human rights as mechanisms which help defuse tension in a society in crisis—but we must never forget they are also *crimes*.

Believers who find in the Book a loving Creator must take very seriously the notion of whether or not any human may take the life of another,

---

15. Khaled Abou El Fadl gives the following definition of *ijtihad*: 'to exert and exhaust oneself in the pursuit of thought and knowledge in search of the Divine Will' ('Foreword', in Amina Wadud, *Inside the Gender Jihad: Women's Reform in Islam* [Oxford: Oneworld Publications, 2006], pp. vii-xiv [xiii]).

16. Austin, TX: University of Texas Press, 2002, p. 3. Other important works on Muslim interpretation and human rights that take the condition of women seriously are Fatima Mernissi, *The Veil and the Male Elite: A Feminist Interpretation of Women's Rights in Islam* (trans. Mary Jo Lakeland; New York: Perseus/Basic Books, 1991; Fedwa Malti-Douglas, *Woman's Body, Woman's Word: Gender and Discourse in Arabo-Islamic Writing* (Princeton, NJ: Princeton University Press, 1991); Leila Ahmed, *Women and Gender in Islam* (New Haven, CT: Yale University Press, 1992); Ann Elizabeth Mayer, *Islam and Human Rights: Tradition and Politics* (Boulder, CO: Westview Press, 4th edn, 2007); Haideh Moghissi, *Feminism and Islamic Fundamentalism: The Limits of Postmodern Analysis* (London: Zed Books, 1999); on-line, the work of Professor Farooq Hassan, a progressive moderate in Shari'a studies is available in full text through any search engine.

especially in cases of transgressions of cultural codes of patriarchal societies. Such entities as states, then and now, thrive on violence, on the consideration of others as prey and property, and privilege above all the ultimate value which they ascribe to their own survival. The Hebrew Bible imagines a restored community, properly ordered, and though we may disagree with the writers' understanding of proper order, we can cling with confidence to the raft of wholeness — restoration — as we toss on the waves of violence that assault us each and every day.

Warriors and women find themselves classed together in the modern literature of trauma survival, the former terrorized by war and the latter by the domestic prisons in which most are held captive and used sexually. It is fitting, then, that in our text we find what the rest of the ancient Near East so politely hid from view: the treatment of women in war. No matter the side where the women stand, they are at greater risk than men, because they bear a heavy and ancient symbolism in the gendered world of war: they are the prey to be hunted, captured, domesticated, consumed. Again, there is not much difference now, although with the addition of female members to the US Armed Forces, we now have the phenomenon of 'command rape': forced sexual relations by one higher up in the chain of command in a combat zone. The stories are reprehensible; the misogyny that underlies them is that of the rapist, the warrior, the Empire.[17] Of the ancient literature surveyed in this volume, only the Hebrew Bible spoke directly of the sexual humiliation faced by women in war, and yet provided us with heroines who not only braved such danger to their honor, but used the gender code to turn the tables on their warrior adversaries.

Another point of contact between the conditions for women and girls during war and captivity and the Hebrew Bible is in the use of legal mechanisms to seek redress and acknowledgment of what must not be allowed to be suppressed. The Book of Job and prophetic texts, while showing little positive attention to women per se, challenge both human and divine communities and call them to account for their role in human suffering. Even where redress and legal remedies can never truly rectify the situation and restore health, they serve the function of modern day tribunals: *they remember and they resist*. While women and children are not used to looking to the laws of men for protections of their rights, the Hebrew Bible stands out as a stark reminder that non-violent actions *can* address the wrongs done, at least symbolically if not materially. In this

---

17. See Sara Rich, 'A Moment of Silence is Not Enough', cited September 7, 2007 <http://www.truthout.org/docs_2006/090707A.shtml>. Her daughter Suzanne Swift, a MP serving in Iraq, experienced Command Rape, was court marshaled and stripped of rank for going AWOL rather than returning to duty under her rapist.

way, the law becomes a form of solidarity the community shows to the survivor. This solidarity creates a culture of support which allows all its members to better resist violent acts against it without losing hope in the face of overwhelming odds, or losing its soul in the thirst for revenge.

The New Testament adds a further dimension to our discussion of the amazing presence of rights for the social underdogs in the Hebrew Bible. Jesus, the Human Rights Messiah, eschews violence repeatedly in the stories about his time among us, yet his spirited defense of human dignity and worth is no less powerful and persuasive for all that. Victor Pizzuto offers a theology of the Cross which cuts across the violence he finds to be intrinsic to biblical texts:

> ...the Bible gives witness to Jesus' own 'posture' toward violence. The cross becomes the chief witness and paradigm of his posture: arms outstretched, embracing the very evil that sought to destroy him... The most central gospel proclamation of 'Christ crucified' challenges us to confront evil not by retaliation or even resistance, but as did Christ—by *absorption*.[18]

Cautioning that nations and other legal entities may not simply ignore violent assaults on large groups of innocent civilians but must act to thwart them, Pizzuto nevertheless calls our attention back to the 'passivism' of Jesus as a guard against national self-delusion on the subject of our own wounded righteousness. Our blind belief in our own goodness as a nation tries to tell us that no act is unacceptable if it is done to protect the 'American people'. If other countries applied similar logic to the decimation of their national life by corporate greed, most of it emanating from our Bible-believing state, then again, 'anything goes' and global interests in justice would repeatedly fall to the powerful impulses of revenge and exploitation.

The Bible and Honor Killings: A Partnership Theology of the Text
Sometimes—at least in our Bible—the Woman lives or the girl comes back to life. We must not forget that most astonishing piece of 'living Torah'. Our use of such texts to establish a broader biblical ethic is an

---

18. Vincent Pizzuto, 'Religious Terror and the Prophetic Voice of Reason: Unmasking our Myths of Righteousness', *BTB* 37 (2007), pp. 47-53 (53). Personally, I do not embrace the idea of pointless sacrifice and find much 'atonement' theology to be profoundly non-biblical and wrong-headed. Depending on one's Christology, the death of Jesus carries radically different meaning for believers. In answer to Pizzuto, whom I assume is suggesting *imitatio dei* as an ethical response, I would note that women have already 'absorbed' male violence inside their bodies, and it does not seem to have produced much liberation, though transformation in the form of pregnancy is certainly an outcome for them and *that* does enhance their status and legal standing, in the ancient world at least.

example of what I call 'Partnership Theology'. A community, a teacher, or a reader can partner a text and a tradition to its best expression, if only they think to try it. The wise man can die, but his wisdom does not, and about this fact, the State can do precisely nothing. If the community rejects the power to terrorize, whether wielded by its own leaders or others, life happens and stories can take an unexpected turn.

While I realize I might be charged with tactical apologetics by those who rightly think that sacred texts ought *not* be used as a Declaration of Universal Complicity, it is nevertheless important—nay, crucial—that in this case we honor the gaps and cracks in the patriarchal state's comfort with violence as a basic means of operation. Too many times made captives themselves, the writers of the Bible had to make room for more flexibility than simple condemnation of all who have the bad fortune to become designated victims of their cultures. At present, we find no other place in ancient Near Eastern law codes where the rights, however limited, of female war captives or injured slaves are given even a gesture of protection; there is no other narrative text than ours where the 'second-born', the designated male 'loser' in the pecking order of patriarchal power relations, is preferred and successful. In no other set of texts is the underdog so consistently favored, the bleeding woman blessed, the adulteress delivered, the father shown up for an aging fool.[19] Simply put, this is our text, and where we can read its departures from the status quo of violent relations under patriarchy as a bulwark against their incessant replication, generation after generation, *we can and we should.*

Honor killings, then, must be one of those cases where we use both positive (Jn 7.53) and negative textual evidence (Num. 5) to enlarge our views and base our objections on the firm foundation of a nuanced biblical interpretation—this is the Straight Path. Elsewhere among the Peoples of the Book, Muslim scholars see no justification for the cultural practice of honor killings in the Qur'an, which protects against female infanticide. Judaism, with its bias against capital punishment, does not practice any sort of execution like this, even though a similar procedure is legislated in Deuteronomy. If we recall that we have seen fictional texts from Egypt which narrate honor killings but no evidence in the legal practice that such ever existed in real life, then we have at least an opening to wonder how much force the Deuteronomic laws really had.

---

19. This is certainly *not* to imply that the Bible (ours) is All Good, and the parallel literature (theirs) is All Bad (consult with witches on this topic for a 'real world' occasion of the Bible being worse than its neighboring traditions!). In the spirit of scrupulous fairness I must observe that Amon-Re gives life to 'the son of the slug', and the Hittite Sun God gives judgment to 'the dog and the pig'. Sumerian Inanna protects prostitutes, but since her temple keeps all the money they make and never frees the sexual slaves, her protection seems only fair.

There can be no such thing as an authentic *Christian* honor killing, no matter the interpreter, text, or tradition. The Gospel says an unequivocal No! to this practice, and this interpreter will take as 'fightin' words' any interpretation that claims otherwise. The shocking participation of Christian communities in the Middle East in this practice can have no justification, and priests and clergy who return girls who have taken refuge with them to their murderous families should be held accountable, dismissed from their positions, taken to the International Criminal Court and tried as accessories to murder. Further, the Gospel's views can be extended to any group of designated victims, especially where the 'crimes' are sexual in nature. Let us take what we learn in John 7.53–8.11 and use it to extend religious protections to those whose violations of gender codes (lesbian, gay, bisexual, and transgendered persons) place them at special risk in our society.

Is John 7.53–8.11 history? Who knows?

Can the text matter, then, even if it's *not* history? Oh, *yes!*

The despised Sotah ritual of Numbers 5 leads us to the conclusion that it is not for the jealous partner or the community to decide on issues of sexual guilt in absence of any proof whatsoever. Even where there *is* proof, investigation and due process are required. It is interesting that the supporters of theocracy (any version) are so at odds with the Bible's 'best practices' on captives, prisoners, and sufferers, as well as ignoring the clear demands to eliminate poverty that fall upon the shoulders of any person who belongs to the Peoples of the Book. Let those who choose the deaths of Others give an account of *their* hermeneutics, if they can.[20] Until they do, we must err on the side of compassion in all cases where religion comes into conflict with basic rights. International human rights law is unequivocal in its statements on honor killings.[21]

God the Abuser: Can This Marriage Metaphor Be Saved?
Sociologists, trauma psychologists, and Human Rights professionals all speak at length about the 'recovery' process for those who have been tortured, traumatized, or even just made into bystanders unwillingly caught up in another's passion play. Likewise, those who have made a study of it know 'what it takes' to be strong under torture and how

---

20. Reader, I think you must be wondering if this view has implications for reproductive choice, capital punishment, diet and ecology. It does, but that is another book, and probably not mine. The United Nations Consultation on the Status of Women's Working Group on Female Infanticide condemns sex-selective abortions, but takes care not to 'rule' on any other form of reproductive choice.

21. For the UN statement on honor killings, available in 19 different languages, please see <http://www.wunrn.com/reference/crimes_honor.htm>.

to cultivate the ability to accept one's own death as a fair price for not contributing to the deaths of others. In Muslim circles, we would speak of such persons as 'martyrs', those who chose death in service of life, as they see it. Among all these experts a few points are called out for special attention.

There is always a tremendous desire to repress what one has seen, to forget the horror one has known. The pain of knowing is too terrible for a fragile psyche, still at risk, to recognize. Only later, after some degree of safety has been achieved, can the abused begin to bring such deep wounding to the surface for reintegration into conscious knowing. Failure to do so means a round of continuing intrusive flashbacks, every bit as horrible as the 'real thing' because the brain can't tell the difference. The wound must be acknowledged and grieved both by the abused *and* the community before healing can begin.

A community remembering — in this sense, both the Bible and Human Rights discourse begin the work of public recognition, reintegration, and reform. It seems insane to members of the Human Rights community that organized religions and personal faith, both of which claim to have so much to do with movement toward wholeness, should hold themselves apart from engagement in the sufferer's return to life based on literalistic interpretations of a fluid and sometimes ambiguous text.

Why is that?

The Hebrew Bible and, after it, the New Testament invite a certain type of analysis because each uses the metaphor of family relations to discuss the mutual duties owed by people to the Divine, and vice versa. Israel is a beloved son; Jerusalem is the Daughter of Zion; the chosen king is an adopted son, and even Moses' Egyptian god-mother becomes part of the family when she is named 'Bithiah', 'my daughter', by the rabbis. Certainly Ezekiel 16 gains its power from the family metaphor, even as it disgusts and horrifies by the violation of that very set of relations when the rescuing midwife God observes that his nursling now has breasts and becomes the sexual partner of the infant he has raised.[22] Family systems therapy to look at why biblical Israel persists in being such an enabling victim to a battering god may be in order. The first victim ideology was formed, at least narratively, under the yoke of slavery; to this, theologian and family systems counselor Jeremy Young adds a second victimization. The people's experience of

---

22. And just where are the practices of Leviticus and Deuteronomy in Ezekiel 16, one might ask! Should God be able to do what is forbidden to human heads of families? Shall not the judge of all the Earth do justice? Ezekiel's god should turn himself in for rehabilitation.

slavery leads them to accept violent behavior as the typical norm for relations between people and groups, deities and their worshippers.[23] The rabbis were clearly on to this fact when they speculated on why God did not give the Torah to the Jews immediately after the Rescue at the Sea: too long held as passive slaves, said the rabbis, Israel was not ready to be a partner to God and could not accept the Law freely, having no sense of themselves as free and responsible. The people had to be weaned away from the bitter lessons of captivity before they could step into a full relationship. Violence attributed to God is the nasty hangover of the experience of the traumatized, and it takes slow and deliberate unlearning.

Ultimately, we must face that taking a 'preferential option' for radical compassion means that we must also reject our easy acceptance of violence as a method hallowed by God as Divine Warrior and replace it with Love Crucified but victorious for all that.[24] In the world of Human Rights and peacemaking, we find a similar concept of a 'good death' that operates in the ancient world, especially for those who die in battle. When one of us dies well, whether executed by the State, an assassin, or in some work-related tragedy—giving nothing critical away and putting no others at risk—we count this in the 'Win' column. A biblically minded person might comment, even in tears, that indeed, Love is *at least* as strong as death. On this insight, Religions and Rights may shake hands and embrace, for we share the same view of 'death with meaning'.

We must reject the violence of God in the Bible, even where it is considered a positive divine attribute, practiced on behalf of the chosen, and presented to us as salvation. This is especially true in texts where God *himself* seems to be the author of that violence; here we are hearing not the voice of a living God but that of the State and its minions, and this holds across all the cultures we have studied. The State needs us to believe in its goodness and that its limitations on human life are there for our protection. In that spirit, deliberately or not, the State projects its violence onto its gods, and its gods project that back as blessing on their chosen ones, who are given leave to execute violent acts as the deity's representative. The result of this ideological feedback loop is that we do not object so strongly as we should, nor act as decisively as we ought when faced with religious violence. A divine glamour has been cast over

---

23. Jeremy Young, *The Violence of God and the War on Terror* (London: Darton, Longman & Todd, 2007). Sadly, this book was turned down by academic publishers in religion in the USA, but features a most useful analysis using family systems methodology to examine God's abuse of Israel and others.

24. Pizzuto, 'Religious Terror', pp. 47-53 (53).

the bleeding body, a glamour that can only be pierced by looking with 'eyes of flesh'. Jesus-our-Rabbi, faithful even unto death, shows us the way, a real Human Rights Hero to rival all the Greats of living memory whose names we speak with gratitude and wonder.

This is the message of the Book of Job.
This is the message of The Woman Who Lived in the Gospel of John.[25]
This is the message.

---

25. I name her this with deep appreciation of author J.K. Rowling's presentation of a perfected Seeker-Victim hero in her stories of the Boy Who Lived.

Epilogue

Only When Women Sing

Do not show me tiny crowds of handpicked men;
do not regale me with films of gunfire in the air—
these mean nothing.

Show me instead the mothers,
pictures of long-dead sons at their breast;
show me their sisters, whose brothers
and husbands never came home;
let me see their joy, if they have it.

Show me battalions of little girls, if you can—
healthy and learned, with futures and names.
Show me their mothers, with homes all arrayed
in abundance and peace, with color and song.

Do not pronounce victories, missions accomplished,
when tyrants go skulking from palace to hole:
show me the women, show me the old,
wreathed now in hope, with a sense of 'it's over',
formerly broken, now a little more whole.

It will only be victory when women sing in the streets,
their veils firmly chosen and anchored in place,
or off and waving, if they have the taste,
but both equally safe—to choose, to live, to learn, to love.
It will only be victory when the women sing.

BIBLIOGRAPHY

Abusch, Tsvi, 'Ishtar's Proposal and Gilgamesh's Refusal: An Interpretation of the Gilgamesh Epic, Tablet 6, Lines 1-79', *HR* 26 (1986), pp. 143-87.
Achtemeier, Elizabeth, *The Old Testament and the Proclamation of the Gospel* (Philadelphia: Westminster Press, 1973).
Adam, A.K.M. (ed.), *Postmodern Interpretations of the Bible: A Reader* (St. Louis, MO: Chalice Press, 2001).
Ahmed, Leila, *Women and Gender in Islam* (New Haven: Yale University Press, 1992).
Al Jazeera.net, 'Al-Qaeda blamed in Iraq sect attack', cited September 27, 2007 <http://english.aljazeera.net/NR/exeres/EED9104C-42E5-4DD8-9B6A-6C92B5B32C43.htm?FRAMELESS=true&NRNODEGUID=%7bEED9104C-42E5-4DD8-9B6A-6C92B5B32C43%7d>.
Albenda, Pauline, 'An Assyrian Relief Depicting a Nude Captive in Wellesley College', *JNES* 29 (1970), pp. 145-50.
Ali, Abdullah Yusuf, *The Holy Qur'an* (Brentwood, MD: Amana Corporation, 1989).
Amnesty International, 'Pakistan: Insufficient Protection of Women', cited February, 2008 <http://archive.amnesty.org/library/Index/ENGASA330062002?open&of=ENG-373>.
Andreu, Guillemettre, Marie-Hélène Rutschowscaya and Christiane Ziegler, *Ancient Egypt at the Louvre* (trans. Lisa Davidson; London and New York: I.B. Tauris, 1999).
Anglo, Sydney, 'Evident Authority and Authoritative Evidence: The *Malleus Maleficarum*', in Anglo (ed.), *The Damned Art: Essays in the Literature of Witchcraft* (London: Routledge & Kegan Paul, 1977), pp. 1-31.
AntiDefamation League, 'Richard Kelly Hoskins', cited February, 2008 <http://www.adl.org/Learn/ext_us/Hoskins.asp?LEARN_Cat=Extremism&LEARN_SubCat=Extremism_in_America&xpicked=2&item=Hoskins>.
Armstrong, Karen, *A History of God: The 4000-Year Quest of Judaism, Christianity, and Islam* (New York: Ballantine, 1993).
Asher-Greve, Julia M., 'The Essential Body: Mesopotamian Conceptions of the Gendered Body', in Wyke (ed.), *Gender and the Body in the Ancient Mediterranean*, pp. 8-37.
Assante, Julia, 'Sex, Magic and the Liminal Body in the Erotic Art and Texts of the Old Babylonian Period', in Parpola and Whiting (eds.), *Sex and Gender in the Ancient Near East*, pp. 27-52.
The Associated Press, 'Army Suicides Highest in 26 Years', cited September 27, 2007 <http://www.truthout.org/docs_2006/081607J.shtml>.
Avalos, Hector, 'Legal and Social Institutions in Canaan and Ancient Israel', in Sasson (ed.), *CANE*, I (1995), pp. 615-31.

—*Fighting Words: The Origins of Religious Violence* (Amherst, NY: Prometheus Books, 2005).
—*The End of Biblical Studies* (Amherst, NY: Prometheus Books, 2007).
Avalos, Hector, Sarah J. Melcher, and Jeremy Schipper (eds.), *This Abled Body: Rethinking Disabilities in Biblical Studies* (Semeia Studies, 55; Atlanta: Society of Biblical Literature, 2007).
Bach, Alice, 'Good to the Last Drop: Viewing the Sotah (Numbers 5:11-31) as the Glass Half Empty and Wondering How to View it Half Full', in Exum and Clines (eds.), *The New Literary Criticism and the Hebrew Bible*, pp. 26-54.
—'A Case History: Numbers 5:11-31', in Bach (ed.), *Women in the Hebrew Bible: A Reader* (New York: Routledge, 1999), pp. 459-522.
Bach, Alice (ed.), *Women in the Hebrew Bible: A Reader* (New York: Routledge, 1999).
Badawi, Jamal A., 'Gender Equity in Islam' (2002), cited September 27, 2007 <http://www.islamicity.com/articles/articles.asp?ref=IC0210-1757&p=1>.
Bahrani, Zainab, *Women of Babylon: Gender and Representation in Mesopotamia* (London and New York: Routledge, 2001).
Bakan, David, *And They Took for Themselves Wives: The Emergence of Patriarchy in Western Civilization* (New York: Harper & Row, 1979).
Bal, Mieke, *Lethal Love: Feminist Literary Readings of Biblical Love Stories* (Bloomington: Indiana University Press, 1987).
—*Death and Dissymmetry: The Politics of Coherence in the Book of Judges* (Chicago: University of Chicago Press, 1988).
—*Murder and Difference: Gender, Genre and Scholarship on Sisera's Death* (trans. Matthew Gumpert; Bloomington: Indiana University Press, 1988).
—'Metaphors He Lives By', *Semeia* 61 (1993), pp. 185-208.
Baltzer, Klaus, 'Women and War in Qoheleth 7:23-8:1a', *HTR* 80 (1987), pp. 127-32.
Barlas, Asma, *'Believing Women' in Islam: Unreading Patriarchal Interpretations of the Qur'an* (Austin, TX: University of Texas Press, 2002).
Barré, Michael (ed.), *'Wisdom, You are My Sister!': Studies in Honor of Roland E. Murphy, O. Carm., on the Occasion of his 80th Birthday* (CBQMS, 29; Washington, DC: Catholic Biblical Association, 1997).
Barstow, Anne Llewellyn, *Witchcraze: A New History of the European Witch Hunts* (San Francisco: Pandora/Harper Row, 1994).
Baumann, Gerlinde, *Love and Violence: Marriage as Metaphor for the Relationship between YHWH and Israel in the Prophetic Books* (trans. Linda M. Maloney; Collegeville, MN: Liturgical Press, 2003).
Beckman, Gary, 'The Anatolian Myth of Illuyanka', *JANES* 14 (1982), pp. 11-25.
Bekkenkamp, Jonneke and Fokkelien van Dijk-Hemmes, 'The Canon of the Old Testament and Women's Cultural Traditions', in Brenner (ed.), *A Feminist Companion to the Song of Songs*, pp. 67-85.
Bellah, Robert, 'Religious Evolution', in Lessa and Vogt (eds.), *Reader in Comparative Religion: An Anthropological Approach*, pp. 36-50.
Bergant, Dianne, '"My Beloved is Mine and I Am His" (Song 2:16): The Song of Songs and Honor and Shame', *Semeia* 68 (1994), pp. 23-40.
Bernard of Clairvaux, *Magnificat: Homilies in Praise of the Blessed Virgin Mary* (trans. Marie-Bernard Saïd and Grace Perigo; Cistercian Fathers Series, 18; Kalamazoo, MI: Cistercian Publications, 1979).
—*On the Song of Songs*, IV (trans. Irene Edmonds; Kalamazoo, MI: Cistercian Publications, 1980).

Bernstein, Ellen, *The Splendor of Creation: A Biblical Ecology* (Cleveland: Pilgrim Press, 2005).
Biale, David, 'The God with Breasts: El Shaddai in the Bible', *History of Religions* 21 (1981–82), pp. 240-56.
Black, Fiona C., 'Nocturnal Egression: Exploring Some Margins of the Song of Songs', in Adam (ed.), *Postmodern Interpretations of the Bible: A Reader*, pp. 93-104.
Blamires, Alcuin (ed.), *Woman Defamed and Woman Defended: An Anthology of Medieval Texts* (Oxford: Clarendon Press, 1992).
Bleibtreu, Erika, 'Grisly Assyrian Record of Torture and Death', *BARev* (January–February, 1991), pp. 52-61.
Blumenthal, David R., *Facing the Abusing God: A Theology of Protest* (Louisville, KY: Westminster/John Knox Press, 1993).
Boyarin, Daniel, *Carnal Israel: Reading Sex in Talmudic Culture* (Berkeley: University of California Press, 1993).
—*Unheroic Conduct: The Rise of Heterosexuality and the Invention of the Jewish Man* (Contraversions—Critical Studies in Jewish Literature, Culture, and Society, 8; Berkeley: University of California Press, 1997).
—'Torah-Study and the Making of Jewish Gender', in Brenner and Fontaine (eds.), *A Feminist Companion to Reading the Bible: Approaches, Methods, Strategies (Second Series)*, pp. 585-621.
Brandon, S.G.F., 'History or Theology? The Basic Problems of the Evidence of the Trial of Jesus', in Cohen (ed.), *Essential Papers on Judaism and Christianity in Conflict: From Late Antiquity to the Reformation* (New York: New York University Press, 1991), pp. 114-30.
Brenner, Athalya, *The Feminist Companion to the Bible* (First Series; Sheffield: Sheffield Academic Press, 1993).
—*A Feminist Companion to the Song of Songs* (FCB, 1; Sheffield: Sheffield Academic Press, 1993).
—'Introduction', in Brenner and Fontaine (eds.), *A Feminist Companion to the Latter Prophets* (FCB, 8; Sheffield: Sheffield Academic Press, 1995), pp. 21-37.
—*The Intercourse of Knowledge: On Gendering Desire and 'Sexuality' in the Hebrew Bible* (BIS, 26; Leiden: E.J. Brill, 1997).
—'Identifying the Speaker in the Text: Isaiah 50', in Brenner and Fontaine (eds.), *The Feminist Companion to Reading the Bible: Approaches, Methods, Strategies (Second Series)* (Sheffield: Sheffield Academic Press, 1997), pp. 136-50.
Brenner, Athalya (ed.), *A Feminist Companion to Samuel and Kings* (FCB, 5; Sheffield: Sheffield Academic Press, 1994).
—*A Feminist Companion to the Hebrew Bible in the New Testament* (FCB, 10; Sheffield: Sheffield Academic Press, 1996).
—*Ruth and Esther: A Feminist Companion to the Bible (Second Series)* (FCB, 3; Sheffield: Sheffield Academic Press, 1999).
Brenner, Athalya and Fokkelien van Dijk-Hemmes (eds.), *On Gendering Texts: Female and Male Voices in the Hebrew Bible* (BIS, 1; Leiden: E.J. Brill, 1993).
Brenner, Athalya and Carole R. Fontaine (eds.), *A Feminist Companion to the Latter Prophets* (FCB, 8; Sheffield: Sheffield Academic Press, 1995).
—*A Feminist Companion to Reading the Bible: Approaches, Methods, Strategies* (Second Series; Sheffield: Sheffield Academic Press, 1997).
—*A Feminist Companion to Wisdom and Psalms (Second Series)* (FCB, 2; Sheffield: Sheffield Academic Press, 1998).

—*The Song of Songs: A Feminist Companion to the Bible (Second Series)* (FCB, 6; Sheffield: Sheffield Academic Press, 2000).
Brock, Rita Nakashima, *Journeys by Heart: A Christology of Erotic Power* (New York: Crossroad, 1991).
Brooks, Peter, *Body Work: Objects of Desire in Modern Narrative* (Cambridge, MA: Harvard University Press, 1993).
Brown, Joanne Carlson and Rebecca Parker, 'For God So Loved the World?', in Brown and Bohn (eds.), *Christianity, Patriarchy, and Abuse: A Feminist Critique*, pp. 1-30.
Brown, Joanne Carlson, and Carole R. Bohn (eds.), *Christianity, Patriarchy and Abuse: A Feminist Critique* (Cleveland: Pilgrim Press, 1989).
Brownlie, Ian (ed.), *Basic Documents on Human Rights* (Oxford: Clarendon Press, 1971).
Brueggemann, Walter, 'A Text That Redescribes', *Theology Today* 58 (2002), pp. 526-40.
Bryant, Darroll (ed.), *Muslim–Christian Dialogue: Problems and Promise* (New York: Paragon Press, 1998).
Burrows, Mark S., '"Peering into the Abyss of the Future": Empire in the Age of Globalization and the Call for a New Ecumenism', *Theologies and Cultures: Church and Empire* 2 (2005), pp. 26-55.
Bussert, Joy M.K., *Battered Women: From a Theology of Suffering to an Ethic of Empowerment* (New York: Lutheran Church in America, 1986).
Butler, Judith, *Gender Trouble: Feminism and the Subversion of Identity* (New York: Routledge, 1990).
Buttrick, George A. (ed.), *The Interpreter's Dictionary of the Bible: An Illustrated Encyclopedia*, I (Nashville: Abingdon Press, 1962).
Cady, Susan, Marian Ronan and Hal Taussig, *Wisdom's Feast: Sophia in Study and Celebration* (San Francisco: Harper & Row, 1989).
Cafferty, Jack, *It's Getting Ugly Out There: The Frauds, Bunglers, Liars, and Losers Who Are Hurting America* (Hoboken, NJ: Wiley Publishers, 2007).
Cairo Declaration on Human Rights in Islam, August 5, 1990, U.N. GAOR, World Conference on Human Rights, 4th Session, Agenda Item 5, U.N. Doc. A/CONF.157/PC/62/Add.18 (1993); for original see <http://www1.umn.edu/humanrts/instree/cairodeclaration.html>
Camp, Claudia V., *Wisdom and the Feminine in the Book of Proverbs* (Bible and Literature, 11; Sheffield: Almond Press, 1985).
—'Understanding a Patriarchy: Women in Second Century Jerusalem through the Eyes of Ben Sira', in Levine (ed.), *'Women like This': New Perspectives on Jewish Women in the Greco-Roman World*, pp. 3-39.
—'Metaphor in Feminist Biblical Interpretation: Theoretical Perspectives', *Semeia* 61 (1993), pp. 3-38.
—'Honor and Shame in Ben Sira: Anthropological and Theological Reflections', a paper read at the First International Conference on Ben Sira (Soesterberg, the Netherlands: July 28-31, 1996).
—'Honor, Shame and the Hermeneutics of Ben Sira's Ms C', in Barré (ed.), *'Wisdom, You are My Sister!': Studies in Honor of Roland E. Murphy, O. Carm., on the Occasion of his 80th Birthday*, pp. 157-71.
—*Wise, Strange and Holy: The Foreign Woman and the Making of the Bible* (JSOTSup, 320; Sheffield: Sheffield Academic Press, 2000).
Camp, Claudia V. and Carole R. Fontaine, 'The Words of the Wise and Their Riddles', in Niditch (ed.), *Text and Tradition: The Hebrew Bible and Folklore*, pp. 127-52.

Camp, Claudia V. and Carole R. Fontaine (eds.), *Women, War and Metaphor: Language and Society in the Study of the Hebrew Bible* (Semeia, 61; Atlanta: Scholars Press, 1993).

Campbell, Colin and Bert A. Rockman (eds.), *The George W. Bush Presidency: Appraisals and Prospects* (Washington, DC: CQ Press, 2003).

Campolo, Tony, *Speaking my Mind: The Radical Evangelical Prophet Tackles the Tough Issues Christians Are Afraid to Face* (Nashville, TN: Thomas Nelson, 2004).

Cannon, Katie, 'Womanist Interpretation and Preaching in the Black Church', in Schüssler Fiorenza (ed.), *Searching the Scriptures*, I, pp. 326-38.

Carmichael, Calum M., 'Women's Offences and Biblical Law', *forum historiae iuris* (February 14, 1998), p. 9; cited September 27, 2007 <http://www.rewi.hu-berlin.de/online/fhi/articles/9802carmi.htm>.

Carroll, James, *Constantine's Sword: The Church and the Jews: A History* (Boston: Houghton Mifflin, 2001).

Carroll, Robert P., 'Desire under the Terebinths: On Pornographic Representation in the Prophets—A Response', in Brenner and Fontaine (eds.), *A Feminist Companion to the Latter Prophets*, pp. 275-307.

Carter, Jimmy, *Endangered Values: America's Moral Crisis* (New York: Simon & Schuster, 2006).

Castelli, Elizabeth A. (ed.), *Women, Gender, Religion: A Reader* (New York: Palgrave, 2001).

Chapman, Cynthia R., *The Gendered Language of Warfare in the Israelite–Assyrian Encounter* (HSM, 62; Winona Lake, IN: Eisenbrauns, 2004).

Chastain, Kimberly Parsons, 'The Dying Art of Demon-Recognition: Victims, Systems, and the Book of Job', in Rigby (ed.), *Power, Powerlessness, and the Divine: New Inquiries in Bible and Theology*, pp. 161-78.

Chernick, Michael (ed.), *Essential Papers on the Talmud* (New York: New York University Press, 1994).

Christianson, Eric S., 'Qoheleth the "Old Boy" and Qoheleth the "New Man": Misogynism, the Womb and a Paradox in Ecclesiastes', in Brenner and Fontaine (eds.), *A Feminist Companion to Wisdom and Psalms (Second Series)*, pp. 109-36.

Clark, Elizabeth A., *Women in the Early Church* (Message of the Fathers of the Church, 13; Wilmington, DE: Michael Glazier, 1983).

Clines, David J.A. (ed.), *The Poetical Books: A Sheffield Reader* (The Biblical Seminar, 41; Sheffield: Sheffield Academic Press, 1997).

Cockburn, Patrick, 'A Wave of Revenge Killers: The Horrific Stoning Death of a Yazidi Girl', cited May 8, 2007 <http://www.counterpunch.org/patrick05082007.html>.

Cohen, Ada (trans.), *The Soncino Talmud: Sotah* (London: Soncino Press, 1936).

—'Portrayals of Abduction in Greek Art: Rape or Metaphor?', in Kampen (ed.), *Sexuality in Ancient Art: Near East, Egypt, Greece, and Italy*, pp. 117-36.

Cohen, Jeremy (ed.), *Essential Papers on Judaism and Christianity in Conflict: From Late Antiquity to the Reformation* (New York: New York University Press, 1991).

Collon, Dominique, *Ancient Near Eastern Art* (Berkeley: University of California Press, 1995).

Convention against Torture, 'Article 1', cited February, 2008 <http://www2.ohchr.org/english/law/cat.htm>.

Cooper, Jerrold S., 'Genre, Gender, and the Sumerian Lamentation', *JCS* 58 (2006), pp. 39-47.

Cosgrove, Charles (ed), *The Meanings We Choose: Hermeneutical Ethics, Indeterminacy and the Conflict of Interpretations* (The Bible in the 21st Century; London: T&T Clark International, 2004).
Craig, Kerry M., and Margaret A. Kristjansson, 'Women Reading as Men/Women Reading as Women: A Structural Analysis for the Historical Project', *Semeia* 51 (1990), pp. 119-36.
Crenshaw, James L., *A Whirlpool of Torment: Israelite Traditions of God as an Oppressive Presence* (OBT, 12; Philadelphia: Fortress Press, 1984).
Crossan, John Dominic, *Who Killed Jesus? Exposing the Roots of Anti-Semitism in the Gospel Story of the Death of Jesus* (San Francisco: HarperCollins, 1995).
—*The Birth of Christianity: Discovering What Happened in the Years Immediately after the Execution of Jesus* (San Francisco: HarperCollins, 1998).
Cunningham, Graham, *'Deliver Me from Evil': Mesopotamian Incantations 2500–1500 BC* (Studia Pohl, Series Maior, 17; Rome: Pontificio Istituto Biblico, 1997).
Davies, Philip R., 'This is What Happens...', in Grabbe, *'Like a Bird in a Cage': The Invasion of Sennacherib in 701 BCE*, pp. 106-19.
Davies, Steve, 'The Canaanite-Hebrew Goddess', in Olson (ed.), pp. 68-79.
Davies, Vivian and Renee Friedman, 'The Narmer Palette: A Forgotten Member', *Nekhen* 10 (1998), p. 22.
Davis, Whitney, *The Canonical Tradition in Ancient Egyptian Art* (Cambridge: Cambridge University Press, 1989).
—*Masking the Blow: The Scene of Representation in Late Prehistoric Egyptian Art* (Berkeley: University of California Press, 1992).
Day, Peggy L. (ed.), *Gender and Difference in Ancient Israel* (Minneapolis: Fortress Press, 1989).
De Troyer, Kristin *et al.* (eds.), *Wholly Woman, Holy Blood: A Feminist Critique of Purity and Impurity* (Studies in Antiquity and Christianity; Harrisburg, PA: Trinity Press International, 2003).
Dean, John W., *Conservatives without Conscience* (New York: Viking, 2006).
Dempsey, Carol L., 'The "Whore" of Ezekiel 16: The Impact and Ramifications of Gender-Specific Metaphors in Light of Biblical Law and Divine Judgment', in Matthews, Levenson, and Frymer-Kensky (eds.), *Gender and Law in the Hebrew Bible and the Ancient Near East*, pp. 57-78.
Dever, William, *Who Were the Israelites and Where Did They Come from?* (Grand Rapids, MI: Eerdmans, 2003).
Dobbs-Allsopp, F.W., *Weep, O Daughter of Zion: A Study of the City-Lament Genre in the Hebrew Bible* (Biblica et orientalia, 44; Rome: Pontificio Istituto Biblico, 1993).
Dodds, Paisley, 'Gitmo Soldier Details Sexual Tactics' (January 27, 2005), cited March 5, 2008 <http://www.truthout.org/docs_05/012905A.shtml>.
Donnelly, Jack, *The Concept of Human Rights* (New York: St. Martin's Press, 1985).
Dunbar, Paul 'An Ante-Bellum Sermon', in Randall (ed.), *The Black Poets*, p. 45.
Dundes, Alan, *The Morphology of North American Indian Folktales* (Helsinki: Folklore Fellows Communications, 1964).
Dundes, Alan (ed.), *The Blood Libel Legend: A Casebook in Anti-Semitic Folklore* (Madison: University of Wisconsin Press, 1991).
—'The Ritual Murder or Blood Libel Legend: A Study of Anti-Semitic Victimization through Projective Inversion', in Dundes (ed.), *The Blood Libel Legend: A Casebook in Anti-Semitic Folklore*, pp. 336-76.

Edmonds, Irene (trans.), *On the Song of Songs*, IV (Kalamazoo, MI: Cistercian Publications, 1980).
Ehrenreich, Barbara, 'Prison Abuse: Feminism's Assumptions Upended', *Los Angeles Times* (May 16, 2004), cited May, 2004; no longer available. <www.latimes.com/news/opinion/commentary/la-op-ehrenreich16may16,1,190206>.
Eilberg-Schwartz, Howard, *God's Phallus and Other Problems for Men and Monotheism* (Boston: Beacon Press, 1994).
El Fadl, Khaled Abou, 'Foreword', in Wadud, *Inside the Gender Jihad: Women's Reform in Islam*, pp. vii-xiv.
Elyon, Ari, 'The Torah as Love Goddess', in Chernick (ed.), *Essential Papers on the Talmud*, pp. 463-76.
Enns, Fernando, Scott Holland and Ann K. Riggs (eds.), *Seeking Cultures of Peace: A Peace Church Conversation* (Telford, PA: Cascadia Publishing House, 2004).
Epstein, Isidore (ed.), *The Soncino Hebrew–English Talmud* (London: Soncino Press, 1935-48).
—*The Babylonian Talmud* (trans. J. Shachter and H. Freedman; Tractate Sanhedrin, 23 vols.; London: Soncino Press, 1935).
Ericksen, Robert P., *Theologians Under Hitler: Gerhard Kittel, Paul Althaus and Emanuel Hirsch* (New Haven: Yale University Press, 1985).
Eskenazi, Tamara C., 'Out from the Shadows: Biblical Women in the Post-Exilic Era', in Brenner (ed.), *A Feminist Companion to Samuel and Kings*, pp. 252-71.
Exum, J. Cheryl, *Fragmented Women: Feminist (Sub)versions of Biblical Narratives* (JSOTSup, 163; Sheffield: Sheffield Academic Press, 1993).
—'Ten Things Every Feminist Should Know about the Song of Songs', in Brenner and Fontaine (eds.), *The Song of Songs: A Feminist Companion to the Bible (Second Series)*, pp. 24-35.
Exum, J. Cheryl and Johanna W.H. Bos (eds.), *Reasoning among the Foxes: Female Wit in a World of Male Power* (Semeia, 42; Atlanta: Scholars Press, 1988).
Exum, J. Cheryl, and David J.A. Clines (eds.), *The New Literary Criticism and the Hebrew Bible* (JSOTSup, 143; Sheffield: Sheffield Academic Press, 1993).
Fackenheim, Emile, *The Jewish Bible after the Holocaust: A Re-reading* (Bloomington: Indiana University Press, 1990).
Fallujah Videos and Accounts, 'Remember Fallujah', cited February, 2008 <http://www.rememberfallujah.org/index.html>.
Fander, Monika, 'Historical Critical Methods', in Schüssler Fiorenza (ed.), *Searching the Scriptures*, I, pp. 205-24.
Faulkner, Raymond (trans.), *The Egyptian Book of the Dead: The Book of Going Forth by Day* (San Francisco: Chronicle Books, 2nd rev. edn, 1998).
Fensham, F. Charles, 'Widow, Orphan and the Poor in Ancient Near Eastern Legal and Wisdom Literature', *JNES* 21 (1962), pp. 129-39.
Fewell, Danna Nolan, and David Gunn, *Gender, Power and Promise: The Subject of the Bible's First Story* (Nashville, TN: Abingdon Press, 1993).
Fischer, Shlomo, '*Kevod Ha'adam, Tzelem Elohim* and *Kevod Habriot (The Dignity of Man, the Image of God, and the Honor of the Fellow-Creature)*', in Seligman (ed.), *Religion and Human Rights: Conflict or Convergence*, pp. 15-26.
Fleming, D.E., *The Installation of Baal's High Priestess at Emar: A Window on Ancient Syrian Religion* (Atlanta: Scholars Press, 1992).
—'More Help from Syria: Introducing Emar to Biblical Study', *BA* 58 (1995), pp. 139-47.

Fontaine, Carole R., 'The Deceptive Goddess in Ancient Near Eastern Myth: Inanna and Inaras', in Exum and Bos (eds.), *Reasoning among the Foxes: Female Wit in a World of Male Power*, pp. 84-102.
—'A Response to the Book of Hosea', in Brenner and Fontaine (eds.), *A Feminist Companion to the Latter Prophets*, pp. 60-69.
—'Disabilities and Chronic Illness in the Bible: A Feminist Perspective', in Brenner (ed.), *A Feminist Companion to the Hebrew Bible in the New Testament*, pp. 286-301.
—'Proverb Performance in the Hebrew Bible', in Clines (ed.), *The Poetical Books: A Sheffield Reader*, pp. 316-32.
—'"Many Devices" (Qoheleth 7.23–8.1): Qoheleth, Misogyny and the *Malleus Maleficarum*', in Brenner and Fontaine (eds.), *A Feminist Companion to Wisdom and Psalms (Second Series)*, pp. 137-68.
—'Facing the Other: Ruth-The-Cat in Medieval Jewish Illuminations', in Brenner (ed.), *Ruth and Esther: A Feminist Companion to the Bible (Second Series)*, pp. 75-92.
—'"A Heifer from thy Stable": On Goddesses and the Status of Women in the Ancient Near East', in Bach (ed.), *Women in the Hebrew Bible: A Reader*, pp. 159-78.
—'"Go Forth into the Fields": An Earth-Centered Reading of the Song of Songs', in Habel and Wurst (eds.), *The Earth Story in the Wisdom Traditions*, pp. 126-42.
—*Smooth Words: Women, Proverbs and Performance in Biblical Wisdom* (JSOTSup, 356; Sheffield: Sheffield Academic Press, 2002).
—'Concluding Semi-Scientific Postscript', in Fontaine, *Smooth Words: Women, Proverbs and Performance in Biblical Wisdom*, pp. 263-71.
—'Strange Bed Fellows: Scriptures, Human Rights and the UU Seven Principles', *Journal of Liberal Religion* 4 (Winter, 2003); <http://www.meadville.edu/journal/2003_fontaine_4_1.pdf>
—'Watching out for the Watchmen (Song of Songs 5:7): How I Hold Myself Accountable', in Cosgrove (ed), *The Meanings We Choose: Hermeneutical Ethics, Indeterminacy and the Conflict of Interpretations*, pp. 102-21.
—'The Proof of the Pudding: Proverbs and Gender in the Performance Arena', *JSOT* 29 (2004), pp. 179-204.
—'Visual Metaphors and Proverbs 5:15-20: Some Archaeological Reflections on Gendered Iconography', in Troxel, Friebel and Margary (eds.), *Seeking out the Wisdom of the Ancients: Essays Offered to Honor Michael V. Fox, on the Occasion of his Sixty-Fifth Birthday*, pp. 185-202.
—'"Be Men, O Philistines!" (1 Sam 4:9): Iconographic Representations and Reflections on Female Gender as Disability in the Ancient World', in Avalos, Melcher, and Schipper (eds.), *This Abled Body: Rethinking Disabilities in Biblical Studies*, pp. 61-72.
Fortune, Marie, *Sexual Violence: The Unmentionable Sin* (New York: Pilgrim Press, 1983).
—*Keeping the Faith: Questions and Answers for the Abused Woman* (San Francisco: Harper & Row Publishers, 1987).
Fortune, Marie, 'Appendix B: Suggestions for Clergy and Laypersons', in Fortune, *Keeping the Faith: Questions and Answers for the Abused Woman*, pp. 81-85.
Foster, Benjamin R., *Before the Muses: An Anthology of Akkadian Literature. I. Archaic, Classical, Mature* (Bethesda, MD: CDL Press, 1993).

Foster, Benjamin R. (trans.), *From Distant Days: Myths, Tales and Poetry of Ancient Mesopotamia* (Bethesda, MD: CDL Press, 1995).
—'Story of the Flood' (Atrahasis Epic), in Foster, *From Distant Days: Myths, Tales and Poetry of Ancient Mesopotamia*, pp. 76-77.
Fox, Michael V., *Qoheleth and his Contradictions* (JSOTSup, 71; Bible and Literature, 18; Sheffield: Almond Press, 1989).
Fox, Michael V., and Bezalel Porten, 'Unsought Discoveries: Qoheleth 7:23–8:1a', *Hebrew Studies* 19 (1978), pp. 26-38.
Franke, Sabina, 'Kings of Akkad: Sargon and Naram-Sin', in Sasson (ed.), *CANE*, II, pp. 831-42.
Frankl, Viktor, *Man's Search for Meaning* (New York: Pocket Books, rev. and updated, 1984).
Frymer-Kensky, Tikva, *In the Wake of the Goddesses* (New York: Fawcett Columbine, 1992).
—'Virginity in the Bible', in Matthews, Levenson, and Frymer-Kensky (eds.), *Gender and Law in the Hebrew Bible and the Ancient Near East*, pp. 79-96.
Gibson, McGuire, *The City and Area of Kish* (Coconut Grove, FL: Field Research Projects, 1972).
Goldstein, Joshua S., *War and Gender: How Gender Shapes the War System and Vice Versa* (Cambridge: Cambridge University Press, 2001).
Goldwasser, Orly, 'The Narmer Palette and the Triumph of Metaphor', in *Lingua Aegyptia (JELS)* 2 (1992), pp. 67-85.
Good, Edwin M., 'Deception and Women: A Response', *Semeia* 42 (1988), pp. 117-32.
Goodman, Felicitas, *Where Spirits Ride the Wind: Trance Journeys and Other Ecstatic Experiences* (Bloomington: Indiana University Press, 1990).
Gordon, Pamela, and Harold C. Washington, 'Rape as a Military Metaphor in the Hebrew Bible', in Brenner and Fontaine (eds.), *A Feminist Companion to the Latter Prophets*, pp. 308-35.
Gottwald, Norman, *The Hebrew Bible: A Socio-literary Introduction* (Philadelphia: Fortress, 1985).
Grabbe, Lester L., *'Like a Bird in a Cage': The Invasion of Sennacherib in 701 BCE* (JSOTSup, 363; European Seminar in Historical Methodology; Sheffield: Sheffield Academic Press, 2003).
Green, Margaret W., 'The Eridu Lament', *JCS* 30 (1978), pp. 127-67.
Green, Miranda, *Celtic Goddesses: Warriors, Virgins and Mothers* (London: British Museum Press, 1995).
Greengus, Samuel, 'Some Issues Relating to the Comparability of Laws and the Coherence of the Legal Tradition', in Levinson (ed.), *Theory and Method in Biblical and Cuneiform Law: Revision, Interpolation and Development*, pp. 60-90.
—'Legal and Social Institutions of Ancient Mesopotamia', in Sasson (ed.), *CANE*, I (1995), pp. 469-84.
Grosz, Elizabeth, *Volatile Bodies: Toward a Corporeal Feminism* (Bloomington: Indiana University Press, 1994).
Gruber, Mayer I., 'Purity and Impurity in Halakic Sources and Qumran Law', in De Troyer *et al.* (eds.), *Wholly Woman, Holy Blood: A Feminist Critique of Purity and Impurity*, pp. 65-76.
Guest, Edgar, 'Home', in John Bartlett, *Bartlett's Familiar Quotations: A Collection of Passages, Phrases and Proverbs* (Boston: Little, Brown & Company, 14th edn and rev., 1968), p. 963.

Gurney, O.R., *The Hittites* (London: Penguin Books, rev. edn, 1981).
Güterbock, H.G., 'An Outline of the Hittite AN.TA.ŠUM Festival', *JNES* 19 (1960), pp. 80-86.
Habel, Norman C., 'Stewardship, Partnership and Kinship I', in Mortensen (ed.), *LWF Studies: A Just Asia*, pp. 45-74.
—'The Implications of God Discovering Wisdom in Earth', in van Wolde (ed.), *Job 28: Cognition in Context*, pp. 281-97.
Habel, Norman C., and Shirley Wurst (eds.), *The Earth Bible* (New York: Pilgrim Press with Sheffield Academic Press, 2001-2004).
— *The Earth Story in the Wisdom Traditions* (Earth Bible, 3; Sheffield: Sheffield Academic Press, 2001).
Hasan-Rokem, Galit, and Alan Dundes (eds.), *The Wandering Jew* (Bloomington: Indiana University Press, 1986).
Hassan, Farooq, Special UN Ambassador for the Family, 'Women in Islam: Distinction between Religious and Fundamentalist Approaches?' (2005), cited August 6, 2007 <http://www.greaterdemocracy.org/archives/000408.html>.
Hassan, Riffat, *Women's Rights and Islam: From the I.C.P.D. to Beijing* (Louisville, KY: NISA Publications, 1995).
—'Religious Human Rights and the Qur'an', in *Religious Human Rights in the World Today* (Emory International Law Review, 10; 1996), pp. 85-96.
—'Women in Muslim Culture', in Bryant (ed.), *Muslim–Christian Dialogue: Problems and Promise*, pp. 187-201.
—'The Issue of Woman–Man Equality in the Islamic Tradition', in Kvam, Schearing and Ziegler (eds.), *Eve and Adam: Jewish, Christian and Muslim Readings on Genesis and Gender*, pp. 463-76.
Hawkes, Terence, *Structuralism and Semiotics* (Berkeley: University of California Press, 1977).
Heidel, Alexander, *The Gilgamesh Epic and Old Testament Parallels* (Chicago: University of Chicago Press, 1946).
Helmick, Raymond G., SJ, and Rodney Petersen (eds.), *Forgiveness and Reconciliation: Religion, Public Policy, and Conflict Transformation, with a Foreword by Desmond Tutu* (Philadelphia: Templeton Foundation, 2001).
Herman, Judith L., *Trauma and Recovery: The Aftermath of Violence from Domestic Abuse to Political Terror* (New York: Basic Books, 1992).
Hersh, Seymour M., *Chain of Command: The Road from 9/11 to Abu Ghraib* (New York: HarperCollins Publishers, 2004).
Hoffner, Harry A., Jr., *Hittite Myths* (WAW, 2; Atlanta: Scholars Press, 2nd edn, 1998).
Hoffner, Harry A., Jr. (trans.), 'The El Kunirsha Myth Reconsidered', *RHA* 23 (1965), pp. 5-16.
Hoglund, Kenneth *et al.* (eds.), *The Listening Heart: Essays in Wisdom and the Psalms in Honor of Roland E. Murphy, O. Carm* (JSOTSup, 58; Sheffield: Sheffield Academic Press, 1987).
Hogue, Arthur R., *Origins of the Common Law* (Indianapolis, IN: Liberty Press, 1985).
Holladay, William L., *Long Ago God Spoke: How Christians May Hear the Old Testament Today* (Minneapolis: Augsburg Fortress, 1995).
Hollis, Susan Tower, 'The Woman in Ancient Examples of the Potiphar's Wife Motif, K2111', in Day (ed.), *Gender and Difference in Ancient Israel*, pp. 28-42.
— *The Ancient Egyptian 'Tale of Two Brothers': The Oldest Fairy Tale in the World* (Norman, OK: University of Oklahoma Press, 1990).

Holmes, Barbara A., and Susan R. Holmes, 'Sex, Stones, and Power Games: A Woman Caught at the Intersection of Law and Religion (John 7.53–8.11)', in Kirk-Duggan (ed.), *Pregnant Passion: Gender, Sex, and Violence in the Bible*, pp. 143-62.

Hoodfar, Homa, 'The Veil in their Minds and on our Heads: Veiling Practices and Muslim Women', in Castelli (ed.), *Women, Gender, Religion: A Reader*, pp. 420-46.

Hornung, Erik, and David Lorton (trans.), *The Ancient Egyptian Books of the Afterlife* (Ithaca, NY: Cornell University Press, 1998).

Hunt, Lynn (ed.), *The New Cultural History: Studies on the History of Society and Culture* (Berkeley: University of California Press, 1989).

Janzen, J. Gerald, *Job* (Interpretation, a Bible Commentary for Teaching and Preaching; Atlanta: John Knox Press, 1985).

Jeremias, Joachim, *New Testament: The Proclamation of Jesus* (New York: Scribner, 1971).

Jilani, Hina, 'Pakistan Women Killed in the Name of Honour' (September 21, 1999), cited February, 2008 <http://asiapacific.amnesty.org/library/Index/ENGAS A330201999?open&of=ENG-325>.

Kamaal, Niam, 'Sociolinguistic Study of the Role of Occupation in Women's Use of Proverbs' (PhD dissertation, University of Mosul, Iraq, 2001).

Kampen, Natalie Boymel (ed.), *Sexuality in Ancient Art: Near East, Egypt, Greece, and Italy* (Cambridge: Cambridge University Press, 1996).

Kane, John, 'American Values or Human Rights? U.S. Foreign Policy and the Fractured Myth of Virtuous Power', *Presidential Studies Quarterly* 33 (2003), pp. 772-800.

Kaplan, Ann E., 'Is the Gaze Male?', in Snitow, Stansell and Thompson (eds.), *Powers of Desire: The Politics of Sexuality*, pp. 309-27.

Katz, Steven T., *The Holocaust in Historical Context. I. The Holocaust and Mass Death before the Modern Age* (New York: Oxford University Press, 1994).

Keel, O., *The Song of Songs: A Continental Commentary* (trans. F.J. Gaiser; Minneapolis: Fortress Press, 1994).

Kellaway, Jean, *The History of Torture and Execution: From Early Civilization through Medieval Times to the Present* (Guildford, CT: Lyons Press, 2003).

Kellenbach, Katharina von, *Anti-Judaism in Feminist Religious Writings* (AAR Cultural Criticism Series, 1; Atlanta: Scholars Press, 1994).

Kimball, Charles, *When Religion Becomes Evil* (San Francisco: HarperCollins, 2002).

Kinnaer, Jacques, 'What is Really Known about the Narmer Palette?', *KMT* 15.1 (2004), pp. 48-54.

Kirk-Duggan, Cheryl A. (ed.), *Pregnant Passion: Gender, Sex, and Violence in the Bible* (Semeia Studies, 44; Atlanta: Scholars Press, 2003).

Kittell, Gerhard (ed.), *Theologisches Wörterbuch zum Neuen Testament* (Stuttgart: W. Kohlhammer, 1957; Grand Rapids, MI: Eerdmann Publishing, 1964).

Klein, Charlotte, *Anti-Judaism in Christian Theology* (trans. Edward Quinn; Philadelphia: Fortress Press, 1978).

Knobel, Peter S., *The Targum of Qohelet, translated with a Critical Introduction, Apparatus and Notes* (The Aramaic Bible, 15; Collegeville, MN: Liturgical Press, 1991).

Koester, Helmut, and Thomas O. Lambdin, 'The Gospel of Thomas (II, 2)', in Robinson (ed.), *The Nag Hammadi Library in English*, pp. 124-38.

Köhler, E. Christiana, 'History or Ideology? New Reflections on the Narmer Palette and the Nature of Foreign Relations in Pre- and Early Dynastic Egypt', in van den Brink and Levy (eds.), *Egypt and the Levant: Interrelations from the 4th through the Early 3rd Millennium BCE*, pp. 505-507.

Kramer, Heinrich, and James Sprenger, *The Malleus Maleficarum* (trans. with an introduction bibliography and notes by Montague Summers; New York: Dover Publications, 1971).

Kramer, S.N. (trans.), 'Lamentation over the Destruction of Sumer and Ur', in Pritchard (ed.), *ANET*, pp. 614-16.

Krüger, Thomas, '"Frau Weisheit" in Koh 7, 26?', *Biblica* 73 (1992), pp. 394-403.

Kuhrt, Amélie, 'Non-Royal Women in the Late Babylonian Period: A Survey', in Lesco (ed.), *Women's Earliest Records: From Ancient Egypt and Western Asia*, pp. 232-37.

Kvam, Kristen E., Linda S. Schearing and Valarie H. Ziegler (eds.), *Eve and Adam: Jewish, Christian and Muslim Readings on Genesis and Gender* (Indianapolis: Indiana University Press, 1999).

Lacocque, André, *Romance, She Wrote: A Hermeneutical Essay on Song of Songs* (Harrisburg, PA: Trinity Press International, 1998).

Lakoff, George, *Women, Fire and Dangerous Things: What Categories Reveal about the Mind* (Chicago: University of Chicago Press, 1987).

Lakoff, George, and Mark Johnson, *Metaphors We Live By, with a New Afterword* (Chicago: University of Chicago Press, 2003).

Laqueur, Thomas W., 'Bodies, Details, and the Humanitarian Narrative', in Hunt (ed.), *The New Cultural History: Studies on the History of Society and Culture*, pp. 176-204.

Laurant, Sophie, 'Megiddo: Questions sur le Royaume de Salomon', *La Monde de la Bible* 180 (Nov-Dec, 2007), pp. 30-33.

Leick, Gwendolyn, *A Dictionary of Ancient Near Eastern Mythology* (London and New York: Routledge, 1991).

Lemche, Niels Peter, *The Israelites in History and Tradition* (Louisville, KY: Westminster/John Knox Press, 1998).

Lemos, T.M., 'Shame and Mutilation of Enemies in the Hebrew Bible', *JBL* 125 (2006), pp. 225-41.

Lerner, Gerda, *The Creation of Patriarchy* (New York: Oxford University Press, 1986).

Lesco, Barbara S. (ed.), *Women's Earliest Records: From Ancient Egypt and Western Asia* (BJS, 166; Atlanta: Scholars Press, 1989).

Lesko, Leonard H., 'Death and the Afterlife in Ancient Egyptian Thought', in Sasson (ed.), *CANE*, III, pp. 1763-74.

Lessa, William A., and Evon Z. Vogt (eds.), *Reader in Comparative Religion: An Anthropological Approach* (New York: Harper & Row, 3rd edn, 1965).

Levack, Brian P. (ed.), *Articles on Witchcraft, Magic and Demonology: A Twelve Volume Anthology of Scholarly Articles. X. Witchcraft, Women and Society* (New York: Garland Publishing, 1992).

Levenson, Jon, 'Is There a Counterpart in the Hebrew Bible to New Testament Anti-Semitism?', *JES* 22 (1985), pp. 242-60.

Levine, A.-J., 'Second Temple Judaism, Jesus, and Women: Yeast of Eden', in Brenner (ed.), *A Feminist Companion to the Hebrew Bible in the New Testament*, pp. 302-31.

Levine, A.-J. (ed.), *'Women like This': New Perspectives on Jewish Women in the Greco-Roman World* (SBL Early Judaism and its Literature, I; Atlanta: Scholars Press, 1991).

Levinson, Bernard M. (ed.), *Theory and Method in Biblical and Cuneiform Law: Revi-*

sion, Interpolation and Development (JSOTSup, 181; Sheffield: Sheffield Academic Press, 1994).

Levy, Thomas E., Edwin C.M. van den Brink, Yuval Goren, and David Alon, 'New Light on King Narmer and the Protodynastic Egyptian Presence in Canaan', *BA* 58 (1995), pp. 26-35.

Levy, Thomas E. and Edwin C.M. van den Brink, 'Interaction Models, Egypt and the Levantine Periphery', in van den Brink and Levy (eds.), *Egypt and the Levant: Interrelations from the 4th through the Early 3rd Millennium BCE* (London: Leicester University Press, 2002), pp. 3-38.

Lewis, C.S., *The Screwtape Letters and Screwtape Proposes a Toast* (New York: Macmillan, 1966).

Lewis, Claudia, 'Requiem for a Jew', *Tikkun* 11 (1996), pp. 77-79.

Lichtheim, Miriam, *Ancient Egyptian Literature: A Book of Readings*. I. *The Old and Middle Kingdoms* (Berkeley: University of California, 1975).

Lincoln, Bruce, 'From Artaxerxes to Abu Ghraib: On Religion and the Pornography of Imperial Violence', Religion and Culture Web Forum (January 2007).

Lorton, David, 'Legal and Social Institutions of Pharaonic Egypt', in Sasson (ed.), *CANE*, I (1995), pp. 345-62.

Luther, Martin, *Luther's Works* (ed. Jaroslav Pelikan; 30 vols.; St Louis: Concordia, 1955–1971).

MacKay, Ernest, *Report on the Excavation of the 'A' Cemetery at Kish, Mesopotamia* (Anthropology Memoirs; Chicago: Field Museum of Natural History, 1925).

McGreal, Chris, 'Murdered in the Name of Family Honour' (June 23, 2005), cited March 5, 2008 <http://www.guardian.co.uk/world/2005/jun/23/israel>.

McKay, Heather, 'On the Future of Feminist Biblical Criticism', in Brenner and Fontaine (eds.), *A Feminist Companion to Reading the Bible: Approaches, Methods, Strategies (Second Series)*, pp. 61-83.

Magdalene, F. Rachel, 'Ancient Near Eastern Treaty–Curses and the Ultimate Texts of Terror: A Study of the Language of Divine Sexual Abuse in the Prophetic Corpus', in Brenner and Fontaine (eds.), *A Feminist Companion to the Latter Prophets*, pp. 326-53.

—'Job's Wife as Hero: A Feminist-Forensic Reading of the Book of Job', *Biblical Interpretation* 14 (2006), pp. 209-49.

Maier, Walter A., III, *'Ašerah: Extrabiblical Evidence* (HSM, 37; Atlanta: Scholars Press, 1986).

Malti-Douglas, Fedwa, *Woman's Body, Woman's Word: Gender and Discourse in Arabo-Islamic Writing* (Princeton, NJ: Princeton University Press, 1991).

Marty, Martin E., 'Religious Dimensions of Human Rights', in Witte, Jr and van der Vyver (eds.), *Religious Human Rights in Global Perspective: Religious Perspectives*, pp. 1-16.

Matthews, Victor H., 'Honor and Shame in Gender-Related Legal Situations in the Hebrew Bible', in Matthews, Levinson, and Frymer-Kensky (eds.), *Gender and Law in the Hebrew Bible and the Ancient Near East*, pp. 97-112.

Matthews, Victor H., Don C. Benjamin and Claudia V. Camp. (eds.), *Honor and Shame in the World of the Bible* (Semeia, 68; Atlanta: Scholars Press, 1994).

Matthews, Victor H., Bernard M. Levinson and Tikva Frymer-Kensky (eds.), *Gender and Law in the Hebrew Bible and the Ancient Near East* (JSOTSup, 262; Sheffield: Sheffield Academic Press, 1998).

Mayer, Ann Elizabeth, *Islam and Human Rights: Tradition and Politics* (Boulder, CO: Westview Press, 4th edn, 2007).

Mernissi, Fatima, *The Veil and the Male Elite: A Feminist Interpretation of Women's Rights in Islam* (trans. Mary Jo Lakeland; New York: Perseus/Basic Books, 1991).
Meshel, Ze'ev, 'Did Yahweh Have a Consort?', *BARev* 5 (1979), pp. 24-35.
Metzger, Bruce M., and Michael D. Coogan (eds.), *Oxford Companion to the Bible* (New York: Oxford University Press, 1993).
Meyers, Carol, 'The Family in Early Israel', in Perdue *et al.*, *Families in Ancient Israel*, pp. 1-47.
Michalowski, Piotr, *The Lamentation over the Destruction of Sumer and Ur* (Mesopotamian Civilizations, 1; Winona Lake, IN: Eisenbrauns, 1989).
Midelfort, H.C. Erik, 'Witchcraft and Religion in Sixteenth-Century Germany: The Formation and Consequences of an Orthodoxy', *Archiv für Reformationsgeschichte* 62 (1971), pp. 266-78.
Miller, Patrick D., Jr, 'El, the Creator of Earth', *BASOR* 239 (1980), pp. 43-46.
—*They Cried to the Lord: The Form and Theology of Biblical Prayer* (Minneapolis: Fortress Press, 1994).
Millet, Nicholas B., 'The Narmer Macehead and Related Objects', *JARCE* 27 (1990), pp. 53-59.
Miroschedji, Pierre de, 'The Socio-Political Dynamics of Egyptian-Canaanite Interaction in the Early Bronze Age', in van den Brink and Levy (eds.), *Egypt and the Levant: Interrelations from the 4th through the Early 3rd Millennium BCE*, pp. 39-57.
Moghissi, Haideh, *Feminism and Islamic Fundamentalism: The Limits of Postmodern Analysis* (London: Zed Books, 1999).
Mohaddessin, Mohammad, *Enemies of the Ayatollahs: The Iranian Opposition's War on Islamic Fundamentalism* (London: Zed Books, 2004).
Moore, George Foot, 'Christian Writers on Judaism', *HTR* 14 (1921), pp. 197-254.
Morton, Donald, and Mas'ud Zavarzadeh (eds.), *Theory/Pedagogy/Politics: Texts for Change* (Chicago: University of Illinois Press, 1991).
Mosala, Itumelang J., 'The Use of the Bible in Black Theology', in Mosala and Tlhagale (eds.), *The Unquestionable Right to Be Free: Black Theology from South Africa*, pp. 175-99.
Mosala, Itumelang J., and Buti Tlhagale (eds.), *The Unquestionable Right to Be Free: Black Theology from South Africa* (Maryknoll, NY: Orbis Books, 1986).
Murphy, Roland E., O. Carm., *The Song of Songs: A Commentary on the Book of Canticles or the Song of Songs* (Hermeneia; Minneapolis: Fortress Press, 1990).
—*Ecclesiastes* (WBC, 23A; Dallas, TX: Word Books, 1992).
Nafisi, Azar, *Reading Lolita in Tehran: A Memoir in Books* (New York: Random House, 2003).
Nathanson, Barbara Geller, 'Reflections on the Silent Woman of Ancient Judaism and her Pagan Roman Counterpart', in Hoglund *et al.* (eds.), *The Listening Heart: Essays in Wisdom and the Psalms in Honor of Roland E. Murphy, O. Carm*, pp. 259-80.
—'Toward a Multicultural Ecumenical History of Women in the First Century/ies C.E.', in Schüssler Fiorenza (ed.) *Searching the Scriptures*, I, pp. 272-89.
Nave, Guy D. Jr, 'No Pax Romana: A Lukan Rejection of Imperial Peace', *Theologies and Cultures: Church and Empire* 2 (2005), pp. 56-72.
Newsom, Carol, 'Woman and the Discourse of Patriarchal Wisdom: A Study of Proverbs 1–9', in Day (ed.), *Gender and Difference in Ancient Israel*, pp. 142-60.
—'The Character of Pain: Job in Light of Elaine Scarry's *The Body in Pain*' (paper presented at the Annual Meeting of the SBL, Orlando, FL, 23 November 1998).

Newsom, Carol and Sharon Ringe (eds.), *The Women's Bible Commentary* (Louisville, KY: Westminster/John Knox Press, 1992).
Niditch, Susan, *War in the Hebrew Bible: A Study in the Ethics of Violence* (New York: Oxford University Press, 1993).
Niditch, Susan (ed.), *Text and Tradition: The Hebrew Bible and Folklore* (Semeia Studies; Atlanta: Scholars Press, 1990).
Noth, Martin, *The History of Israel* (New York: HarperCollins College Division, 2nd edn, 1960).
O'Connor, David, 'Context, Function and Program: Understanding Ceremonial Slate Palettes', *JARCE* 39 (2004), pp. 5-25.
—'Narmer's Enigmatic Palette', *Archaeology Odyssey* (September–October, 2004), pp. 16-52.
O'Day, Gail R., 'John 7.53–8.11: A Study in Misreading', *JBL* 111 (1992), pp. 631-40.
Oepke, George, 'Der Dienst der Frau in der urchristlichen Gemeinde', *Neue allgemeine Missionszeitschrift* 16 (1939), pp. 39-53.
Ogden, Graham, *Qoheleth* (Readings; Sheffield: JSOT Press, 1987).
Olson, Carl (ed.), *The Book of the Goddess: Past and Present* (New York: Crossroad, 1985).
Olyan, Saul M., *Asherah and the Cult of Yahweh in Israel* (SBLMS, 34; Atlanta: Scholars Press, 1988).
Oppenheim, A. Leo (trans.), 'Babylonian and Assyrian Historical Texts', in Pritchard, *ANET* (1969), pp. 265-317.
Ostriker, Alicia, 'A Holy of Holies: The Song of Songs as Countertext', in Brenner and Fontaine (eds.), *The Song of Songs: A Feminist Companion to the Bible (Second Series)*, pp. 36-54.
Otten, H., 'Ein kanaanäischer Mythus aus Bogaszköy', *MIO* 1 (1953), pp. 125-50.
Parpola, Simo, and R.M. Whiting (eds.), *Sex and Gender in the Ancient Near East* (Proceedings of the 47th Rencontre Assyriologique Internationale, Helsinki, July 2-6, 2001; University of Helsinki: Neo-Assyrian Text Corpus Project, 2002).
Patte, Daniel, *Ethics of Biblical Interpretation: A Reevaluation* (Louisville, KY: Westminster/John Knox Press, 1995).
Pelikan, Jaroslav (ed.), *Luther's Works* (30 vols.; St. Louis: Concordia, 1955–1971).
Perdue, Leo G., Joseph Blenkinsopp, John J. Collins, and Carol Meyers, *Families in Ancient Israel* (Louisville, KY: Westminster/John Knox Press, 1997).
Perry, Michael J., *The Idea of Human Rights: Four Inquiries* (Oxford: Oxford University Press, 1998).
Perry, T.A., *Dialogues with Koheleth: The Book of Ecclesiastes* (University Park, PA: Pennsylvania State University Press, 1993).
Phillips, John A., *Eve: The History of an Idea* (San Francisco: Harper & Row, 1984).
Pilch, John J., 'Family Violence in Cross-Cultural Perspective: An Approach for Feminist Interpreters of the Bible', in Brenner and Fontaine (eds.), *A Feminist Companion to Reading the Bible: Approaches, Methods, Strategies (Second Series)*, pp. 306-25.
Pizzuto, Vincent, 'Religious Terror and the Prophetic Voice of Reason: Unmasking our Myths of Righteousness', *BTB* 37 (2007), pp. 47-53.
Plaskow, Judith, 'Blaming Jews for Inventing Patriarchy', *Lilith* 7 (1979), pp. 9-11, 14-17.
—'Feminist Anti-Judaism and the Christian God', *JFS* 7 (1991), pp. 99-109.
—'Anti-Judaism in Feminist Christian Interpretation', in Schüssler Fiorenza (ed.), *Searching the Scriptures*, I, pp. 117-29.

Plaskow, Judith and Carol P. Christ (eds.), *Weaving the Visions: New Patterns in Feminist Spirituality* (San Francisco: Harper, 1989).
Pollock, Susan and Reinhard Bernbeck, 'And They Said, Let Us Make Gods in our Image: Gendered Ideologies in Ancient Mesopotamia', in Rautman, *Reading the Body: Representations and Remains in the Archaeological Record*, pp. 150-64.
Pomeroy, Sarah B., *Goddesses, Whores, Wives, and Slaves: Women in Classical Antiquity* (New York: Schocken Books, 1975).
—*Women in Hellenistic Egypt from Alexander to Cleopatra* (New York: Schocken Books, 1984).
Pope, Marvin, *Song of Songs* (AB; Garden City, New York: Doubleday, 1977).
Price, Janet and Margrit Shildrick (eds.), *Feminist Theory and the Body: A Reader* (New York: Routledge, 1999).
Pritchard, James B. (ed.), *The Ancient Near East in Pictures Relating to the Old Testament* (Princeton, NJ: Princeton University Press, 2nd edn, 1974).
—*Ancient Near Eastern Texts Relating to the Old Testament* (Princeton, NJ: Princeton University Press, 3rd edn, 1969).
Propp, Vladimir, *Morphology of the Folktale* (Publications of the American Folklore Society, 9; Austin: University of Texas Press, 1968).
Puar, Jashir K., 'Abu Ghraib: Arguing against Exceptionalism', *Feminist Studies* 30.2 (Summer, 2004), pp. 522-34.
Pui-Lan, Kwok, 'Racism and Ethnocentrism in Feminist Biblical Interpretation', in Schüssler Fiorenza (ed.), *Searching the Scriptures: A Feminist Introduction*, I, pp. 101-16.
Rajavi, Maryam, *Islamic Fundamentalism and the Question of Women* (Auvers-sur-Oise: Women's Committee of the National Conference of Resistance of Iran, 2004).
Randall, Dudley (ed.), *The Black Poets* (New York: Bantam, 1971).
Rappoport, Angelo S., *Myth and Legend of Ancient Israel*, III (New York: Ktav, 1966).
Rautman, Alison E. (ed.), *Reading the Body: Representations and Remains in the Archaeological Record* (Philadelphia: University of Pennsylvania Press, 2000).
Raza, Raheel, *Their Jihad is Not my Jihad: A Muslim Canadian Woman Speaks out* (Ingersoll, Ontario: Basileia Books, 2005).
Reed, Betsey (ed.), with intro. by Katha Pollitt, *Nothing Sacred: Women Respond to Religious Fundamentalism and Terror* (New York: Thunder's Mouth Press/Nation Books, 2002).
Rich, Sara, 'A Moment of Silence is Not Enough', cited September 7, 2007 <http://www.truthout.org/docs_2006/090707A.shtml>.
Rigby, Cynthia L. (ed.), *Power, Powerlessness, and the Divine: New Inquiries in Bible and Theology* (Scholars Press Studies in Theological Education; Atlanta: Scholars Press, 1997).
Riggs, Ann K., 'Inculturation: Building on the Cultures of our Past', in Enns, Holland and Riggs (eds.), *Seeking Cultures of Peace: A Peace Church Conversation*, pp. 97-108.
Ritner, Robert K., 'Book of the Dead 125: "The Negative Confession" ', in Simpson, *LAE*, pp. 267-77.
Riverbend, *Baghdad Burning: Girl Blogger from Iraq* (New York: Feminist Press at CUNY, 2005); for more see <http://riverbend.blogspot.com/>.
Robins, Gay, *Women in Ancient Egypt* (Cambridge, MA: Harvard University Press, 1993).
Robinson, James M. (ed.), *The Nag Hammadi Library in English* (San Francisco: Harper & Row, 1977).

Roth, Martha T., *Law Collections from Mesopotamia and Asia Minor* (WAW, 6; Atlanta: Scholars Press, 2nd edn, 1997).
Ruether, Rosemary, *Faith and Fratricide: The Theological Roots of Anti-Semitism* (New York: Seabury Press, 1974).
Russell, Letty M. (ed.), *Feminist Interpretation of the Bible* (Philadelphia: Westminster Press, 1985).
Sanders, E.P., *Paul and Palestinian Judaism* (Philadelphia: Fortress Press, 1977).
Sasson, Jack M., *Civilizations of the Ancient Near East* (4 vols.; New York: Scribner, 1995).
Satrapi, Marjane, *Persepolis: The Story of a Childhood* (New York: Pantheon Books, 2003).
—*Persepolis 2: The Story of a Return* (New York: Pantheon Books, 2004).
Savran, George, ' "How Can We Sing a Song of the Lord?": The Strategy of Lament in Psalm 137', *ZAW* 112 (2000), pp. 43-58.
Scarry, Elaine, *The Body in Pain: The Making and Unmaking of the World* (Oxford: Oxford University Press, 1985).
Schmitt, J.J., 'Like Eve, like Adam: *mšl* in Gen 3, 16', *Biblica* 72 (1991), pp. 1-22.
Schneider, Matthew, 'Writing in the Dust: Irony and Lynch-Law in the Gospel of John', *Anthropoetics* 3 (Spring/Summer 1997), cited June 8, 2007 <http://www.anthropoetics.ucla.edu/Ap0301/Dust.htm>.
Schottroff, Luise, *Lydia's Impatient Sisters: A Feminist Social History of Early Christianity* (trans. Barbara and Martin Rumscheidt; Louisville, KY: Westminster/John Knox Press, 1991).
Schüssler Fiorenza, Elisabeth, *In Memory of Her: A Feminist Theological Reconstruction of Christian Origins* (New York: Crossroad, 1983).
—*Searching the Scriptures: A Feminist Introduction* (2 vols.; New York: Crossroad, 1993-1994).
Seitel, Peter, *The Powers of Genre: Interpreting Haya Oral Literature* (Oxford Studies in Anthropological Linguistics 22; New York: Oxford University Press, 1999).
Seligman, Adam B. (ed.), *Religion and Human Rights: Conflict or Convergence* (Interreligious Center on Public Life; Hollis, NH: Hollis Publishing, 2004).
Setel, T. Drorah, 'Prophets and Pornography: Female Sexual Imagery in Hosea', in Russell (ed.), *Feminist Interpretation of the Bible*, pp. 86-95.
Sharma, Arvind, and Katherine K. Young (eds.), *Through her Eyes: Women's Perspectives on World Religions* (Boulder, CO: Westview Press, 1999).
Simon, Maurice (trans.), *The Soncino Talmud: Berakhot* (London: Soncino Press, 1948).
—*The Soncino Talmud: Gittin* (London: Soncino Press, 1936).
Simpson, W.K. (ed.), *The Literature of Ancient Egypt: An Anthology of Stories, Instructions, Stelae, Autobiographies, and Poetry* (New Haven: Yale University Press, 3rd edn, 2003).
—'The Contendings of Horus and Seth', in Simpson (ed.), *LAE*, pp. 91-103.
—'The Maxims of Ptahhotep', in Simpson (ed.), *LAE*, pp. 129-48.
—'King Cheops and the Magicians', in Simpson (ed.), *LAE*, pp. 13-24.
Slotki, Israel W. (trans.), *The Soncino Talmud: Yebamot*, I (London: Soncino Press, 1936).
Smalley, Beryl, *Medieval Exegesis of Wisdom Literature* (ed. Roland E. Murphy; Atlanta: Scholars Press, 1986).
Snitow, Ann, Christine Stansell and Sharon Thompson (eds.), *Powers of Desire: The Politics of Sexuality* (New York: Monthly Review Press, 1983).

Speiser, E.A., 'The Epic of Gilgamesh', in Pritchard, *ANET* (1969), pp. 72-99.
Stanley, Jean-Daniel, 'Configuration of the Egypt-to-Canaan Coastal Margin and the North Sinai Byway in the Bronze Age', in van den Brink and Levy (eds.), *Egypt and the Levant: Interrelations from the 4th through the Early 3rd Millennium BCE*, pp. 98-117.
Stendahl, Krister, 'Biblical Theology, Contemporary', in Buttrick (ed.), *The Interpreter's Dictionary of the Bible: An Illustrated Encyclopedia*, I, pp. 418-32.
—'Anti-Semitism', in Metzger and Coogan (eds.), *Oxford Companion to the Bible*, pp. 32-34.
Sterba, James P., *Three Challenges to Ethics: Environmentalism, Feminism, and Multiculturalism* (Oxford: Oxford University Press, 2001).
Stoning Video, cited August 21, 2007 <http://farkous.blog.ca/2007/05/17/stoning~2289644>.
Sugirtharajah, R.S. (ed.), *The Postcolonial Bible* (The Bible and Postcolonialism Series, 1; Sheffield: Sheffield Academic Press, 1998).
Sunder, Madhavi, 'A Culture of One's Own: Learning from Women Living under Muslim Laws', in Reed (ed.), *Nothing Sacred: Women Respond to Religious Fundamentalism and Terror*, pp. 149-63.
Tamez, Elsa, *Bible of the Oppressed* (Maryknoll, NY: Orbis Books, 1982).
Thistlethwaite, Susan Brooks, 'Every Two Minutes: Battered Women and Feminist Interpretation', in Russell (ed.), *Feminist Interpretation of the Bible*, pp. 96-110.
—*Sex, Race, and God: Christian Feminism in Black and White* (New York: Crossroad, 1989).
—'"You May Enjoy the Spoil of your Enemies": Rape as a Biblical Metaphor for War', in Camp and Fontaine (eds.), *Women, War and Metaphor: Language and Society in the Study of the Hebrew Bible*, pp. 59-78.
Tigay, Jeffrey, *The Evolution of the Gilgamesh Epic* (Philadelphia: University of Pennsylvania, 1982).
Torjesen, Karen Jo, *When Women Were Priests: Women's Leadership in the Early Church and the Scandal of their Subordination in the Rise of Christianity* (San Francisco: Harper, 1993).
Trachtenberg, Joshua, *The Devil and the Jews: The Medieval Conception of the Jew and its Relation to Modern AntiSemitism* (New Haven: Yale University Press, 1943).
Tracy, David, *The Analogical Imagination: Christian Theology and the Culture of Pluralism* (New York: Crossroad, 1981).
Traer, Robert, *Faith in Human Rights: Support in Religious Traditions for a Global Struggle* (Washington, DC: Georgetown University Press, 1991).
Trenchard, Luise, *Ben Sira's View of Women: A Literary Analysis* (BJS, 38; Chico, CA: Scholars Press, 1982).
Trible, Phyllis, *Texts of Terror: Literary-Feminist Readings of Biblical Narratives* (OBT; Philadelphia: Fortress Press, 1984).
Troxel, Ronald L., Kelvin G. Friebel and Dennis R. Margary (eds.), *Seeking out the Wisdom of the Ancients: Essays Offered to Honor Michael V. Fox, on the Occasion of his Sixty-Fifth Birthday* (Winona Lake, IN: Eisenbrauns, 2005).
Uehlinger, Christoph, 'Clio in a World of Pictures—Another Look at the Lachish Reliefs from Sennacherib's Southwest Palace at Nineveh', in Grabbe, *'Like a Bird in a Cage': The Invasion of Sennacherib in 701 BCE*, pp. 221-307.
Umansky, Ellen M., 'Creating a Jewish Feminist Theology: Possibilities and Problems', in Plaskow and Christ (eds.), *Weaving the Visions: New Patterns in Feminist Spirituality*, pp. 187-98.

UN Doc. E/CN.4/2004/66; §55 (b) (2003), 'Integration of the Human Rights of Women and the Gender Perspective: Violence against Women', cited September 26, 2007 <http://www.unhchr.ch/Huridocda/Huridoca.nsf/TestFrame/b0ec728d91b871d8c1256e610040591e>.

UN Doc. A/CONF.157/PC/62/Add.18 (1993), 'Cairo Declaration on Human Rights in Islam' (August 5, 1990), U.N. GAOR, World Conference on Human Rights, 4th Session, Agenda Item 5, original cited September 26, 2007 <http://www1.umn.edu/humanrts/instree/cairodeclaration.html>.

UN statement on honor killings, cited September 26, 2007 <http://www.wunrn.com/reference/crimes_honor.htm>.

United Nations Economic and Social Commission for Asia and the Pacific, 'Hidden Sisters: Women and Girls with Disabilities in the Asian and Pacific Region' (Population and Social Integration section; Bangkok, Thailand, 2006), cited September, 2007 <http://www.unescap.org/esid/psis/disability/decade/publications/wwd1.asp>.

van den Brink, Edwin C.M., and Thomas E. Levy (eds.), *Egypt and the Levant: Interrelations from the 4th through the Early 3rd Millennium BCE* (London: Leicester University Press, 2002).

Wadud, Amina, *Inside the Gender Jihad: Women's Reform in Islam* (Oxford: Oneworld Publications, 2006).

Wallis, Jim, *God's Politics: Why the Right Gets It Wrong and the Left Doesn't Get It* (San Francisco: HarperOne, 2005).

Walsh, Cary Ellen, *Exquisite Desire: Religion, the Erotic, and the Song of Songs* (Minneapolis: Fortress Press, 2000).

Wantchekon, Leonard and Andrew Healy, 'The "Game" of Torture', *Journal of Conflict Resolution* 43 (1999), pp. 596-609.

Waskow, Arthur, 'Falluja is the Birthplace of the Talmud' (December 1, 2004), cited February 2008 <http://www.shalomctr.org/node/729>.

Watelin, L.Ch. and Stephen Langdon, *Excavations at Kish* (Field Museum, Oxford University Joint Expedition to Mesopotamia; Paris: Librairie Orientaliste Paul Geuthner, 1930).

Watson, Alan, 'Jesus and the Adulteress', *Biblica* 80 (1999), pp. 100-108.

Watt, W. Montgomery, *Muhammad: Prophet and Statesman* (Oxford: Oxford University Press, 1961).

Weedon, Chris, 'Post-structuralist Feminist Practice', in Morton and Zavarzadeh (eds.), *Theory/Pedagogy/Politics: Texts for Change*, pp. 47-63.

Weems, Renita J., *Battered Love: Marriage, Sex, and Violence in the Hebrew Prophets* (OBT; Minneapolis: Augsburg-Fortress, 1995).

Westermann, Claus, *The Old Testament and Jesus Christ* (trans. Omar Kaste; Minneapolis: Augsburg Press, 1970).

—*Genesis 1–11: A Commentary* (trans. John J. Scullion; Minneapolis: Augsburg Publishing, 1984).

—*Die Klagelieder* (Neukirchen–Vluyn: Neukirchener Verlag, 1990).

—'Beauty in the Hebrew Bible', Üte Oestringer and Carole R. Fontaine (trans.), in Brenner and Fontaine (eds.), *A Feminist Companion to Reading the Bible: Approaches, Methods, Strategies (Second Series)*, pp. 584-602.

White, Randall, *Prehistoric Art: The Symbolic Journey of Humankind* (New York: Harry Abrams, 2003).

Whybray, R.N., *Ecclesiastes* (Old Testament Guides; Sheffield: JSOT Press, 1989).

Whyte, M.T., *The Status of Women in Preindustrial Societies* (Princeton: Princeton University Press, 1978).
Wikipedia contributors, 'Crime against Humanity', Wikipedia, The Free Encyclopedia, cited August 6, 2007 <http://en.wikipedia.org/w/index.php?title=Crime_against_humanity&oldid=36696265>.
—'Habeas Corpus', Wikipedia, The Free Encyclopedia, cited January 14, 2008 <http://en.wikipedia.org/wiki/Habeas_corpus>.
—'Peremptory Norm', Wikipedia, The Free Encyclopedia, cited August 6, 2007 <http://en.wikipedia.org/w/index.php?title=Peremptory_norm&oldid=35680056>.
Wilckens, Robert (ed.), *Aspects of Wisdom in Judaism and Early Christianity* (Notre Dame: Notre Dame University Press, 1975).
Wilkinson, Richard H., *Symbol and Magic in Egyptian Art* (London: Thames & Hudson, 1999).
Wilson, John A. (trans.), 'Campaign of Seti I in Asia', in Pritchard, *ANET* (1969), pp. 254-55.
Winter, Irene J., 'Sex, Rhetoric, and the Public Monument: The Alluring Body of Naram-Sin of Agade', in Kampen (ed.), *Sexuality in Ancient Art: Near East, Egypt, Greece, and Italy*, pp. 11-36.
Winter, M.T., *Woman Prayer, Woman Song: Resources for Ritual* (Oak Park, IL: Meyer-Stone Books, 1987).
Witte, John, Jr, and Johan D. van der Vyver (eds.), *Religious Human Rights in Global Perspective: Religious Perspectives* (The Hague: Martinus Nijhoff Publishers, 1996).
Wolde, Ellen van (ed.), *Job 28: Cognition in Context* (BIS, 64; Leiden: E.J. Brill, 2003).
Women's United Nations Report Network (WUNRN), Resources on Honor Killings and Human Rights, cited September 26, 2007 <http://www.soas.ac.uk/honourcrimes/Directory_Contents.htm>.
—Special Rapporteur Asma Jahangir's report 'Civil and Political Rights, Including the Question of Disappearances and Summary Executions: Extrajudicial, Summary or Arbitrary Executions', cited September 26, 2007 <http://www.wunrn.com/research/factual_aspects/stories/04-20-04ReportUNHRCommis04full.htm> para. 66-71, para. 96.
Woolman, John, *Considerations on Keeping Negroes (Part 2), 1762* (New York: Grossman Publishers, 1976).
WorldWar4Report, 'Iraq: Yazidi Workers Massacred in Mosul', cited September 27, 2007 <http://ww4report.com/node/3681>.
—'Another Account from Issam Shukri', posted May 3, 2007; cited September 27, 2007 <http://ww4report.com/node/3681>.
Wyke, Maria (ed.), *Gender and the Body in the Ancient Mediterranean* (Oxford: Blackwell Publishers, 1998).
Young, Brad H., '"Save the Adulteress!": Ancient Jewish Responsa in the Gospels?', *NTS* 41 (1995), pp. 59-70.
Young, Jeremy, *The Violence of God and the War on Terror* (London: Darton, Longman & Todd, 2007).
Zilboorg, Gregory, *The Medical Man and the Witch during the Renaissance* (The Hideyo Noguchi Lectures; Publications of the Institute of the History of Medicine, the Johns Hopkins University, 3/2, 1935; repr., New York: Cooper Square Publishers, 1969).

Zina Ordinance, 'Pakistan: Insufficient Protection of Women', cited February, 2008 <http://www.amnesty.org/en/library/info/ASA33/006/2002>,'Legal Reform' §2.5.

Zornberg, Avivah, *The Beginning of Desire: Reflections on Genesis* (New York: Doubleday, 1996).

INDEXES

INDEX OF REFERENCES

OLD TESTAMENT

Genesis		15.1b-3	161	Deuteronomy	
1.27	26, 198	15.3	32	5.15	17 n. 35
1.31	26	21.7-8	71 n. 74	15.7-11	17 n. 35
1–11	193, 196	21.20-21	85	15.12-18	17 n. 35
3.16b	173	21.22-23	85	21.10-14	17, 69
3.22	198	21.24	84	22.13-21	76 n. 82, 85
4.1	77 n. 86	21.26-27	32 n. 4, 85		
4.10-11	4	22.4	110	22.22-24	84
14.19	231 n. 28	22.7	110	22.23-29	164, 226
17	106	22.9	110	22.25	84
19.30-38	171	22.20-24	111	23.15-16	85
19.32	226	22.21	112	23.15-17	17 n. 35
22	150	22.22-25	112	25.12	84
24.65	253	23.1-2	112		
27	194 n. 38	23.4-5	112	Judges	
28	106	23.9	112	1.6	58 n. 50
30.2	170 n. 56	23.11	112	5	64 n. 62, 67
34.1-2	226				
35	106	Leviticus		5.29-30	68
37.7	225	19	xix, xxiii	11.30-31	171
37.12	225	19.16	27, 251 n. 59	11.35	171
37.14	225			14–16	171
38.11	168	19.20-22	85	19	68, 125, 150, 217
38.14	253	20	84, 264		
38.16	171, 225	20.18	84 n. 22	19–21	215, 217
38.19	253	21.20	5	20.48	68
38.24	171	25.45-46	85	21.19-22	68
38.26	260				
39	228, 230, 237, 240	Numbers		1 Samuel	
		5	xxi, 39, 275, 276	2.5-6	161
40	90 n. 31			4.9	185 n. 11
49	106	5.11-13	255	5.4	90 n. 32
		5.14	255	9	194 n. 38
Exodus		25.14	70 n. 73	10.27–11.11	91
4.9	166	25.26-28	70 n. 73	11.2	91
7.17-21	166	31.6-18	56		

14–15	102		103, 110,	27.15-16	191
17.51	90 n. 32		111	30.20	191
21.9	90 n. 32	31.5	112	30.21-23	192
		31.9-10	111	31	60 n. 51,
2 Samuel		31.13-15	114		182, 206
4	89	31.16-22	111	31.2-3	192
4.12	90 n. 32	31.26-28	112	31.10	190
6.20-23	150	31.29-30	112		
11.2	171	31.32	112	*Qoheleth*	
13	150, 171	31.38-40	112	1.4-7	188
13.3	260	38.1	110	1.9	195 n. 42
13.11	226	38–42	177	1.12	193 n. 35
13.15	171	42.10	110	2.4-10	188
16.21-22	260			2.8	196 n. 48
16.23	260	*Psalms*		2.16	207
18	90	45	163	7	192, 203,
20	89	45.10-11	163		206
22	111 n. 64	62.8-10	103	7.23-24	197, 207
		68	111 n. 64	7.23-29	189
1 Kings		85.10-11	xxiii	7.23–8.1	190, 195
5.13-18	171	97	111 n. 64	7.23–8.1a	184, 185
11	189 n. 25	104	111 n. 64	7.24	186
11.1-6	172	121.4	191 n. 28	7.25	189
		137	93, 270	7.25b	186
2 Chronicles				7.25–8.1a	186
35.25	96 n. 42	*Proverbs*		7.26	187
		1–9	182	7.27	186, 193,
Esther		5.3	191		195
1	150	5.18	190	7.27-28	194
1.13-22	168	7.10-11	191	7.28	193, 196,
		7.27	191		197
Job		8	177	7.28b	193
6.4	106	11.16	190	7.29	187, 189,
7.1-4	113	11.22	191		193, 198
7.5	106	12.4	190	9.9	190
9.14-24	108	16.11	103	9.11	195
10.4-5	29	17.3	103	12.8	193 n. 35
10.4-9	106	18.22	190, 195	12.8-14	187
10.9-13	29	19.14	190	12.10	193 n. 35
16.6-9	107	20.9-10	103		
16.11-17	107	21.9	191	*Song of Songs*	
19.8-12	108	21.19	191	1.6	248, 254,
23.15-17	109	22.10	191 n. 29,		259
25	109		198	2.7	247
27.2-6	109	22.14	191	2.10	226
29–30	113	23.27-28	191	2.13	226
30.28-29	109	24.10-12	103, 268	2.15	248
31	xx, 102,	25.24	191	3.1-5	194, 247

Song of Songs (cont.)		5.3	69	7.4	90
3.2	248	5.11	169	15.30	90
3.3	249				
3.5	247	*Ezekiel*		NEW TESTAMENT	
3.6-11	247	16	277	*Matthew*	
4.1	253	23.25-26	85	5.31-32	264
4.1-7	247	32.16	96 n. 42	7	175
4.3	253			14	90
4.8	226	*Daniel*		19.3-9	264
4.16	226	5.27	103	23.9	121 n. 5
5.1	226			23.29-33	31 n. 2
5.2-8	194, 247	*Hosea*		25	31
5.7	248, 249, 259	2.3	255	25.40	5
		2.9-10	255		
5.10-16	247	11.9	157	*Mark*	
6.5	253	11.9b	256	6	90
6.5a-7	247			10.2-9	264
6.6	253	*Amos*			
6.7	253	1.3	72	*Luke*	
7.1-9	247	1.6	72	1.52-53	161
7.10-13	254	1.9	72	10.27	27
7.11	226	1.13	72	11.27-28	150
8.2	254				
8.6	206, 247, 257	*Micah*		*John*	
		2.6	xii	7.53	275
8.6-7	247, 258			7.53–8.11	263, 276
8.8-9	248, 254	*Nahum*		8.1-11	157
		3.13	57 n. 49		
Isaiah				*1 Corinthians*	
3.22	254	APOCRYPHA		6.15-16	164
3.23	254	AND PSEUDEPIGRAPHA			
19	111 n. 64	*1 Esdras*		*1 Timothy*	
19.16	57 n.49	4.13-32	168	2.11-14	168
49.15	157			2.12-14	198
		Judith		2.14-15	154
Jeremiah		9.2-4	90		
9.17	96 n. 42	12-13	90	*Hebrews*	
9.23-24	xxiv	15.2	90	12.6	249
50.37	57 n. 49				
51.30	57 n. 49	*Ben Sira*		*1 Peter*	
		25.24	199 n. 54	3.15	178
Lamentations					
2.1a	111	*1 Maccabees*		*Revelation*	
2.20	69	7.47	90 n. 32	6	103
2.21	69	11.17	90 n. 32	20.4	90 n. 32
3.34-36	268, 269				
3.36	269	*2 Maccabees*			
4.10	69	1.16	90 n. 32		

Other Ancient Texts

CHRISTIAN TEXTS
Gospel of Thomas
114.20   24

EGYPTIAN TEXTS
Book of the Dead
              xx, 53, 82,
              98, 100,
              101, 102,
              103, 104,
              110, 111,
              269

Tale of Two Brothers
              219, 225,
              228, 230,
              240

JEWISH TEXTS
MIDRASH
Exodus Rabbah
1.12   246

Qoheleth Rabbah
              195
7.29   198

MISHNAH
Pirqe Avot
5   124

TALMUD
b. Berakhot
8a   195

b. Yebamot
63a   195
63b   195, 198

b. Sotah
8b   195
11b   246

b. Gittin
45a   195

68a   196 nn. 48,
              50

b. Sanhedrin
21a   171 n. 60

QUR'AN
Sura
2.62   27
4.124   27
6.151   27
9.97   27
11   27

INDEX OF AUTHORS

Abusch, T., 227
Achtemeier, E., 119
Adam, A.K.M., 248
Ahmed, L., 272
Albenda, P., 88
Ali, A.Y., 27
Andreu, G., 44
Anglo, S., 201, 202
Armstrong, K., 15
Asher-Greve, J.M., 61
Assante, J., 60, 61
Avalos, H., 17, 31, 40, 84

Bach, A., 22, 32, 154, 165, 256
Badawi, J.A., 21
Bahrani, Z., 40
Bakan, D., 170
Bal, M., 67, 130, 154, 174, 253
Baltzer, K., 205, 206
Barlas, A., 21, 25, 272
Barré, M., 184
Barstow, A.L., 200, 201
Bartlett, J., 190
Baumann, G., 59, 255
Beckman, G., 233, 235
Bekkenkamp, J., 162, 167
Bellah, R., 151
Benjamin, D.C., 184
Bergant, D., 194
Bernbeck, R., 21
Bernstein, E., 26
Biale, D., 161
Black, F.C., 248, 250, 253
Blamires, A., 183, 199
Bleibtreu, E., 88, 89
Blumenthal, D.R., 153, 158
Bohn, C.R., 156, 249
Bos, J.W.H., 32, 234
Boyarin, D., 141, 145, 146, 148, 170
Brandon, S.G.F., 140

Brenner, A., xxi, 12, 23, 59, 74, 125, 127, 138, 142, 147, 152, 154, 157, 162, 163, 165, 174, 184, 199, 205, 222, 247, 249, 251, 266
Brink, E.C.M. van der, 43, 48
Brock, R.N., 170
Brooks, P., 38, 39
Brown, J.C., 156, 249
Brownlie, I., 13
Brueggemann, W., 125
Bryant, M.D., 251
Burrows, M.S., 178
Bussert, J.M.K., 153, 167
Butler, J., 33, 218, 220, 237
Buttrick, G.A., 119

Cady, S., 144, 161, 182
Cafferty, J., 179
Camp, C.V., 18, 63, 174, 182, 183, 184, 206
Campbell, C., 178
Campolo, T., 180
Cannon, K., 160
Carmichael, C.M., 31
Carroll, J., 19
Carroll, R.P., 174
Carter, J., 178
Castelli, E.A., 149
Chapman, C.R., 54, 61, 62, 114
Chastain, K.P., 109
Chernick, M., 123
Christ, C.P., 130, 146, 160
Christianson, E.S., 205
Clairvaux, B. of, 154, 249
Clark, E.A., 199
Clines, D.J.A., 3, 154, 182
Cockburn, P., 216
Cohen, A., 63, 195
Cohen, J., 140
Collon, D., 46, 89

Coogan, M.D., 130
Cooper, J.S., 93, 95, 96
Cosgrove, C., xx, xxii
Craig, K.M., 150
Crenshaw, J.L., 104, 158, 199, 200
Cross, F., 231
Crossan, J.D., 19, 129, 131, 140
Cunningham, G., 74

Davies, P.R., 63
Davies, S., 168
Davies, V., 48, 50
Davis, W., 43, 44, 45, 46, 48
Day, P.L., 192, 223
De Troyer, K., 38
Dean, J.W., 178
Dempsey, C.L., 253
Dever, W., 17
Dijk-Hemmes, F. van, 162, 165, 167, 222
Dobbs-Allsopp, F.W., 94, 95, 110, 111
Dodds, P., 268
Dunbar, P., 175
Dundes, A., 127, 141, 220

Ehrenreich, B., 79
Eilberg-Schwartz, H., 169
El Fadl, K.A., 272
Elyon, A., 123
Enns, F., 9
Epstein, I., 172
Ericksen, R.P., 145
Ertürk, Y., 5
Eskenazi, T.C., 184
Exum, J.C., 32, 150, 154, 234, 247, 248

Fackenheim, E., 134
Fander, M., 159
Faulkner, R., 98, 100
Fensham, F.C., 167
Fewell, D.N., 158, 159, 161
Fischer, S., 27
Fleming, D.E., 165
Fontaine, C.R., xix, xxi, 2, 9, 12, 22, 23, 32, 36, 37, 40, 59, 63, 124, 125, 127, 138, 142, 147, 152, 154, 157, 163, 165, 167, 169, 174, 182, 205, 206, 207, 234, 246, 247, 249, 251, 254, 266
Fortune, M., 152, 155, 160

Foster, B.R., 156, 271
Fox, M.V., 186, 187, 193, 194
Franke, S., 33
Frankl, V., 177
Friebel, K.G., 2, 36
Friedman, R., 48, 50
Frymer-Kensky, T., 168, 253

Gibson, M., 37
Goldstein, J.S., 56
Goldwasser, O., 48
Good, E.M., 158
Goodman, F., 43
Gordon, P., 59
Gottwald, N., 18
Grabbe, L.L., 63
Green, M., 145
Green, M.W., 93, 94
Greengus, S., 80
Grosz, E., 33
Gruber, M.I., 38
Guest, E., 190
Gunn, D., 158, 159, 161
Gurney, O.R., 186
Güterbock, H.G., 165

Habel, N.C., 26, 75, 246
Hasan-Rokem, G., 141
Hassan, F., 25, 272
Hassan, R., 24, 251
Hawkes, T., 142
Healy, A., 79
Heidel, A., 227
Helmick, R.G., 178
Herman, J.L., 76, 77, 153
Hersh, S.M., 65
Hoffner, H.A., Jr, 225, 230, 231, 232, 233, 234, 235, 236
Hoglund, K., 190
Hogue, A.R., 10
Holladay, W.L., 136, 137, 138
Holland, S., 9
Hollis, S.T., 221, 222, 223, 230
Holmes, B.A., 264
Holmes, S.R., 264
Hoodfar, H., 149
Hornung, E., 98
Hunt, L., 105

Jahangir, A., 12
Janzen, J.G., 110
Jeremias, J., 133, 134
Jilani, H., 251
Johnson, M., 38

Kamaal, N., 207, 208
Kampen, N.B., 33, 63
Kane, J., 65
Kaplan, A.E., 172
Katz, S.T., 147
Keel, O., 247
Kellaway, J., 88
Kellenbach, K. von, 122, 138, 140, 143, 145, 146
Kimball, C., 31
Kinnaer, J., 48
Kirk-Duggan, C.A., 264
Kittel, G., 145
Klein, C., 133, 134, 135
Knobel, P.S., 196, 197, 198
Koester, H., 24
Köhler, E.C., 48
Kramer, H., 202, 204, 205, 206
Kramer, S.N., 94
Kristjansson, M.A., 151
Krüger, T., 185, 205, 206, 207
Kuhrt, A., 166
Kvam, K.E., 252

Lacocque, A., 246
Lakoff, G., 38
Lambdin, T.O., 24
Langdon, S., 37
Laqueur, T.W., 105, 106
Laurant, S., 50
Leick, G., 271
Lemche, N.P., 18
Lemos, T.M., 55, 88, 91
Lerner, G., 130, 146, 159, 168
Lesco, B.S., 166
Lesko, L.H., 100
Lessa, W.A., 151
Levack, B.P., 201
Levenson, J., 130, 132, 135, 136
Levine, A.-J., 184, 199
Levinson, B.M., 80, 253
Levy, T.E., 43, 48
Lewis, C., 200

Lewis, C.S., 123
Lichtheim, M., 192, 193
Lincoln, B., 54, 88
Lorton, D., 82, 83, 84, 98
Luther, M., 130, 138, 146, 154, 155

MacKay, E., 36
Magdalene, F.R., 59, 109, 112
Maier, W.A., 168
Malti-Douglas, F., 272
Margary, D.R., 2, 36
Marty, M.E., 8
Matthews, V.H., 184, 253
Mayer, A.E., 272
McGreal, C., 216
McKay, H., 127
Melcher, S.J., 40
Mernissi, F., 272
Meshel, Z., 168
Metzger, B.M., 130
Michalowski, P., 64, 94, 95
Midelfort, H.C.E., 200
Miller, P.D., 164, 231
Millet, N.B., 48
Miroschedji, P. de, 43
Moghissi, H., 272
Mohaddessin, M., 209
Moore, G.F., 134, 136
Morton, D., 147
Mosala, I.J., 119, 160
Murphy, R.E., 187, 188, 193, 194, 195, 196, 197, 205, 247, 248

Nafisi, A., 210
Nathanson, B.G., 156, 190
Nave, G.D., 178
Newsom, C., 23, 109, 192
Niditch, S., 66, 67, 206
Noth, M., 135

O'Connor, D., 48
O'Day, G.R., 264
Ogden, G., 186, 193
Olson, C., 168
Olyan, S.M., 168
Oppenheim, A.L., 271
Ostriker, A., 247
Otten, H., 231

Parker, R., 156
Parpola, S., 60
Patte, D., 121, 130, 142
Perdue, L.G., 219
Perry, M.J., 8, 13, 16
Perry, T.A., 187, 188, 189
Petersen, R., 178
Phillips, J.A., 199
Pilch, J.J., 12, 251
Pizzuto, V., 274, 278
Plaskow, J., 144, 156, 160, 170
Pollock, S., 21
Pomeroy, S.B., 183
Pope, M., 247, 248, 254
Porten, B., 187, 193, 194
Price, J., 33
Pritchard, J.B., 44, 86, 92, 94, 167, 223, 271
Propp, V., 234
Puar, J.K., 79
Pui-Lan, K., 152, 159

Rajavi, M., 209, 211, 212
Randall, D., 175
Rappoport, A.S., 197
Rautman, A.E., 21, 33
Raza, R., 208
Reed, B., 5, 210
Rich, S., 273
Rigby, C.L., 109
Riggs, A.K., 9, 10
Ringe, S., 23
Ritner, R.K., 53, 103
Riverbend, 2, 3, 87
Robins, G., 85
Robinson, J.M., 24
Rockman, B.A., 178
Ronan, M., 144, 161
Roth, M.T., 64, 80, 81
Ruether, R., 130, 132, 140
Russell, L.M., 157, 159
Rutschowscaya, M-H., 44

Sanders, E.P., 134
Sasson, J.M., 33, 80, 82, 84, 100
Satrapi, M., 210
Savran, G., 94
Scarry, E., 39, 107, 109
Schearing, L.S., 252

Schipper, J., 40
Schmitt, J.J., 173
Schneider, M., 264
Schottroff, L., 183, 199, 200
Schüssler Fiorenza, E., 23, 123, 144, 152, 156, 159, 160, 163
Seitel, P., 207
Seligman, A.B., 27
Setel, T.D., 157
Sharma, A., 25
Shildrick, M., 33
Simon, M., 195, 196
Simpson, W.K., 53, 96, 97, 103, 123, 238
Slotki, I.W., 195
Smalley, B., 195
Snitow, A., 172
Speiser, E.A., 223, 227
Sprenger, J., 202, 204, 205, 206
Stanley, J-D., 43
Stansell, C., 172
Stendahl, K., 119, 130, 131
Sterba, J.P., 7, 8
Sugirtharajah, R.S., 119
Sunder, M., 5, 6

Tamez, E., 159
Taussig, H., 144, 161, 182
Thistlethwaite, S.B., 63, 144, 159, 184
Thompson, S., 172
Tigay, J., 227
Tlhagale, B., 119, 160
Torjesen, K.J., 199
Trachtenberg, J., 3, 131, 132, 138, 144, 147
Tracy, D., 16
Traer, R., 13
Trenchard, L., 183
Trible, P., 143, 158, 171
Troxel, R.L., 2, 36

Uehlinger, C., 63
Umansky, E.M., 160

Vogt, E.Z., 151
Vyver, J.D. van der, 8

Wadud, A., 272
Wallis, J., 180

Walsh, C.E., 248
Wantchekon, L., 79
Washington, H.C., 59
Waskow, A., 3
Watelin, L.Ch., 37
Watson, A., 264
Watt, W.M., 20
Weedon, C., 147
Weems, R.J., 59, 174, 249
Westermann, C., 111, 125, 139, 176
Weyer, J., 202, 203, 205
White, R., 34, 35, 41, 42
Whiting, R.M., 60
Whybray, R.N., 188, 193
Whyte, M.T., 7
Wilckens, R., 182
Wilkinson, R.H., 101

Wilson, J.A., 92
Winter, I.J., 33
Winter, M.T., 161
Witte, J., 8
Wolde, E. van, 75
Woolman, J., 10
Wurst, S., 26, 246
Wyke, M., 61

Young, B.H., 264, 266
Young, J., 277, 278
Young, K.K., 25

Zavarzadeh, M., 147
Ziegler, V.H., 44, 252
Zilboorg, G., 202, 203, 205, 207
Zornberg, A., 219

SUBJECT INDEX

Abolition, 173
Abu Ghraib, xi, xii, xiv-xv, xvii, xix, 2-3, 54, 63, 65, 78 n. 2, 79, 82 n. 14, 267-68, 271
Abuse, xvii, xxi, 31, 32, 39, 76, 109, 155, 162, 175-76, 190 n. 29
   Divine, 249
   Domestic, 151, 178
   Prisoner, 267-68, 271
   Sexual, xi, xvii, 33, 87 n. 25, 152, 184, 273
   Textual, xx
   Theological, 5, 178-90
   Verbal, xx
Adultery, 77, 80, 83-84, 103, 190, 195, 197, 255, 264; adulteress, 59, 191
Ajeeban, 263, 265
'Allah, 20, 27, 128
American Exceptionalism, xii, 178-79, 274
Animal Imagery, 41-43, 46-47, 51-54, 58, 138
Anti-Judaism, 122, 126, 130-35, 138-42, 154, 160
Anti-Semitism, 127-28, 130-31, 133-35, 145, 147
'Apiru, 17
Art, 39-41, 267
   Combat, xix, xx, 61, 270
   Literary, 174
   Monumental, 70, 270
   Primitive, 41
   Public, 32, 39
Ashurbanipal, 89-90
Ashurnasiripal II, 88, 271
Assyria, xix, 61-62, 267, 270; see also Empires

Babylonian Exile, 67, 93, 134, 136, 270
Beauty, 124, 125 n. 20, 191, 211, 223, 227, 230, 232, 238

Beloved, 194, 247
Ben Sira, 182
Bernard of Clairvaux, 154, 203, 249-50
Bias, xvii, 11, 14, 23, 87, 118, 120, 133-34, 147
Big Man, see Social Perspective
Blood, xxiii, 4-5, 90, 223, 229
Blood guilt, 132
Body, 5, 23-24, 28-29, 32, 37-39, 73, 74, 78-79, 91, 93, 96, 98-99, 103-107, 114, 172, 179, 203, 210, 238-39; see also Embodiment
Book of the Dead, see Egypt 53, 98-104
Brothers, 254
Bystanders, 76, 105-106, 116, 209, 269, 276; see also Empathy
Bull, 44, 50-52, 227, 229-30, 239, 267

Canaan, 43, 136
   Canaanites, 17, 67
Capital Punishment, xxii, 80, 82, 84, 97-98, 115, 200, 251; see also Death
Captives, xii, xix, 40, 44, 50, 57-58, 60, 64, 68-70, 73, 76, 81, 85, 86 fig. 19, 92, 109, 112, 115, 196, 202, 266-69, 275
Castration, see Torture
Children, 26, 55 figs. 10-11, 56, 68, 112, 130 n. 30, 134, 193, 196; see also Widows and Orphans; Brothers
   Daughter Zion, 69, 111, 270, 277
   Daughters of Jerusalem, 194, 258
   Fetus, 81, 85
Choice, 219, 246, 257, 259, 276 n. 20
Chosen, see Election
Christianity, xvi, 6, 11, 13, 16, 19-20, 27, 139-43, 148, 179, 249; Christians, 198, 221, 268; conservative Christians, xiii
Circumcision, 50 n. 42, 52
   Foreskin, 91

Cities, 59, 94
  Gods, 94
  Imaged as female, 71 n. 76
  Adulterous raped female, 3, 59 n. 51, 69, 71, 76-77
  Laments, 69, 71 n. 76, 93-96, 107, 110 n. 63, 269
Citizen army, 17-18
City laments, *see* Cities
Contextual criticism, 1, 129, 162 n. 36, 213
Corporeal studies, 37-39; *see also* Embodiment; Body
Corpse, 4-5, 50, 53, 96, 99, 102; *see also* Death
Crimes against Humanity, 28, 79, 205, 267, 271; *see also* War crimes

Daughters, *see* Children
Death, 24, 27, 39, 56, 74, 80, 102-103, 105, 109, 115, 185, 192, 196-97, 203, 217, 235-36, 237, 239, 251, 257, 259-60, 264, 265
Death Penalty, *see* Capital Punishment
Decalogue, *see* Ten Commandments
Deir al Medinah, 82 n. 16, 83
Desire, xxi, 215-17, 218-19, 221, 233, 235-36, 237, 238-39, 246, 250, 257-58, 261, 277
Deuteronomistic Historians, 62, 66-67
Dialogue, 103, 109, 187-88; interfaith, 147-48
Divorce, 151
Domestic violence, *see* Violence against women *and* Abuse, domestic
Due Process, 76, 78-79, 218, 264, 276
Dynamic Analogy, 119

Earth, *see* Gaia
Ecology, *see* Gaia
Egypt, xix, xxi, 35, 275
  Book of the Dead, xx, 53, 82, 98-104, 269
  Instruction of Amenemope, 268
  Westcar Papyrus, 96-98
  Tale of Two Brothers, 219, 225, 228-30, 238, 240-45
El Kunirsha, 219, 238

El, Ashertu and the Storm God, 219, 225, 230-33, 240-45
Elders, xix, 84, 114, 165
Election/Chosen, xiv, 6, 77, 120, 126, 132, 137, 139, 249, 278
Embodiment, 28-30, 37-41, 87, 105-106, 112, 154, 178; *see also* Body
  Boundaries/Margins, 32-33, 74, 75, 76, 78, 88, 106, 109, 112, 254
  Integrity, 6, 73, 77, 79, 81, 85, 96, 102, 268
  Perception/vision, 30, 34-41, 73, 106, 114, 125, 159, 211, 237, 257
  Resurrection of, 98-101
Empathy/Compassion, 105-106, 153
Empires, xx, 18, 20, 42, 64, 91, 182, 273
  American, xv-xvii, 3, 11, 178 n. 74
  Assyrian, 61
  Egyptian, 43, 48-53, 83
  Hellenistic, 206
  Mesopotamian, 40, 83, 88
  Persian, 18, 20, 206
  Roman, 18-20, 140, 264
Enemy, 49-50, 51-52, 55, 57, 60, 70, 81, 88, 92, 102, 112, 113, 203, 205, 250;
  combatant, 181
Entity rights, 27-28, 102-115
Erotic, 33, 38, 60, 247
  Coitus a tergo, 60 fig. 15
  Sado-homerotic, 54, 60
Ethics, (ancient), xx, 14, 27, 76, 103, 114-15; feminist, 6
Ethnicity/race, 239
Exodus, 18

Fallujah, 2-3, 87
Fathers, 133, 150, 168-71; *see also* Patriarchy
Fertility, 154, 170, 201, 204, 227;
  commodification of, 172-73;
  potency/virility, 232, 236, 238
Folklore, 80 n. 60, 127, 132, 212
  Folktale, 220
  Folktale motifs
    Banquet, 46, 234
    Dragon/snake, 75, 234, 242
    Helper, 236
    Lack, 220, 230-31

Spurned woman, 219, 222, 228, 230, 235
   K 2111 motif, 222, 230
   Method, xxi
Foreigners, *see* Others
Foundationalism, Human Rights, 6-9
Fundamentalism, 5, 20, 118, 210

Gaia, xxiii, 26, 170, 179, 221, 232
Gaps, 120, 122-23, 231 n. 30, 253, 255, 272, 275
Gay Bomb, 57
Gebel el-Arak, xviii, 44-46, 49
Gender, xv, xix, xxiii, 26-27, 30-38, 40, 56, 160, 168-69, 198-204, 222, 237; and war, 56-62
Gender jihad/gender war, 206, 218
Gendered authority, 81, 168-79, 223, 238
Genitals, xix, 48, 51-52, 57, 59, 62, 201, 204
   Penis, 50, 52-53, 229, 232, 238
   Pudenda, 57-58 figs. 12-13
Genocide, 4, 63, 116 n. 69
Gilgamesh, 219, 223-28, 230, 235, 239, 240-45
Girl Blogger of Baghdad, xviii, 2-3, 87
God, Biblical, 16, 77, 153, 158-59, 269, 270; *see also* YHWH
   Creator, 16, 30, 114, 124 n. 16, 125 n. 20, 193, 231 n. 28, 272
   Deus Absconditus, 110
   Divine Watcher, 107, 109
   Divine Warrior, 106-107, 109, 153, 278
   Enraged Spouse, 69
   God of the Fathers, 16-17
   Midwife, 277
   Judge, 256
   Patriarchal god, 158, 168-70
   Presence, 123, 125 nn. 21-22
   Redeemer, 30
   Shaddai/Almighty, 106, 109, 116, 160
Gods, assorted, 158 n. 21
   Amon Re, 98, 275
   Anubis, 233, 239
   Apophis, 100
   Assyrian, 270

   Bata, 228-30, 239
   Chemosh, 66
   Horus, 86
   Nergal, 106
   Osiris, 86, 98
   Resheph, 106
   Seth, 86
   Thoth, 99
   Weather gods, 110-11, 219; Ba'al, 225, 231-33, 238-39; Emar, 165; Enlil, 94, 110 n. 63
Goddesses, 21 n. 46, 32, 71 n. 76, 87, 94, 143, 146, 165-66, 168, 233, 236, 271
   Anat-Astarte, 87, 158 n. 21, 232, 238
   Asherah/Ashertu, 168 n. 50, 219, 225, 230-33
   Inanna, 158 n. 21
   Inara, 234-37
   Ishtar, 32, 223-28, 235
   Isis, 86
   Kali-Ma, 87
   Lilith, 226
   Ma'at, 99, 102
   Weeping Goddess (Sumerian), 270
   Woman Stranger, 182
   Woman Wisdom, 21-25, 56, 63, 65-67, 69-70, 74, 80-81, 83, 85, 90, 113, 138, 143, 145, 154, 164-67, 183, 192, 207
Guantanamo Bay, xii-xiii, 63, 78 n. 2, 181, 268
Gynophobia, 23-24, 74-76, 154; *see also* Misogyny

Habeas Corpus, xvi, 29
Harlotry, harlot; *see* Prostitute
Hermeneutics, xxi, 119, 121; aesthetic, 124; 129-42, 246; feminist, xiv, xxi, 118; iconographic, xx, 1; *see also* Interpretation; Text
Historical criticism, 119-20, 131, 137, 158
Hittites, xxi, 92 n. 34, 135, 185 n. 11, 219, 233
Holocaust, 127, 134, 176, 177 n. 71
Homosexuality, 4 n. 5, 9, 53, 57, 65, 84, 119, 152, 179, 201
   Homoerotic, xii

Homophobia, xii, 75, 78 n. 2, 116 n. 69
Honor and shame, xii, 32, 54 n. 45, 56-57, 60, 64-66, 68-70, 74-76, 82, 84, 90-91, 113, 184-85, 190, 194, 228, 230, 233, 239, 248, 250, 254, 256, 260-61, 268
Honor killings, xxviii, xxix, 11-12 n. 23, 66, 83, 138, 215-19, 230, 251, 260, 263, 272, 274-75; Christian, 216 n. 1, 276
Human dignity and worth, xix, 5-6, 13, 16, 24, 26-27, 28, 31, 37, 55, 67, 73, 77, 81, 98, 101-102, 114, 151, 268
Human Rights, 4, 6-8, 9, 13-16, 26-29, 113-14, 115, 220, 268
   Duty bearer, 8, 18, 28, 76, 116
   Rights bearer, 8, 18, 28, 76
Human trafficking, 22
Humanitarian narrative, xx, 38, 102, 104-17
Hunt, hunter, xix, 41-49, 58, 270

Ideology, 5, 32, 38-9, 43, 57-58, 64, 65 n. 66, 66, 71, 87, 92-93, 114, 131-36, 278
Ijtihad, 272
Images, 107, 266
Imago dei, 13, 16, 26, 124 n. 16, 140, 274
Imitatio dei, 274
Incest, 84, 114, 153, 171
Infanticide, female, 21, 275, 276 n. 20
International law, 11, 28, 78, 276
   Geneva Conventions, 65
      Peremptory norms, 28
   UN Convention against Torture and Other Cruel, Inhuman, or Degrading Treatment or Punishment, 78
   UNDUHR, 4, 113, 148
Interpretation, 12, 15, 21, 23, 62-63, 119-26, 153, 155, 159, 174, 186, 247
   Feminist, 128, 142
   Masculinist, 219, 221
   Oral, 265-66, 272
   Patriarchal, 13, 21-22, 23, 218, 221
   Post-modern, xv, 14, 250
   see also Hermeneutics; Text
Iran, xxi, 5, 12, 207, 210

Iraq, xii-xiii, xvi-vii, 2-3, 5, 65, 82 n. 14, 87, 215
   Yazidi sect, 215-17
Islam, 6, 12-13, 16, 20-24, 212 n. 89
   Hadith, Ahadith (pl.), 21, 25 n. 51, 252 n. 61
   Islamic Fundamentalism, 20, 25 n. 51, 210
Israel, modern state of, 12

Jesus, xxii, 24, 62, 121-22, 130, 132, 134-36, 138-39, 143, 146, 177, 199, 220, 262-64, 265-66, 274, 279
Jews, xii-xiii, 23, 129, 131-32, 146, 148, 264
Jihad, 12
Job (character), 29, 103, 107, 110, 273
Judah, 17, 67, 85, 113, 182
Judaism, 6, 13, 16-18, 20, 27, 132-34, 136, 144-45, 147, 156, 199 n. 55, 201, 221, 272
Judean Pillar Figures (JPF), 35 n. 13
Judgment, 31, 99, 102-103, 110-12, 139
Jus cogens, 28
Justice, 4, 66, 69, 106, 112, 116, 269, 274

Kingdom of God, 19
   Heaven, 22
Kingship, 46, 54, 64, 102
Kish, 2-3, 36-37 fig. 1

Lachish, xviii-xix, 55 figs. 10-11, 63 n. 57, 70, 71 fig. 17, 72 fig. 18, 84, 266
Law Codes, 1, 17, 71 n. 75, 79, 80, 84, 268
   Covenant Code, 111-12
   Eshnunna, 80
   Hammurabi, 80, 143 n. 70
   Leviticus, 264
   Middle Assyrian Laws, 81
   Ten Commandments, 11, 17 n. 35
   Ur-Namma, 64, 80
Legal traditions, 12, 28, 64, 71 n. 75, 79-85, 102, 110-12, 114-15, 273; oral, 265-66; Inheritance law, 38, 81, 184; Property rights, 268
Lion, 47-48 fig. 4, 52-53, 54 fig. 9, 97

Magical texts, 57, 60, 74-75, 80, 98-104, 110

Malleus maleficarum, xxi, 198-205
Marriage, 18, 21-22, 25, 80-81, 84, 253
    Forced, 68, 113, 164, 196
    Mixed, 184
    Remarriage, 198, 264
    Sacred, 227, 236
    Temporary (*sigheh*), 25
Mesopotamia, xxi, 2, 40, 60, 87, 93
Misogyny, xxi, 122, 183, 186, 198-99, 202, 207, 213, 272
Moabite inscription, 66, 135
Moses, 56, 277
Motherhood, Mothers, 24-25, 64, 69, 74, 154, 164, 192, 222, 228, 237, 260, 269
Muhammad, 20, 22
Multivalence, 174-75; polyvalence, 119
Muslims, xvi, 128, 148, 208-14, 272
Mythology, xxi, 11, 22, 84, 98, 234

Naked, nakedness, *see* Nudity
Napalm, 3, 87
Naqada Period, xviii, 43-44, 267
Naram-Sin, 33, 46, 95
Nazis, 11, 78 n. 1, 143-44, 145 nn. 74-75
NCRI, 211-13
New Testament, 5, 24, 26, 30, 62, 133, 135, 137-38, 154; NT Theology, 156 n. 14, 220-21, 268, 274
Nineveh, 55, 70, 89, 267, 271
Nudity, 33, 61, 75, 254; *see also* Torture, Stripping and Display

Occupied Palestinian Territories, 12
Orphans, *see* Widows and Orphans
Other, Others, xv, xix, 6, 15-17, 28-30, 50-53, 59, 66, 72, 82, 89, 111-13, 121, 126, 148, 210, 218, 220, 239, 247, 257-58, 267, 276

Partnership Theology, xxi, xxii, 246, 257-58, 275
Paul, Apostle, 143-44, 220
Paganism, 135, 159, Neo-paganism, 22, 146
Pain, 39, 78, 93, 107
Pakistan, 263
Palettes, ritual, 43-54
    Battlefield, 51-54
    Bull, 51-52, 54
    Hunter, 46-48
    Narmer, 49-51, 54, 62
    Oxford, xviii, 46
Pashtunistan, 263
Patriarchy, 6, 21-24, 26, 69-77, 81, 115, 120, 145-46, 155, 158-59, 169-70, 220, 239, 250, 252, 259, 265, 275
Pharaoh, 43, 46, 82, 85, 89, 92, 229
    Akhenaton, 33
    Cheops/Khufu, 96-98
    Narmer, xviii, 49-52
    Seti I, 92
PMOI, 208-214
Post-Traumatic Stress, 76, 93, 114, 152-53
Potiphar's wife, xxi, 222, 228-30, 240-45, 260; *see also* Folklore motif, Spurned woman; Seductress
Poverty, xxi, 119, 276
Priestly Source, 67
Prisoners, xx, 78, 92, 97, 109, 269; *see also* Captives
Prostitute, prostitution, 80-81, 191, 228, 253-54, 275 n. 19
Proverbs, xxi, 181, 188, 207, 211-13; Book of, 190; *see also* Scripture Index
Pubic triangle, *see* Genitals
Punishments, legal, 78, 80-85, 255; *see also* Capital Punishment
Purity, 91, 96, 102, 115, 271; impurity, 200

Qoheleth, xxi, 104, 185-200, 271; *see also* Scripture Index
Quaker traditions, 9-11
Qur'an, 20, 21, 24-25, 27, 149, 251, 268, 272, 275

Rajavi, Maryam, xxviii, 209, 211-12
Rape, 48, 53-54, 57, 59 n. 51, 60-63, 65, 67-68, 70-71, 84, 90, 94, 112, 125, 150, 152, 164, 184, 209, 222, 227, 250, 252, 260; *see also* Torture
Reader response criticism, 127-28, 142, 174, 177; *see also* Hermeneutics; Interpretation
Readers, 106

Christian, 128, 136-38, 163
Elite, xv, 118-21, 124-27, 132-36, 206
Ordinary, 128-29, 136, 220
Reading Other-ly, 148, 177-78, 250, 255
Representation, 32-43, 267
Respect for life, 27, 96-98
Restoration, xxiii, 83-84, 111, 115, 256, 273
Retribution, 81, 85, 90, 113, 203, 270
Role reversal, 161, 168, 170-72
Ritual sin, 102, 115

Sages, 183, 187-88
Scribes, 94, 96, 97 fig. 21, 98, 100 fig. 22, 101, 103-104
'Scripture', 7 n. 11, 9, 13-14, 21, 23, 30, 31, 131, 151, 186; sacred text, 262; see also Text
Seduction, seductress, xxi, 223, 227
Sennacherib, xviii, 70, 84, 267
September 11, 2001 terrorist attacks, xii, xiii, 11, 79, 126, 128, 178, 210
Shalmaneser III, 61
Shaman, 41, 46
Shari'a, 13
Shasu, 92-93
Silence, 70, 73, 116, 199, 233, 150, 178, 246, 248, 259; voice, 105
Slavery, slaves, 10-11, 17-19, 21-22, 25-26, 37, 64 n. 62, 70-71, 80-81, 83, 85, 88, 92, 113-15, 120, 164 n. 40, 166 n. 45, 174, 190, 239, 268, 275, 277
Social perspective, 44-46, 49, 51
Sojourner, 17 see also Others
Song of Songs, xx, 194, 226, 240-45, 246; see also Scripture Index
Sotah, xxi, 39, 138, 195, 246, 255-56, 275, 276
Spatial representation, 35-37, 45
Spectral evidence, 181, 200
State violence, xxi, 39, 48-53, 57-59, 88, 200, 273, 275, 278
Stranger, see Others
Sumer and Akkad, xix, 36, 80, 93-94, 95, 166; see also Kish
Survivors, 73, 150-55, 164, 175-76, 274, 276-77
Talmud, 3 n. 4, 123 n. 13, 145, 195

Taverns, 80
Text
Content, 167-73
Function, 173, 176
Nature of, xx, 122-23, 151-52
Plain sense, 186-87, 195-96, 205, 207, 217, 246, 250, 265, 271
Surprise, 121, 124
Transformation, 125 n. 22, 223
Transparency, 126
Tiglath-Pileser I, 270
Torah, xxiv, 15, 17-19, 27, 116, 123-25, 190, 197, 265, 274, 278
Torture, xxiii, 78-79, 83, 87-88, 100-101, 202-203, 205, 209, 212, 271; see also Abuse
Beating/Smiting, 49, 250
Beheading, 49-50, 70, 86 fig. 20, 87-89, 90, 92, 266
Burning, 88, 100
Castration, 50, 52, 91, 229-30
Degrading treatment/humiliation, 59 fig. 14, 59 n. 51, 70-71, 80, 100, 202, 267, 273
Feminizing/gendering, xii, 50-51, 53, 56-58, 65, 75, 267, 268 n. 9
Flaying, 55 fig. 11, 70, 88, 266
Impaling, 61-62, 71 fig. 17, 86, 266
Mutilation and dismemberment, 50, 80-81, 83-86, 88-89, 91, 98, 100, 150
Stoning, 84
Stripping/Trophy-taking and Display, 58, 76, 87, 88-90, 108, 254-55
'Torture porn', 87 n. 25
Trauma, 153, 205, 255, 272
Trauma studies, 76, 276
Treaty curses, 59 n. 51
Tree, 197, 229, 233
Tribunals, 28, 82, 99, 115, 273

United States, xii-iii, xvi, 3, 11, 63, 178
State Department, 208-209, 262
Ur, 46, 64, 107, see also Sumer and Akkad
Lamentation over the Destruction of, 93-95
Ur Standard, 46
Ur-Namma, 64

Violence against women, 21, 59 n. 51, 194, 250, 252 n. 62, 253, 257, 265
Veil, Veiling, 80, 149 n. 87, 211, 253, 259
Vicarious liability, 80, 112
Victim ideology/subjectivity, 15, 73, 77, 83, 152, 220, 277; *see also* Survivor
War, 56, 63-69, 73, 75, 87, 92, 94-96, 273
    Holy war (ban, *herem*), 66-67, 179
War captives, *see* Captives
War crimes, xiii, xxii, xiii, 72-73; *see also* Crimes against Humanity
Watchmen/sentinels, xx, 194, 247-48, 249, 250, 252, 254
Western philosophy, 6-7, 8-11, 16, 199
    Enlightenment, 6-7
    Hellenistic, 23-24
Widows and orphans, 17-18, 24, 64, 69, 90, 103, 111, 167 n. 48, 201; *see also* Children
Wife, 22, 59, 80-81, 111-12, 190; *see also* Woman

Wisdom, Wisdom literature, 29, 69, 101, 103, 144, 182, 185, 187, 190, 192, 206, 238, 268
Witches, 146, 147 n. 83
    Witchcraze/hunt, xxi, 146, 147, 200, 202, 214
    — and Jews, 146-47 n. 83
Witchcraft, 80, 201, 206
Woman, women, xv, xxi, 5, 21-25, 56, 63, 65-67, 69-70, 74, 80-81, 83, 84, 85, 90, 113, 138, 143, 145, 154, 164-67, 184-85, 187, 191-93, 197-99, 200-201, 203, 206-211, 263-64, 265
Woman stranger, 182
WUNRN, xxii, 210
WWJD?, 121, 122 n. 7
Xenophobia, 15, 63, 116 n. 69

YHWH, 18, 32, 103-104; *see also* God, Biblical
    'Yahweh-alone' group, 67, 111

www.ingramcontent.com/pod-product-compliance
Lightning Source LLC
Chambersburg PA
CBHW052050230426
43671CB00011B/1850